face2face

Teacher's Book

Chris Redston & Rachel Clark
with Gillie Cunningham & Belinda Cerda

Tests by Anthea Bazin

CAMBRIDGE
UNIVERSITY PRESS

CAMBRIDGE UNIVERSITY PRESS

Cambridge, New York, Melbourne, Madrid, Cape Town, Singapore, São Paulo

Cambridge University Press
The Edinburgh Building, Cambridge CB2 2RU, UK

www.cambridge.org
Information on this title: www.cambridge.org/9780521613712

First published 2005
3rd printing 2006

Printed in the United Kingdom at the University Press, Cambridge

A catalogue record for this publication is available from the British Library

ISBN-13   978-0-521-61371-2 Teacher's Book
ISBN-10   0-521-61371-X Teacher's Book

ISBN-13   978-0-521-60061-3 Student's Book with CD-ROM/Audio CD
ISBN-10   0-521-60061-8 Student's Book with CD-ROM/Audio CD

ISBN-13   978-0-521-60792-6 Workbook with Key
ISBN-10   0-521-60792-2 Workbook with Key

ISBN-13   978-0-521-60338-6 Class Audio CDs
ISBN-10   0-521-60338-2 Class Audio CDs

ISBN-13   978-0-521-60342-3 Class Audio Cassettes
ISBN-10   0-521-60342-0 Class Audio Cassettes

ISBN-13   978-0-521-61400-9 Network CD-ROM
ISBN-10   0-521-61400-7 Network CD-ROM

ISBN-13   978-8-483-233-689 Student's Book with CD-ROM/Audio CD, Spanish Edition
ISBN-10   8-483-23368-1 Student's Book with CD-ROM/Audio CD, Spanish Edition

ISBN-13   978-312-539731-6 Student's Book with CD-ROM/Audio CD, Klett Edition
ISBN-10   3-12-539731-6 Student's Book with CD-ROM/Audio CD, Klett Edition

Teacher's Book Contents

Welcome to face2face!

Teaching Notes

Photocopiable Materials

Class Activities

Vocabulary Plus

Study Skills

Progress Tests

Welcome to face2face!

face2face

face2face is a general English course for adults and young adults who want to learn to communicate quickly and effectively in today's world.

face2face is based on the communicative approach and it combines the best in current methodology with special new features designed to make learning and teaching easier.

The face2face syllabus integrates the learning of new language with skills development, and places equal emphasis on vocabulary and grammar.

face2face uses a guided discovery approach to learning, first allowing students to check what they know, then helping them to work out the rules for themselves through carefully structured examples and concept questions.

All new language is included in the interactive *Language Summaries* in the back of the face2face Student's Book and is regularly recycled and reviewed.

There is a strong focus on listening and speaking throughout face2face.

Innovative *Help with Listening* sections help students to understand natural spoken English in context and there are numerous opportunities for communicative, personalised speaking practice in face2face. *The Real World* lessons in each unit focus on the functional and situational language students need for day-to-day life.

The face2face Student's Book provides approximately 80 hours of core teaching material, which can be extended to 120 hours with the photocopiable resources and extra ideas in this Teacher's Book. Each self-contained double-page lesson is easily teachable off the page with minimal preparation.

The vocabulary selection in face2face has been informed by the *Cambridge International Corpus* and the *Cambridge Learner Corpus*.

face2face is fully compatible with the *Common European Framework of Reference for Languages* (CEF) and gives students regular opportunities to evaluate their progress. face2face Elementary reviews CEF A1 and takes students to the end of A2 (see p13).

face2face Elementary Components

Student's Book with CD-ROM/Audio CD

The Student's Book provides 49 double-page lessons: a Welcome to the class! lesson and 12 thematically linked units, each with 4 lessons of 2 pages. Each lesson takes approximately 90 minutes.

The CD-ROM/Audio CD is an invaluable resource for students with over 200 exercises in all language areas, plus video, recording and playback capability, a fully searchable *Grammar Reference* section and *Word List*, all the sounds in English, customisable *My Activities* and *My Test* sections, and *Progress* sections where students evaluate their progress. Help students get the most out of the CD-ROM/ Audio CD by giving them the photocopiable instructions on p10–p12.

Class Audio Cassettes and Class Audio CDs

The two Class Audio Cassettes and three Class Audio CDs contain all the listening material for the Student's Book, including conversations, drills, songs and the listening sections of the *Progress Tests* for units 6 and 12.

Workbook

The Workbook provides further practice of all language presented in the Student's Book. It also includes a 24-page *Reading and Writing Portfolio* based on the *Common European Framework of Reference for Languages*, which can be used either for homework or for extra work in class.

Teacher's Book

This Teacher's Book includes *Teaching Tips*, *Teaching Notes* and photocopiable materials: 35 *Class Activities*, 12 *Vocabulary Plus* and 5 *Study Skills* worksheets, and 12 *Progress Tests*.

Network CD-ROM

The Network CD-ROM is a network version of the CD-ROM material from the Student's Book CD-ROM/ Audio CD for use in school computer laboratories by up to 30 users.

Elementary and Pre-intermediate DVD

The Elementary and Pre-intermediate DVD contains all the video sequences from the Elementary and Pre-intermediate Student's Book CD-ROMs. The user guide accompanying the DVD gives ideas for exploiting the video material in class.

Website

Visit the face2face website www.cambridge.org/elt/face2face for downloadable activities, sample materials and more information about how face2face covers the language areas specified by the CEF.

The face2face Approach

Listening

A typical listening practice activity checks students' understanding of gist and then asks questions about specific details. The innovative *Help with Listening* sections take students a step further by focusing on the underlying reasons why listening to English can be so problematic. Activities in these sections:

- focus on the stress system in English and its relationship to the main information in a text.
- examine features of connected speech.
- prepare students for what people in public places say.
- highlight how intonation conveys mood and feelings.
- encourage students to make the link between the written and the spoken word by asking them to work with the *Recording Scripts* while they listen.

For *Teaching Tips* on Listening, see p18.

Speaking

All the lessons in **face2face** Elementary and the *Class Activities* photocopiables provide students with numerous speaking opportunities. Many of these activities focus on accuracy, while the fluency activities help students to gain confidence, take risks and try out what they have learned. For fluency activities to be truly 'fluent', however, students often need time to formulate their ideas before they speak, and this preparation is incorporated into the *Get ready ... Get it right!* activities.

For *Teaching Tips* on Speaking, see p18.

Reading and Writing

In the **face2face** Elementary Student's Book, reading texts from a wide variety of genres are used both to present new language and to provide reading practice. Reading sub-skills, such as skimming and scanning, are also extensively practised. In addition there are a number of writing activities, which consolidate the language input of the lesson.

For classes that require more practice of reading and writing skills, there is the 24-page *Reading and Writing Portfolio* in the **face2face** Elementary Workbook. This section contains 12 double-page stand-alone lessons, one for each unit of the Student's Book, which are designed for students to do at home or in class. The topics and content of these lessons are based closely on the CEF reading and writing competences for levels A1 and A2. At the end of the section there is a list of 'can do' statements allowing students to track their progress.

Vocabulary

face2face Elementary recognises the importance of vocabulary in successful communication. There is lexical input in every lesson, all of which is consolidated for student reference in the interactive *Language Summaries* in the back of the Student's Book. The areas of vocabulary include:

- lexical fields (*bus, car, train*, etc.)
- collocations (*go swimming, play tennis*, etc.)
- sentence stems (*Would you like ... ?, Can I have ... ?*, etc.)
- fixed and semi-fixed phrases (*See you soon., Have a nice evening.*, etc.)

When students meet a new vocabulary area, they are often asked to tick the words they know before doing a matching exercise or checking in the *Language Summaries*. This is usually followed by communicative practice of the vocabulary. In addition, each unit in **face2face** Elementary includes at least one *Help with Vocabulary* section, designed to guide students towards a better understanding of the lexical systems of English. Students study contextualised examples and answer guided discovery questions before checking in the *Language Summaries*.

For longer courses and/or more able students, this Teacher's Book also contains one *Vocabulary Plus* worksheet for each unit. These worksheets introduce and practise new vocabulary that is <u>not</u> included in the Student's Book.

For *Teaching Tips* on Vocabulary, see p18.

Grammar

Grammar is a central strand in the **face2face** Elementary syllabus and new grammar structures are always introduced in context in a listening or a reading text. We believe students are more likely to understand and remember new language if they have actively tried to work out the rules for themselves. Therefore in the *Help with Grammar* sections students work out the meaning and form of the structure for themselves before checking in the *Language Summaries*. All new grammar forms are practised in regular recorded pronunciation drills and communicative speaking activities and consolidated through written practice.

For *Teaching Tips* on Grammar, see p19.

Functional and Situational Language

face2face Elementary places great emphasis on the functional and situational language students need to use immediately in their daily lives. Each unit has a double-page *Real World* lesson that introduces and practises this language in a variety of situations. Typical functions and situations include:

- functions: suggestions, requests and offers, giving advice.
- situations: in a restaurant, in a shop, planning a day out.

Pronunciation

Pronunciation is integrated throughout **face2face** Elementary. Drills for every new grammar structure and all new *Real World* language are included on the Class Audio Cassettes/CDs and indicated in the Student's Book and Teacher's Book by the icon **P**. These drills focus on sentence stress, weak forms, intonation and other phonological features.

For *Teaching Tips* on Pronunciation, see p19.

Reviewing and Recycling

We believe that regular reviewing and recycling of language are essential and language is recycled in every lesson. Opportunities for review are also provided in the *Quick Review* sections at the beginning of every lesson, the comprehensive *Review* sections at the end of each unit and the 12 photocopiable *Progress Tests* in this Teacher's Book.

For *Teaching Tips* on Reviewing and Recycling, see p20.

The Student's Book

Lessons A and B in each unit introduce and practise new vocabulary and grammar in realistic contexts.

Menu boxes list the language taught and reviewed in each lesson.

Help with Grammar sections encourage students to work out the rules of form and use for themselves before checking their answers in the interactive *Language Summary* for the unit.

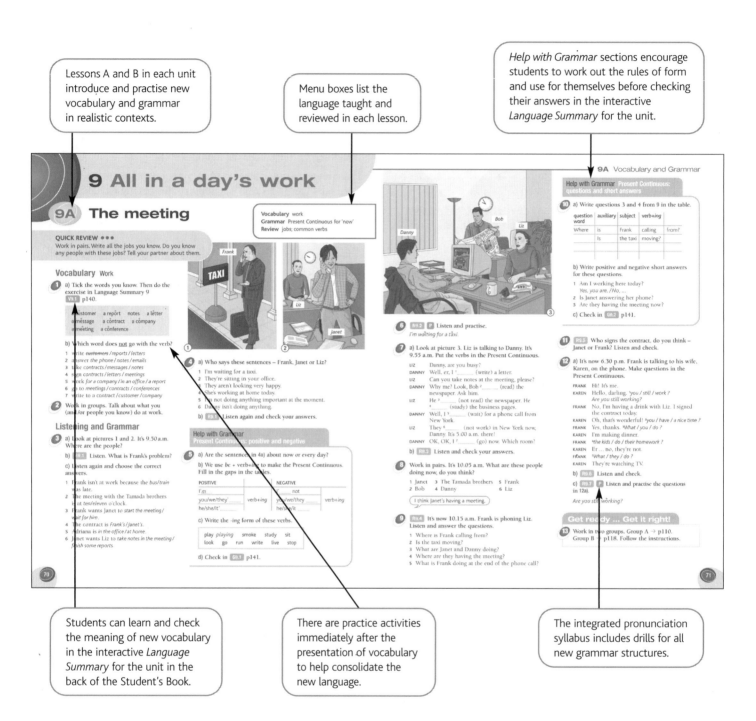

Students can learn and check the meaning of new vocabulary in the interactive *Language Summary* for the unit in the back of the Student's Book.

There are practice activities immediately after the presentation of vocabulary to help consolidate the new language.

The integrated pronunciation syllabus includes drills for all new grammar structures.

Reduced sample pages from **face2face** Elementary Student's Book

Quick Reviews at the beginning of each lesson recycle previously learned language and get the class off to a lively, student-centred start.

Help with Listening sections focus on the areas that make spoken English so difficult to understand and teach students how to listen more effectively.

Students are often encouraged to refer to the Recording Scripts in the back of the Student's Book to help develop their ability in both listening and pronunciation.

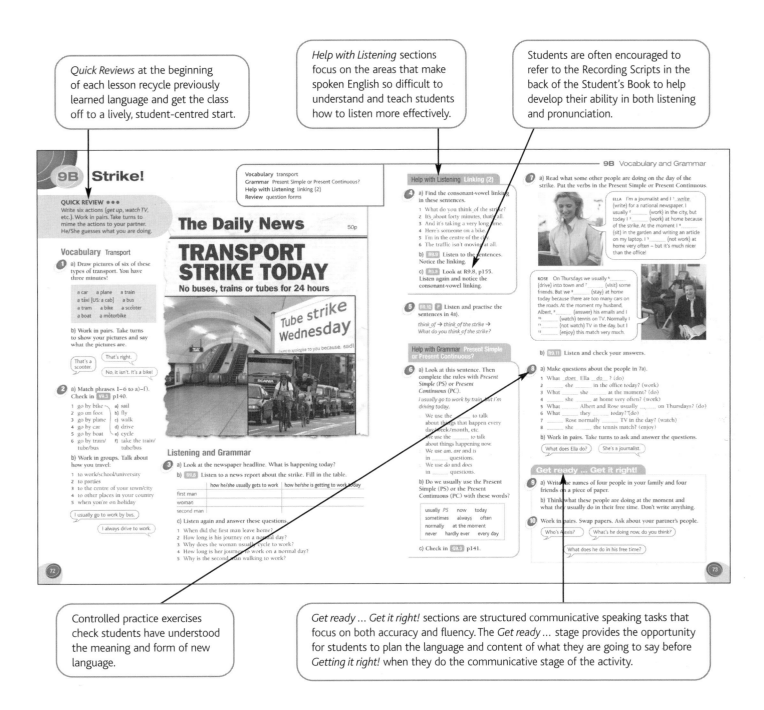

Controlled practice exercises check students have understood the meaning and form of new language.

Get ready ... Get it right! sections are structured communicative speaking tasks that focus on both accuracy and fluency. The *Get ready ...* stage provides the opportunity for students to plan the language and content of what they are going to say before *Getting it right!* when they do the communicative stage of the activity.

The Student's Book

Lesson C *Real World* lessons focus on the functional/situational language students need for day-to-day life.

Real World sections help students to analyse the functional and situational language for themselves before checking in the interactive *Language Summary* for the unit.

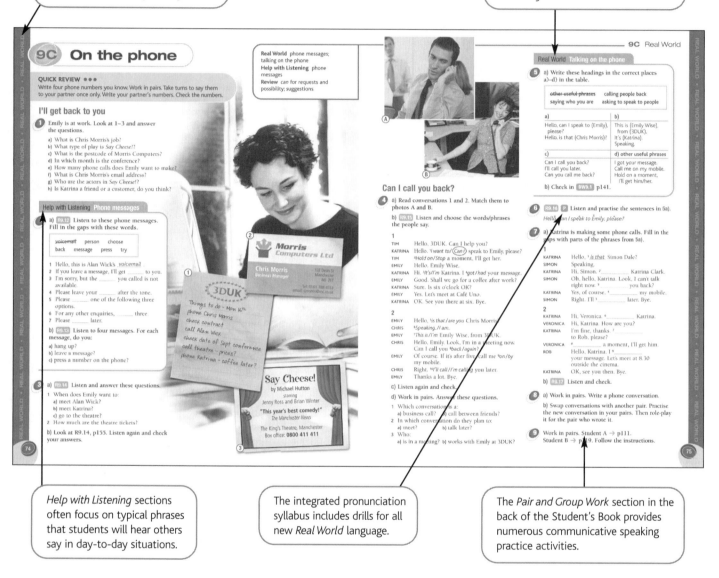

Help with Listening sections often focus on typical phrases that students will hear others say in day-to-day situations.

The integrated pronunciation syllabus includes drills for all new *Real World* language.

The *Pair and Group Work* section in the back of the Student's Book provides numerous communicative speaking practice activities.

Lesson D *Vocabulary in Context* lessons develop students' range of receptive skills by providing opportunities to see and hear new words and phrases in extended reading and listening texts.

The *Review* sections at the end of every D lesson provide revision of key language from the unit. These activities can be done in class or for homework and help students prepare for the *Progress Test* for the unit.

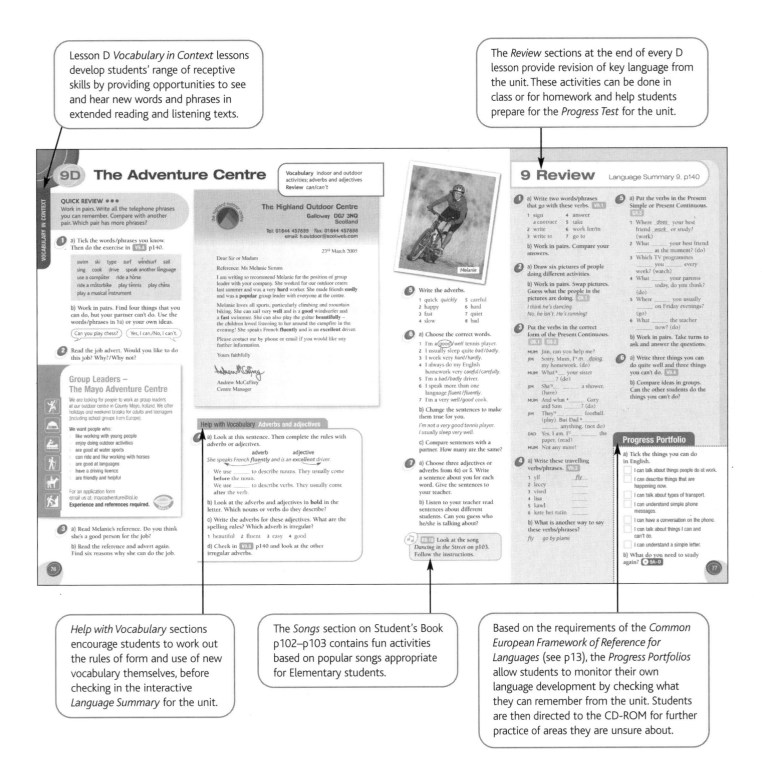

Help with Vocabulary sections encourage students to work out the rules of form and use of new vocabulary themselves, before checking in the interactive *Language Summary* for the unit.

The *Songs* section on Student's Book p102–p103 contains fun activities based on popular songs appropriate for Elementary students.

Based on the requirements of the *Common European Framework of Reference for Languages* (see p13), the *Progress Portfolios* allow students to monitor their own language development by checking what they can remember from the unit. Students are then directed to the CD-ROM for further practice of areas they are unsure about.

The CD-ROM/Audio CD: Instructions

- Use the CD-ROM/Audio CD in your computer to practise language from the Student's Book and to review language at the end of each lesson.

- Use the CD-ROM/Audio CD in CD players at home or in your car. Listen to and repeat the day-to-day language from the *Real World* lessons (lesson C in each unit).

Look at the *Language Summary* reference for the *Grammar* and *Real World* language you have learned in the lessons. You can also add your own notes.

Read, listen and record yourselves saying any word or phrase from the Student's Book.

Learn the phonemic symbols and practise saying the sounds.

Check your progress.

Make your own *Tests* from over 600 questions.

Practise the language from the Student's Book in over 200 different activities.

Read and listen again to the main recordings from the Student's Book.

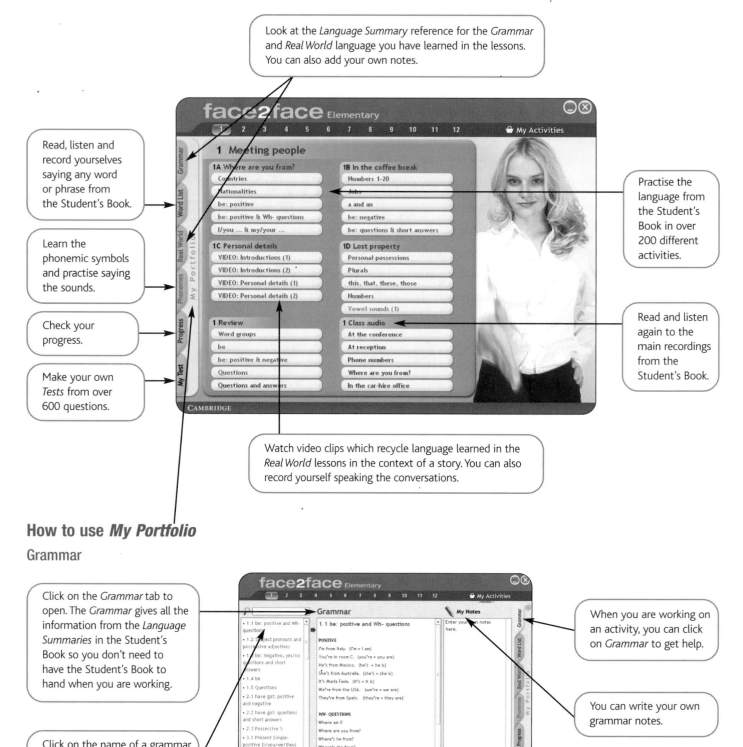

Watch video clips which recycle language learned in the *Real World* lessons in the context of a story. You can also record yourself speaking the conversations.

How to use *My Portfolio*

Grammar

Click on the *Grammar* tab to open. The *Grammar* gives all the information from the *Language Summaries* in the Student's Book so you don't need to have the Student's Book to hand when you are working.

Click on the name of a grammar area to find the information you need.

When you are working on an activity, you can click on *Grammar* to get help.

You can write your own grammar notes.

Two screen grabs from **face2face** Elementary CD-ROM/Audio CD

Phonemes

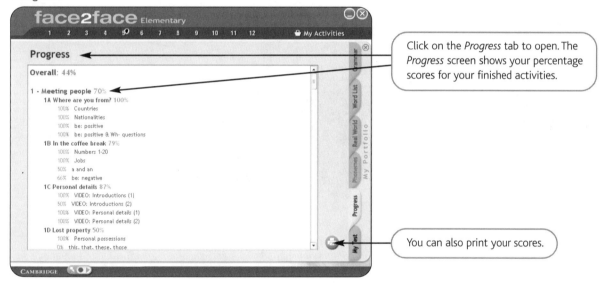

Click on the *Phonemes* tab to open. The *Phonemic Symbols* screen shows all the sounds in English. It is the same list as on Student's Book p159.

You can click on the sounds to listen to and compare them.

You can also record your pronunciation of the words and sounds.

Progress

Click on the *Progress* tab to open. The *Progress* screen shows your percentage scores for your finished activities.

You can also print your scores.

My Test

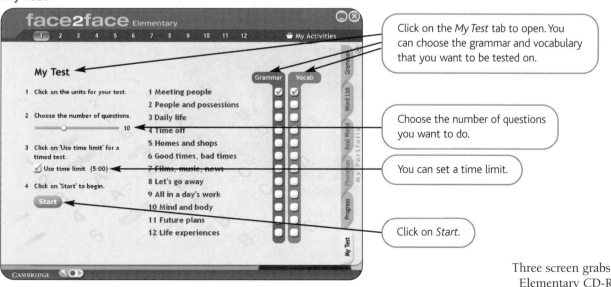

Click on the *My Test* tab to open. You can choose the grammar and vocabulary that you want to be tested on.

Choose the number of questions you want to do.

You can set a time limit.

Click on *Start*.

Three screen grabs from **face2face** Elementary CD-ROM/Audio CD

face2face Elementary Photocopiable

The CD-ROM/Audio CD

How to practise new language

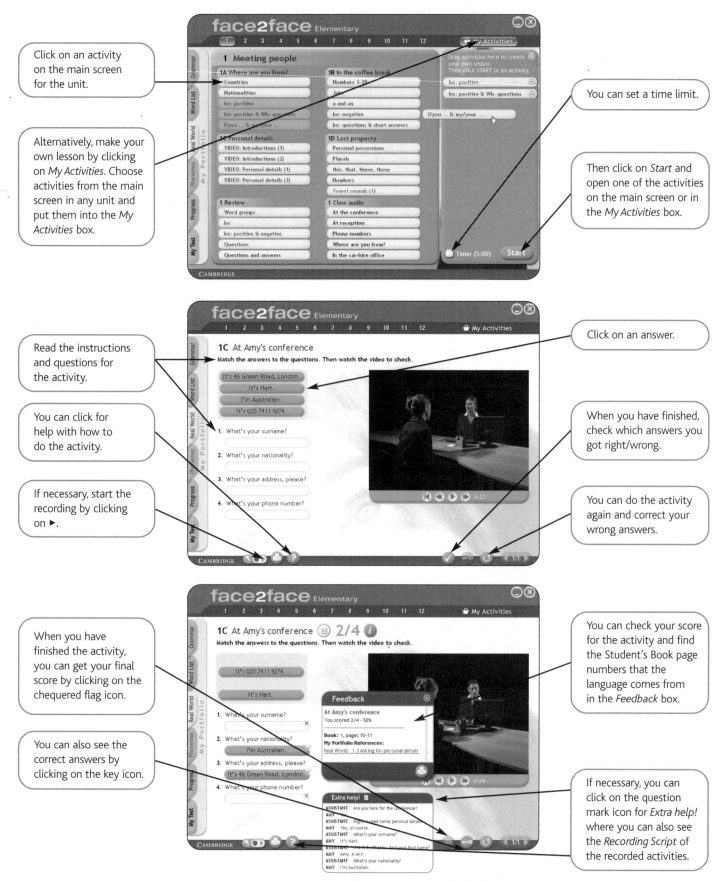

Click on an activity on the main screen for the unit.

Alternatively, make your own lesson by clicking on *My Activities*. Choose activities from the main screen in any unit and put them into the *My Activities* box.

You can set a time limit.

Then click on *Start* and open one of the activities on the main screen or in the *My Activities* box.

Read the instructions and questions for the activity.

You can click for help with how to do the activity.

If necessary, start the recording by clicking on ▶.

Click on an answer.

When you have finished, check which answers you got right/wrong.

You can do the activity again and correct your wrong answers.

When you have finished the activity, you can get your final score by clicking on the chequered flag icon.

You can also see the correct answers by clicking on the key icon.

You can check your score for the activity and find the Student's Book page numbers that the language comes from in the *Feedback* box.

If necessary, you can click on the question mark icon for *Extra help!* where you can also see the *Recording Script* of the recorded activities.

Three screen grabs from **face2face** Elementary CD-ROM/Audio CD

The Common European Framework (CEF)

What is the Common European Framework?

Since the early 1970s, a series of Council of Europe initiatives has developed a description of the language knowledge and skills that people need to live, work and survive in any European country. *Waystage 1990*[1], *Threshold 1990*[2] and *Vantage*[3] detail the knowledge and skills required at different levels of ability.

In 2001, the contents of these documents were further developed into sets of 'can do' statements or 'competences' and officially launched as the *Common European Framework of Reference for Languages: Learning, teaching, assessment* (CEF)[4]. A related document, *The European Language Portfolio*, encourages learners to assess their progress by matching their competences against the 'can do' statements.

The **face2face** series has been developed to include comprehensive coverage of the requirements of the CEF. The table above right shows how **face2face** relates to the CEF and the examinations which can be taken at each level through University of Cambridge ESOL Examinations (Cambridge ESOL), which is a member of ALTE (The Association of Language Testers in Europe).

face2face Student's Book	CEF level	Related examinations	Council of Europe document
Elementary	A1		*Breakthrough*
	A2	KET Key English Test	*Waystage*
Pre-intermediate / Intermediate	B1	PET Preliminary English Test	*Threshold*
Upper Intermediate	B2		*Vantage*
		FCE First Certificate in English	

In the spirit of *The European Language Portfolio* developed from the CEF, **face2face** provides a *Progress Portfolio* at the end of every Student's Book unit. Students are encouraged to assess their ability to use the language they have learned and to review any aspects they are unsure of by using the CD-ROM/ Audio CD. In the Workbook there is a 24-page *Reading and Writing Portfolio* section linked to the CEF and a comprehensive list of 'can do' statements in the *Reading and Writing Progress Portfolio*, which allows students to track their own progress.

face2face Elementary and CEF levels A1 and A2

		A1	A2
UNDERSTANDING	Listening	I can recognise familiar words and very basic phrases concerning myself, my family and immediate concrete surroundings when people speak slowly and clearly.	I can understand phrases and the highest frequency vocabulary related to areas of most immediate personal relevance, (e.g. very basic personal and family information, shopping, local area, employment). I can catch the main point in short, clear, simple messages and announcements.
	Reading	I can understand familiar names, words and very simple sentences, for example on notices and posters or in catalogues.	I can read very short, simple texts. I can find specific, predictable information in simple everyday material such as advertisements, prospectuses, menus and timetables and I can understand short simple personal letters.
SPEAKING	Spoken Interaction	I can interact in a simple way provided the other person is prepared to repeat or rephrase things at a slower rate of speech and help me formulate what I'm trying to say. I can ask and answer simple questions in areas of immediate need or on very familiar topics.	I can communicate in simple and routine tasks requiring a simple and direct exchange of information on familiar topics and activities. I can handle very short social exchanges, even though I can't usually understand enough to keep the conversation going myself.
	Spoken Production	I can use simple phrases and sentences to describe where I live and people I know.	I can use a series of phrases and sentences to describe in simple terms my family and other people, living conditions, my educational background and my present or most recent job.
WRITING	Writing	I can write a short, simple postcard, for example sending holiday greetings. I can fill in forms with personal details, for example entering my name, nationality and address on a hotel registration form.	I can write short, simple notes and messages relating to matters in areas of immediate need. I can write a very simple personal letter, for example thanking someone for something.

The table above describes the general degree of skill required at levels A1 and A2 of the CEF. Details of the language knowledge required for A2 are listed in *Waystage 1990* and the 'can do' statements for both A1 and A2 are listed in the *Common European Framework of Reference for Languages: Learning, teaching, assessment.*

The Listening, Reading, Speaking and Writing tables on p14–p17 show where the required competences for levels A1 and A2 are covered in **face2face** Elementary. For more information about how **face2face** covers the areas specified by the Common European Framework, see our website www.cambridge.org/elt/face2face.

[1] *Waystage 1990* J A van Ek and J L M Trim, Council of Europe, Cambridge University Press
[2] *Threshold 1990* J A van Ek and J L M Trim, Council of Europe, Cambridge University Press
[3] *Vantage* J A van Ek and J L M Trim, Council of Europe, Cambridge University Press
[4] *Common European Framework of Reference for Languages: Learning, teaching, assessment* (2001) Council of Europe Modern Languages Division, Strasbourg, Cambridge University Press

The CEF

Listening

A language user at A1 and A2 can:	W	1	2	3
manage simple, routine exchanges	W	1A 1B 1C	2C 2D	3A 3B
identify the topic of/information in a discussion				3C
handle simple business in shops, post offices or banks			2C	
understand directions				
extract essential information from short recorded passages		1B 1C	2A 2C 2D	3A 3B 3C 3D
identify the main points of TV news items				
understand the main point in short, clear messages and announcements				

Reading

A language user at A1 and A2 can understand and find simple information in these types of text:	W	1	2	3
directions, signs, notices and instructions	W		2C	
posters and advertisements				
brochures, leaflets, guides				
price lists, tickets, menus				
radio, theatre, TV programmes, timetables				
maps				
forms		1C WB1C WBP1		
personal correspondence: letters, notes, postcards, etc.				WB3B WBP3
articles			WB2D	3A 3D
weather forecasts				

W = **face2face** Elementary Student's Book Welcome to the class! lesson
1A = **face2face** Elementary Student's Book unit 1 lesson A

WB1A = **face2face** Elementary Workbook Unit 1 lesson A
WBP1 = **face2face** Elementary Workbook Reading and Writing Portfolio 1

14

4	5	6	7	8	9	10	11	12
4A 4B 4D	5A	6A 6B 6C		8A	9B 9C	10C	11A 11B 11C	12A 12C
	5A	6C	7A 7C		9A	10A 10B	11B	12B
4C	5C							12C
							11C	
4A 4B 4D	5B	6A	7B 7C	8A 8B 8C	9C	10B	11A 11B 11C	12A 12B
			7C		9A 9B			
4C								

4	5	6	7	8	9	10	11	12
				WB8A		WB10A		WBP12
WBP4	5B WBP5		WBP7		9C 9D WBP9	10A	11C	12C
	WB5D		WB7B	8B 8C WB8B WB8C WBP8			WBP11	
4C								
			WBP7					WBP12
							11C WB11C	
WB4B								
4C WBP4	WBP5	WB6D WBP6	WBP7	8D WB8A	9C 9D WB9A WB9D WBP9		11A 11C WB11B WBP11	WBP12
WB4D	5D	6B 6D WB6B	7A 7B 7C WB7A WB7C	WB8D		10D WBP10	11D WB11D	12A WB12A
						10D		

The CEF

Speaking

A language user at A1 and A2 can:	W	1	2	3
make an introduction and use basic greetings and leave-taking expressions	W	1A		
ask how people are and react to news		1A		
make and respond to invitations, suggestions and apologies	W			3C 3D
say what he/she likes and dislikes			2A	3B
discuss what to do in the evening/at the weekend				
agree and disagree with others				3B 3C
exchange relevant information and give his/her opinion				
make simple purchases by stating what is wanted and asking the price				
get simple information about travel and buy tickets			2C	
give and receive information about quantities, numbers and prices		1B 1C 1D	2C 2D	3C
order a meal				
ask and answer questions about themselves and other people, where they live, people they know, things they have		1A 1B	2A 2B 2C	3A 3B 3C 3D
indicate time by such phrases as *next week*, *last Friday*, *in November*, *three o'clock*			2C 2D	3B 3C 3D
ask for and give directions referring to a map or plan			2D	
ask for and provide personal information	W	1A 1B 1C	2A 2B	
use simple techniques to start, maintain or end a short conversation			2A	3C
ask for repetition and say he/she didn't follow		1C		

Writing

A language user at A1 and A2 can write these simple types of text and perform the following written functions:	1	2	3
forms	1C WBP1		
standard letters			
personal correspondence			WBP3
notes and messages relating to everyday life			
describe events and activities			
describe plans and arrangements			
express likes and dislikes		WBP2	
describe family and living conditions			WBP3
relate personal experiences			

W = **face2face** Elementary Student's Book Welcome to the class! lesson   WBP1 = **face2face** Elementary Workbook Reading and Writing Portfolio 1
1A = **face2face** Elementary Student's Book unit 1 lesson A

4	5	6	7	8	9	10	11	12
					9C 9D			12C
		6C	7C			10C		
4C				8C	9C			
4B 4D	5C 5D	6A	7A 7B 7C 7D			10D	11D	12A
4A	5A	6D		8A 8B 8C	9D		11A 11B	12C
4B 4D		6D	7A	8C	9B			
4B	5A	6A 6C 6D	7C	8A 8B 8C 8D	9A 9D	10A 10B 10D	11A 11B 11C 1D	12A
4C	5D							
					9B			12C
	5B	6B			9C	10D		12A
4C								
4A 4B 4C	5A 5B 5C 5D	6A 6B	7A 7B 7C 7D	8A	9A 9B 9D	10A 10B 10C	11B 11D	12A 12B 12C
4A		6A 6B 6C	7B			10A	11A 11B	12C
							11C 11D	
						10C		
		6C	7C		9C 9D			

4	5	6	7	8	9	10	11	12
	WBP5				WBP9			
	WBP5				WBP9		WBP11	WBP12
			WBP7	8D		WBP10		
		WBP6					WBP11	
WBP4							WBP11	WBP12
	WBP5							
		WBP6					WBP11	WBP12

Teaching Tips

Listening

- Make full use of the *Help with Listening* sections in the Student's Book, which are designed to help students understand natural spoken English and develop their ability to anticipate and understand what is being said.

- Before asking students to listen to a recording, establish the context, the characters and what information you want them to listen for.

- Give students time to read the comprehension questions in the Student's Book. Deal with any problems or new language in these questions before playing a recording.

- Be sensitive to the difficulties that students might be having and play a recording several times if necessary.

- If you use a cassette recorder in class, don't forget to set the counter to zero each time.

- When you play a recording for a second or third time, you can ask students to read the *Recording Scripts* at the back of the Student's Book while they listen. This helps them to 'tune in' to spoken English and connect what they hear with what they read.

- When students need to listen and write their answers, you can stop the recording after each answer in second and subsequent listenings to give them time to write.

- Use the activities for the *Songs* on Student's Book p102–p103 at the points suggested in the course.

- Encourage students to listen to the classroom recordings again on their CD-ROM/Audio CD on their computer at home. Note that students can only listen to these classroom recordings on a computer, not on a CD player.

Speaking

Pair and Group Work

- Make full use of all the communicative speaking activities in the Student's Book, particularly the *Get ready ... Get it right!* sections.

- Help students with the language they need to do speaking tasks by drawing their attention to the 'transactional language' in the speech bubbles. If necessary, drill this language with the class before they do the speaking activity in their pairs or groups.

- Try to ensure that students work with a number of different partners during a class. If it is difficult for students to swap places in class, you can ask them to work with students in front of or behind them as well as on either side of them.

- It is often useful to provide a model of the tasks you expect students to do. For example, before asking students to talk about their family in pairs, you can talk about your family with the whole class to give students a model of what they are expected to do.

- Remember that students often find speaking activities much easier if they are personalised, as they don't need to think of ideas as well as language.

- Go around the class and monitor students while they are speaking in their pairs or groups. At this stage you can provide extra language or ideas and correct any language or pronunciation which is impeding communication.

- Avoid becoming too involved in speaking activities yourself unless you see students have misunderstood your instructions or you are asked for help. As soon as you join a group, students often stop talking to each other and talk to you instead.

- When giving feedback on speaking, remember to praise good communication as well as good English and focus on the result of the task as well as the language used.

Correction

- When you hear a mistake, it is often useful to correct it immediately and ask the student to say the word or phrase again in the correct form. This is particularly effective if the mistake relates to the language you have been working on in the lesson.

- Alternatively, when you point out a mistake to a student you can encourage him/her to correct it himself/herself before giving him/her the correct version.

- Another approach to correction during a freer speaking activity is to note down any mistakes you hear, but not correct them immediately. At the end of the activity write the mistakes on the board. Students can then work in pairs and correct the mistakes. Alternatively, you can discuss the mistakes with the whole class.

- You don't have to correct every mistake when students are doing a freer speaking activity, particularly when the mistake is not specifically in the language they have been asked to practise. Effective communication is often just as important as accuracy.

Vocabulary

- Give students time to work through the exercises in the *Help with Vocabulary* sections on their own or in pairs, rather than doing this with the whole class. This gives students the opportunity to try and work out the rules themselves before checking their answers in the *Language Summaries*. You can then check students have understood the main points with the whole class.

- Point out the stress marks (*) on all new words and phrases in the vocabulary boxes in the lessons and the *Language Summaries*. These show the main stress only.

- When you write a new vocabulary item on the board, make sure students know the stress and part of speech. Students then copy new vocabulary into their notebooks.

- Make students aware of collocations in English (for example, *go swimming*, *go dancing*) by pointing them out when they occur and encouraging students to record them as one phrase in their notebooks.

- Encourage students to notice patterns in new vocabulary, for example, *twenty*, *thirty*, *forty*.

- Review and recycle vocabulary at every opportunity in class, using the *Reviews*, the *Language Summaries*, the *Classroom Activities and Games* and the *Class Activities*.

- Use the photocopiable *Vocabulary Plus* worksheets to introduce and practise extra vocabulary which is not included in the Student's Book. They can be used for self-study in class or as homework, or as the basis of a classroom lesson. There is one *Vocabulary Plus* worksheet for each unit in the Student's Book.

- Use the photocopiable *Study Skills* worksheets in class to help students understand other aspects of vocabulary, such as grammatical terms, using a dictionary and how to record vocabulary items.

Grammar

- Give students time to work through the exercises in the *Help with Grammar* sections on their own or in pairs, rather than doing this with the whole class. This gives students the opportunity to try and work out the grammar rules themselves before checking their answers in the *Language Summaries*. You can then check students have understood the main points with the whole class.

- Teach your students useful grammatical terms (for example, auxiliary, etc.) when the opportunity arises. This helps students become more independent and allows them to use grammar reference books more effectively.

- Use different colour pens for different parts of speech when writing sentences on the board (for example, Present Simple questions). This helps students see the patterns in grammar structures.

- If you know the students' first language, highlight grammatical differences between their language and English. This raises their awareness of potential problems if they try to translate. It is also useful to highlight grammatical similarities to show students when a structure in English is the same as in their own language.

- After teaching a grammatical item, use reading and listening texts as reinforcement by asking students to find examples of that grammatical item in the text. This helps students to see the language in a realistic context.

Pronunciation

- Make full use of the pronunciation drills on the Class Audio CDs/Class Audio Cassettes. These drills are marked with the pronunciation icon **P** in the Student's Book and Teacher's Book, and give standard British native-speaker models of the language being taught.

- Point out the stress marks on all new vocabulary in the vocabulary boxes in the lessons and the *Language Summaries*. Note that only the main stress in each new word or phrase is shown. For example, in the phrase *listen to music*, the main stress on *music* is shown, but the secondary stress on *listen* is not. We feel this is the most effective way of encouraging students to stress words and phrases correctly.

- Also point out the example sentences in the Student's Book before using the pronunciation drills. Note that in the examples of sentences in *Grammar* or *Real World* drills, all stresses in the sentences are shown.

- When using the recordings of these drills, there are usually sufficient pauses for students to repeat chorally without stopping the recording. Alternatively, you can pause the recording and ask each student to repeat individually before continuing.

- For variety, model and drill the sentences yourself instead of using the recordings.

- Point out the stress, linking and weak forms marked in some of the *Recording Scripts* (Student's Book p148).

- Encourage students to listen to the audio component of the CD-ROM/Audio CD on their CD player. This contains *Real World* drills from each lesson C in the Student's Book.

Helping students with sounds

- Consider teaching your students the phonemic symbols (Student's Book p159). This allows students to look up the pronunciation of the words and record difficult pronunciation in their notebooks. It is often easier to take a 'little and often' approach to teaching these symbols, rather than trying to teach them all in one lesson.

- Encourage students to use the phonemes section of the CD-ROM/Audio CD at home. This will help them to learn the symbols and allow them to practise the sounds.

- Highlight the phonemic transcriptions in the *Language Summaries*. Note that transcriptions are only given for vocabulary that is particularly problematic.

- Write the phonemic transcription for difficult words on the board. Ask students to work out the pronunciation.

- For sounds students often have problems with (for example, /θ/) you can demonstrate the shape of the mouth and the position of the tongue (or draw this on the board). Often students can't say these sounds simply because they don't know the mouth position required.

- Draw students' attention to the English sounds which are the same in their own language(s) as well as highlighting the ones that are different.

Helping students with stress and intonation

- Drill all new words, phrases and sentences, and pay particular attention to words that sound different from how they are spelt.

- When you write words or sentences on the board, mark the stress in the correct place or ask the students to tell you which syllables or words are stressed.

- When you model sentences yourself it may be helpful to over-emphasise the stress pattern to help students hear the stress. You can also 'beat' the stress with your hand.

- Emphasise that intonation is an important part of meaning in English and often shows how we feel. For example, a falling intonation on the word *please* can sound very impolite to a native English speaker.

- Show the intonation pattern of model sentences by drawing arrows on the board or making hand gestures.

- Hum the sentences you are focusing on. It is sometimes easier for students to hear the stress or intonation pattern when there are no words.

Teaching Tips

Drilling

- Make sure students know the meaning of new language before drilling this with the class.

- When you model a phrase or sentence, speak at normal speed with natural stress and contractions. Repeat the target language two or three times before asking the whole class to repeat after you in a 'choral drill'.

- After choral drilling it is usually helpful to do some individual drilling. Start with the strongest students and drill around the class in random order.

- As the aim of drilling is accuracy, you should correct students when they make a mistake. However, avoid making the students feel uncomfortable and don't spend too long with one student.

- Praise students for good/comprehensible pronunciation and acknowledge weak students' improvement, even if their pronunciation is not perfect.

- Use 'mumble' drills. Ask students to say the phrase or sentence to themselves initially, then increase the volume each time until they are speaking at a normal volume. Shy students often appreciate the chance to say things quietly until they feel more confident.

- Use chain drills to revise vocabulary. Students sit in a semi-circle. Give an object (or a picture) to the student at one end and ask *What's this?*. The student replies *It's a ...* , takes the object, turns to the next student, asks *What's this?* and so on. Meanwhile, give a new object to the student at the other end and repeat the process. At regular intervals, feed in more objects at each end so that there are several going around at the same time.

Reviewing and Recycling

- Use the *Quick Reviews* at the beginning of each lesson. They are easy to set up and should take no more than five to ten minutes. They are a good way of getting the class to speak immediately as well as reviewing what students learned in previous lessons.

- Exploit the *Review* sections at the end of each unit. They can be done in class when students have finished the unit, or set for homework (see the Extra practice and homework boxes in the *Teaching Notes*). Alternatively, individual exercises can be used as quick fillers at the beginning or end of a lesson, as the *Review* exercises are organised in lesson order.

- After a mid-lesson break, ask students to write down in one minute all the words they can remember from the first part of the lesson. These quick *What have we just learned?* activities help students to transfer information from their short-term to their long-term memory.

- Start a class vocabulary box. You or the students write each new vocabulary item on a separate card and put it in the box. The cards can be used for activities which review vocabulary, for example, Know, Might Know, Don't Know (see p21).

- Encourage students to use the **face2face** CD-ROM/Audio CD to review each lesson at home and to review new language by reading the *Language Summary* for the lesson.

- Set homework after every class. The **face2face** Elementary Workbook has a section for each lesson in the Student's Book, which reviews all the key language taught in that lesson.

Teaching Mixed Level Classes

In Elementary classes, teachers are often faced with a mixture of complete beginners, false beginners and Elementary students. If this is the case in your class, try some of the following suggestions.

- Work at the pace of the average student. Try not to let the fastest or slowest students dictate the pace.

- To avoid stronger students dominating, nominate the quieter ones to answer easier questions.

- Allow time for students to check their answers in pairs or groups before checking with the whole class.

- Encourage stronger students to help weaker ones, for example, if a student has finished an activity, ask him/her to work with a slower student.

- Give students time to think by asking students to write down the answers rather than shouting them out. This helps avoid the more able students dominating the class.

- When monitoring during pair and group work, go to the weaker students first to check if they have understood the instructions and are doing the activity correctly.

- Plan which students are going to work together in pair and group work. Mix stronger students with weaker ones when they can give help, for example, in a vocabulary matching activity. On other occasions, for example, in freer speaking activities, it is often a good idea to place stronger students in the same group. Weaker students may feel more confident speaking with other students at their own level.

- In activities where students work on their own, ask them to put up their hands as they finish. Fast finishers can check answers together while they are waiting.

- Have ideas for extra activities to give early finishers to do while the slower ones are still working, for example, an exercise from a *Review* section or the Workbook.

- Don't feel that you have to wait for everyone in the class to finish an exercise. It is usually best to stop an activity when the majority of the class have finished.

- Vary the amount and type of correction you give according to the level of the student, in order to push stronger students and avoid overwhelming those who are less confident. Remember to praise successful communication as well as correct language.

- Grade the tasks you set students, for example, when students are practising conversations on the recordings, weaker ones can read the recording script for support.

- Be flexible in the number of questions, sentences, etc. you expect different levels of students to produce.

- In progress checks, acknowledge improvement as well as final performance.

- Set weaker students extra homework from the Workbook or the CD-ROM/Audio CD to help them catch up with areas of language the rest of the class is confident with.

Classroom Activities and Games

These *Classroom Activities and Games* can be used to practise a variety of different language areas in class. The *Teaching Notes* suggest when they can be used alongside the lessons in the Student's Book.

Board Race

This activity is useful for revising vocabulary. You need a classroom where students can stand in two lines in the centre of the room, facing the board.

- Divide the class into two teams. Each team stands in a line facing the board. Divide the board into two columns with the headings *Team A* and *Team B*.
- Give the first student in each team a board pen.
- Give students a topic (for example, food/drink or places in a town/city) and a time limit (for example, three minutes).
- Say *Go*. The first student in each team runs to the board, writes a word associated with the topic in his/her team's column, runs back and gives the pen to the second student, who does the same and so on. Students can help other members of their team.
- When the time is up, students sit down. Check answers with the whole class. Teams get one point for each answer, one point for each word/phrase that is spelt correctly and one point for each answer not in the other team's list. The team with the most points wins.

Know, Might Know, Don't Know

This activity helps you to find out what vocabulary students already know. It is a good activity for mixed level classes, as stronger students can teach weaker students vocabulary that they don't know.

- Before the lesson, write a worksheet containing 15–20 words or phrases you want to teach or review.
- Photocopy one worksheet for each student.
- In class, give each student a copy of the worksheet. Tell students to divide the words into three groups: *Know* (I know this word/phrase and can give an example or definition), *Might Know* (I think I know this word/phrase but I'm not sure) and *Don't Know* (I don't know this word/phrase).
- Students work in pairs or groups and compare their answers. If one student knows a word, he/she should teach it to his/her partner or the other members of the group. Alternatively, students can move around the room and talk to various students.
- When they have finished, students say which word/phrases they still don't know. Encourage other groups to give definitions to help them, or give the meanings and examples yourself.
- Allow time for students to record any new vocabulary in their notebooks.

Bingo!

This popular activity can be used to revise any large lexical group, such as numbers, irregular verbs, dates, free time activities, etc.

- Before the class, choose a language area that you would like to practise and make a list of words/phrases.
- Make one card for each student and divide each card into 8 or 10 equal squares.
- Write one word/phrase taken from your list in each square, ensuring that no two cards have exactly the same words on them.
- In class, give one card to each student.
- Dictate the words on your list. Students cross out any words they hear which are on their cards.
- The first student to cross out all their words shouts *Bingo!*. Ask the student to dictate back all the words. If they are correct, that student wins.

Noughts and Crosses

This is a quick revision activity which can be used for vocabulary, grammar or students' common mistakes.

- ✎ Draw a noughts and crosses grid on the board and fill in the boxes with examples of your chosen language area, for example:

under	behind	from
on	in	by
at	in front of	to

- Divide the class into two teams: a noughts (0) team and a crosses (X) team. The purpose of the game is to be the first team to complete a line of either three noughts or three crosses in any direction (horizontal, vertical or diagonal).
- Teams toss a coin to see who starts. Each team takes it in turns to choose a word/phrase from a square on the grid. Students then try to make a sentence with it that shows they know the meaning. If they are successful, mark a nought or a cross in that square.
- Play continues until a horizontal, vertical or diagonal line is complete. The team that completes the line wins the game.
- Alternatively, prepare nine questions for students to answer and write numbers 1–9 on the grid. Again, toss a coin to see who starts. Each team takes it in turns to choose a number and you ask the team the corresponding question from your list. If students answer the question correctly, mark a nought or a cross in the numbered square.

Classroom Activities and Games

Pelmanism

This is a student-centred activity which can be used to review vocabulary or grammar.

- Before the lesson, prepare a set of 10 pairs of cards for each pair of students (for example, *happy/sad*, *boring/interesting*, etc.).
- In class, put one set of cards on the table arranged face-down in five rows of four cards each.
- Demonstrate how to play the game by turning over two cards. If they don't match, put them back in the same places, face-down. Explain that if a student has a successful match, he/she has another turn.
- Give a set of cards to each pair. Students take turns to turn over two cards until all the pairs are matched. The student with the most pairs of cards wins.

Grammar Auction

This is a fun grammar revision activity which involves the whole class.

- Before the class, prepare a worksheet with 10–12 sentences on it, based on the grammar areas you have covered with your class. Some of the sentences should be correct English and some should contain mistakes.
- Photocopy one worksheet for each student.
- In the lesson, divide the class into teams of four or five. Give one worksheet to each student. Students discuss in their groups which sentences are correct and which are incorrect. Students should speak quietly so that other teams can't hear them.
- Check that they know what an auction is and how to buy something. Tell the class each group has £20,000 to spend. Act as the auctioneer and sell the sentences one at a time.
- Students try to buy the correct sentences. They can also use tactics to persuade other teams to buy the incorrect ones, for example, bidding for incorrect sentences to put doubt into the minds of the other students.
- When a group buys a sentence, they mark that sentence on their worksheet. Students must stop bidding when they have no more money.
- When all the sentences have been sold, check which are correct with the class. The team with the most correct sentences wins. In the case of a tie, the team with the most money left wins.
- At the end of the auction, students work in their groups and correct the incorrect sentences. Check answers with the class.

Dialogue Build

This activity focuses on grammatical accuracy as well as giving students confidence in speaking.

- Before the lesson, prepare a 6–8 line conversation based on language the students should know. Find a magazine picture of each person in the conversation (or draw two people on the board).
- In class, set the context (for example, in a restaurant). Put the pictures of the two speakers on either side of the board.
- Draw a speech bubble from the person who speaks first and insert a prompt, for example, *order?*. Elicit the target sentence, for example, *Would you like to order now?*. Model and drill the target language with the whole class and then individually. Don't write the sentence on the board at this stage.
- Draw a reply speech bubble from the person on the other side of the board and insert a prompt, for example, *burger + chips*. Elicit the target sentence and continue as above, establishing one line each time until the conversation is complete.
- Students practise the conversation in pairs. They then change roles and practise the conversation again.
- Re-elicit the whole conversation, writing each line on the board by the appropriate prompt. Give students time to copy the conversation into their notebooks.

Running Dictation

This activity involves all four skills (reading, writing, speaking and listening) and is a good way to inject some energy into a class.

- Before the lesson, choose a short text. This text can be used to introduce a topic in a lesson, provide a context for new language, revise a language area already covered or simply provide extra reading practice.
- Photocopy one copy of the text for each student.
- In class, divide students into pairs, one reporter and one secretary. Secretaries sit near the back of the class with pen and paper.
- Put one copy of the text on the board. With larger classes, put other copies on the wall at the front of the class.
- When you say *Go*, the reporters go to the board, remember as much as they can of the text, then run back to their partners, who must write down the exact words they hear. When a reporter has told his/her secretary all he/she can remember, he/she goes back to the board and repeats the process.
- In the middle of the activity, clap your hands and tell students to change roles.
- The first pair to complete the text wins. Allow the activity to continue until most or all of the students have finished.
- Give a copy of the text to each student. Students then check their version of the text against the original.

Welcome to the class!

Student's Book p4–p5

Hello!

1 a) [R0.1] Focus students on the photo and teach *a teacher* and *a student*. Play the recording. Students listen and read conversation 1. Play the recording again if necessary.

Drill the conversation with the class, either by playing the recording again and pausing after each phrase/ sentence or by modelling the phrases/sentences yourself. Point out that *My name's ...* and *I'm ...* have the same meaning.

Note: for tips on drilling in class, see p20.

b) Practise conversation 1 with individual students. Students should use their own names.

2 a) [R0.2] Focus students on Marco and Lin in the photo. Establish that they don't know each other.

Play the recording. Students listen and read conversation 2. Play the recording again if necessary. Point out that *Hi* is more informal than *Hello*.

Drill the conversation chorally and individually with the class, either by playing the recording again and pausing after each phrase/sentence or by modelling the phrases/ sentences yourself.

b) Demonstrate the conversation with a few confident students. Then ask students to practise the conversation with six other students, either by moving around the room or talking to people sitting near them. Students should use their own names.

Colours

3 Students work on their own or in pairs and match the words to the colours. Check answers with the class. Model and drill the colours. Note that the colours are in Language Summary Welcome [V0.1] SB (Student's Book) p121.

> **EXTRA IDEAS**
> - If you have a class of complete beginners, pre-teach the colours using items in the classroom before doing **3**.
> - Teach *What colour is it?*. Put students into pairs. Students take turns to point to a colour and ask their partner what colour it is.

The alphabet

4 a) [R0.3] [P] Pre-teach or elicit *the alphabet*. Play the recording. Students listen and say the alphabet.

Play the recording again if necessary. Pay particular attention to the pronunciation of the letters *g* /dʒiː/, *h* /eɪtʃ/, *j* /dʒeɪ/ *r* /ɑː/ and *w* /ˈdʌbəljuː/. Note that students often confuse the letters *e* /iː/ and *i* /aɪ/, and the letters *a* /eɪ/ and *r* /ɑː/.

> **Vocabulary** colours; the alphabet and spelling; days of the week
> **Real World** saying hello and goodbye; introducing yourself; classroom instructions

b) Do question 1 (the grey letters) with the class to show that all the letters in that colour have the same vowel sound /eɪ/. Students then work in pairs and decide how we say the other sound groupings. Check answers with the class.

> 1 /eɪ/: A, H, J, K
> 2 /iː/: B, C, D, E, G, P, T, V
> 3 /e/: F, L, M, N, S, X, Z
> 4 /aɪ/: I, Y
> 5 /uː/: Q, U, W
> 6 /əʊ/: O /ɑː/: R

c) [R0.4] [P] Play the recording (see Student's Book p148 for the recording script) and ask students to repeat. You could ask students to look at the table in Language Summary Welcome [V0.2] SB p121 while they are listening.

d) Point out the **TIP!** (ee = *double e*). Drill the word *double*. Spell out *hello* and ask students to write it down.

[R0.5] Play the recording (SB p148). Students write down the words they hear. Check answers with the class.

> yellow; please; green; class; teacher; student; welcome

> **EXTRA IDEAS**
> - If you have a strong class, draw the table from Language Summary Welcome [V0.2] SB p121 on the board without the letters of the alphabet filled in. Then drill the seven symbols at the top of the columns. When you check the answers to **4b)**, write the letters in the correct place in the table. Use the completed table to highlight that the same vowel sound is used in each column of letters, then drill the letters in their groups as in **4c)**. You can also point out that there is a full list of phonemic symbols on SB p159.
> - Students work in pairs. Student A says a letter, and student B has to point to the letter in the Student's Book. Alternatively, students can take turns to say each letter of the alphabet in pairs.
> - Students take turns to say the letters of the alphabet in order. If a student makes a mistake, he/she is 'out' and stops playing. The last student to stay 'in' wins. This game can be played with the whole class or in small groups. The game can be made more challenging by asking students to say the alphabet backwards!

Classroom instructions

 5 a) Students work on their own and tick the instructions they understand.

Ask students to turn to Language Summary Welcome RW0.2 (SB p121) and do the matching exercise. Check answers with the class, demonstrating any instructions to the whole class if necessary.

Note: explain to students that the Language Summaries in **face2face** contain <u>all</u> the new language taught in each lesson/unit of the Student's Book and are a useful reference when students are working in class or at home.

> RW0.2 2h) 3j) 4d) 5a) 6i) 7l) 8k) 9e) 10c) 11b) 12g)

b) R0.6 Play the recording (SB p148). Students underline the instructions in **5a)** when they hear them. Play the recording again if necessary.

— EXTRA IDEA —
* If you have a class of complete beginners, teach the instructions yourself first and use the matching exercise in Language Summary Welcome RW0.2 (SB p121) as practice.

Spelling

 6 a) Pre-teach *late*, *first name*, *surname* and *spell*. Drill these words with the class.

Focus students on Pablo in the photo and ask students to read conversation 3. Students then match questions 1–3 to answers a)–c).

b) R0.7 Play the recording (SB p148). Students listen and check.

> 1c) 2b) 3a)

c) R0.8 Play the recording. Students write down the students' names. Ask students to check answers in pairs.

d) Students turn to recording script R0.8 on SB p148. Play the recording again and allow students to listen and read. Check answers with the whole class. Note: in **face2face** students are often directed to the recording scripts in the back of the Student's Book, as listening and reading at the same time can help students 'tune in' to sound-spelling relationships in English.

> 1 Isabel Boutron 2 Pavel Stepanov

7 a) R0.9 P Play the recording and ask students to repeat the questions.

b) Students ask four other students the questions in **6a)** and write down the answers. Students can either move around the room or talk to students sitting near them.

— EXTRA IDEA —
* Students spell out their names to you. Write them on a large sheet of paper and put it on the classroom wall to help students remember one another's names.

Goodbye!

 8 a) Pre-teach *day* and *week*. Students work in pairs and put the days of the week in order.

b) R0.10 Play the recording.
Students check their answers.

P Play the recording again and ask students to repeat the days. Pay particular attention to the pronunciation of *Tuesday* /'tjuːzdeɪ/ and *Thursday* /'θɜːzdeɪ/ which students often confuse, and *Wednesday* /'wenzdeɪ/ which is two syllables not three.

9 R0.11 Play the recording. Students listen and write the day (Thursday). Play the recording again and ask the students to repeat each word/phrase. Check students understand that we say *Hello/Hi* when we meet someone and *Goodbye/Bye* when we leave them.

Students practise the conversation with other students.

Progress Portfolio

* Progress Portfolio boxes encourage students to reflect on what they have learned. This approach is consistent with the need for students to think about their own language learning as required by the *Common European Framework of Reference for Languages* (CEF). There is a Personal Progress box at the end of each unit in the Student's Book. More information on how to use these boxes is given in the teaching notes for unit 1, p32.

10 Students can also work on their own and tick the things they can do. Encourage students to check new language in Language Summary Welcome, SB p121.

Students can also work in pairs or groups and compare which statements they have ticked.

— EXTRA IDEA —
* If you have a class of complete beginners, use the pictures in Language Summary Welcome RW0.4 SB p121 to teach the meaning of *I can ...* before students begin ticking the things they can do in the Progress Portfolio box.

11 Students close their books, then work in pairs and tell their partner three things they can do in English. Students should demonstrate their ability to do these things to their partners.

Finally, suggest to students that they review the language they have learned in the lesson in the Language Summary Welcome SB p121 at home.

— EXTRA PRACTICE AND HOMEWORK —
 Study Skills 1 Classroom language p202 (Instructions p199)
Workbook Welcome to the class! p3

1 Meeting people

1A Where are you from?

QUICK REVIEW ●●●

- Quick Reviews begin each lesson in a fun, student-centred way. They are short activities which revise previously taught language and are designed to last about five or ten minutes. For more information on Reviewing and Recycling, see p20.

This activity reviews spelling and vocabulary. Students write six words on their own, then work in pairs and take turns to spell the words to each other. They should write down their partner's words. Finally, students check their spelling is correct. Check any problem words with the class.

> **Vocabulary** countries and nationalities
> **Grammar** *be* (1): positive and *Wh-* questions; subject pronouns and possessive adjectives
> **Real World** introducing people
> **Help with Listening** word stress
> **Review** saying hello; the alphabet

Introducing people

1 a) Focus students on Carol and John in the photo. Elicit where they are (at a conference in a hotel).

R1.1 Play the recording. Students listen and read conversation 1.

P Play the recording again, pausing after each phrase/sentence for students to repeat. Check students understand the meaning of *How are you?* and *I'm fine/ OK, thanks.*

b) Demonstrate the conversation with a few confident students. Then ask students to practise the conversation with four other students, either by moving around the room or talking to students sitting near them. Students should use their own names. Encourage students to do this without looking at their books if possible.

2 a) R1.2 Focus students on Monica, Roberto and Elena in the photo. Play the recording. Students listen and read conversation 2. Check students understand that Monica is introducing Elena to Roberto.

P Play the recording again, pausing after each phrase/ sentence for students to repeat. Check students understand that they can say either *And you.* or *Nice to meet you too.* You can also teach *You too.* as another possible response.

b) Demonstrate the conversation with a few confident students. Then put students into groups of six and ask them to practise introducing one another. Alternatively, students can practise this conversation by moving around the room.

> — **EXTRA IDEA** —
> - If students know each other well, give them false identities of famous people on cards before they practise the conversation.

Vocabulary Countries and nationalities

3 a) Pre-teach *country*. Students then work on their own and tick the countries they know in the first column. Check students know where each country is. Point out that all countries and nationalities are spelt with a capital letter. Also point out the use of the article *the* with *USA* and *UK*. The USA is often called *the US*, *the States* or *America*. Note that *the UK* refers to England, Scotland, Wales and Northern Ireland, whereas *Great Britain/Britain* refers to England, Scotland and Wales only.

b) Write on the board *I'm from Brazil. I'm … .* Elicit the missing word (*Brazilian*). Use this example to establish the difference between *country* and *nationality*.

Focus on the examples in the table in **3a)**. Students then fill in the missing letters in the nationalities column.

Students check answers in **V1.1** SB (Student's Book) p122. Check they have noticed the spelling pattern in each section.

Point out that the third column in the table in **V1.1** is a list of the languages spoken in these countries. Drill these words with the class.

Help with Listening Word stress

- Help with Listening boxes are designed to help students understand natural spoken English. They often focus on phonological aspects of spoken English which make listening problematic for students. For more information on the **face2face** approach to Listening, see p5. This Help with Listening section introduces students to word stress.

4 R1.3 Focus students on the table in **3a)** and point out how stress is marked in the Student's Book (●). Play the recording. Students listen and notice the word stress.

Use the countries and nationalities to teach *syllable* and ask how many syllables there are in some of the words.

Point out that the same syllable is stressed in most countries and nationalities, for example, *Brazil/Brazilian*. Elicit which countries and nationalities don't follow this pattern: *Italy/Italian*; *China/Chinese*; *Japan/Japanese*.

Also highlight that *Spain* and *France* don't have a stress mark as they are one-syllable words.

5 R1.3 P Play the recording again and ask students to repeat the pairs of words. Pay particular attention to the pronunciation of *Australia* /ɒ'streɪliə/ and *Turkey* /tɜːrki/, and the word stress on *Italy/Italian*, *China/Chinese* and *Japan/Japanese*.

— EXTRA IDEA —

- Students work in pairs, student A and student B. Student B closes his/her book. Student A says a country from the list in **3a)** and student B says the nationality. After a few minutes, students swap roles.

Listening and Grammar

6 ✍ Write on the board *Where are you from? I'm from (the UK)*. Drill the question with the class, then practise with individual students.

Focus students on the rest of the people in the photo and pre-teach *receptionist*.

R1.4 Play the recording. Students listen and fill in the countries in conversations 3, 4 and 5. Play the recording again if necessary. Check answers with the class.

> 3 Italy 4 the USA 5 Mexico; Australia; Spain

Help with Grammar *be*: positive and *Wh*- questions

- Help with Grammar boxes help students to examine examples of language and discover the rules of meaning, form and use for themselves. Students should usually do the exercises on their own or in pairs, then check their answers in the Language Summaries. You can then check the main points with the whole class as necessary. For more information on the **face2face** approach to Grammar, see p5.

7 a)–c) Students do the exercises on their own or in pairs, then check their answers in G1.1 SB p123. Check answers with the class.

> - a) 1 'm 2 're 3 's 4 's 5 's 6 're 7 're
> - Highlight that *'m* is the contracted form of *am*, etc., and that contractions are very common in spoken English and informal writing. Encourage students always to use contracted forms when speaking.
> - Check students understand the subject pronouns *I, you, he, she, it, we, they* and point out that *you* is both singular and plural in English.
> - Highlight which part of *be* (*am/is/are*) goes with each subject pronoun.
>
> - b) 1 are 2 's 3 's 4 's 5 are 6 are
> - Highlight the word order in questions: question word + *am/is/are* + subject + … , and that *'s* in questions 2, 3 and 4 is the contracted form of *is*.
> - Highlight that we don't contract *are* to *'re* in questions: *Where are you from?* not ~~*Where're you from?*~~

8 a) R1.5 P Play the recording and ask student to repeat. Check students pronounce the contractions correctly.

b) R1.6 P Play the recordings and ask student to repeat. Point out the pronunciation of *Where are* /weərə/ and *What are* /wɒtə/. Also check students are pronouncing the weak form of *are* /ə/ and the contracted forms *Where's* and *What's* correctly.

c) Students work in pairs and practise conversations 3, 4 and 5. Monitor and correct pronunciation as necessary.

9 Students do the exercise on their own, then check their answers in pairs. Check answers with the class.

Point out that we don't contract *are* after a noun, for example, names: *Our names are …* not ~~*Our names're …*~~.

> 2 're 3 are 4 's 5 's 6 are 7 are 8 are 9 'm 10 's

Help with Grammar Subject pronouns and possessive adjectives

10 a)–b) Students do **10a)** on their own or in pairs, then check their answers in G1.2 SB p123. Check answers with the class.

- The possessive adjectives are: *my, your, his, her, its, our, their*.
- We use subject pronouns with verbs: *I'm from France, They're both from Germany*, etc.
- We use possessive adjectives with nouns: *my name, his book*, etc.
- Point out that *you* and *your* are both singular and plural in English, and that we always use a capital *I* for the subject pronoun.
- Also highlight that verbs in English always need a subject: *It's my book.* not ~~*Is my book.*~~

11 R1.7 P Play the recording (SB p148) and ask students to repeat. Check students pronounce the contractions, pronouns and possessive adjectives correctly.

12 Focus students on the photo again and point out the name cards that the people are wearing. Tell students that the receptionists are giving out these name cards to people arriving at the conference.

R1.8 Play the recording (SB p148). Students listen to three conversations and fill in the gaps on the name cards. Play the recording again, pausing if necessary to give students time to write. Check answers with the class.

> A Jansen, the UK; Iveson, the UK B Demirlek, Turkey C Koprowska, Poland

— EXTRA IDEA —

- When students have completed the name cards, ask them to turn to R1.8, SB p148. Play the recording again. Students listen and read at the same time to check their answers.

Get ready ... Get it right!

- There is a Get ready ... Get it right! activity at the end of every A and B lesson. The Get ready ... stage helps students to collect their ideas and prepare the language they need to complete the task. The Get it right! stage gives students the opportunity to use the language they have learned in the lesson in a communicative (and often personalised) context. These two-stage activities help students to become more fluent without losing the accuracy they have built up during the controlled practice stages of the lesson. For more on the **face2face** approach to Speaking, see p5.

13 Put students into pairs, student A and student B. Student As turn to SB p104 and student Bs turn to SB p112.

a) Focus students on the example questions above the cards. Point out that the people on cards C and D and on cards E and F are together so students should ask questions with *they/their*. Remind students of the question: *How do you spell that?*.

Students work on their own and prepare the rest of the questions they need to ask in order to complete the name cards. While students are working, check their questions for accuracy and help with any problems.

Students work in their pairs and take turns to ask questions and complete their name cards. Students are not allowed to look at their partner's cards.

b) Students check their answers (and spelling) with their partners.

EXTRA PRACTICE AND HOMEWORK

Ph Class Activity 1A At the conference p137 (Instructions p122)
1 Review Exercises 1 and 2 SB p13
CD-ROM Lesson 1A
Workbook Lesson 1A p5

1B In the coffee break

QUICK REVIEW ●●●

This activity reviews the question *What's his/her name?* and the names of the students in the class. Check students understand *I think* and *I can't remember*. Model and drill these phrases if necessary. Put the students in pairs. They take turns to ask the names of the other students in the class. Finally, check the students' names with the class.

Vocabulary numbers 0–20; phone numbers; jobs; *a* and *an*
Grammar *be* (2): negative, *yes/no* questions and short answers
Review *be*; positive; countries

EXTRA IDEA

- Students work in pairs and count from 0–20, taking turns to say a number. They can then count backwards from 20–0.

Vocabulary Numbers 0–20

1 Students work in pairs and see how many of the numbers they can say, then check in **V1.2** SB p122. Highlight that we can say *zero* or *nought* for 0.

Model and drill the numbers. Highlight the pronunciation of *nought* /nɔːt/, *three* /θriː/ and *eight* /eɪt/, and the stress on the *-teen* words (*thirteen*, *fourteen*, etc.).

2 a) Set the context by reminding students of the hotel in lesson 1A.

R1.9 Play the recording (SB p148). Students listen and write down the hotel room numbers. Play the recording again if necessary. Check answers with the class.

> A 19 B 427 C 15 D 319 E 316

b) Students work in pairs and take turns to dictate five numbers. Their partner writes down the numbers. Students check their answers with their partner.

3 a) Pre-teach *phone number* and point out the **TIP!** on how to say 0 and double digits in phone numbers.

Students work in pairs and try to work out how to say the four phone numbers on the yellow note.

b) **R1.10** Play the recording. Students listen and check. Play the recording again and ask students to repeat. Check students pause between numbers at the appropriate places.

Point out that in phone numbers the digits are said individually and are grouped together in 'chunks' separated by pauses.

4 a) **R1.11** Play the recording (SB p148). Students listen and write the phone numbers. Play the recording again, pausing if necessary to allow time for students to write.

Students check their answers in pairs by saying them to their partner. Check answers with the class.

> A 01622 654331 B 07931 516087 C 01902 785664
> D 0034 96 3922 959

b) Focus students on the pictures and use these to teach *phone* and *mobile phone*. Drill the questions in the speech bubbles and point out that we often say *It's …* before saying our phone number.

Students ask three other people for their phone numbers. They can invent numbers if they prefer. Students should check they have written each number down correctly before moving on to the next person.

Vocabulary Jobs; *a* and *an*

5 a) Pre-teach the word *job*. Students work on their own and tick the jobs they know, then do the exercise in **V1.3** SB p122. They can then check answers in pairs. Check answers with the whole class. Point out that *a waiter/an actor* is for men and *a waitress/an actress* is for women (although *actor* is now often used for both men and women).

Draw students' attention to the **TIP!** and point out that only the <u>main</u> stress is shown in the vocabulary boxes and Language Summaries. We feel this is the simplest and most effective way to make sure students put the main stress in the right place. For example, the main stress in *shop assistant* is on *shop*, not on the second syllable of *assistant* (which is also stressed).

> **V1.3** 1c) 2f) 3i) 4l) 5n) 6h) 7e) 8p) 9j) 10o) 11b) 13g) 14m) 15d) 16k)

b) **R1.12** **P** Play the recording and ask students to repeat. Check students stress the words/phrases correctly. Highlight the pronunciation of *musician* /mjuːˈzɪʃən/, *manager* /ˈmænɪdʒə/, *lawyer* /ˈlɔɪə/ and *retired* /rɪˈtaɪəd/.

Help with Vocabulary *a* and *an*

- Help with Vocabulary boxes help students to explore and understand how vocabulary works, and often focus on aspects of lexical grammar. Students should usually do the exercises on their own or in pairs, then check in the Language Summaries. Check the main points with the class as necessary. For more information on the **face2face** approach to Vocabulary, see p5.

6 a) Pre-teach *consonant* and *vowel*. Students work on their own and complete the rules by referring to the vocabulary in **5a)**. Check answers with the class.

- We use *a* with nouns that begin with a consonant sound.
- We use *an* with nouns that begin with a vowel sound.
- Highlight that we always use an article with jobs: *I'm a doctor.* not *I'm doctor.*
- Point out that *unemployed* and *retired* are adjectives, and so don't take *a* or *an*. We say *He's unemployed.* not *He's an unemployed.*

b) Students work in pairs. Check answers with the class.

> 1 a 2 a 3 an 4 a 5 an 6 a

7 a) Teach and drill the questions *What's his job?* and *What's her job?* and the answer *He/She's a/an … .* Students look at the pictures in **V1.3** SB p122. Ask students to cover the words.

Put students into pairs. Students take turns to point to a picture and ask their partner what the person's job is. Remind students of the phrase *I can't remember*.

b) Tell students that *What's your job?* and *What do you do?* have the same meaning. Model and drill both questions.

Students ask each other what their jobs are. Help students with any job words they need at this stage.

Ask students to share interesting answers with the class.

Listening and Grammar

8 a) Focus students on the photo and the lesson title. Ask where the people are (at the conference in the coffee break). **R1.13** Play the recording. Students read, listen and fill in the gaps. Play the recording again if necessary. Check answers with the class.

> 1 engineer; lawyer 2 musician 3 doctor; teacher

b) Students work on their own or in pairs and match conversations 1–3 in **8a)** to the groups of people A–C in the photo. Check answers with the class.

> 1B 2C 3A

Help with Grammar *be*: negative, *yes/no* questions and short answers

9 a)–d) Students do the exercises on their own or in pairs, then check their answers in **G1.3** SB p123. Check answers with the class.

- **b)** 1 'm 2 aren't 3 isn't
- We make negatives of *be* with *not*. *Not* comes after the verb.
- Point out that *aren't* is the contracted form of *are not* and *isn't* is the contracted form of *is not*. Encourage students always to use the contracted forms in speaking and writing.
- We can say *you/we/they aren't* or *you're not/we're not/ they're not*, and *he/she/it isn't* or *he's not/she's not/it's not*.

- **c)** 1 'm 2 Is; isn't 3 Are; aren't
- Highlight the inverted word order in *yes/no* questions: *be* + subject + … .
- Point out that we don't usually just answer these questions with *Yes* or *No* as this can sound impolite.
- We don't use the contracted form in positive short answers: *Yes, I am.* not *Yes, I'm.*
- We don't usually use the uncontracted form in negative short answers: *No, I'm not.* not *No, I am not.*
- For negative short answers we can say: *No, you/we/ they aren't.* or *No, you're not/we're not/they're not*, and *No, he/she/it isn't.* or *No, he's not/she's not/it's not.*

10 R1.14 P Play the recording and ask students to repeat. Check students are pronouncing the contracted forms correctly. Students can also follow the stressed words in the recording script (SB p148).

11 **a)** Write *I'm from (France).* on the board (or another country if you are from France). Ask if this is true for you. Elicit the negative sentence *I'm not from (France).* Add *I'm from (your country).*

Students do the exercise on their own.

b) Students compare sentences in groups. Ask students to share interesting sentences with the class.

Get ready ... Get it right!

12 Put students into pairs, student A and student B. Student As turn to SB p104 and student Bs turn to SB p112.

a) Tell students that they are receptionists at the conference hotel. They have a conference guest list, but some of the information that is circled is wrong. All the information that is <u>not</u> circled is correct.

Teach and drill *Mr* /'mɪstə/ and *Mrs* /'mɪsɪz/.

Focus students on the examples. Students then work on their own and write *yes/no* questions to check the rest of the information in the circles.

b) Check students understand that five of the pieces of information circled are correct and five are wrong.

Students work with their partners and take turns to ask and answer their questions. Students are not allowed to look at their partner's guest list.

Encourage students to use the correct short answers. Students should correct any wrong information on their version of the conference guest list.

c) Students work in pairs with another student from the same group and check their answers.

> **EXTRA IDEA**
>
> • With a class of complete beginners, ask students to check their *yes/no* questions with a student from the same group before they work with their partner in **12b)**.

> **EXTRA PRACTICE AND HOMEWORK**
>
> **Ph** **Vocabulary Plus** 1 Jobs p187 (Instructions p182)
> **Ph** **Class Activity** 1B Short answer dominoes p138 (Instructions p122)
> **1 Review** Exercises 3, 4 and 5 SB p13
> **CD-ROM** Lesson 1B
> **Workbook** Lesson 1B p6

1C Personal details

QUICK REVIEW ●●●
This activity reviews jobs. Students do the activity in pairs. Set a time limit of two minutes. Find out which pair has the most words and write them on the board. Ask students to spell any difficult words. Find out if other pairs have any different words and add them to the list.

> **Real World** asking for and giving personal details; asking people to repeat things
> **Vocabulary** numbers 20–100; age
> **Help with Listening** numbers with *-teen* and *-ty*; sentence stress (1)
> **Review** *be*; phone numbers

What number is it?

1 Start with a quick revision of numbers 0–20.

Students work in pairs and try to say the numbers, then check in V1.5 SB p122. Highlight the use of hyphens (-) in compound numbers like *twenty-one*.

Model and drill the numbers. Pay particular attention to the pronunciation of *thirty* /'θɜːti/ and *forty* /'fɔːti/.

2 Students work in pairs and practise saying the numbers. Check answers with the class. Drill any problematic words.

Help with Listening Numbers with *-teen* and *-ty*

• This Help with Listening section helps students to hear the difference between numbers that end in *-teen* and those that end in *-ty*.

3 **a)** Remind students of word stress by writing some words on the board and asking them which syllable is stressed.

R1.15 Play the recording. Students look at the numbers and listen to the stress. Highlight that for *thirteen, fifteen,* etc. the stress is usually on the *-teen* syllable and for *thirty, fifty,* etc. the stress is on the first syllable.

b) Students work on their own or in pairs and mark where they think the stress is in the numbers.

c) R1.16 Play the recording and ask students to check their answers.

fórty; seventéen; éighty; síxty; eightéen; fourtéen; sixtéen; séventy

4 **a)** **R1.16** **P** Play the recording again. Ask students to repeat. Check they are stressing the numbers correctly.

b) Demonstrate this by saying a number between 1 and 100. Ask a confident student to say the next three numbers. Students work in pairs and take turns to say a number between 1 and 100. Their partners then say the next three numbers.

Hiring a car

5 **a)** Focus students on the photo. See if students remember the names of the two people from lesson 1A (Molly and David) and ask where they are now (at a car hire office).

Students match the words to Molly's things 1–4. Check answers with the class.

Model and drill the words, paying particular attention to the pronunciation of *business* /'bɪznɪs/.

> 1 a passport 2 a letter 3 a credit card 4 a business card

b) Pre-teach *married, single* and *How old is she?/How old are you?*. Point out that we use the verb *be* to talk about age, not *have*. We say *She's 26 (years old)*. not ~~She has 26 years old~~.

Students answer questions 1–4 on their own or in pairs. Check answers with the class. Point out that we can say *She's 26 years old.* or *She's 26.*, but not ~~She's 26 years~~.

> 1 No, she's British. 2 She's a lawyer. 3 She's married.
> 4 Students will need to calculate Molly's age using her date of birth (23rd June 1980).

> ── EXTRA IDEA ──
> • Drill the question *How old are you?*, then ask students to practise asking each other their ages. Students can find out if anyone is the same age as them. Note that this activity might not be suitable if you think your students will be reluctant to talk about their age.

6 **a)** Students do the exercise on their own.

b) Focus students on the speech bubbles. Students check answers in pairs by asking questions with *What's her … ?*.

Check answers with the class. Point out that *postcode* is British English and *zip code* is American English.

Use Molly's email address to teach students how we say . (*dot*) and @ (*at*): *molly dot blackwell at w j l dot com*. (Students practise saying their email addresses in **10b**).)

> 2a) 3b) 4d) 5i) 6e) 7c) 8h) 9j) 10f)

Help with Listening Sentence stress (1)

• This Help with Listening section introduces students to sentence stress and highlights that we stress the important words.

7 **a)** **R1.17** Play the recording. Students listen and notice the sentence stress in the questions.

Check students can hear that these words/syllables are said louder than other words/syllables. Use sentences 1–7 to highlight that we stress the important words in sentences (the words that carry the meaning).

b) Play the recording again. Students listen for the pronunciation of *your* /jə/ and *and* /ən/.

Use the sentences in **7a)** to show how the sound of unstressed words often changes in sentences and are not pronounced as students might expect. Point out that the alternative ways to say these words are called 'weak forms'.

You may wish to highlight the schwa /ə/ in the weak forms of *your* and *and*. Note that the schwa is dealt with in detail in lesson 2B, and that weak forms in general are dealt with at various points in the Help with Listening syllabus.

8 **a)** Focus students on David in the photo of the car hire office. Ask what he wants to do (hire a car). Pre-teach *fill in* and *form*.

R1.18 Play the recording (SB p148). Students fill in the form while they listen to the conversation. Play the recording again if necessary.

Students check answers in pairs. Check answers with the class.

> **Surname:** Holmes **Nationality:** British
> **Address:** 57 Green (Road) (Birmingham) B22 4LJ
> **Home phone number:** 0121 787 6544
> **Mobile phone number:** (07810) 056678

b) Students look at R1.18, SB p148. Play the recording again and ask students to follow the stress on the woman's sentences. This activity will help students 'tune in' to sentence stress in spoken English. Note that only the woman's sentences are marked for stress.

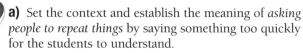

Real World Asking people to repeat things

9 **a)** Set the context and establish the meaning of *asking people to repeat things* by saying something too quickly for the students to understand.

R1.19 Allow students time to read the exercise, then play the recording. Students fill in the gaps using the words in the box. Play the recording again if necessary.

Students check answers in **RW1.2** SB p123. Point out that *say again* and *repeat* mean the same thing, but *repeat* is more formal. Also point out that we often say *sorry* when we ask people to repeat things.

> 1 say; again
> 2 sorry
> 3 could; repeat

b) Establish that intonation is very important in English and that the correct intonation pattern can help students sound polite. Say the sentences in **9a)** with rising and flat intonation to demonstrate how a rising intonation makes you sound polite and flat intonation makes you sound impolite or bored.

P Play the recording again and ask students to repeat. Check they are copying the rising intonation pattern correctly. Drill students individually if necessary.

10 a) R1.20 P Focus students on questions 1–7 in **7a)**, then play the recording and ask students to repeat. Check students use the correct stress in the questions.

b) Put students in pairs, if possible with people they don't know very well. Students take turns to interview their partner and fill in the form. Remind them of the questions in **9a)** and *How do you spell that?* before they begin.

When both students have filled in their form, they check that all the information on their partner's form is correct.

Note that the language needed for asking about people's personal details is in RW1.3 p123.

EXTRA PRACTICE AND HOMEWORK

Ph **Class Activity** 1C At the car hire office p139 (Instructions p122)
1 Review Exercise 6 SB p13
CD-ROM Lesson 1C
Workbook Lesson 1C p8

1D Lost property

QUICK REVIEW ●●●
This activity reviews numbers 0–100. Demonstrate both parts of the activity with a confident student before asking students to do the activity in pairs.

Focus students on the picture and the title of the lesson. Establish the meaning of *lost property*. Ask them where the lost property room is (in the hotel).

Students work on their own or in pairs and match the words to the pictures. Check answers with the class.

Model and drill the words. Pay particular attention to the pronunciation of *suitcases* /ˈsuːtkeisiz/, *watches* /ˈwɒtʃiz/, *dresses* /ˈdresiz/ and *teeth* /tiːθ/.

suitcases 5; wallets 13; shoes 7; coats 4; an umbrella 9; a CD player 2; ID (identity) cards 11; watches 12; a camera 8; dresses 1; bags 6; a bike 10; false teeth 3

Help with Vocabulary Plurals

2 a)–b) Pre-teach *plural, man, woman, child* and *person*. Students do **2a)** on their own or in pairs by referring to the words in **1**, then check their answers in V1.7 SB p122. Check answers with the class.

- To make most nouns plural we add *-s*: *bags, shoes, suitcases*, etc.
- If the noun ends in *-ch, -sh, -s, -ss, -x* or *-z*, we add *-es*: *watches, dresses*, etc.
- If the noun ends in consonant + *y*, we change *-y* to *-ies*: *diaries*, etc.
- A few common nouns have irregular plural forms: *men, women, children, people, teeth*, etc.
- *Persons* does exist but it is very formal. Point out that we use a plural verb form after *people*. We say *British people are friendly*. not ~~British people is friendly~~.

Vocabulary personal possessions (1); plurals; *this, that, these, those*
Review *be*

3 R1.21 P Play the recording and ask students to repeat. Pay particular attention to the *-es* /ɪz/ endings in *suitcases, watches* and *dresses*, and the pronunciation of *women* /ˈwɪmɪn/, *children* /ˈtʃɪldrən/ and *teeth* /tiːθ/.

4 Students do the exercise on their own, then check their answers in pairs.

Check answers with the class.

Ask students how they think these plural forms are pronounced. Drill the plural forms with the class, focusing on the extra /ɪz/ syllables in *waitresses* and *addresses*.

b) credit cards c) nationalities d) waitresses
e) countries f) addresses g) cameras h) colours

5 Tell students to cover the vocabulary box in **1** and the table in **2a)**. Say the number of two or three items in the picture and ask students to say what they are.

Use the speech bubbles to remind students of the difference between *It's* and *They're* for singular and plural nouns.

Students work in pairs and take turns to test each other on the items in the picture.

6 Focus on the main picture and establish that Eva has got a job at the hotel. Then focus on the four smaller pictures 1–4. Tell students that Eva isn't a native English speaker and so she is asking how to say things in English.

Students work on their own and fill in the gaps in the conversations.

Check answers with the class.

1 umbrella 2 watches 3 CD player 4 false teeth

---

7 Help with Vocabulary *this, that, these, those*

Students fill in the gaps in the table by referring back to pictures 1–4 in **6**. They then check answers in **V1.8** SB p122. Check answers with the class.

- Check the table with the class (see the table in **V1.8** SB p122).
- We use *this* and *these* to indicate something that is close to us.
- We use *that* and *those* to indicate something that is further away from us.
- We use *this* and *that* to refer to singular nouns and *these* and *those* to refer to plural nouns.
- Point out that we often use *over there* with *that* and *those* if something is a long way from us: *What's that over there?*.

8 a) R1.22 **P** Play the recording (SB p149). Ask students to repeat. This is a 'chain drill' which helps students build up correct stress patterns in longer sentences.

b) Give students time to choose three things in the classroom or in their bags that they want to know the English word for.

Students ask you what the things are in English, using the questions in **6**. Tell students the answers. Write new words on the board and mark the stress.

EXTRA PRACTICE AND HOMEWORK

1 Review SB p13
CD-ROM Lesson 1D
Workbook Lesson 1D p9
Workbook Reading and Writing Portfolio 1 p64
Progress Test 1 p211

---

1 Review

- The Review section reviews the key language taught in the unit. It includes communicative and personalised speaking stages as well as controlled grammar, vocabulary and writing practice.
- This section is designed to be used in class after students have finished lesson D, but individual exercises can be used as 'fillers' if you have a few minutes left at the end of a lesson. The Extra practice and homework boxes list which exercises are relevant to each lesson.
- The icons refer to the relevant sections of the Language Summary. Students can refer to these if they need help when doing the exercises.
- For more information on the **face2face** approach to Reviewing and Recycling, see p5.

1a)

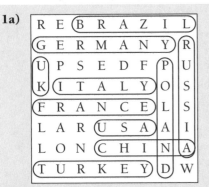

1b) Brazilian; German; Italian; French; American; Chinese; Turkish; British; Polish; Russian

1c) Brazil, Brazilian; Germany, German; Italy, Italian; France, French; the USA, American; China, Chinese; Turkey, Turkish; the UK, British; Poland, Polish; Russia, Russian

2a) 1 His name's Boris. 2 They're from Italy. 3 I'm from England. 4 Her surname's Owen. 5 My name's Amanda. 6 He's from Germany.

2b) 1 What's his name? 2 Where are they from? 3 Where are you from? 4 What's her surname? 5 What's your name? 6 Where's he from?

3 2 an **actor** 3 a **musician** 4 a **waitress** 5 an **accountant** 6 a **manager** 7 an **engineer** 8 a **police officer**

5a) 2 Brad Pitt isn't an accountant. He's an actor. 3 Venus and Serena Williams aren't from Spain. They're from the USA. 4 Nike and Ford aren't British companies. They're American (companies). 5 Ferraris aren't German cars. They're Italian (cars).

6a) 2 What's your (first) name? 3 What's your nationality? 4 What's your phone number? 5 What's your email address? 6 What's your address? 7 How old are you? 8 Are you married?

Progress Portfolio

- Progress Portfolio boxes encourage students to reflect on what they have learned and help them decide which areas they need to study again.
- Note that the *I can ...* statements reflect communicative competences as set out in the *Common European Framework of Reference for Languages* (CEF) for levels A1 and A2. For more information on the CEF, see p13.

a) Students work through the list of *I can ...* statements on their own and tick the things they feel they can do. They can refer to Language Summary 1 if they wish.

b) Students work on their own or in pairs/groups and decide which areas they need to study again. Encourage students to use the CD-ROM/Audio CD, lessons 1A–D to help them improve in these areas. For more information on the CD-ROM/Audio CD, see p10.

2A   What's important to you?

QUICK REVIEW ●●●
This activity reviews personal possessions (1). Remind students of the lost property room at the hotel. Students work on their own and write all the things they can remember that were in the room. Set a time limit of three minutes. Students compare answers in pairs, then check in the picture on p12.

Vocabulary adjectives (1); adjectives with *very*; personal possessions (2)
Grammar *have got*
Review *be*; possessive adjectives

Vocabulary Adjectives (1)

1 ✍ Write *a red dress* on the board and use this to teach the words *noun* and *adjective*.

Students tick the adjectives they know, then do the exercise in **V2.1** SB p124.

Check answers with the class. Point out the two opposites of *old* (*new* and *young*) and teach the word *opposite*.

Model and drill the words, focusing on word stress. Pay particular attention to the pronunciation of *ugly* /ˈʌgli/ and *favourite* /ˈfeɪvrɪt/.

> **V2.1** 2a) 3i) 4f) 5e) 6d) 7b) 8g) 9j) 10c) 12k) 13l) 14n)

Help with Vocabulary Adjectives with *very*

2 **a)–b)** ✍ Write the example sentences on the board. Ask a student to underline the adjectives and circle the nouns. Check students understand the meaning of *very*.
Students do the exercise on their own and check their answers in **V2.2** SB p124. Check answers with the class.

- We put adjectives after the verb *be*: *She's old.* not *She old is*.
- We put adjectives before a noun: *It's a small bag.* not *It's a bag small*.
- We put *very* before adjectives: *He's a very happy child.* not *He's a happy very child*.
- Adjectives aren't plural with plural nouns: *Those are my new shoes.* not *Those are my news shoes*.

3 **a)** Students work on their own and use the rules in **2a)** to put the words in the correct order.

b) Students check answers in pairs. Check answers with the class.

> **2** It's my old camera. **3** The dresses are very beautiful.
> **4** It's a very cheap watch. **5** They're your new books.

Reading, Listening and Grammar

4 **a)** Focus students on the photos of Sally and her grandfather, Bill. Tell students that Sally and Bill are talking about the things that are important to them.

R2.1 Play the recording. Students listen and read to find four important things for each person. Play the recording again if necessary.

> **SALLY** a great CD player; an old bike; a beautiful long dress; a new mobile phone
>
> **BILL** a very old car (a Toyota); a dog; an expensive digital camera; a very good DVD player

b) Check students understand *true* and *false*. Students do the exercise on their own, then check their answers in pairs or groups.

Check answers with the class, and ask students to correct the false sentences.

> **2T 3F 4F 5T 6F**

Help with Grammar *have got*: positive and negative

5 **a)–c)** Students do the exercises on their own or in pairs, then check their answers in **G2.1** SB p125. Check answers with the class.

- The positive form of *have got* is: *I/you/we/they've got* and *He/she/it's got*.
- The negative form of *have got* is: *I/you/we/they haven't got* and *he/she/it hasn't got*.
- Highlight the contractions *I've, he's, haven't, hasn't,* etc. in the positive and negative forms.
- Highlight that the *'s* in *he's got,* etc. is a contraction of *has,* not *is*.
- Point out that we don't contract *have* with names: *Bill and Sally have got …* not *Bill and Sally've got …* .
- *Have got* is very common in British English to talk about possession, family, illnesses, etc. In American English, *have* is often used rather than *have got*: *I've got a new car.* (UK) = *I have a new car.* (US). *Have* and *have got* are dealt with in more detail in unit 4.

6 **R2.2** **P** Play the recording and ask students to repeat. Help students reproduce the correct sentence stress and contractions. Students can follow the stressed words in the recording script (SB p149).

7 **a)** Complete question 1 with the whole class and use this to teach the meaning of *but*. Students do the exercise on their own, then check answers in pairs. Check answers with the class. Make sure students have used the contracted forms of *have*.

> 1 ve got 2 ve got 3 ve got 4 ve got 5 s got; hasn't got

b) Use the speech bubbles to teach *Really?* and highlight the example of a follow-up question.

Model a rising intonation of *Really?* to show interest. Say *I've got an old car.* and encourage students to ask questions about it using adjectives from **1**.

Students work on their own and write down four things that are important to them.

Students work in groups of three or four and take turns to exchange information. Encourage them to ask questions about each thing.

Ask students to share interesting answers with the class.

Vocabulary Personal possessions (2)

8 Students work in pairs and tick the words they know, then check the new words in **V2.3** SB p124.

Model and drill the vocabulary, focusing on correct stress. Highlight the pronunciation of *videos* /'vɪdiəuz/, *digital camera* /ˌdɪdʒɪtl 'kæmərə/ and *radio* /'reɪdiəu/.

Note that only the main stress in words/phrases is shown in vocabulary boxes and the Language Summaries.

Point out the American English words *a cell phone* (or *a cell*) and *a VCR*.

Listening and Grammar

9 **a)** Focus students on the picture and ask where Bill and Sally are (an electrical shop). Establish who the other man is (a shop assistant) and that he is doing a survey to find out what electrical products people have got.

Students look at the product survey forms and guess which things Bill and Sally have got by writing *yes* or *no* in the *your guess* columns.

b) **R2.3** Play the recording (SB p149). Students complete the *his/her answer* columns and compare the answers with their guesses.

Play the recording again if necessary. Check answers with the class.

Product	Bill	Sally
computer	yes	no
mobile phone	no	yes
digital camera	yes	no
personal stereo	yes	no
DVD player	yes	no

EXTRA IDEA
- When the students have completed the listening, ask them to turn to R2.3, SB p149, then play the recording again. Students listen and read the conversation at the same time.

 Help with Grammar *have got*: questions and short answers

10 **a)–b)** Students do **10a)** on their own or in pairs, then check their answers in **G2.2** SB p125.

Check answers with the class.

- Check the questions and short answers with the class (see **G2.2** SB p125).
- Highlight the word order of questions: (question word) + *have/has* + subject + *got* + … .
- We don't use contractions in positive short answers: *Yes, I have.* not *Yes, I've.*
- We don't use *got* in short answers: *No, he hasn't.* not *No, he hasn't got.*
- We often use *any* in plural negatives and questions with *have got*. *Any* is dealt with in more detail in unit 5. At this stage we suggest you just teach it as an item of vocabulary.

11 **R2.4** **P** Play the recording and ask students to repeat. Point out that *have* is stressed in short answers but not in questions.

12 Students work in pairs and take turns to ask and answer questions about Bill and Sally. Students can check their partner's answers in **4a)** and **9a)**.

EXTRA IDEA
- If you have a class of complete beginners, ask students to write their questions before putting them in pairs.

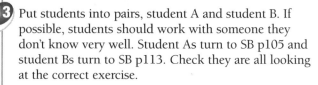 **Get ready … Get it right!**

13 Put students into pairs, student A and student B. If possible, students should work with someone they don't know very well. Student As turn to SB p105 and student Bs turn to SB p113. Check they are all looking at the correct exercise.

a) Students work on their own and guess which things their partner has got by putting a tick or a cross in the *your guess* column. Students are not allowed to talk to each other at this stage.

b) Students work on their own and write questions with *you* about the pictures. While students are working, check their questions for accuracy and help with any problems.

c) Students work with their partner and take turns to ask and answer their questions. They should fill in the *your partner's answer* column with a tick or a cross and check if their guesses were correct.

d) Students work with a new partner and say five things their first partner has/hasn't got.

Finally, ask the class who had the most correct guesses.

EXTRA PRACTICE AND HOMEWORK

Ph **Vocabulary Plus** 2 Personal possessions p188 (Instructions p182)

Ph **Class Activity** 2A Harry and Harriet p140 (Instructions p123)

2 Review Exercises 1, 2 and 3 SB p21

CD-ROM Lesson 2A

Workbook Lesson 2A p10

2B Meet the Robinsons

QUICK REVIEW ●●●

This activity reviews *have got* and personal possessions. Students work in pairs and ask questions with *Have you got ... ?* to find five things they've got that their partner hasn't got. Ask students to share interesting information with the class.

Vocabulary family; *How many ...?*
Help with Listening the schwa /ə/ in words and sentences
Grammar possessive *'s*
Review *be*; *have got*; jobs

Vocabulary Family

1 **a)** Focus on the title of the lesson and elicit the name of the family in the family tree (the Robinsons). Point out the photos of Bill and Sally from lesson 2A. Check students understand the organisation of the family tree and that the two-rings symbol means the people are married.

Students work on their own and fill in the gaps in each paragraph. Check answers with the class.

— EXTRA IDEAS —
- To generate interest at the beginning of the lesson, bring in photos of your family and talk about them to the class.
- If you have a class of complete beginners, teach the words in the boxes yourself first by drawing your own family tree on the board. Then use **1a)** as a practice activity.

b) **R2.5** Play the recording. Students listen and check their answers. Check answers with the class.

With a strong class you can also teach *typical, baby, kids* and *divorced* from the texts.

LISA 2 children 4 son 5 father 6 mother 7 brother
MAX 9 sisters 11 grandchildren 12 granddaughters
13 grandson SALLY 15 uncle 16 cousins
18 grandfather 19 grandmother

2 Draw a three-column table on the board with the headings *male, female* and *male and female*. Tell students to copy the table into their notebooks. Write the examples from the Student's Book in the correct places in the table.

Students work in pairs and complete the table with the words from the three vocabulary boxes in the family tree. Students then check answers in **V2.4** SB p124.

Point out that only your mother and father are your *parents*, other family members are *relatives*. Also point out that *dad, mum* and *kids* are informal words for *father, mother* and *children*. You can also teach the words *a boyfriend/a girlfriend*.

Model and drill the words, focusing on word stress. Pay particular attention to the pronunciation of *parents* /'peərənts/, *daughter* /'dɔːtə/ and *aunt* /ɑːnt/. Also focus on the /ʌ/ sound in *mother* /'mʌðə/, *son* /sʌn/, *brother* /'brʌðə/, *husband* /'hʌzbənd/, *grandmother* /'grændmʌðə/, *uncle* /'ʌŋkəl/ and *cousin* /'kʌzən/.

Help with Listening The schwa /ə/ in words

- This Help with Listening section introduces the schwa /ə/ sound in words and highlights that we don't stress this sound.

3 **a)** Point out the schwas in the words in the box (the schwa is the most common sound in English).

R2.6 Play the recording. Ask students to listen to the words and notice the schwas. Elicit that the schwa is not stressed.

b) **R2.7** Play the recording and ask students to identify where the schwas are in the words in the box. Check answers with the class. Alternatively, students can try to work out where the schwas are first, then listen and check.

Highlight the relationship between the stressed syllables in each word and the schwa, which is never stressed. Also point out that *-or/-er* word endings in English are often pronounced as a schwa.

doctor	address	woman	musician	manager
/ə/ /ə/		/ə/	/ə/	/ə/

4 Write *Lisa's got … brothers and sisters.* and *Bill and Pat have got … children.* on the board. Use these sentences to elicit the example questions with *How many … ?* in the Student's Book. Tell students that we use *How many … ?* to ask about a number and that the noun used with *How many … ?* is always plural.

Also point out that *brothers* is only for men/boys, so we ask *How many brothers and sisters (have you got)?*.

Model and drill the example questions and elicit similar questions from the class.

Students work in pairs and ask each other six *How many … ?* questions about the Robinsons. Monitor and correct any mistakes you hear.

> ── EXTRA IDEAS ──
>
> * Students prepare their questions with *How many … ?* on their own first before working in pairs.
> * Students do the activity with their books closed as a memory game.

Grammar and Listening

5 Go through the examples with the class. Students then do the exercise on their own, using the family tree to help them. Check answers with the class.

> 3 ✓ 4 ✓ 5 Kate is Sally's aunt. 6 ✓

Help with Grammar Possessive *'s*

6 **a)–c)** Students do the exercises on their own or in pairs, then check answers in **G2.3** SB p125. Check answers with the class.

> * **a)** We use name + *'s* for the possessive.
> * **b)** 1c) 2a) 3b)
> * We say *Kate is Lisa's sister.* not ~~*Kate is the sister of Lisa*~~.
> * When there are two names, we put the apostrophe after the second name only: *Pat is Chris and Emma's grandmother.* not ~~*Pat is Chris's and Emma's grandmother*~~.
> * For plural nouns, the apostrophe is after the *s*: *My parents' names …* not ~~*My parent's names …*~~ .

7 Students work on their own and make sentences about the people. Check answers with the class.

> 2 Max is Anna's husband. 3 Pat is Bill's wife. 4 Chris is Bill and Pat's grandson. 5 Emma is Chris's sister. 6 Sally is Anne and Max's daughter.

8 **R2.8** **P** Play the recording (SB p149) and ask students to repeat. Point out the extra /ɪz/ syllable in *Chris's* and *Max's*. This is because *Chris* and *Max* end in a /s/ sound.

9 **a)** Ask students to find Kate on the family tree. Ask *Is she married?* and elicit/teach *No, she's divorced.*

Tell students she's got a new boyfriend, Tim, and she wants to show him some photos of her family.

Ask students to name the people in photos A–C.

> **A** Max, Anna, Sally, Pat, Bill, Fred the dog
> **B** Emma, Chris
> **C** Lisa, Tom

b) **R2.9** Play the recording. Students listen and put the photos in the order they hear them.
Check answers with the class.

> 1C 2B 3A

c) Give students time to read sentences 1–7, then play the recording again. Students listen and choose the correct words.

> 2 musician 3 seven 4 lawyer 5 Italian
> 6 a teacher 7 seventy-three

Help with Listening The schwa /ə/ in sentences

* This Help with Listening section introduces the schwa /ə/ sound in sentences and highlights that we often say many small unstressed words (*and, are,* etc.) with this sound.

10 **a)** Write the sentence *Come and look at these photos of my family.* on the board. Elicit which words are stressed.

Tell students that the vowel sounds in small 'grammar' words like *and, are, a, of, to* and *the* are often pronounced as schwas in sentences. Point out the words with schwas in the example sentence (*and, at, of*) and tell students that these are called 'weak forms'.

R2.9 Play the first sentence of the recording and ask students to listen for the words with the schwas. Ask students if the words with the schwas are stressed (they aren't). Tell students that the schwa is a weak sound and is never stressed.

b) Students turn to R2.9, SB p149. Play the whole recording again. Students listen and notice the stressed words and the unstressed schwas.

Note that the small words like *are, and,* etc. which Kate and Tim pronounce in their strong form are not marked with a schwa in the recording script.

> ── EXTRA IDEA ──
>
> * Students read the recording and make a list of all the words that are pronounced with a schwa.

Get ready ... Get it right!

11 a) Students write their names and the names of five family members of a piece of paper.

Give students two minutes to think about what they can say about these people. Students must not write this information.

b) If possible, put students into pairs with someone they don't know very well. Ask them to swap papers. Point out the example questions and elicit more topic areas: age, job, nationality, possessions, etc.

Students then work on their own and write questions about the people on their partner's paper. While students are working, check their questions for accuracy and help with any problems.

12 a) Students take turns to ask their partner their questions. Students should make notes on their partner's answers.

b) Students work in new pairs and swap information about their partner's family.

Finally, students can share any interesting information with the class.

EXTRA PRACTICE AND HOMEWORK

2 Review Exercises 4 and 5 SB p21
CD-ROM Lesson 2B
Workbook Lesson 2B p11

2C Time and money

QUICK REVIEW ●●●
This activity reviews family vocabulary. Students do the activity in pairs. Set a time limit of three minutes. Students decide whether the words on their list are for men/boys, women/girls, or both. Students then compare lists with another pair. You could do this as a Board Race (see p21).

Real World talking about times and prices; buying tickets
Vocabulary time words (*minute, year*, etc.); *How much ... ?*
Review numbers

What's the time?

1 Students work in pairs and try to put the words in order, then check in **V2.5** SB p124.

Model and drill the words. Highlight the pronunciation of *minute* /ˈmɪnɪt/ and the silent *h* in *hour* /aʊə/.

> 2 a minute 3 a hour 4 a day 5 a week 6 a month
> 7 a year

2 a) Pre-teach *cooker* and check students remember the other words in the vocabulary box.

Use the speech bubbles to teach *I think ...* and *Me too*. Say *I think A is a radio.* and invite students to respond with the language in the speech bubbles.

Students work in pairs and decide what the things are in pictures A–F.

> A a cooker B a mobile (phone) C a TV D a laptop
> E a digital camera F a radio

b) Students match the times to photos A–F, then check their answers in pairs. Check answers with the class.

Model and drill the times. Note that only the main stress on each time is given in the Student's Book. Highlight the schwa in *o'clock* /əˈklɒk/.

> B ten forty C eight fifteen D three forty-five
> E nine twenty F two thirty

c) Tell students that there are two ways to tell the time in English. Students work on their own or in pairs and match the times to photos B–F. Check answers with the class.

Check students understand the meaning of *quarter, half, past* and *to* in times. Point out that we can say *quarter past six* or *a quarter past six*, but not ~~fifteen past six~~.

Model and drill the times. Highlight the pronunciation of *quarter* /ˈkwɔːtə/ and *half* /haːf/, and point out the weak form of *to* /tə/ in *quarter to four*, etc.

> B twenty to eleven C quarter past eight D quarter
> to four E twenty past nine F half past two

3 Use the pictures to teach the difference between *a watch* and *a clock*.

Students work on their own or in pairs and write the times, then check their answers in **RW2.1** SB p125. Model and drill the times.

> 1 five past **one** 2 twenty-five to **seven** 3 ten past **eight**
> 4 ten to **twelve** 5 twenty-five past **ten** 6 five to **three**

4 **R2.10** Refer students back to photos A–F in **2a)**. Play the recording (SB p149). Students listen and match the conversations to three of the photos. Check answers with the class.

> 1A 2F 3C

Real World Talking about the time

5 **a)–c)** Students do the exercises on their own or in pairs, then check their answers in [RW2.2] SB p125. Check answers with the class.

- 1 is 2 clock 3 time 4 past 5 got
- Point out that all three questions have the same meaning, but the third question is more polite.

- 1 at 2 from; to
- Point out that we use *at* with individual times and we use *from … to* for lengths of times.
- Teach the meaning of *a.m., p.m., noon, midday* and *midnight*. Model and drill these words/phrases.

6 **a)** [R2.11] [P] Play the recording. Ask students to repeat. Check students copy the polite intonation correctly.

Also check students understand *Thanks a lot.* (an informal way to say *Thank you.*) and *You're welcome.* (a polite response to *Thank you.*).

b) Give students one minute to work on their own and write down six times.

Students work in pairs and take turns ask and answer the questions in **5a)**. Their partner should write down the times. Encourage students to use all three questions. Students check they have written down the correct times with their partner.

An evening out

7 **a)** Use adverts A–C to teach *adverts*. You can teach students that *advert* and *ad* are short forms of *advertisement* /ad'vɜːtɪsmənt/.

Students do the exercise on their own, then check in pairs. Check answers with the class.

A an exhibition B a concert C a cinema

— EXTRA IDEAS —
- Ask students to find more detail in the adverts, (the names of the exhibition, singer and films, the months the exhibition/concert/films are on, etc.).
- Point out that a booking fee is often added to the price of a ticket bought by phone or credit card and that the numbers (12) and (15) after the film titles in advert C give the minimum age that a child must be to see the film.

b) Tell students they are going to hear two recorded messages and one conversation about the adverts A–C. Focus students on the gaps 1–5 for the times.

[R2.12] Play the recording (SB p149). Students listen and write the times. Play the recording again if necessary. Check answers with the class.

1 5.30 (p.m.) 2 4.30 (p.m.) 3 7.30 4 5.40 5 2.50

8 **a)** Pre-teach *price*. Elicit what the money symbols represent (£ = *pound*, p = *pence*, € = *Euro*, $ = *dollar*, c = *cents*). Students work in pairs and try to say the prices.

b) [R2.13] Play the recording. Students listen and check their answers.

[P] Play the recording again and ask students to repeat. Highlight the pronunciation of *p* /piː/, *euros* /'jʊərəʊz/ and *cents* /sents/.

Point out that in the UK it is much more common to say *forty p* than *forty pence*, although both are correct. Also point out that the currency words are often missed out if the context is clear, for example, *twenty-nine ninety-nine*.

Note that how to say the prices in **8a)** is given in [RW2.3] SB p125.

c) Refer students back to adverts A–C. Focus students on the gaps a)–f) for the prices.

[R2.14] Pre-teach *ticket*, then play the recording (SB p149). Students listen and write the prices. Play the recording again if necessary. Check answers with the class.

a) 7 b) 5 c) 19.50 d) 17.50 e) 6.50 f) 4

9 **a)** Focus students on the photo. Elicit the name of the woman (Kate from lesson 2B), where she is (at the cinema) and what she wants to do (buy tickets). Use the photo to teach *ticket office* and *ticket seller*.

Point out that Kate's sentences 1–4 are in the correct order. Students do the exercise on their own or in pairs.

b) [R2.15] Play the recording. Students listen and check their answers. Check students understand the phrases *How much is that?, Here you are., Right.* (= OK), *Thanks a lot.* and *You're welcome.* (a common response to *Thank you.*).

1c) 2a) 3d) 4b)

c) Students practise the conversation in pairs. They then swap roles and practise the conversation again.

After a few minutes, ask students to close their books and see if they can remember the conversation. You can also ask pairs of students to role-play the conversation for the class.

— EXTRA IDEA —
- With a beginner's class, you can practise the conversation as a Dialogue Build (see p22).

Real World Asking about prices

10 **a)–b)** Students fill in the gaps on their own, then check answers in [RW2.3] SB p125. Check answers with the class.

- 1 is 2 are 3 is 4 are
- Remind students that we use *How much … ?* to ask about prices.

11 Put students into pairs, student A and student B. Student As turn to SB p105 and student Bs turn to SB p113.

a) Allow students time to read about their roles. Students then work in their pairs and student A buys tickets from student B. Students should write the time and how much their tickets cost.

b) Students read about their new roles. Students repeat the role-play with student B as the customer.

c) Students role-play the conversations again. Customers buy tickets for a different film and write the times and how much their tickets cost. Encourage students to buy different types and numbers of tickets each time.

You can finish by asking a few pairs of students to role-play their conversations for the class.

EXTRA PRACTICE AND HOMEWORK

Ph **Class Activity** 2C Time and money p141 (Instructions p123)
2 Review Exercises 6 SB p21
CD-ROM Lesson 2C
Workbook Lesson 2C p13

2D Where's the baby?

QUICK REVIEW ●●●
This activity reviews times and prices. Students write four times and prices on their own, then work in pairs and dictate them to their partner, who writes them down. Students check their answers in pairs.

Vocabulary things in a house; prepositions of place; *Whose ... ?*
Review possessive *'s*; possessive adjectives; personal possessions

1 Students work in pairs and tick the words they know, then do the exercise in **V2.6** SB p124. They can then check answers with another pair.
Check answers with the class. Model and drill the words.

V2.6 1j) 2g) 3f) 4h) 5e) 6c) 7d) 8b) 9a) 10i)

Help with Vocabulary *Prepositions of place*

2 Students do the exercise on their own or in pairs, then check answers in **V2.7** SB p124. Check answers with the class.
Note that *by* is taught here, rather than *next to*, as it is more commonly used in this context. *Next to* is introduced later in the course.

1 in front of 2 behind 3 under 4 by 5 on 6 in

3 Focus students on the picture. Establish that the people in the picture, Lisa, Emma and Tom, are the people from the Robinson family tree in lesson 2B. You can use the picture to teach *living room*.
Focus students on the speech bubble below the box. Ask students to find Lisa's DVDs in the picture.
Students work in pairs and take turns to say where the other things in the box are in the picture. Check students are using the correct prepositions at this stage.

Check answers by asking individual students to tell the class where things are.

Tom's suitcase is behind the sofa. Tom's keys are on the coffee table. Tom's mobile phone is under the coat. The DVD player is under the TV. Lisa's coat is on the sofa. Emma's new shoes are under the chair. The cat is on the chair. Emma's bag is by the door. Emma's books are in the bag. Tom's passport is on the TV. Emma's personal stereo is on the coffee table.

— **EXTRA IDEA** —
● To revise the vocabulary in **1**, students work in pairs and take turns to point to things in the picture. Their partner must say what the item is.

4 Use the speech bubbles to teach *Whose ... is it/are they?*. Point out the use of *It's ... /They're ...* and the possessive *'s* in the answers. Drill the questions and answers with the class.
Ask students to cover the box in **3** and then put students into pairs. Students take turns to point to things in the picture and ask their partner questions with *Whose ... ?*.

— **EXTRA IDEA** —
● Go around the class and ask each student to put one of their possessions in a bag. Then ask students to take turns to take an object out of the bag and ask *Whose ... is this?*. The other students answer *(I think) it's (student's name + 's)*.

5 a) Focus students on the picture. Tell students that the Robinson family are having a busy Monday morning. R2.16 Play the recording (SB p149). Students listen and tick the things in the box in **3** that the family talk about. Check answers with the class.

> Tom's suitcase; Tom's keys; Tom's mobile phone; Lisa's coat; Emma's new shoes; Emma's bag; Emma's books; Tom's passport

b) Check students understand that three things are in the wrong place in the picture. Play the recording again. Students listen and find the three things.

Students check answers in pairs. Check answers with the class.

> **1** Tom's keys: in the picture they're on the coffee table, but in the recording they're on the desk by the computer. **2** Emma's shoes: in the picture they're under the chair by the sofa, but in the recording they're under the chair by the window. **3** Tom's passport: in the picture it's on the TV, but in the recording it's on the table by the window, in front of the plant.

c) Ask students to find the baby (he's under the desk).

6 R2.16 Students look at R2.16, SB p149. Play the recording again. Students listen and underline all the prepositions of place.

Students check answers in pairs. Check answers with the class. You can do this by playing the recording again and asking student to shout *stop* when they hear a preposition. Pause the recording briefly each time they shout *stop* before continuing.

> on; By; under; on; under; by; by; in; on; by; in front of

7 Drill the questions and answers in the speech bubbles to remind students of the language they need to do the exercise.

Allow students two minutes to look at the picture. They are not allowed to make notes.

Students close their books. Put students into pairs. Students take turns to ask each other where things are in the living room.

— EXTRA IDEA —

- Students work on their own and write eight questions about things in the picture. Students close their books and work in pairs. They take turns to ask their questions and give their partner one point for each question he/she gets right. The student with the most correct answers is the winner.

— EXTRA PRACTICE AND HOMEWORK —

Ph Class Activity 2D Where is it? p142 (Instructions p124)
2 Review SB p21
CD-ROM Lesson 2D
Workbook Lesson 2D p14
Workbook Reading and Writing Portfolio 2 p66
Progress Test 2 p212

2 Review

See p32 for ideas on how to use this section.

1a) 2 cheap 3 small 4 slow 5 beautiful 6 easy 7 young 8 good

1b) 2 expensive 3 big 4 fast 5 ugly 6 difficult 7 old 8 bad

3a) 2 Has 3 Have 4 Have 5 Have

4 2 your sister 3 your grandchildren 4 your uncle 5 your grandfather 6 your aunt 7 your grandparents 8 your cousin

5 2 has 3 is 4 possessive 5 is 6 is; possessive

6a) 2 quarter to ten 3 ten to ten 4 five to ten 5 ten past ten 6 quarter past ten 7 twenty-five past ten 8 half past ten

6b) nine forty-five; nine fifty; nine fifty-five; ten ten; ten fifteen; ten twenty-five; ten thirty

Progress Portfolio

See p32 for ideas on how to use this section.

3 Daily life

Student's Book p22–p29

3A   A glamorous life?

QUICK REVIEW ●●●
This activity reviews prepositions of place. Do one or two examples with the class before putting them in pairs. Students take turns to tell their partner where something is in the room. Their partner guesses what the thing is.

Vocabulary daily routines
Grammar Present Simple (1): positive and *Wh-* questions (*I/you/we/they*)
Review the time

Vocabulary Daily routines

a) Students work on their own and tick the words/phrases they know, then do the exercise in **V3.1** SB p126. They can then check answers in pairs.

Check answers with the class. Point out that *get in get home* means *arrive* and that we usually say *have breakfast/ lunch/dinner* not *eat breakfast*, etc. Use the words/phrases in the box to teach the phrase *daily routine*.

Focus students on the **TIP!** under the vocabulary box. Point out that only the main stress in phrases is shown in the vocabulary boxes and in the Language Summaries. We only show the main stress (*finish work*), not the secondary stress (*finish work*) as we feel this is the simplest and most effective way to make sure students put the main stress in the right place.

Model and drill the words/phrases. Highlight the pronunciation of *breakfast* /'brekfəst/, *lunch* /lʌntʃ/, *work* /wɜːk/ (often confused with *walk* /wɔːk/) and the different vowel sounds in *leave* /liːv/ and *live* /lɪv/.

> **V3.1** 1b) 2n) 3c) 4i) 5m) 6e) 7f) 8k) 9j) 10d)
> 11l) 14o) 15a)

b) Pre-teach *in the morning/afternoon/evening* and *at night*. Point out that we don't say ~~in the night~~. Check students understand what parts of the day these are. Drill these phrases with the class.

Students do the exercise on their own or in pairs. Check answers with the class.

> 1 have breakfast; leave home; start work/classes; work; study 2 have lunch; work; study; finish work/classes; (get home) 3 (get home); have dinner; (work); (study) 4 go to bed; sleep

Reading and Grammar

a) Focus students on the photos. Ask students what Sam Dane's job is (he's a film actor). Pre-teach *early, late, before, after, at home* and *at the studio*.

b) Tell students to cover the article. Students do the exercise on their own or in pairs. ✏️ Write students' suggestions for the times film actors do these things on the board.

c) Students read the interview and check their answers. Check answers with the class.

> 1 five o'clock in the morning
> 2 about 7.30
> 3 about 5.45
> 4 twelve

Students read the interview again to find out if sentences 1–6 are true or false. Remind students to correct the false sentences. Check answers with the class.

> 2F They get up very early. 3T 4F They have half an hour for breakfast. 5T 6T

— EXTRA IDEA —
* With a strong class, teach the other new words in the article: *a party, a holiday, glamorous, star, long, get to (= arrive at), first*.

Help with Grammar Present Simple: positive (*I/you/we/they*)

a)–c) Students do the exercises on their own or in pairs, then check answers in **G3.1** SB p127. Check answers with the class.

* 2 get up 3 start 4 have
* Point out the word order: subject + verb + ...

* The form of the Present Simple is the same after *I, you, we* and *they* and it is the same as the infinitive.
* Check students understand that we often use the Present Simple to talk about routines.

5 **R3.1** **P** Point out the stress on the example sentence, then play the recording and ask students to repeat. Check they stress the sentences correctly.

You can also point out the schwas in the weak forms of *at, an* and *for* in sentences 1, 3 and 4.

6 Students do the exercise on their own. While they are working, monitor and check for accuracy.

Students can compare sentences in pairs or groups. Ask each student to tell the class one of their sentences.

7 a) Pre-teach *get back to (the hotel)*.

Students read the sentences about the rest of Sam's daily routine and guess which answers are correct. Students can compare guesses in pairs.

b) **R3.2** Play the recording (SB p150). Students listen and check answers. Play the recording again if necessary. Check answers with the class.

> 1 9 2 an hour or two 3 9.30 4 10.30 5 six hours

c) This exercise introduces students to the question form of the Present Simple. Ask students to look at R3.2, SB p150.

Play the recording again. Students listen and find all the questions. Check answers with the class.

Remind students that *When* and *What time* can both be used to ask about times.

> When do you finish work? And when do you have dinner? What time do you get back to the hotel? And what time do you go to bed? So, *do* you have a glamorous life?

Help with Grammar Present Simple:
Wh- questions (*I/you/we/they*)

8 a) Draw the table on the board and write in the example questions.

Teach the meanings of the grammar headings: *question word, auxiliary, subject* and *infinitive* by referring to the examples in the table.

Use the examples to highlight the word order of Present Simple questions with *I/you/we/they*: question word + *do* + subject + infinitive + … .

Establish that the auxiliary *do* has no meaning but is used to make the question form of the Present Simple with *I/you/we/they*.

b)–c) Students do the exercise on their own, then check answers in **G3.2** SB p127. Check answers with the class.

- Focus students on the table on the board. Elicit which words in sentences 1–3 in **8b)** go in each column and complete the table (see the table in **G3.2** SB p127). Use these examples to highlight the word order in Present Simple questions.
- You may also wish to highlight the difference in word order between Present Simple questions and questions with *be* and *have got*.

9 a) Students do the exercise on their own, referring back to the table in **8a)** if necessary. You can do the first question with the class as an example.

b) **G3.3** Play the recording. Students listen and check their answers.

Focus students on the stressed words in the example and point out that *do you* is often pronounced /dʒə/ in natural spoken English. Note that *do you* is also pronounced /djə/.

P Play the recording again and ask students to repeat. Encourage students to copy the sentence stress and the weak form of *do you*.

> 1 Where do you live? 2 Where do you work?
> 3 What time do you get up? 4 When do you start work or classes? 5 What time do you get home?
> 6 When do you have dinner?

c) Students work in pairs and take turns to ask and answer the questions in **9a)**. Encourage students to use natural short answers, for example, *In Madrid. At about 8 o'clock.*, not whole sentences. Monitor and correct pronunciation as necessary.

Get ready … Get it right!

10 Focus students on the examples and teach the phrases *in the week* and *at the weekend*. Students work on their own and write eight questions about people's daily and weekend routines, using words/phrases from **1a)**.

While students are working, check their questions for accuracy and help with any problems.

11 a) Remind students of the phrase *Me too.* and teach *What about you?*.

Students move around the room asking other students their questions or ask as many people as they can sitting near them.

When they find a student who does something at the same time as them, they write the person's name down next to the question. Students should try and find a different student for each question. While students are working, monitor and help with any problems.

b) Use the speech bubble to teach *both*. Point out that *both* can go after the subjects (*Petra and I both …*) or at the beginning of the sentence (*Both Petra and I …*).

Students take turns to tell the class two things they have found out.

EXTRA PRACTICE AND HOMEWORK

Ph **Vocabulary Plus** 3 Daily routines p189 (Instructions p183)

Ph **Class Activity** 3A World routines p143 (Instructions p124)

3 Review Exercise 1 SB p29

CD-ROM Lesson 3A

Workbook Lesson 3A p15

3B Evenings and weekends

Vocabulary free time activities (1); time phrases with *on, in, at, every*
Grammar Present Simple (2): negative and *yes/no* questions (*I/you/we/they*)
Help with Listening questions with *do you ... ?*
Review Present Simple: positive

QUICK REVIEW ●●●

This activity practises daily routine vocabulary and the Present Simple. Students work on their own and make notes on their daily routines (*get up – 8.30*, etc.). Put students into pairs. Students compare their daily routines. Check students are saying whole sentences at this stage (*I get up at 8.30*, etc.). Students find out how many of the times are the same.

Vocabulary Free time activities (1)

1 a) Check students understand the meaning of *free time* (when you're not working).

Students work on their own and tick the phrases they know, then do the exercise in V3.2 SB p126. They can then check answers in pairs.

Check answers with the class. Point out that *go for a drink* means a drink in a pub/bar, not in a café, and that we say *Do you want to go for a drink?* not ~~Do you want to drink something?~~.

Also note that we can say *eat out* or *go out to eat*, and *stay in* or *stay at home*.

Highlight the different phrases that follow *go*: *go **for a** drink, go **to the** cinema, go **to** concerts*, and *go shopping* not ~~go to shopping~~.

Model and drill the phrases, focusing on stress. Note that only the main stress in words/phrases is shown in vocabulary boxes and the Language Summaries.

> V3.2 1d) 3f) 4j) 5h) 6b) 7g) 8k) 9i) 10c) 11l) 12a)

b) Give students a few moments to think of their answers to the question. They can use phrases from **1a)** or their own ideas. Help students with new vocabulary as necessary.

Students work in pairs and compare answers.

Ask students to share interesting answers with the class.

Listening and Grammar

2 Focus students on the photo and ask where the people are (at an office party). Ask students if they think Tanya and Robert, the people in the foreground, are good friends.

> ### Help with Listening Questions with *do you ... ?*

- This Help with Listening section helps students to understand Present Simple questions with *do you ... ?* and highlights the weak pronunciation /dʒə/ of this phrase.

3 a) Tell students they are going to listen to five questions that Robert asks Tanya at the office party. Give students time to read questions 1–5.

R3.4 Play the recording. Students listen and fill in the gaps. Check answers with the class. Point out that in sentences 2 and 4 *do* is both the auxiliary verb and the infinitive.

> 2 do; evenings 3 eat 4 do; weekends 5 go; concerts

b) Play the recording again. Highlight the pronunciation of *do you* /dʒə/ in questions and point out that this is how these questions are normally pronounced in natural spoken English.

─ EXTRA IDEA ─
- Ask students which words are stressed in questions 1–5 in **3a)**. Play the recording again for students to check their answers. Ask students if *do you* is stressed (it isn't).

4 a) Give students time to read the sentences and check students understand the new words *same, office, a lot* and *together*.

R3.5 Play the recording (SB p150). Students listen and tick the true sentences. Check answers with the class. Ask students to correct the false sentences.

> 1 ✗ Robert and Tanya work in different offices.
> 2 ✓ 3 ✗ Tanya doesn't go out on Saturday evenings.
> 4 ✗ Tanya doesn't want to go to a concert with Robert. 5 ✗ Tanya's married.

b) Point out that the a) and b) options in 1–5 in **4a)** are Tanya's possible answers to Robert's questions in **3a)**.

Play the recording again. Students listen and choose the correct answers, a) or b). Check answers with the class.

> 2b) 3b) 4a) 5a)

─ EXTRA IDEA ─
- Ask students to look at R3.5, p150 and play the recording again. Students listen and read, noticing the pronunciation of *do you* in the questions. This is useful consolidation for students and helps them see the relationship between sounds and spelling.

Help with Grammar Present Simple: negative (*I/you/we/they*)

5 **a)–c)** Students do the exercises on their own or in pairs, then check their answers in **G3.3** SB p127.

While they are working, draw the table from **5a)** on the board so you are ready to check students' answers. Check answers with the class.

- Focus students on the table on the board. Check students understand that *don't* is the contracted form of *do not*. Point out that we usually use the contracted form in speaking and writing.
- Use the example to illustrate the word order of the Present Simple negative with *I/you/we/they*: subject + *don't* + infinitive + … .
- Elicit which words in sentences 1 and 2 in **5b)** go in each column and complete the table (see the table in **G3.3** SB p127).

6 **a)** Go through the example with the class. Students do the exercise on their own.

b) Focus on the speech bubbles. Ask students which of the sentences in the blue speech bubbles is positive (*I go shopping on Saturdays.*) and which is negative (*I don't watch TV every evening.*). Check students understand *every*.

Use these examples to teach/review *Me too./I don't.*, which are ways to agree or disagree with a positive sentence, and *Me neither./Oh, I do.*, which are ways to agree or disagree with a negative sentence.

Students work in pairs and compare their sentences from **6a)**. Encourage students to respond by using the language in the speech bubbles.

Ask students to share any interesting ideas with the class.

Help with Grammar Present Simple: *yes/no* questions and short answers (*I/you/we/they*)

7 **a)–c)** Students do the exercises on their own or in pairs, then check answers in **G3.4** SB p127.

While they are working, draw the table from **7a)** on the board so you are ready to check students' answers. Check answers with the class.

- Focus students on the table on the board. Elicit which words in questions 1 and 2 in **7b)** go in each column and complete the table (see the table in **G3.4** SB p127).
- Use the examples to illustrate the word order in Present Simple *yes/no* questions: *Do* + subject + infinitive + … .
- Point out that we use the auxiliary *do* or *don't* in the short answers, but we don't repeat the infinitive: *Yes, I do.* not ~~Yes, I do go.~~
- Remind students that short answers are very common in spoken English.

8 **a)** Pre-teach *sometimes*. Do the first example with the class, then ask students to finish the exercise on their own. Students can compare their answers in pairs or groups.

b) **R3.6** Play the recording. Students listen and check their answers.

P Play the recording again. Ask students to repeat. Focus on word stress and the pronunciation of *do you* /dʒə/.

> **1** A Do; go B visit **2** A Do; have **3** A Do; go B do
> **4** A Do; eat B don't; stay; watch **5** A Do; do B don't

c) Demonstrate this activity with a confident student. Make it clear that students answer about themselves.

Students work in pairs and take turns to ask and answer the questions in **8a)**.

Ask students to share interesting answers with the class.

Vocabulary Time phrases

9 **a)** Student do the exercise on their own or in pairs, then check answers in **V3.3** SB p126.

While they are working, draw the four circles on the board so you are ready to check student's answers.

Check answers with the class. Help students see the following patterns: we use *on* with days; we use *in* with *the morning, the afternoon, the evening* (but we say *at night* not ~~in the night~~); we use *at* with times. Highlight the use of *at* with *night* and *the weekend*.

Point out that we can use the singular or plural of days, parts of days and the weekend: *I play tennis on Monday/Mondays.*, etc. Note that we don't use plurals with *every*. We say *every week* not ~~every weeks~~.

Also point out that in American and Australian English we say *on the weekend*.

> **on** Thursday; Mondays; Monday mornings; Sunday afternoon
> **in** the afternoon; the evening; the week
> **at** half past three; night; the weekend
> **every** Thursday; day; month; night; morning

b) Students work in pairs and take turns to test each other on the time phrases, as in the speech bubbles.

Get ready … Get it right!

10 Put students in three groups, group A, group B and group C. Ask students to turn to the appropriate pages in the back of the Student's Book.

a) Students work on their own and choose the correct words in the phrases.

Students check answers with someone from the same group. If they disagree, ask them to check any queries in **V3.3** SB p126. Monitor and deal with any problems.

> **GROUP A** **2** on **3** in **4** every **5** at **GROUP B** **2** every
> **3** on **4** at **5** every **GROUP C** **2** in **3** at **4** on **5** every

b) Students work on their own (or in pairs with someone from the same group) and write the questions.

c) Students move around the room asking their questions or ask as many people as possible sitting near them. They must find two people who answer *yes* for each question. When they find a person who answers *yes*, they must write his/her name in their table.

Tell students to change partners when they have written down a student's name.

d) Students take turns to tell the class about the people in their table, as in the examples.

EXTRA PRACTICE AND HOMEWORK

Ph **Class Activity** 3B Time phrase snap p144 (Instructions p124)
3 Review Exercises 2 and 3 SB p29
CD-ROM Lesson 3B
Workbook Lesson 3B p16

3C Special days

QUICK REVIEW ●●●

This activity reviews the Present Simple (positive and negative). ✎ Write *On a perfect day I ...* on the board and teach the meaning of *perfect*. Write the positive and negative examples or give two of your own. Students then work on their own and think of four ways to finish the sentence. Students compare their perfect days in pairs. Ask students to share their ideas with the class.

Real World phrases for special days; suggestions
Vocabulary months and dates
Help with Listening dates
Review *be*; Present Simple

Congratulations!

1 a) Focus students on the photos of the five cards and teach *card*.

Students do the exercise on their own, then check in pairs.

Check answers with the class and use the cards to teach *wedding, New Year's Eve, birthday* and *wedding anniversary*. Drill these words/phrases with the class, paying particular attention to the pronunciation of *birthday* /ˈbɜːθdeɪ/.

1C 2E 3D 4B 5A

b) **R3.7** Play the recording (SB p150). Students match the conversations 1–5 to the special days in **1a)**. Play the recording again if necessary. Check answers with the class.

1 a New Year's Eve party 2 the birth of a new baby
3 a wedding anniversary 4 a birthday 5 a wedding

Real World Phrases for special days

2 Tell students we say these phrases on special days. Students do the exercise on their own. Check answers with the class. Point out that we usually write these phrases with exclamation marks.

Happy birthday! 3 Happy New Year! 2
Congratulations! 1; 5 Happy anniversary! 4

3 a) **R3.8** **P** Play the recording. Students copy the stress and intonation so that they sound enthusiastic!

b) **R3.9** Play the recording (SB p150). Students should respond to each sentence with the appropriate phrase.

1 Happy birthday! 2 Congratulations! 3 Happy anniversary! 4 Congratulations! 5 Happy New Year!

When's your birthday?

4 a) Students work in pairs and put the months in the correct order. Point out that months always begin with capital letters. Teach these common abbreviations: *Jan, Feb, Mar, Apr, Aug, Sept, Oct, Nov, Dec.*

b) **R3.10** Play the recording. Students listen and check their answers.

Draw students' attention to the stress marks in **4a)**.
P Play the recording again and ask students to repeat. Pay particular attention to the pronunciation of *February* /ˈfebruəri/, *June* /dʒuːn/, *July* /dʒʊˈlaɪ/ and *August* /ˈɔːgəst/.

5 a) ✎ To establish the difference between *date* and *day*, write today's day and date and on the board and elicit which is which.

Students do the exercise on their own, then check answers in **V3.5** SB p126.

Check answers with the class. Point out the use of the letters *st, nd, rd* and *th* when we write dates using numbers, and the hyphens (-) in numbers written as words.

2nd = second; 3rd = third; 4th = fourth; 5th = fifth; 20th = twentieth; 22nd = twenty-second; 23rd = twenty-third; 31st = thirty-first

- Write each date (*1ˢᵗ*, etc.) and word (*first*, etc.) on separate cards. Give one to each student. Students move around the room to find their partner.
- Students count round the class using ordinal numbers (*first, second*, etc.). If they make a mistake, they are 'out'. The last student 'in' wins.

b) R3.11 P Play the recording and ask students to repeat the dates. Pay particular attention to the 'consonant clusters' at the ends of words (*fif**th**, thirteen**th***, etc.). You may want to drill the other dates with your class.

Help with Listening Dates

- This Help with Listening section helps students to understand questions about dates and the different ways we say dates.

6 a) R3.12 Play the recording. Students fill in the gaps. Check answers with the class. Highlight that we use *on* with dates. Point out that we say **the** *fifth* **of** May or May **the** *fifth* (or *May fifth* in American English), but we write *5ᵗʰ May* or *May 5ᵗʰ*.

Also point out that dates are written differently in the UK and the USA. The date 1/9/07 is the first of September 2007 in the UK, but the ninth of January 2007 in the USA.

> 1 April 2 July 3 May

b) Play the recording again. Students listen and notice the weak forms of *the* /ðə/ and *of* /əv/. Point out the schwas /ə/ in these weak forms.

7 a) R3.13 Play the recording (SB p150). Students listen and circle the dates they hear. Play the recording again if necessary. Check answers with the class.

> 2 December 13ᵗʰ 3 March 14ᵗʰ 4 July 2ⁿᵈ
> 5 October 20ᵗʰ 6 February 1ˢᵗ

b) R3.14 P Play the recording. Students repeat the correct answers from **7a)**. Encourage students to use the weak forms of *the* /ðə/ and *of* /əv/ when saying dates.

- After **7b)**, students practise saying the other dates in **7a)**.
- Pre-teach *When's your birthday?*. Students move around the room asking the question with the aim of standing in a line in order of their birthdays. At the end, each student says his/her birthday in turn to check everyone is standing in the correct place.

8 a) Students work on their own and write four important dates for them.

b) Use the speech bubbles to teach *Why … ?* and *Because … .*

Put students into pairs. Students take turns to say their dates to each other. They should write down their partner's dates.

Student then ask their partner why these dates are important. While they are working, monitor and help with any new vocabulary students need.

Ask students to share interesting information with the class.

What shall we get him?

9 a) Focus students on the photo and ask students if they recognise Tanya (from lesson 3B). Elicit that Simon is her husband and tell students that they are talking about their friend Tom's birthday.

Pre-teach *(birthday) present* and focus on the title of the section to establish that *get* means *buy* in this context.

R3.15 Play the recording. Students listen to find out what Tanya and Simon decide to buy.

Check the answer with the class (they decide to buy the new Simpsons DVD).

b) Give students time to read the conversation. Play the recording again. Students listen and fill in the gaps. Play the recording again if necessary.

Students check answers in pairs. Check answers with the class.

> 1 tenth 2 birthday 3 book 4 DVD 5 DVD 6 good
> 7 watch

- Write the words that go in the gaps on the board in random order before students listen. Students predict which gaps they go in, then listen and check.

Real World Suggestions

10 a)–b) Students look at the conversation in **9b)** and fill in the gaps in the table, then check their answers in RW3.2 SB p127. Check answers with the class.

- Check the table with the class (see the table in RW3.2 SB p127).
- Check students understand the meaning of *suggestions* and the headings in the table.
- Check students understand the meaning of *get*, *buy* and *give*. We say *give someone a present* not *present someone*.
- Point out that *What shall we … ?* and *Let's … *are followed by the infinitive. *Let's* is a short form of *Let us*, although this is very rarely used.
- Teach *How about … ?* as an alternative to *What about … ?*.
- Highlight the negative answer *No, I don't think so.* which isn't in the conversation.

11 **a)** R3.16 P Play the recording (SB p150) and ask students to repeat. Encourage students to copy the stress and intonation. Note we use the weak form of *shall* /ʃəl/.

b) Students work in pairs and choose a role, Tanya or Simon. They practise the conversation in pairs and try to memorise it. Students should use today's date.

c) Students close their books and practise the conversation again to see if they can remember it.

Ask a few pairs of students to role-play the conversation in front of the rest of the class.

12 **a)** Students work in groups of four and make a list of typical birthday presents. Make sure you have an <u>even</u> number of groups, so if you have extra students have some groups of five. Help students with vocabulary as necessary and encourage them to write as many things as possible.

b) Tell students to imagine that it is everyone's birthday today and that they are going to give presents to students in another group. Pair up the groups so that students know who they are giving presents to.

Students discuss in their groups which presents from their list to give the people in the other group. Encourage students to use the language from **10a)** in their discussion.

When they have decided on their presents, each student should draw one of the presents on a piece of paper to give to a person in the other group.

c) Drill the phrases in the speech bubbles. Teach *lovely*.

Put the matching groups together. Students take turns to give their presents and say thank you.

EXTRA PRACTICE AND HOMEWORK

1 Review Exercises 4 and 5 SB p29
CD-ROM Lesson 3C
Workbook Lesson 3C p18

3D Early bird or night owl?

QUICK REVIEW ●●●
This activity revises asking for, making and responding to suggestions. Students do the activity in groups of four. Ask each group to share their plans with the class. The class decides which plan is the best.

Vocabulary frequency adverbs
Grammar subject and object pronouns
Review Present Simple; routines

Help with Vocabulary Word order of frequency adverbs

1 Focus students on the line and check they have noticed the 100% and 0% at each end. Use the position of *hardly ever* on the line to teach its meaning. Tell students that the words in the box are called *frequency adverbs*.

Students do the exercise on their own or in pairs, then check in V3.6 SB p126. Check answers with the class.

Model and drill the frequency adverbs. Pay particular attention to the pronunciation of *usually* /ˈjuːʒuəli/ and *hardly ever* /ˈhɑːdli ˌevə/.

2 **a)** Focus students on the questionnaire and the pictures. Pre-teach *(I'm an) early bird.* (someone who likes getting up early) and *(I'm a) night owl.* (someone who prefers being awake and active at night).

Pre-teach *happy, have (a lot of) energy, record a TV programme, the end (of a party, film, etc.)*

Students do the questionnaire on their own.

b) Ask students to turn to SB p158. Students work out their score and read their profile. Help students with vocabulary as necessary.

c) Students compare scores in groups, then find out how many of their answers are the same. Ask students to share their results with the class.

3 **a)–c)** Students do the exercises on their own or in pairs by referring back to the questionnaire. They then check answers in V3.7 SB p126. Check answers with the class.

- Frequency adverbs go after the verb *be*:
  *I'm **always** happy when I get up.*
- Frequency adverbs go before other verbs:
  *I **sometimes** get up before 9.*
- Point out that we can only use *always, usually* and *often* in negative sentences. We can say *I don't always/usually/often go out on Sunday evenings.* but not ~~I don't sometimes/hardly ever/never go out on Sunday evenings.~~

4 **a)** Pre-teach *tired*, then go through the example with the class.

Students do the exercise on their own, referring to the rules in **3b)** as necessary. Monitor and check for word order.

b) Students check answers in pairs and find out how many sentences are the same.

Ask each pair to tell the class one or two sentences that are the same for both students.

Help with Grammar Subject and object pronouns

5 **a)–c)** 🖊 Establish the concept of subject and object by drawing a man and a woman on the board with a speech bubble from one person saying *I love you*. Ask students to identify the subject and object (subject = *I*, object = *you*). Use the sentence to point out the typical subject + verb + object word order in sentences.

Students then do the exercises on their own or in pairs before checking their answers in **G3.5** SB 127.

🖊 While they are working, draw the table in **5b)** on the board so you are ready to check students' answers. Check answers with the class.

- In the example sentences in **5a)** *I* and *We* are subject pronouns, *her* and *him* are object pronouns.
- Elicit the answers to **5b)** and fill in the table on the board: *you; him; her; it; us; them*.
- Point out that in positive and negative sentences, subject pronouns come before the verb and object pronouns come after the verb: **I** *often phone <u>her</u> at 11 p.m.* **We** *don't usually see <u>him</u> in the mornings.*

6 Focus on the example from the questionnaire. Point out the object pronoun *it* in the second sentence and show how it represents the noun phrase *a good film* in the first sentence.

Students do the exercise on their own or in pairs.

> **3b)** it → a good film
> **5a), 5b), 5c)** them → friends
> **6a), 6b)** him/her → a friend

7 **a)** Remind students who Tanya is (the woman from lessons 3B and 3C). Ask if she's married (she is) and what her husband's name is (Simon). Tell students Tanya is doing the questionnaire.

R3.17 Focus students on the questionnaire and play the recording (SB p150). Students listen and write *T* next to Tanya's answers. Play the recording again if necessary.

b) Students check answers in pairs. Check answers with the class.

> **1b) 2c) 3c) 4c) 5a) 6a)**
> **Score: 11** Tanya's an afternoon person.

3 Review

See p32 for ideas on how to use this section.

1a) **2** When/What time do you get up?
3 Where do you work?
4 When/What time do you start work?
5 When/What time do you have lunch?
6 When/What time do you finish work?
7 Where do you have dinner?
8 When/What time do you go to bed?

2 have coffee with friends; watch TV; go to the cinema/shopping; go shopping/to the cinema; visit your family; stay in; do sport

3a) **2** at **3** on **4** on **5** at **6** on **7** in **8** at

4a) **2** Feb 28th **3** Mar 16th **4** Apr 7th **5** May 31st **6** June 19th **7** July 13th **8** Aug 22nd **9** Sept 10th **10** Oct 4th **11** Nov 30th **12** Dec 25th

5a) **2** I hardly ever sleep in the afternoons. **3** I'm sometimes at home on Friday evenings. **4** My friends don't often go out in the week. **5** My friends always remember my birthday.

Progress Portfolio

See p32 for ideas on how to use this section.

4 Time off

4A   Away from home

Vocabulary free time activities (2)
Grammar Present Simple (3): positive and negative
(*he/she/it*)
Help with Listening linking (1)
Review Present Simple (*I/you/we/they*); frequency adverbs

QUICK REVIEW ●●●
This activity reviews frequency adverbs and the Present
Simple. Students write the sentences on their own. Then
put students in pairs to compare sentences. Finally, each
pair tells the class any sentences that are the same.

Vocabulary Free time activities (2)

 a) Students work on their own and tick the phrases they
know, then do the matching exercise in **V4.1** SB p128.

Check answers with the class. Highlight the pattern: *go* +
verb+*ing*, (*go skiing, go swimming*, etc.) and that we say
listen to music but *listen to the radio*.

Model and drill the phrases. Pay particular attention to
the pronunciation of *skiing* /ˈskiːɪŋ/ and *listen* /ˈlɪsən/.

Note that only the main stress in words/phrases is shown
in vocabulary boxes and the Language Summaries.

> **V4.1** 1e) 2h) 3d) 4j) 5g) 6k) 7b) 8i) 9c)
> 10a) 11f)

b) Use the speech bubbles to remind students how
to make Present Simple questions with *you*. Drill the
question and the answers and elicit other possible
answers, for example, *Yes, on Mondays. No, I don't. Yes,
sometimes*, etc.

Students work in pairs and ask each other about their free
time activities. Ask students to share interesting answers
with the class.

--- EXTRA IDEA ---
• Students work in pairs and test each other on the
collocations in **1a)**. For example, student A says
photos and student B says *take photos*.

Listening and Grammar

 a) Focus students on the photo. Ask students where they
think it is (Antarctica), who the man is (Paul) and who
Alison and Erin are (his wife and daughter).

b) Pre-teach *weather station* and *two/three months off
a year*.

R4.1 Give students time to read sentences 1–4, then play
the recording (SB p150). Students work on their own and
circle the correct answers.

Students check answers in pairs. Check answers with
the class.

> 2 engineer 3 six 4 three

3 a) Students work in pairs and choose four free time
activities for Paul from **1a)**.

b) **R4.2** Play the recording (SB p150) of the rest of Alison
and Vicky's conversation. Students listen and check if
their guesses are correct. Check answers with the class.

> watches sport on TV goes skiing goes running
> takes photos goes swimming (on New Year's Day)

Help with Listening Linking (1)

• This Help with Listening section introduces
consonant-vowel linking and helps students to
understand that we often link words together in
natural spoken English.

4 a) Write the example sentence on the board. Point
out the linking between the final consonant sounds
and the initial vowel sounds. Show how this makes
two words sound like one word. Highlight that it is
the initial and final sounds that are important, not
the spelling, for example, *people_at* links, even though
people ends in a vowel.

Students turn to R4.2, SB p150. Focus students on the
links shown in the recording script. Point out that only
Alison's sentences are linked.

R4.2 Play the recording again. Students listen and read,
noticing the linking.

Note that vowel-vowel links which have an extra
linking sound (for example, *So_/w/_it's* and
he_/j/_emails) are not marked in the recording script
for R4.2. Extra linking sounds are dealt with in
face2face Pre-intermediate.

b) Students work in pairs and find four consonant-
vowel links in Vicky's sentences. Check answers with
the class. You can play the recording again so that
students can hear the links.

Note: *does he* in *So what does he do?* is also linked as
the /h/ is not pronounced.

> What_about his free time? So what does_he do?
> In_Antarctica?! Do you talk to him_a lot?
> And what do *you* think_about his job?

Help with Grammar Present Simple: positive and negative (*he/she/it*)

5 **a)–c)** Students do the exercises on their own or in pairs before checking their answers in **G4.1** SB p130. Check answers with the class.

- In positive sentences with *he/she/it* (and names of people or places) we add **-s** or **-es** to the infinitive.
- In negative sentences with *he/she/it* we use **doesn't** + infinitive.
- In negative sentences we don't add -s or -es to the infinitive: *He doesn't like ...* not ~~He doesn't likes ...~~ .
- We use *doesn't* in negative sentences with *he/she/it*. We use *don't* in negative sentences with *I/you/we/they*.

6 **a)** Students look at **G4.2** SB p130. Go through the spelling rules with the whole class. Note that the *he/she/it* form of *have* is *has*, not ~~haves~~.

Students work on their own and write the *he/she/it* forms of the verbs. Students then check answers in pairs.

✏ Draw a four-column table on the board with the headings -s, -es, -ies and *irregular*. Check answers with the whole class and write them in the correct column.

-s: plays; gets; writes; phones; lives; starts **-es**: watches; goes; finishes; does **-ies**: studies **irregular**: has

b) **R4.3** **P** Play the recording and ask students to repeat the verb forms. Ask students which *he/she/it* forms end in the sound /ɪz/ (*watches* /'wɒtʃɪz/, *finishes* /'fɪnɪʃɪz/ and *studies* /stʌdɪz/). Remind students that this is how we make the *he/she/it* form of all verbs ending in -ch and -sh, for example, *matches*, *washes*, etc.

Note: this is also true for all verbs ending in -s, -ss, -x or -z, for example, *miss*, *fix*, etc., but these have not been included in the exercise as students have not met any of these verbs at this point in the course.

— EXTRA IDEA —

- Students work in pairs and write as many *he/she/it* forms of other verbs they can think of. Set a time limit of three minutes. ✏ Check answers with the class by writing the *he/she/it* forms in the table on the board. The pair with the most new verbs wins.

7 Ask students to read the text quickly without filling in the gaps to find out what it is about (how Alison, Paul and Erin spend their time when Paul comes home to Canada). Students do the exercise on their own, then check answers in pairs. Check answers with the class.

2 works 3 meets 4 gets 5 comes 6 buys 7 go
8 play 9 watches 10 doesn't watch 11 doesn't have
12 go 13 goes

8 Focus students on the example and ask them why the words *live in* are linked (because *live* ends in a consonant sound and *in* begins with a vowel sound).

R4.4 **P** Play the recording (SB p151) and ask students to repeat. Check students copy the linking correctly. You can ask students to turn to R4.4, SB p151. They can then follow the linking while they listen.

Get ready ... Get it right!

9 **a)** Pre-teach *very active*, *quite active* and *not very active* by referring back to the activities in **1a**).

Allow students to choose their own partners or put students into pairs yourself. If possible, students should work with someone they don't know very well.

Focus students on the example in the *How active is your partner?* box. Students then work on their own and guess whether their partner does or doesn't do these things. They should then complete the sentences with the positive or negative form of the verb in brackets. Students are not allowed to talk to their partner at this stage of the activity.

b) Students work on their own and make *yes/no* questions with *you* for each sentence in the box, as in the example. While they are working, check their questions for accuracy and help with any problems. Check these questions with the whole class before continuing and drill if necessary.

10 **a)** Use the speech bubbles to remind students of possible answers to *Do you ... ?* questions.

Students then work in their pairs and take turns to ask and answer their questions from **9b**). They should tick any sentences in the box that they have guessed correctly. While they are working, monitor and help with any problems.

b) Students decide if their partner is very active, quite active or not very active.

c) Students work in new pairs and take turns to share information about their first partner. Encourage students to use the *he/she* forms of the verbs in the box during this stage, for example, *Marco doesn't play tennis, but he goes running*, etc.

Finally, students tell the class what they have found out about their partners. The class can then decide who they think is the most active student in the class.

— EXTRA PRACTICE AND HOMEWORK —

Ph **Class Activity** 4A Verb-noun collocations p146 (Instructions p125)
4 Review Exercises 1 and 2 SB p37
CD-ROM Lesson 4A
Workbook Lesson 4A p20

4B · First Date!

QUICK REVIEW ●●●

This activity reviews the Present Simple, free time activities and time phrases. Students write their list of activities on their own. Put students into pairs. Students take turns to tell their partner when they do the things on their list. Ask students to share interesting sentences with the class.

> **Vocabulary** things you like and don't like; verb+*ing*
> **Grammar** Present Simple (4): questions and short answers (*he/she/it*)
> **Review** free time activities

Vocabulary Things you like and don't like

1 Students work on their own and tick the words/phrases they know, then do the exercise in **V4.2** SB p128.

Check answers with the class. Note that in the UK *dance music* usually refers to a particular style of music, not any music you can dance to.

Model and drill the phrases. Pay particular attention to the pronunciation of *clothes* /kləʊðz/, which is only one syllable. You could point out that many native speakers pronounce this word the same as *close* /kləʊz/.

> **V4.2** 1i) 2a) 3l) 4c) 5g) 6b) 7k) 8f) 9o)
> 10n) 11h) 12d) 13m) 14j) 15e)

> — EXTRA IDEA —
> • Students can do a *Know, Might Know, Don't Know* activity (see p21) instead of ticking the words/ phrases in **1**.

2 Draw this line on the board. Ask students to copy it into their notebooks. Then ask students where to put *I love* and *I hate* on the line (1 and 7).

| 1 | 2 | 3 | 4 | 5 | 6 | 7 |

Students work on their own and put the other phrases in **2** on the line, then check answers in **V4.3** SB p128. Model and drill the phrases.

Help with Vocabulary Verb+*ing*

3 a) Focus students on the example sentences. Highlight how the verb+*ing* acts as a noun after the verbs in **2**. Also highlight that we use a plural noun without *the* when talking about things we like or don't like in general: *I like books.* not ~~I like book~~ or ~~I like the books~~.

b) Students work on their own and circle the verb+*ing* words in **1**.

Check answers with the class (see **V4.4** SB p128). Note: at this point in the course we are not asking students to make verb+*ing* forms, only to recognise them. The spelling of verb+*ing* forms is dealt with in lesson 9A.

> reading; travelling; shopping; dancing; cooking

4 Use the speech bubbles to teach students how to respond to *I like …* sentences and *Do you like … ?* questions. Highlight the use of object pronouns in the answers, for example, *Do you like dance music? Yes, I love it. Do you like cats? No, I hate them.* Drill this language with the class.

Students work in pairs and discuss what they like and don't like. Ask students to share interesting answers with the class.

Reading and Grammar

5 Focus students on the photo and ask students what they think *First Date!* is (a TV dating programme). Use the photo to pre-teach *date* and *a presenter*.

R4.5 Play the recording. Students read and listen to find four things Mark likes and one thing he doesn't like. Check answers with the class.

> **Mark likes:**
> watching TV
> playing computer games
> going to the cinema
> playing football and tennis
> rock music
> Chinese food
> animals
>
> **Mark doesn't like:**
> shopping for clothes

> — EXTRA IDEA —
> • If you think your students need extra listening practice, play the recording first with their books closed. Then ask students to check their answers by reading the text.

6 a) Check students understand that on the TV programme Mark is not talking to the women, but asking the presenter about them. Elicit which woman he is asking about in questions 1–6 (Kim).

Pre-teach *vet*. Students then work on their own and match Mark's questions and the presenter's answers. Early finishers can check their answers in pairs.

b) **R4.6** Play the recording. Students listen and check their answers.

> 1d) 2e) 3b) 4c) 5a) 6f)

Help with Grammar Present Simple: questions and short answers (*he/she/it*)

7 **a)–d)** Students do the exercises on their own or in pairs, then check their answers in G4.3 SB p130.

While they are working, draw the table from **7b)** on the board so that you are ready to check students' answers. Check answers with the class.

- **a)** 1 *Does she like animals?* 2 *Does she watch TV a lot?* 3 *What does she do in her free time?*
- Highlight that we use *does* in questions with *he/she/it* and that in questions we don't add *-s* or *-es* to the infinitive: *Does she watch …* not ~~*Does she watches …*~~ .
- Point out that the short answers to the *yes/no* questions in 1 and 2 are: *Yes, he/she/it does.* and *No, he/she/it doesn't.*
- Also highlight that we don't repeat the verb in short answers: *Yes, he/she/it does.* not ~~*Yes, he/she/it likes.*~~
- **b)** Focus students on the table on the board. Elicit which words in sentences 3 and 4 from **6a)** go in each column and fill in the table (see the table in G4.3 SB p130).
- Use the table to highlight the word order of questions in the Present Simple: question word + auxiliary + subject + infinitive + … .
- **c)** We use *does* in questions with *he/she/it*. We use *do* in questions with *I/you/we/they*.

Note: students are also asked to read G4.4 SB p130, which focuses on the differences between *have* and *have got*. Highlight these points with the class.
- We can use *have* or *have got* to talk about possessions and family: *She's got/She has two dogs. I haven't got/I don't have any children.*
- We can only use *have* to talk about meals and other activities: *We often have coffee with friends.* not ~~*We often have got coffee with friends.*~~

8 **a)** Students work on their own and write questions with *she* from the prompts.

b) R4.7 Play the recording (SB p151). Students listen and check.

P Play the recording again and ask students to repeat. Point out that *does* is not stressed and is pronounced /dəz/.

c) Students work in pairs and take turns to answer the questions in **8a)**. Before they start, remind students that all the information about Kim is in **6a)**.

While students are working, draw the table from the answer key on the board, but without the answers for Kim, Jo or Susie.

Check the answers for Kim with the class and write them in the *Kim* column of the table. Elicit any other information students know about Kim and write it next to *other information* in Kim's column. Ask students to copy the table into their notebooks.

	Kim	Jo	Susie
do?	a vet	a journalist	a waitress
rock music?	no	yes	no
food?	Italian food	Chinese food	fast food
sport?	yes, tennis	no, hates football	yes, swimming
animals?	yes, two dogs	no, but likes animals	yes, seven cats
Saturday evenings?	goes to the cinema	goes to the cinema or eats out	goes dancing watches TV all night
other information	eats out a lot hates watching TV loves dance music doesn't like rock music	29 years old watches TV goes shopping reads a lot likes jazz	23 years old loves dance music doesn't eat out very often doesn't like watching sport on TV

9 **a)** Focus students on the picture of the TV programme on SB p32 and ask students the names of the other two women on the programme (Jo and Susie.)

Pre-teach *journalist* and *a pet*. Then divide the class into pairs: student A and student B. Student As turn to SB p104 and read about Jo. Student Bs turn to SB p112 and read about Susie. Students find the answers to questions 1–6 in **8a)** in their texts and fill in the correct column in their tables.

b)–c) Students work with their partner and take turns to ask and answer questions 1–6 in **8a)** about Jo and Susie. They should write the answers in the correct column in the tables in their notebooks.

Students tell their partner three more things about the woman they read about and fill in the correct column next to *other information*.

Check answers with the class and write them in the table on the board. See the answer key for **8c)**.

10 **a)** Students work in groups and decide which woman would be the best for Mark's first date. Encourage students to look at the text about Mark on SB p32, and their tables about the three women, to help them decide. Students should also think of reasons for their choice.

b) The groups share their choices and reasons with the class. The whole class must agree on <u>one</u> woman to go on a date with Mark. Ask the class to vote on this if necessary.

c) Tell students that Mark and the woman they chose went on a date last night and ask them if they want to know what happened. If the class chose Kim, students should all turn to SB p109 to read about the date. If the class chose Jo, they should all turn to SB p117. If the class chose Susie, they should all turn to SB p120. The students should <u>not</u> read about the dates with the other two women.

Students read about the date and answer questions 1–3.

Check answers with the class. Students can then discuss if they made the right choice for Mark's first date.

> **KIM** 1 Yes. They both go to the cinema and like animals, and he thinks she's very beautiful. 2 No. He talks about football and TV all the time, and they don't like the same music. 3 Mark: yes; Kim: no
>
> **JO** 1 No. She talks about books and shopping all the time, and she hates sport. 2 Yes. They like different things and she thinks that's a good thing. 3 Mark: no; Jo: yes
>
> **SUSIE** 1 Yes. They both like watching TV, sport and cats. 2 Yes. They both do a lot of sport and like watching TV and DVDs. 3 Mark: yes; Jo: yes

Get ready … Get it right!

11 **a)** Allow students to choose their own partners or put students into pairs yourself. If possible, students should work with someone they don't know very well.

Students choose a friend to introduce to their partner and write his/her name in the box. Students then tick and circle things in the box that this friend does or likes.

b) Students choose eight things from the box that they do or like themselves. They write *yes/no* questions with *he/she* about these things, as in the examples.

12 **a)** Students work with their partners and take turns to ask questions about each other's friends. Encourage students to ask questions about the person's name, age, job and where he/she lives before asking the questions they prepared in **11b)**. Students should make brief notes on their partner's answers at this stage. While students are working, monitor and help with any problems.

b) Put students into new pairs. Students tell their new partner about their first partner's friend and the things they have (or don't have) in common, as shown in the speech bubbles. Make sure students use *he/she/it* verb forms in this stage of the activity.

Finally, students tell the class if they would like to meet their partner's friend, giving reasons for their answers.

EXTRA PRACTICE AND HOMEWORK

 Class Activity 4B A TV presenter's weekend p147 (Instructions p125)

4 Review Exercises 3 and 4 SB p37

CD-ROM Lesson 4B

Workbook Lesson 4B p21

 ## Eating out

QUICK REVIEW ●●●

This activity reviews Present Simple questions and free time activities. Give students a few moments to write the names of three people in their family, then put students into pairs. Students swap papers and ask what the people on their partner's paper do in their free time. Ask students to share interesting answers with the class.

Let's go to the Jazz Café

1 Students work in groups of three and discuss the questions. Ask students to share interesting answers with the class.

2 Pre-teach *an answerphone*. Focus students on the answerphone message and the different possible answers. Ask them who the message is from (Jack).

R4.8 Play the recording (SB p151). Students listen and circle the correct answers.

Check answers with the class. Play the recording again if necessary.

> **Time:** 6 **Message:** 1 I'm at 2 two 3 eat out

Real World requests and offers with *Can I/we have …?, I'd/We'd like … , Would you like …?*
Vocabulary food and drink (1)
Help with Listening questions with *Would you like … ?*
Review *How much …?*; prices; Present Simple

3 **R4.9** Tell students that Emma got Jack's message and phones him back on his mobile. Give students time to read sentences 1–5. Then play the recording (SB p151). Students decide if the sentences are true or false.

Students work in pairs and check answers. Check answers with the class.

> 1F 2F 3T 4F 5F

4 **a)** Focus students on the Jazz Café menu. Students work in pairs and match the photos to the things on the menu, then check their answers in **V4.5** SB p129.

Check students understand that *chips* are hot and are often eaten as part of a main meal. Students may confuse *chips* with *crisps* /krɪsps/, which are cold and usually come in bags. *Chips* are often called *French fries* in American English.

Model and drill the words/phrases. Pay particular attention to the pronunciation of *chicken* /ˈtʃɪkɪn/, *sandwich* /ˈsænwɪdʒ/, *burger* /ˈbɜːgə/ and *mixed* /mɪkst/.

> **2** a glass of red/white wine **3** a pizza **4** a cheese and tomato sandwich **5** a bottle of beer **6** a burger and chips **7** a bottle of red wine **8** a coffee **9** bottles of/a glass of mineral water **10** a mixed salad

b) Students work in pairs and take turns to test each other on the food and drink.

Check students understand the other food vocabulary on the menu. Students can check any new words/phrases in **V4.5** SB p129.

5 Focus students on the menu again. Model and drill the prices. Ask questions with *How much ... ?* about items on the menu to check students can say the prices.

Students work in pairs. They take turns to choose something to eat and drink and then ask their partner how much it is. Before students start, draw attention to the example in the speech bubbles.

Help with Listening
Questions with *Would you like ... ?*

- This Help with Listening section helps students to understand questions with *Would you like ... ?* and highlights the pronunciation of *would you* /wʊdʒə/.

6 a) Focus students on the photo and use it to pre-teach *waiter* and *customer*. Tell students that questions 1–4 are typical questions a waiter asks in a restaurant.

R4.10 Play the recording. Students fill in the gaps with the words in the box. Alternatively, students can fill in the gaps before they listen and check their answers by listening to the recording.

Check answers with the class.

> **1** red **2** anything **3** order **4** drink

b) Play the recording again and highlight the pronunciation of *would you* /wʊdʒə/.

7 a) Students work on their own or in pairs. They read and then complete the conversation using questions 1–4 from **6a)**. Ask students if they can guess the meaning of *bill* from the context.

b) **R4.11** Play the recording (SB p151). Students listen and check their answers. Ask students what Emma and Jack order.

> **1** Would you like to order now? **2** What would you like to drink? **3** Would you like red or white? **4** Would you like anything else?
>
> Emma and Jack order: a tuna salad; a cheeseburger and chips; a bottle of white wine; a bottle of sparkling mineral water

Real World Requests and offers

8 a)–b) Use the examples in **8a)** to teach *request* and *offer*. Students work on their own or in pairs and complete the rules before checking answers in **RW4.1** SB p130.

- We use *I'd/We'd like ...* and *Can I/we have ... ?* for requests. Check students understand that *'d = would* in these phrases.
- We use *Would you like ... ?* for offers.
- Use the examples in **8a)** to show students that we use a noun after *Can I/we have ... ?* and we use a noun or an infinitive with *to* after *Would you like ... ?* and *I'd/We'd like ... ?*
- Check students understand the difference between *I like* and *I'd like*. We use *I like* to talk about things we like in general: *I like burgers*. We use *I'd like* to mean *want*: *I'd like (a burger), please*. Point out that *I'd like* is more polite than *I want* and that it is impolite to say *I want (a burger)* in English.

c) Students work on their own and underline three more requests in **7a)**. Check answers with the class.

> I'd like a tuna salad, please. And can I have a cheeseburger and chips, please? Can we have a bottle of wine? And we'd like a bottle of sparkling mineral water, please.

9 a) **R4.12** Play the recording (SB p151). Ask students to notice the stress pattern, and highlight the high pitch and the rise on *please*, both of which show politeness. You can also ask students to turn to R4.12, SB p151. They can then follow the stress pattern while they listen.

b) **R4.13** Play the recording (SB p151). Students decide which is more polite, a) or b). Play the recording again if necessary. Check answers with the class.

> **2**b) **3**b) **4**a) **5**b) **6**a)

c) **R4.14** **P** Play the recording and ask students to repeat. Check that they copy the polite intonation pattern correctly. Play the recording again if necessary.

10 a) Put students into groups of three. Students choose roles, then practise the conversation in **7a)** until they can remember it.

b) Students practise the conversation again with their books closed.

─ EXTRA IDEAS ─

- If you have beginners, you can put cues on the board to help students remember each line in the conversation: WAITER *order?* EMMA *tuna salad* JACK *cheeseburger / chips*, etc.
- When students feel confident, ask for volunteers to role-play the conversation for the rest of the class.

11 a) Students work in the same groups and write their own restaurant conversation. Set a time limit of five minutes. While they are working, check their conversations for accuracy and help with any problems.

b) Students give their conversations to another group to read and correct. Help students with any language problems at this stage and encourage groups to check any queries with the group who wrote the conversation.

c) Students practise the new conversation in their groups until they can remember it.

4D Breakfast time

QUICK REVIEW ●●●
This activity reviews food and drink vocabulary. Students do the activity in pairs. Students check their answers on SB p35. Check answers with the class.

1 Students work on their own and tick the food and drink they know, then do the matching exercise in **V4.6** SB p129. You can also teach *marmalade*, which is usually made from oranges and eaten for breakfast. Students often confuse this word with *jam*, which is usually made from soft fruit such as strawberries, etc.
Model and drill the words with the class. Pay particular attention to the pronunciation of *biscuits* /ˈbɪskɪts/, *toast* /təʊst/, *sausages* /ˈsɒsɪdʒɪz/, *vegetables* /ˈvedʒtəblz/, *orange juice* /ˈɒrɪndʒ dʒuːs/, *fruit* /fruːt/ and *cereal* /ˈsɪərɪəl/. Point out the silent letters in *biscuits* and *vegetables*.

> **V4.6** 1j) 2e) 3h) 4r) 5n) 6b) 7i) 8m) 9f) 10s) 11c) 12q) 13l) 14o) 15t) 16g) 17p) 18a) 19k) 20d)

2 Give examples of what you eat for breakfast from **1**. Highlight that we usually use the verb *have* in this context (not *eat* or *drink*), for example, *I usually have coffee and toast*. Students do the exercise in groups. Ask students to share answers with the class.

3 a) Focus students on the photo and ask students what the people do (they're cooks/chefs). Tell students that the cooks, Kevin and Andy, work in an international language school. They want to make typical breakfasts for the four nationalities written on the blackboard in the photo.
Students work in pairs and make a list of what they think is in each breakfast, using words from **1**. Do not check their ideas at this stage.

b) **R4.15** Play the recording (SB p151). Students listen and tick the food and drink on their own lists that Kevin and Andy talk about.

c) Play the recording again. Students add any missing items that Kevin and Andy talk about to their lists for each breakfast.

Each group takes it in turns to role-play the conversation for the group that wrote the original script.
While students are working, monitor and help with any problems.
Finally, ask one or two pairs to role-play the conversations for the class.

> ┌─ **EXTRA PRACTICE AND HOMEWORK** ─────
> **4 Review** Exercise 5 SB p37
> **CD-ROM** Lesson 4C
> **Workbook** Lesson 4C p23

> **Vocabulary** food and drink (2); countable and uncountable nouns
> **Review** Present Simple; likes and dislikes; frequency adverbs

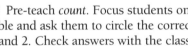 Check answers by writing the four headings from the answer key on the board. Elicit the answers from the students and fill in the table. Ask students which of these breakfasts they would like.

Japanese	Brazilian	Spanish	English
rice	bread	biscuits	eggs
fish	cheese	toast	sausages
soup	orange juice	a sandwich	toast
green tea	coffee	coffee	jam
			tea

4 a) Pre-teach *count*. Focus students on the pictures in the table and ask them to circle the correct answers in rules 1 and 2. Check answers with the class.

> 1 can 2 can't

b) Check students understand *singular* and *plural*, then focus on the examples in the table.
Students work in pairs and complete the table with words from **1**. Check answers with the class.

Point out that some words are uncountable in English but countable in other languages, for example, *bread*, *toast*. Elicit any other uncountable words from **1** that are countable in the students' language(s).

COUNTABLE NOUNS		UNCOUNTABLE NOUNS	
singular	**plural**	toast	bread
a sausage	sausages	fish	coffee
an egg	eggs	soup	cheese
a vegetable	vegetables	orange juice	tea
a banana	bananas	jam	meat
		fruit	cereal

5 **a)–b)** Students do **5a)** on their own or in pairs, then check their answers in **R4.7** SB p129. Check answers with the class.

- Countable nouns can be plural.
- We use *a* or *an* with singular countable nouns.
- We don't use *a* or *an* with plural countable nouns.
- Uncountable nouns aren't usually plural.
- We don't use *a* or *an* with uncountable nouns.
- Point out that many drinks can be countable if we mean *a cup/glass of*, for example, *a coffee = a cup of coffee*, *an orange juice = a glass of orange juice*, etc.

6 **a)** Pre-teach *meal* and *main meal*. Use the example to check students understand that a dash (–) means no article. Students do the exercise on their own, then check answers with the class. Elicit the reason for each choice.

> 2 a 3 – ; – 4 – 5 – 6 an 7 a

b) Focus students on the example and use this to show how students can make the sentences in **6a)** true for them by changing the underlined word (*rice* to *chips*).

Students work on their own, ticking the sentences in **6a)** that are true for them and changing the underlined word in the other sentences.

c) Students work in pairs and compare sentences. Ask students to share interesting information with the class.

7 Focus students on the speech bubbles. Use these to elicit when we use *it* (singular or uncountable) and *them* (plural) in the answers. Model and drill the questions and answers with the class.

Students work in groups of four and discuss the food they like/don't like.

8 **a)** Start by describing your own perfect breakfast.

Students then work on their own and use the questions to make notes about their own perfect breakfast.

b) Students work in groups and tell one another about their perfect breakfast. Each group can then choose which student has the best breakfast. Finally, ask these students to tell the class about their breakfasts.

EXTRA PRACTICE AND HOMEWORK

Ph **Vocabulary Plus** 4 Food p190 (Instructions p183)

Ph **Class Activity** 4D Food habits p149 (Instructions p126)

4 Review SB p37

CD-ROM Lesson 4D

Workbook Lesson 4D p24

Workbook Reading and Writing Portfolio 4 p70

Progress Test 4 p214

---

4 Review

See p32 for ideas on how to use this section.

1a) listen to music/the radio; watch DVDs/sport on TV; take photos; go running/dancing; read books/magazines

2a) 2 plays 3 lives 4 work 5 goes 6 like 7 starts

2b) 2 Ed doesn't play golf on Sundays
3 My sister doesn't live in the USA.
4 Jo and Liz don't work at home.
5 She doesn't go out a lot.
6 Tim's parents don't like jazz.
7 Our class doesn't start at six.

4a) 2 What food does he like?
3 Does he like shopping for clothes?
4 What does he do at the weekend?
5 What music does he like?
6 Does he like animals?

4c) 1 He's a teacher.
2 He likes/loves Chinese food.
3 No, he doesn't.
4 He plays football and tennis.
5 He likes/ loves rock music.
6 Yes, he does.

6a)
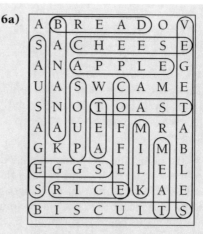

6b) Uncountable: bread, cheese, toast, rice, soup, tea, coffee, milk, meat
Countable: sausages, apple, eggs, biscuits, banana, vegetables

Progress Portfolio

See p32 for ideas on how to use this section.

5 Homes and shops

5A My kind of place

QUICK REVIEW ●●●

This activity revises food and drink vocabulary. Students do the activity in pairs. Set a time limit of three minutes. Draw a two-column table with the headings *countable* and *uncountable* on the board. Find out which pair has the most words. Elicit which words go in each column. Ask if other pairs have any different words and put them under the correct heading.

Vocabulary Places in a town/the country

1 a) Students work on their own and tick the words they know, then do the exercise in **V5.1** SB p131. They can then check answers in pairs. Check answers with the class. You may also wish to teach the words *a pub* and *a building*.

Point out that British people often use *a station* to mean *a train station*. Check students understand the difference between *a country* (the UK, Spain, etc.) and *the country* (undeveloped land or farmland not in towns and cities).

Also tell students that *a bed and breakfast* (or *a B & B*) is a place to stay in someone's house where you get breakfast but no other meals. They are very common in the UK and are usually cheaper than hotels.

Model and drill the words. Pay particular attention to the pronunciation of *station* /ˈsteɪʃən/, *beach* /biːtʃ/, *museum* /mjuːˈziːəm/, *mountains* /ˈmaʊntɪnz/ and the stress on the first syllable of *café* /ˈkæfeɪ/.

Note that only the main stress in words/phrases is shown in vocabulary boxes and the Language Summaries.

> **V5.1** 1t) 2s) 4l) 5i) 6c) 7p) 8g) 9r) 10m) 11b) 12j) 13o) 14e) 15q) 16h) 17f) 18d) 19n) 20k)

b) Students work on their own and choose four things from **1a)** for where they live and four things for where they go on holiday.

Put students into groups to compare their ideas. Ask them to share interesting ideas with the class.

Listening and Grammar

2 Focus students on the photos and ask if they know where the places are. Elicit which is a big city (Auckland, New Zealand), a small town (Keswick, The Lake District in England), and a village (Eyeries, Ireland). Drill *village* /ˈvɪlɪdʒ/ with the class. Note the pronunciation of: *Auckland* /ˈɔːklənd/, *Keswick* /ˈkəsɪk/, *Eyeries* /ˈaɪriːz/.

Elicit the things from **1a)** that are in the photos.

> Auckland: the sea, flats Keswick: a lake, mountains
> Eyeries: a road, houses, a bar

> **Vocabulary** places in a town/the country
> **Grammar** *there is/there are*
> **Help with Listening** sentence stress (2)
> **Review** adjectives

Help with Listening Sentence stress (2)

- This Help with Listening section reviews sentence stress and helps students to understand what type of words are usually stressed.

3 a) Remind students what sentence stress is by writing one or two sentences on the board and asking them to tell you which words are stressed. Ask them why these words are stressed (because they're the important words that carry meaning).

Tell students that they are going to listen to sentences from three conversations about the places in the photos.

R5.1 Play the recording. Students listen and read, noticing the stressed words.

b) Ask students to give you examples of nouns, verbs and adjectives to check they remember these terms.

Students work on their own and look at the sentences in **3a)** in order to answer the question.

Check the answer with the class.

> Nouns, adjectives and negatives all carry important information and are usually stressed. Main verbs are also usually stressed, but not the verb *be* in its positive and question forms.

4 Check students understand that they have to match the three conversations A–C to the photos and to the things people talk about 1–3.

R5.2 Play the recording (SB p151). Students listen and match the conversations. Check answers with the class.

> A Keswick; 3 B Eyeries; 2 C Auckland; 1

5 a) Focus students on sentences 1–9 in **3a)**. Students do the exercise in pairs.

b) **R5.2** Play the recording again. Students listen and check answers. Check answers with the class.

> Auckland: 3, 7, 9
> Keswick: 1, 5, 8
> Eyeries: 2, 4, 6

6 a) Students work in groups and discuss which place they would like to visit. Encourage students to give reasons, using vocabulary from **1a)** or their own ideas.

b) Ask students to share answers with the class, again giving reasons for their choices. Find out which place is the most popular.

Help with Grammar *there is/there are*

7 a)–b) Students do **7a)** on their own by referring back to the sentences in **3a)**. They then check answers in **G5.1** SB p133. Check answers with the class.

- Check the tables with the class (see the tables in **G5.1** SB p133).
- We use *there is/are* to say that things exist in a place. Students sometimes confuse *there is/are* with *it is/they are*. ✍ If this is a problem for your students, write *There's a lake. It's beautiful.* and *There are two hotels. They're expensive.* on the board to highlight the difference. Note that the **face2face** Elementary Workbook practises this distinction in exercise 4, p26.
- Point out that *'s* in *there's …* is the contracted form of *there is …* . Note that we don't contract *there are … to there're …* and we don't use contractions in positive short answers. We say *Yes, there is.* not *Yes, there's.*
- Highlight the inverted word order of questions: *Is/Are + there + …* , and the use of *any* in negatives and questions with *there are*. Note that the difference between *some* and *any* is dealt with in lesson 5B.

8 a) Focus students on the photo of Keswick and elicit what students can remember about the place.

Go through the two examples with the class to check they understand that a tick means they should write a positive sentence and a cross means they should write a negative sentence.

Students fill in the gaps on their own, then check answers in pairs. Check answers with the class.

> 3 's 4 aren't 5 are 6 's 7 isn't 8 are

b) **R5.3** **P** Play the recording and ask students to repeat. Highlight the pronunciation of *there's* /ðəz/ and *there are* /ðeərə/, and point out that these phrases are not stressed. Repeat the drill if necessary.

9 a) Focus students on the table. Do questions 1 and 2 with the class.

Students then complete questions 3–8 on their own. Check answers with the class.

> 1 Is there 2 Are there 3 Are there 4 Is there
> 5 Are there 6 Is there 7 Are there 8 Is there

EXTRA IDEA

- Instead of checking answers with the class, ask students to check answers to **9a)** by listening to **R5.4** .

b) **R5.4** **P** Focus on the examples. Play the recording and ask students to repeat.

Point out that *Is there* and *Are there* are not stressed in questions, but that *is* and *are* are stressed in positive short answers: *Yes, there is. Yes, there are.* Repeat the drill if necessary.

c) Students think about places near their own home and write *yes* or *no* in the *me* column in the table.

d) Use the speech bubbles to teach *(five minutes) away.*

Students do the exercise in pairs. Encourage students to give more information about the places if possible. Each pair should decide if they live in similar places, or if they are very different.

Ask students to share interesting information with the class.

Get ready … Get it right!

10 Give students time to think about their favourite place. Tell students that this place shouldn't be the place they are in at the moment. Ask students to write down the name of the place.

Students work in their own and tick/cross the things in the box that are/aren't in their favourite place.

11 a) Students work in groups of three or four and take turns to tell their partners about their favourite places. While students are working, monitor and help with any problems.

EXTRA IDEA

- If you have a class of beginners, ask students to make sentences with *there is/there are* about the things in the box in **10** before moving on to **11a)**.

b) Students stay in their groups and decide which of their partners' places they would like to visit and why they would like to go there. Ask students to share their ideas with the class.

EXTRA IDEA

- Ask students to write a paragraph about their favourite place.

EXTRA PRACTICE AND HOMEWORK

Ph **Vocabulary Plus** 5 Places in a town p191 (Instructions p184)

Ph **Class Activity** 5A Places bingo p150 (Instructions p126)

5 Review Exercises 1 and 2 SB p45

CD-ROM Lesson 5A

Workbook Lesson 5A p25

5B Renting a flat

> **Vocabulary** rooms and things in a house
> **Grammar** *How much ... ?/How many ... ?*; *some, any, a*
> **Review** *there is/there are*; *have got*

Vocabulary Rooms and things in a house

1 Focus students on the photo of Alex and his wife, Martina on p41. Ask what they want to do (find/rent a flat). Focus students on the plan of the flat and the advert on p40.

Students do the exercise on their own, then check in pairs. Check answers with the class. Point out that we can also say *sitting room* instead of *living room*.

Model and drill the words, paying particular attention to the pronunciation of *kitchen* /'kɪtʃɪn/.

> **A** balcony **B** kitchen **C** living room **D** bedrooms
> **E** bathroom

2 Check the two examples with the class and point out that *furniture* is an uncountable noun.

Students work on their own and match the words with the things in the flat, then check answers in pairs.

Check answers with the class. Point out that *a sink* is in the kitchen and *a washbasin* is in the bathroom, and highlight the difference between *a chair* and *an armchair*. Also establish the difference between *a cooker* and *a cook* (a person).

Model and drill the new words. Pay particular attention to the pronunciation of *furniture* /'fɜːnɪtʃə/, *double bed* /'dʌbl bed/, *fridge* /frɪdʒ/, *bath* /baːθ/ and *washing machine* /'wɒʃɪŋ məˌʃiːn/.

> a single bed 8; a fridge 4; a coffee table 15; a bath 14;
> a chair 7; a shower 11; a cooker 3; a toilet 12; a sink 2;
> an armchair 16; a desk 9; a plant 17; a sofa 18;
> a washing machine 5; a washbasin 13; a table 6

--- EXTRA IDEAS ---

● Students cover the words in the vocabulary box and test each other by pointing to things on the plan and asking *What's this?*.

● Students look at the plan of the flat for two minutes and try to remember what is in each room. Students close their books. Ask students to work in pairs and write down what is each room. They can check answers with the plan on SB p40 or in **V5.2** SB p131.

Grammar and Listening

3 Pre-teach *rent* as a noun (*How much is your rent?*) and as a verb (*I rent a flat.*), *space* and *information*.

Students do the exercise on their own. Set a time limit of two minutes.

Students check answers in pairs. Check answers with the class. Point out that we often use *a* to mean *every*: *The rent is £700 a month.*

> **1** In Park Street. **2** £700. **3** Two. **4** 80m² (square metres).
> **5** Nine (including two armchairs and the two chairs on the balcony). **6** A sofa, two armchairs and a coffee table.
> **7** Call Rent-a-Home on 020 7655 4311.

> **Help with Grammar** *How much ... ?/*
> *How many ... ?*

4 **a)–c)** Check students remember the meaning of *countable noun* and *uncountable noun*. Use words for food and drink to remind them of the difference if necessary.

Students do the exercises on their own or in pairs, then check answers in **G5.2** SB p133. Check answers with the class.

> ● **a)** *Table, bedroom, people, chair, phone* are countable nouns (*people* is the plural of *a person*). *Furniture, money, space, time* are uncountable nouns.
> ● We use *How many ... ?* with plural countable nouns: *How many bedrooms are there?*.
> ● We use *How much ... ?* with uncountable nouns: *How much space is there in the flat?*.
> ● Point out that we don't usually say the word *money* when we're talking about prices: *How much is that?*.

5 **a)** Pre-teach *spend time*, then ask students to do the exercise on their own. Check answers with the class.

> **2** How many **3** How much **4** How many **5** How much
> **6** How many **7** How much **8** How many

b) Students work in pairs and take turns to ask and answer the questions.

Ask students to share any surprising answers with the class.

--- EXTRA IDEA ---

● Before they do the questionnaire, ask students to predict their partner's answers. Students then ask the questions to check if they are correct.

6 a) Students read the advert again and find two things they think are good about the flat. Compare answers with the class.

b) Pre-teach *estate agent* by referring to Rent-a-Home in the advert. Focus students on the photo of Alex and Martina and establish that Alex is on the phone to an estate agent who works for Rent-a-Home.

R5.5 Play the recording (SB p151). Students listen and put the things a)–f) in order. Check answers with the class.

2d) 3b) 4c) 5f) 6e)

7 R5.5 Give students time to read sentences 1–8, then play the recording again. Students listen and decide if the sentences are true or false.

Check answers with the class. Ask students to correct the false sentences.

2T 3F One bedroom is quite small. 4T 5F There is a cooker. 6F There are some shops only five minutes away. 7F The rent is £800 a month. 8T

— EXTRA IDEAS —

- With a strong class, ask students to try and remember which sentences in **7** are true or false before they listen again, then play the recording to check.
- After **7**, ask students to look at R5.5, SB p151 and play the recording again. Students listen, read and check their answers.

Help with Grammar *some, any, a*

8 a)–c) Students do the exercises on their own or in pairs, then check answers in G5.3 SB p133. They can refer to R5.5, SB p151 if they wish. Check answers with the class.

- Check the table with the class (see the table in G5.3 SB p133).
- We usually use *some* in positive sentences with plural countable nouns and uncountable nouns.
- We usually use *any* in negatives and questions with plural countable nouns and uncountable nouns.
- We use *a* (or *an*) in positive sentences, negatives and questions with singular countable nouns.
- Point out that we can often use *there is/there are* or *have got* to talk about things in the house: *Has it got a shower?* = *Is there a shower?*.

9 a) Tell students that Alex and Martina now live in the flat. Martina is at the supermarket and phones Alex to ask about food. Pre-teach *butter* and *need*.

Students work on their own and fill in the gaps, then check answers in pairs.

b) R5.6 Play the recording. Students listen and check answers. Check answers with the class and ask students to explain their answers.

2 some 3 any 4 some 5 any 6 some 7 some
8 any 9 a 10 any 11 some 12 some 13 a

Get ready … Get it right!

10 Put students into two groups, group A and group B. Students in group A turn to SB p106 and students in group B turn to SB p114. Check they are all looking at the correct exercise.

a) Students work in pairs with someone from their own group and take turns to describe things in the picture using *there is/there are* and *some/any/a*. Draw students' attention to the examples in the box before they start.

b) Tell the class that there are twelve differences between group A's picture and group B's picture. Students stay in their pairs and make questions to ask students in the other group about their picture. Focus students' attention on the examples in the box before they start. While students are working, check their questions for accuracy and help with any problems.

c) Put students in pairs, with one student from group A and one student from group B in each pair. Students are not allowed to look at their partner's picture.

Students take turns to ask and answer questions about the pictures in order to find the twelve differences. Remind them to use short answers (*Yes, there is. No, there aren't.*, etc.) where appropriate. Set a time limit of ten minutes.

d) Students work with their partner from their own group and compare the differences they have found. Check answers with the class.

1 A: two windows; B: one window 2 A: a CD player on the fridge; B: a TV on the fridge 3 A: three chairs; B: four chairs 4 A: two plants; B: no plants 5 A: a cat; B: a dog 6 A: one bag on the floor; B: three bags on the floor 7 A: four bananas in the fruit bowl; B: no bananas 8 A: nine eggs in the fridge; B: six eggs in the fridge 9 A: milk in the fridge door; B: no milk 10 A: four bottles of water; B: two bottles of water 11 A: no rice; B: rice on the table 12 A: three pizzas on the table; B: two pizzas on the table

— EXTRA PRACTICE AND HOMEWORK —

Ph **Class Activity** 5B A place to rent p151 (Instructions p127)
5 Review Exercises 3, 4 and 5 SB p45
CD-ROM Lesson 5B
Workbook Lesson 5B p26

5C At the shops

Real World shop language
Vocabulary shops; *one* and *ones*; things to buy
Help with Listening in a shop
Review *Have you got ... ?*; *Can I have ... ?*; *this/that/these/those*

Shopping

 1 Students discuss the questions in groups. Ask students to compare answers with the class.

2 Students work on their own and tick the words they know, then do the exercise in V5.3 SB p131. They can then check answers in pairs.

Check answers with the class. Point out the possessive *'s* at the end of many shops (*a chemist's, a baker's*, etc.) and that the person who owns the shop is called *a chemist, a baker*, etc. Also highlight that we use *in* or *at* with shops: *You buy food in/at a supermarket*, but we say *at a kiosk* not ~~in a kiosk~~.

Model and drill the words. Pay particular attention to the pronunciation of *chemist's* /ˈkemɪsts/, *pharmacy* /ˈfɑːməsi/, *newsagent's* /ˈnjuːzˌeɪdʒənts/, *butcher's* /ˈbʊtʃəz/ and *greengrocer's* /ˈgriːngrəʊsəz/.

> V5.3 **2** a greengrocer's **3** a butcher's **4** a bank **5** a department store **6** a baker's **7** a chemist's [US: a pharmacy] **8** A dry cleaner's **9** a bookshop **10** a post office **11** a kiosk; a newsagent's

3 Focus students on the photo on p43 and ask who the two customers are (Alex and Martina from lesson 5B). Ask students what they remember about them. Then focus students on the shopping list on p42 and pre-teach *aspirin, cigarettes, dictionary* and *pasta* if necessary. Point out that in the example sentence *You* = people in general.

Students work on their own or in pairs and make sentences to say where you buy each of the things on the list. Check answers with the class.

> aspirin: chemist's; cigarettes: newsagent's/kiosk; dictionary: bookshop; sausages: butcher's/supermarket; bread: baker's/supermarket; apples, bananas: greengrocer's/supermarket; pasta: supermarket; TV, new sofa: department store

4 a) R5.7 Tell students that Martina and Alex are now at the shops, then play the recording. Students listen and decide which shops they are in. Check answers with the class.

> **1** a department store **2** a greengrocer's

b) Play the recording again. Students listen and fill in the gaps in the conversations. Play it again if necessary.

Students check answers in pairs. Check answers with the class and ask what Martina and Alex bought.

You can also point out that *Let me see* and *Er* are expressions that allow us time to think, and that *I'll think about it.* is a polite way to say that we don't want to buy something at the moment.

> **2** 600 **3** 550 **4** think **5** apples **6** green **7** red **8** bananas Martina didn't buy a sofa. Alex bought a kilo of apples and some bananas.

— EXTRA IDEA —
● Students practise the conversations in pairs. Ask students to swap roles after a few minutes.

Help with Vocabulary *one* and *ones*

5 Establish that in English we try to avoid repeating words in a sentence. Use the examples to show students that one way of doing this is to replace a noun with *one* or *ones*.

Student complete the rules on their own. Check answers with the class.

> We use *one* in place of a singular noun.
> We use *ones* in place of a plural noun.

6 a) Students read the conversations and decide which shops Martina and Alex are in. Check answers with the class.

> **1** a department store **2** a butcher's/a supermarket **3** a bookshop

b) Students do the exercise on their own, then check answers in pairs.

c) R5.8 Play the recording. Students check their answers. Check answers with the class.

> **1** one; ones **2** ones **3** one; one

— EXTRA IDEA —
● Students write their own shop conversations and practise them in pairs. They can then act them out for the class.

At the newsagent's

7 **a)** Focus students on the photo. Ask where Martina and Alex are (at a newsagent's). Students work on their own and tick the words they know, then do the exercise in **V5.5** SB p132. They can then check answers in pairs. Check answers with the class. Model and drill the words. Highlight the pronunciation of *envelopes* /'envələʊps/, *tissues* /'tɪʃuːz/ and *chocolate* /'tʃɒklət/.

> **V5.5** 1j) 2b) 3e) 4n) 5d) 6l) 7h) 8k) 9g) 10i)
> 11a) 12f) 13c) 14m)

b) Students do the exercise on their own or in pairs. Check answers with the class.

> stamps; maps; batteries; cigarettes; films; postcards; tissues; magazines; lighters; newspapers; chocolate

c) Students make their lists on their own. Help students with any new vocabulary at this stage.
Students work in groups and compare lists.

8 **R5.9** Focus students on the photo again, then play the recording. Students listen and write down the things Alex and Martina buy. Check answers with the class.

> some batteries; a £10 phone card; some postcards; four stamps (for Europe)

Help with Listening In a shop

- This Help with Listening section helps students to understand typical phrases they will hear in shops.

9 **a)** Pre-teach *change, receipt* /rɪ'siːt/, *Here you are.* and *Anything else?*. Drill these words/phrases with the class.
R5.9 Students read sentences a)–h). Play the recording again. Students listen and put a)–h) in the correct order.

b) Ask students to look at R5.9, SB p152. Play the recording again. Students read, listen and check answers.

> 2b) 3g) 4c) 5h) 6f) 7a) 8e)

Real World Shop language

10 **a)–b)** Students do **10a)** on their own or in pairs, then check answers in **RW5.1** SB p133. Check answers with the class.

> any; Can; much; that

11 **a)** **R5.10** **P** Play the recording. Ask students to repeat. Check that students copy the stress and intonation correctly. Play the recording again if necessary.

b) Ask students to look again at R5.9, SB p152.
Students work in pairs and practise the conversation. Ask students to change roles after a few minutes. While they are working, monitor and correct pronunciation where necessary.

12 Put students into pairs, student A and student B. Student As turn to SB p107 and student Bs turn to SB p115. Check they are all looking at the correct exercise.

a) Allow students time to read the information about their roles and point out the prompts in the boxes. Focus student As on the shopping list and student Bs on the picture of the shop. Check students understand *spend money* and that *Sure.* means *OK.*
Students do the role-play with their partner, with student A buying things from student B's shop. Student B starts the conversation with *Hello, can I help you?*. While students are working, monitor and help with any problems.

b) Give students time to read about their new roles. Focus student As on the picture of the shop and student Bs on the shopping list. Students then role-play another conversation, with student B buying things from student A's shop.
Finally, ask students how much they spent and what they didn't buy (student A: a film; student B: tissues).

┌─ **EXTRA PRACTICE AND HOMEWORK** ─
5 Review Exercise 6 SB p45
CD-ROM Lesson 5C
Workbook Lesson 5C p28

5D In fashion

Vocabulary clothes; plural nouns
Review *have got*; *some, any, a*; colours

This activity practises shops and shopping vocabulary. Students do the activity in pairs.  While they are working, write the headings *newsagent's, greengrocer's, department store, supermarket* on the board. Students tell you things you can buy in these shops. Write them on the board. Check which things students buy every week.

1 Use what you are wearing to elicit the word *clothes* /kləʊðz/.
Students work on their own and tick the words they know, then do the exercise in **V5.6** SB p132. They can then check answers in pairs.

Check answers with the class. Model and drill the words. Pay particular attention to the pronunciation of *trousers* /'traʊzəz/, *jeans* /dʒiːnz/, *suit* /suːt/, *skirt* /skɜːt/, *jumper* /'dʒʌmpə/, *jacket* /'dʒækɪt/ and *shirt* /ʃɜːt/.

V5.6 1f) 2d) 3g) 4h) 5r) 7e) 8b) 9s) 10o) 11j) 12m) 13p) 14i) 15l) 16c) 17n) 18k) 19q)

 2 a) Elicit all the colours students know and write them on the board. Pre-teach *wear*.

Students work on their own and make their own lists with words from **1** or their own ideas. Help students with vocabulary as necessary.

b) Focus students on the speech bubbles and drill these examples with the class. Remind students of the phrases *in the week* and *at the weekend*.

Students work in groups of three or four and talk about their lists from **2a)**. While students are working, correct any mistakes you hear and help with any problems.

Help with Vocabulary Plural nouns

3 a) Focus students on the first example and point out that the word *jeans* looks plural and takes a plural verb (*are*), but is actually 'one thing'. Tell students that it is not possible to say *a jean*. Compare this with the second example, where *shoes* is a plural word and refers to two shoes. Elicit that it is possible to use the singular form (*a shoe*).

b)–d) Students do the exercises on their own or in pairs, then check their answers in **V5.7** SB p132. Check answers with the class.

- **b)** *Jeans, shorts* and *trousers* can mean 'one thing'. *Shoes, socks, boots* and *trainers* can be singular.
- **c)** 1 are 2 's 3 some 4 a
- We can use *a pair of* with both types of plural noun: *I've got a new pair of shoes/jeans.*
- The word *clothes* /kləʊðz/ is always plural. If we want to use the singular, we can say *an item of clothing.*

 4 a) Check students remember how we use *some, any* and *a*, and refer them to **G5.3** SB p133 if necessary. Students then do the exercise on their own.

Students check answers in pairs. Check answers with the class.

1 any 2 some 3 a 4 some 5 a 6 any 7 some

b) Make 1 and 2 from **4a)** true for you. Remind students how to agree and disagree with positive sentences (*Me too./Oh, I don't.*) and negative sentences (*Me neither./Oh, I do.*). Demonstrate how to compare sentences with a few confident students.

Students work on their own and make the statements true for themselves, then compare sentences in pairs.

5 Focus students on the article and check they understand the headline. Then ask students to read the article and match paragraphs 1–3 to the people in the photos. Check answers with the class.

1 Libby 2 Yolanda 3 Michael

6 Students read the article again and match 1–6 to the people in the photos. Students check answers in pairs. Check answers with the class.

1 Yolanda 2 Michael 3 Yolanda 4 Libby 5 Libby 6 Yolanda

7 Students discuss the questions in groups of four. Include a mixture of men and women in each group if possible. Ask students to share interesting points with the class from their discussions. You can also find out how many people think they are most like Yolanda, Michael or Libby in their attitudes to clothes.

┌─ **EXTRA PRACTICE AND HOMEWORK** ─────
Ph **Class Activity** 5D Shopping crossword p153 (Instructions p127)
5 Review SB p45
CD-ROM Lesson 5D
Workbook Lesson 5D p29
Workbook Reading and Writing Portfolio 5 p72
Progress Test 5 p215
└──────────────────────────────────

5 Review

See p32 for ideas on how to use this section.

1a)–b) 2 market 3 station 4 airport 5 river 6 museum 7 hotel 8 mountains

3a) 2 bed: it isn't in the kitchen
3 shower: it isn't a room
4 desk: it isn't in the bathroom
5 living room: it's a room, not something in the bathroom
6 bedroom: it's a room, not a place to live
7 washing machine: it isn't in the living room

5a) 2 How much coffee do you drink? 3 How many hours do you spend travelling? 4 How much TV do you watch? 5 How much time do you spend on a computer? 6 How many emails do you write?

7 dress; shoes; suit; shirt; trousers; skirt; tie; hat; top; jeans; shorts; socks; jumper

Progress Portfolio

See p32 for ideas on how to use this section.

6 Good times, bad times

Student's Book p46–p53

6A Three generations

QUICK REVIEW ●●●

This activity reviews clothes vocabulary. Students work on their own and write all the clothes they know. Set a time limit of two minutes. Students compare lists in pairs, then tell their partner about their favourite clothes.

Vocabulary adjectives (2); years
Grammar Past Simple (1); *be*
Help with Listening *was* and *were*
Review clothes

Vocabulary Adjectives (2)

1 Focus students on photo A and the title of this lesson. Establish that the people in the photo are three generations of the same family.

Students discuss the questions in pairs. Check answers with the class.

> 1 Margaret is Helen's mother. Rebecca is Helen's daughter. **2** Margaret was born in 1940. Helen was born in 1962. Rebecca is thirteen. **3** A Rebecca; B Margaret

2 a) Students work on their own and match the adjectives and their opposites, then check answers in pairs.

Students then do the exercise in **V6.1** SB p134. Check answers with the class. Point out the prefix *un-* in *unhappy* and *unfriendly* means *not*.

Model and drill the words. Pay particular attention to the pronunciation of *friendly* /'frendli/, *crowded* /'kraʊdɪd/, *interesting* /'ɪntrəstɪŋ/, *dirty* /'dɜːti/ and *quiet* /kwaɪət/. Point out that *interesting* only has three syllables.

> **V6.1** 2d) 3g) 4c) 5j) 6i) 7k) 8b) 9e) 10a) 11f)

b) Focus students on photos A and B and the sentences in the speech bubbles. Teach the difference between *Margaret is friendly.* (I know her) and *Margaret looks friendly.* (I don't know her but I think she is friendly from her photo).

Students work in pairs and use the adjectives in **2a)** to talk about the photos. Ask students to share interesting ideas with the class.

> — **EXTRA IDEA** —
> • Write the adjectives in **2a)** on cards. Put students into pairs and give a set of cards to each pair. Students try to match up the pairs of adjectives, then check in **V6.1** p134. Alternatively, this idea can be used for revision next class.

Listening, Reading and Grammar

3 a) Tell students they are going to hear about a birthday party. Pre-teach *yesterday* to establish that the text is in the past.

R6.1 Focus students on the text in the speech bubble, then play the recording. Students listen and read. Ask students who they think is talking (Rebecca).

b) Students read about the party again and underline the things in the box in the text. Do the first answer as an example with the class.

Students check answers in pairs. Check answers with the class.

> **place:** Perth, Australia
> **number of people:** about forty
> **food:** burgers, chicken
> **drink:** Coke, orange juice
> **people not at the party:** Rebecca's grandfather and her other two brothers

Help with Grammar
was/were/wasn't/weren't

4 a) Students do the exercise on their own, then check in pairs. Check answers with the class.

b)–c) Students do **4b)** on their own, then check in **G6.1** SB p135.

 While they are working, draw the table from **4b)** on the board so that you are ready to check their answers. Check answers with the class.

• Check students understand that Rebecca's text is in the past, and that *was*, *were*, *wasn't* and *weren't* are all past forms of the verb *be*.
• Focus students on the table on the board. Elicit which words go in the gaps and fill in the table (see the table in **G6.1** SB p135). Highlight the relationship between the pronouns and the past forms of *be*.
• Highlight that *wasn't* and *weren't* are the contracted form of *was not* and *were not*. Tell students that we usually use the contracted forms when speaking and writing.
• Point out that the past of *there is/there are* is *there was/there were*.
• Teach students the phrase *I was born in ...* (place/year). Point out that we can't say *I borned in ...* .

5 Check students remember who Helen is (Rebecca's mother). Students do the exercise on their own, referring back to the table in **4a)** if necessary, then check in pairs. Check answers with the class.

> 1 was 2 was 3 wasn't 4 was 5 wasn't 6 wasn't 7 were
> 8 weren't 9 was

 6 a) Check students remember who Rebecca's grandmother is (Margaret) and ask which photo shows her thirteenth birthday party (photo B). Ask students why they think her party was in the street and teach *a coronation* (the ceremony when a king or queen is crowned).

R6.2 Play the recording (SB p152). Students listen and decide if it was a good party and why/why not. Check answers with the class.

> Yes, it was a good party. It was the same day as Queen Elizabeth's coronation and there was a big party in the street with lots of food and about 300 people.

b) Give students time to read the questions. Then play the recording again. Students check answers in pairs. Check answers with the class. Note that in 1953 it wasn't easy to buy meat in the UK, so chicken sandwiches were a big treat.

> 1 June 2nd 1953. 2 In a street in London. 3 No, not very. 4 Chicken sandwiches. 5 No, they weren't. 6 About 300.

Help with Listening *was* and *were*

- This Help with Listening section helps students to understand the weak and strong forms of *was* and *were* in questions, statements and short answers.

 7 a) Tell students that there are two ways to pronounce *was* and *were*: the 'strong form' and the 'weak form'.

R6.3 Play the recording. Students listen and notice the difference between the strong and weak forms. Play the recording again if necessary. Note that the recording includes the strong and weak forms of *was* and *were* in the table and the example sentences under the table.

b) Students complete the rules on their own or in pairs, referring to the examples in **7a)** if necessary.

Check answers with the class. Highlight that the strong forms of *was* and *were* are stressed in sentences, whereas the weak forms are unstressed. Point out the schwa /ə/ in the weak forms and remind students that this sound is always unstressed.

Also point out that there is only one pronunciation of the negative forms *wasn't* /ˈwɒzənt/ and *weren't* /wɜːnt/, and that these words are always stressed.

- In statements and questions *was* and *were* are usually weak (and therefore unstressed).
- In short answers *was* and *were* are strong (and therefore stressed).

Help with Grammar Questions and short answers with *was/were*

 8 a)–c) Students do the exercises on their own or in pairs, then check their answers in G6.2 SB p135.

 While they are working, draw the table from **8a)** on the board so that you are ready to check their answers. Check answers with the class.

- Focus students on the table on the board. Elicit which words in questions 2 and 3 from **6b)** go in each column and complete the table (see the table in G6.2 SB p135).
- Highlight the word order of questions with *was/were*: (question word) + *was/were* + subject + ... You may wish to compare the questions in the table to questions with *be* in the present, (*Where is he from?*, *What are their jobs?*, etc.) to show that the word order is the same.
- Check students have written the correct short answers: *Yes, I/he/she/it was.*, *No, he/she/it wasn't.*, *Yes, you/we/they were.* and *No, you/we/they weren't.* Point out that we use contractions in negative short answers.

9 R6.4 P Play the recording (SB p152) and ask students to repeat. Encourage students to copy the sentence stress and the weak forms of *was* and *were*. You may wish students to look at R6.4, SB p152 while they practise.

10 a) Students work in pairs and see if they can work out how to say the years.

b) Students check their answers in V6.2 SB p134. Model and drill the years. Point out the *and* in *two thousand and five*. Note that for earlier dates, for example, 1704, we say *seventeen oh four* not ~~*seventeen and four*~~.

c) Use the speech bubbles to teach the questions *When/Where was Ana born?* and *When/Where were you born?*. Drill these questions with the class.

Students work on their own and write the names of five people in their family.

Students work in pairs and take turns to ask about the people their partner has written down. Encourage students to ask more questions about the people (*Who's Ana? What does she do?*, etc.).

— **EXTRA IDEA** —
- Students move around the room asking where other students were born. Students should find the person who was born nearest to them geographically.

11 a) Use the example to highlight that the students should make questions with the subject *you*. Students make questions on their own.

Check the questions with the class. Drill the questions with the class.

2 Where were you last night? 3 Were you at home yesterday afternoon? 4 Where were you on your last birthday? 5 Were you in this class last month? 6 Where were you last New Year's Eve?

b) Students work in pairs and take turns to ask and answer the questions. Encourage students to give more information and ask more questions if possible.

Ask students to share any interesting information with the class.

Get ready … Get it right!

12 Put students into pairs, student A and student B. Student As turn to SB p111 and student Bs turn to SB p119. Check they are all looking at the correct exercise.

a) Students work on their own and write questions with *you* or *your* about when they were thirteen from the prompts. While students are working, check their questions for accuracy and help with any problems.

b) Students write their answers in the *you* column.

c) Students work with their partner and take turns to ask and answer their questions. Students should write their partner's answers in the *your partner* column.

d) ✍ Write *Tom and I were both happy at school.* on the board to show students that *both* comes after the verb *be*. Then write *I was happy at school, but Vanessa wasn't happy.* on the board. Cross out the second *happy* to show students that we don't repeat this word.

Students work with a new partner from either group A or group B. They take turns to talk about themselves and their partner, using the information from their table in **a)**. Again monitor for accuracy and help students with any problems.

EXTRA PRACTICE AND HOMEWORK

Ph **Class Activity** Famous people quiz p154 (Instructions p127)
6 Review Exercises 1, 2 and 3 SB p53
CD-ROM Lesson 6A
Workbook Lesson 6A p30

6B People who changed the world

QUICK REVIEW ●●●
This activity practises questions with *was/were* and times. Students make a list of six times of the day on their own. Students then work in pairs and ask each other where they were at these times yesterday. Ask students to share interesting answers with the class.

Vocabulary life events
Grammar Past Simple (2): regular and irregular verbs; positive and *Wh-* questions
Review *was/were*; dates; years

Vocabulary Life events

 Students do the exercise in pairs, then check answers in V6.3 SB p134.

Check answers with the class. Point out that we *get married to someone*, not ~~get married with someone~~.

Check that students understand the meaning of *university* /juːnɪˈvɜːsɪti/, *divorced* /dɪˈvɔːst/ and *law* /lɔː/.

Model and drill the collocations.

2 **finish** school/university 3 **meet** my husband/my wife
4 **get** married/divorced
6 **become** a lawyer/president 7 **write** a book/a letter
8 **study** languages/law

— EXTRA IDEA —
● Students work in pairs and take turns to test each other on the collocations. One student says the noun, for example, *law* and his/her partner says the whole collocation, for example, *study law*.

Reading and Grammar

 a) Focus students on the photo of Nelson Mandela. Elicit what students know about him. Use this information to pre-teach *prison* and *politics*.

b) Students work on their own and fill in the gaps in the text with the dates and numbers in the box. Students check their answers in pairs.

c) R6.5 Play the recording. Students read, listen and check their answers.

1 18th July 2 1943 3 1957 4 two 5 eighteen 6 four
7 1996

— EXTRA IDEA —
● ✍ While doing **2a)**, write up students' ideas on the board to build up a profile of Nelson Mandela. Students can then read the text to check if the information on the board is correct.

3 Students do the exercise on their own, then check answers in pairs. Check answers with the class.

2c) 3b) 4a) 5e) 6g) 7f)

Help with Grammar Past Simple regular and irregular verbs: positive

4 a) Focus students on the boxes and teach students the difference between regular verbs and irregular verbs.

Teach any new words, for example, *stay, forget*. Ask the class to find the Past Simple of the first two verbs (*start* and *study*) in the text.

Students then work on their own or in pairs and find the Past Simple of the other verbs. While they are working, write the infinitives on the board in two columns: *Regular verbs* and *Irregular verbs*.

Check answers with the class and write the Past Simple forms on the board next to their infinitives. Leave these on the board to help students with **4b)** and **5**.

- Check students understand that we use the Past Simple to talk about the past and that we know when these things happened.
- Regular verbs: *started; studied; finished; lived; worked; wanted; stayed; married*
- Irregular verbs: *became; had, got; met; went; forgot; left; write*
- Also compare *marry* (which must have an object: *She married **him** last year.*) to *get married* (which we can use without an object: *I got married in 1999.* or with *to*: *She got married to Richard.*).

b)–c) Students do **4b)** on their own or in pairs by referring to the verbs and their Past Simple forms in **4a)**, then check answers in G6.3 SB p135 and the Irregular Verb List, SB p159. Check answers with the class.

- **b)** **1** *-ed* **2** regular verbs that end in *-e*: *-d*; regular verbs that end in consonant + *y*: *-y* → *-i* and add *-ed* **3** Yes, it is.
- Check students have understood the spelling rules in the table in G6.3 SB p135 and the reason for doubling the *p* in *stopped* (*stop* ends in consonant + vowel + consonant).
- Highlight that the Past Simple is the same for all subjects.
- Point out that there are no rules for the Past Simple of irregular verbs.
- Draw students' attention to the Irregular Verb List, SB p159.

5 a) R6.6 P Play the recording of the regular Past Simple forms from **4a)** and ask students to repeat.

Ask students which of the Past Simple forms end with the sound /ɪd/ (*started, studied, wanted, married*).

Point out that for regular verbs ending in a /t/ or a /d/ sound, the *-ed* ending in the Past Simple is pronounced as an extra syllable /ɪd/ (*started, needed*, etc.) Pay particular attention to the pronunciation of *finished* /ˈfɪnɪʃd/ and *worked* /wɜːkt/ as students often have problems pronouncing the consonant clusters.

b) R6.7 P Play the recording of the irregular Past Simple forms from **4a)** and ask students to repeat.

6 Pre-teach *prize, win* (Past Simple: *won*).

Students work on their own and fill in the gaps with the correct form of the Past Simple.

Students check answers in pairs. Check answers with the class.

2 studied; was **3** had **4** left; went **5** became; won

7 a) Focus students on the title of the quiz and ask students if they can name any of the people in the photos. Pre-teach *fly* and *explorer*.

Students do the quiz in groups.

b) Students check answers on SB p158. Find out which group got the most answers right.

1b) **2**a) **3**b) **4**a) **5**a)

Help with Grammar Past Simple: Wh- questions

8 a) Check students understand the headings in the table. Use the example to illustrate the word order of Past Simple questions.

b)–c) Students do **8b)** on their own, then check answers in G6.4 SB p135.

 While they are working, draw the table from **8a)** on the board so that you are ready to check their answers.

Check answers with the class.

- Focus students on the table on the board. Elicit which words in questions 2 and 3 from the quiz go in each column and complete the table (see the table in G6.4 SB p135).
- Use these examples to illustrate the word order in Past Simple questions: question word + *did* + subject + infinitive + ...
- Point out that the auxiliary *did* has no meaning but is used to make the question form of the Past Simple.
- Show students the similarity between Past Simple and Present Simple questions by writing some Present Simple questions on the board (*Where do you come from? What does he do?*, etc.). Point out that the only difference in form is the auxiliary *do/does* in the Present Simple and *did* in the Past Simple.
- Also highlight that we use *did* for all subjects, including *he/she/it*.

9 a) Students do the exercise on their own, then check in pairs.

b) R6.8 Play the recording. Students listen and check. P Play the recording again and ask students to repeat.

Focus on sentence stress and point out that *did* isn't usually stressed.

> **2** Where did you meet your best friend? **3** Where did your parents meet? **4** When did you first go to another country? **5** What did you do last weekend?

c) Students work in pairs and take turns to ask and answer the questions in **9a)**.

While they are working, correct any mistakes you hear and help students with any vocabulary they need.

Ask students to share interesting answers with the class.

Get ready … Get it right!

10 Ask students to look at SB p120.

a) Draw your own timeline on the board and write a few years or dates on it which mark important events in your life. Tell the students about these events.

Students then work on their own and choose five to eight things from the list that they want to talk about. They write the event and the time when it happened on their timeline.

b) Students work in pairs and talk about their timelines. Encourage students to ask follow-up questions and to remember as much as they can about their partner's life.

While students are working, monitor and help with any problems.

c) Put students into new pairs. Students take turns to tell their new partner three things about the person they talked to in **b)**.

Finally, ask students to share any interesting information with the class.

EXTRA PRACTICE AND HOMEWORK

Ph **Vocabulary Plus** 6 Irregular Verbs p192 (Instructions p184)

Ph **Class Activity** 6B Antonio's honeymoon p155 (Instructions p128)

6 Review Exercises 4 and 5 SB p53

CD-ROM Lesson 6B

Workbook Lesson 6B p31

6C Four weekends

QUICK REVIEW ●●●

This activity reviews Past Simple forms. Students work on their own and write a list of ten verbs and their Past Simple forms. Remind them of the Irregular Verb List, SB p159. Put students into pairs. Students take turns to say a Past Simple form from their list. Their partner says the infinitive.

Real World showing interest and continuing a conversation
Vocabulary weekend activities
Help with Listening showing interest
Review Past Simple

How was your weekend?

1 **a)** Focus the students on the picture and ask where the people are (in an office/a meeting). Tell students that the meeting is on Monday morning.

Pre-teach *busy* /ˈbɪzi/ and *terrible*, and check students remember *great* and *quiet*.

Students work on their own or in pairs and try to match the people to the types of weekend they had.

b) Focus students on the four texts A–D around the picture and ask students what they are (a letter, a list, an email, a diary). Students read the texts and check their guesses in **1a)**.

Check answers with the class and ask students to give reasons for their choices. Note that the diary entry (D) was written by Jane.

> 1 Sarah 2 Jane 3 Mick 4 Henry

2 **a)** Focus students on the phrases 1–8 (*work every evening, clean the car,* etc.). Check students understand the phrases and teach *the washing, go away* and *wonderful* if necessary.

Students work on their own and fill in the gaps with words/phrases from the box, then check in **V6.4** SB p134.

Check answers with the class. Check students understand the new words/phrases *all day, a bad cold, a couple of days* and *until*.

Establish the difference between these phrases: *be cold* (not hot) and *have (got) a cold* (ill); *all day* (all the hours in one day) and *every day* (all the days in one week, month, etc.); *do the washing* (clothes) and *do the washing up* (plates, cutlery, etc.); *go shopping* (for clothes, shoes, CDs, etc.) and *do the shopping* (for food and for other necessities).

Model and drill the phrases. Pay particular attention to the pronunciation of *tired* /taɪəd/ and *couple* /ˈkʌpəl/.

2 clean the house **3** write an email **4** do the shopping
5 go away for a couple of days **6** sleep until 11 a.m.
7 be tired **8** have a bad cold

EXTRA IDEA

- Write the words and phrases from **2a)** on sets of coloured cards (one colour for the verbs and another colour for the other words/phrases). Put students into groups. Give one set of cards with the verbs and the words/phrases to each group. Students match the verbs to the words/phrases, then check in **V6.4** SB p134.

---

b) Students work in pairs and take turns to test each other on the collocations, as shown in the speech bubbles.

c) Students read texts A–D again and underline all the collocations from **2a)** they can find in the texts. Point out that the verbs may be in the infinitive or the Past Simple. Check answers with the class.

A go away for the weekend; had a wonderful time
B clean the car; do the shopping; write report
C was ill; worked every evening
D Slept until 11 a.m.; did the washing

d) Focus students on the collocations in **2a)**. Elicit the Past Simple forms of the verbs and write them on the board for students to copy.

1 worked **2** cleaned **3** wrote **4** did **5** went away
6 slept **7** was/were **8** had

3 a) Students work on their own and write six things they did last weekend. While they are working, help with any new vocabulary as necessary.

b) Use the speech bubbles to remind students of *Me too.* as a way of agreeing with a positive sentence. Check students understand *last weekend.*

Students work in pairs and talk about what they did last weekend. Students must find three things they both did.

Ask each pair to tell the class what they both did last weekend.

EXTRA IDEA

- Students work in pairs. Give students three minutes to think of as many other words/phrases that collocate with the verbs in **2a)** as they can. The pair that thinks of the most words/phrases wins. Write students' phrases on the board next to the verbs for other students to copy.

Being a good listener

4 Focus students on the people in the picture again and check students know their names.

R6.9 Play the recording (SB p152). Students listen and decide who is speaking in each conversation.

1 Jane; Henry **2** Mick; Sarah

Help with Listening Showing interest

- This Help with Listening section helps students to be a good listener by introducing useful phrases for showing interest during a conversation.

5 a) Give students time to read sentences 1–8 and responses a)–h).

R6.10 Play the recording. Students listen and match the sentences to the responses. Check answers with the class.

2d) **3**a) **4**b) **5**e) **6**g) **7**h) **8**f)

b) Pre-teach *be sorry* and *be surprised.*
Students work on their own and fill in the table, then check answers in **RW6.1** SB p135.
Check answers with the class.

I'm happy for you: Oh, great! Oh, nice.
I'm sorry for you: Oh, dear. What a shame.
I'm surprised: Wow! You're joking! Really?

6 Establish the importance of intonation in showing interest by saying *Oh, really?* in an interested way and then in an uninterested way.

R6.11 **P** Play the recording and ask students to repeat. Focus on the intonation of each phrase and ask students to exaggerate the intonation pattern if necessary.

7 Put students into pairs, student A and student B. Student As turn to SB p105 and student Bs turn to SB p113. Check they are all looking at the correct exercise.

Give students a few moments to study the words/phrases in the box and read sentences 1–6.

Students work in pairs and take turns to say the sentences. His/her partner should respond with one of the phrases in the box. While students are working, monitor and help with any problems.

Real World Continuing a conversation

8 a) Tell students that, after showing interest, we often continue conversations by asking 'follow-up' questions to find out more information.

Students work on their own and fill in the gaps in the questions. Check answers with the class.

Highlight that *What was it like?* is asking for a description or an opinion about a place or thing.
Point out that we don't use *like* in the answer. We say *It was …* (*great/expensive/boring*, etc.), not ~~*It was like*~~ (*great*, etc.). This language point is dealt with in more detail in lesson 10B.

Model and drill the questions.

1 was 2 Are 3 did 4 did 6 did 7 did 8 did

b)–c) Students do **8b)** on their own or in pairs, then check in RW6.2 SB p135.

a) 4; 5; 7 b) 3 c) 1; 2 d) 5; 6; 7; 8

d) R6.9 Ask students to look at R6.9, SB p152, then play the recording. Students listen, read and underline the follow-up questions. You can also ask students to circle the phrases for showing interest from **5a)**. Students check answers in pairs.

Play the recording again, pausing after each follow-up question and asking students to repeat.

 a) Students do the exercise on their own. While they are working, move around the room and help with any new vocabulary as necessary.

b) Focus students on the conversation in the speech bubbles. Point out that the conversation uses both aspects of being a good listener studied in the lesson: showing interest and continuing a conversation.

Demonstrate the activity with a confident student and try to continue the conversation for as long as possible.

Put students into pairs. Students take turns to ask their partner what they did at times 1–5 in **9a)**. Encourage students to continue each conversation for as long as possible. While students are working, correct any mistakes you hear and help with any problems.

Finally, ask students to tell the class one interesting thing their partner told them.

┌─ **EXTRA PRACTICE AND HOMEWORK** ─
6 Review Exercise 6 SB p53
CD-ROM Lesson 6C
Workbook Lesson 6C p33

6D The good and the bad

QUICK REVIEW ●●●
This activity reviews ways of showing interest and continuing a conversation. Give students a few moments to think of five things they did last week. Students then do the activity in pairs. ✏ If necessary, elicit/write the language from RW6.1 and RW6.2 on the board before pairs start.

> **Vocabulary** adjectives with *very, really, quite, too*
> **Review** Past Simple; Present Simple

 Pre-teach and drill *competition* /ˌkɒmpɪˈtɪʃən/. Students discuss the questions in groups. Ask groups to share their ideas with the class.

 Focus students on the title of the article and teach *winners* and *losers*. Allow students a few moments to read the first paragraph of the article only, then ask the class what they think the rest of the article is about.

 a) Focus students on the photos in the article and the names of the people. Ask who they think had a good experience (Jim) and who had a bad experience (Sandra).

Students work in pairs, student A and student B. Student As read about Jim and student Bs read about Sandra. All students answer the same questions 1–6. Ask students to cover the text about the other person before they start.

b) Student work with their partner. Student A asks student B questions 1–6 about Sandra. When student B has finished answering the questions, student B asks student A questions 1–6 about Jim.

Early finishers can tell their partners any other interesting things from their part of the article.

Check answers with the class.

JIM 1 A weekend for two in Paris. 2 His girlfriend, Naomi. 3 In a very expensive hotel near the River Seine. 4 Quite hot. 5 They had coffee by the river and went to the Louvre Museum. 6 He asked Naomi to marry him.
SANDRA 1 A weekend for two in Scotland. 2 Her boyfriend, Logan. 3 A really cheap, ugly hotel. 4 Really bad and too cold. 5 They didn't go out and they had a fight in the evening. She went to bed early and he talked to the receptionist for hours. 6 He left Sandra and went away with the receptionist.

a) Students read their part of the article again and find all the adjectives.

JIM big, expensive, hot, good, long, crowded, interesting, wonderful, beautiful
SANDRA happy, empty, cheap, ugly, dirty, small, bad, cold, boring, early, young, friendly, terrible

b) Students compare lists with their partner and find as many opposite pairs as they can. ✏ Check answers with the class and write the opposite pairs on the board.

Give students time to read the other part of the article and ask about any new vocabulary.

big/small; expensive/cheap; hot/cold; good/bad; crowded/empty; interesting/boring; wonderful/terrible; beautiful/ugly

Help with Vocabulary Adjectives with *very, really, quite, too*

5 **a)** Students work on their own and match sentences 1–3 to pictures A–C.

Check answers with the class. Highlight that *too* has a negative meaning and means *more than you want*. Point out that we don't use *too* to mean *very very*. We say *She's really happy.* not ~~*She's too happy*~~. Check students understand *very* and *really* mean the same.

> 1C 2A 3B

b) Students work on their own and find examples of *very, really, quite* and *too* + adjective in the article. Students check answers in pairs.

c)–d) Students complete the rule in **5c)**, then check in **V6.5** SB p134. Check the answer with the class.

> • *Very, really, quite* and *too* come after the verb *be* and before adjectives.

6 Pre-teach *plane* and *drive*. Students do the exercise on their own, then check in pairs. Check answers with the class.

> 2 very 3 really 4 very 5 too 6 really 7 quite 8 too

7 **a)** Students work on their own and write the name of a place in their town/city for the phrases in 1–6.

b) Focus on the speech bubbles to show students how to structure the conversation. Students work in groups and discuss the places they have written down. Encourage students to comment on the places. Finally, ask students to tell the class about two of the places their group discussed.

♪ Ask students to turn to SB p102 and look at *Da Do Ron Ron*. This song was originally recorded by the American group The Crystals in 1963.

1 Students work on their own and write the Past Simple forms. Remind them of the Irregular Verb List, SB p159.

✎ Check answers with the class. Write them on the board. Students need these Past Simple forms for **2a)**. Check students understand the literal meanings of *stand* and *catch*. Drill their Past Simple forms *stood* /stʊd/ and *caught* /kɔːt/. Pre-teach *stand still* and *catch someone's eye*.

> 2 stood 3 told 4 was/were 5 walked 6 knew
> 7 caught 8 looked

2 **a)** Give students time to read the song. Play the recording. Students listen and fill in the gaps using some words more than once. Play it again if necessary.

b) Students check answers in pairs. Play the recording again, pausing after each line for students to check.

> 2 stood 3 told 4 was 5 stood 6 was 7 walked
> 8 knew 9 caught 10 looked 11 caught 12 walked
> 13 looked 14 looked 15 walked

3 **a)** ✎ Write rhyming pairs of words on the board (*do/shoe*, etc.) to teach students *rhyme* /raɪm/. Students work on their own and find two more pairs of words in the song that rhyme.

> eye/my; fine/mine

b) Students do the exercise on their own or in pairs. Check answers with the class.

> 2 heart 3 name 4 when 5 make 6 what 7 seven 8 day

EXTRA PRACTICE AND HOMEWORK

Ph **Study Skills** 3 Using your English dictionary p204 (Instructions p200)

Ph **Class Activity** 6D Money, money, money! p156 (Instructions p128)

6 Review SB p53

CD-ROM Lesson 6D

Workbook Lesson 6D p34

Workbook Reading and Writing Portfolio p74

Progress Test 6 p216–p217

---

6 Review

See p32 for ideas on how to use this section.

1 2 unhappy 3 poor 4 empty 5 dirty 6 short
7 unfriendly 8 intelligent 9 noisy 10 interesting

2a) 1 was/wasn't 2 were/weren't 3 was/wasn't
4 were/weren't 5 was/wasn't

3a) 2 Were your family all together last New Year's Eve?
3 Were you with your friends on Saturday evening?
4 Were both your parents born in the same country?
5 Were you born in the place you live in now?

4 2 lived 3 met 4 got 5 had 6 went 7 met 8 moved 9 was

5a) 3 Where did Stan meet Margaret? 4 When did they get married? 5 When did they have Helen? 6 Where did Helen go in 1986? 7 Who did she meet there? 8 Where did they move to in 1990? 9 When was Rebecca born?

6a) 2 Oh, great! 3 Oh, nice. 4 You're joking! 5 Oh, right.

Progress Portfolio

See p32 for ideas on how to use this section.

7 Films, music, news

7A Licence to kill

Vocabulary types of film
Grammar Past Simple (3): negative, *yes/no* questions and short answers
Help with Listening Past Simple questions
Review Past Simple: positive and *Wh-* questions

Vocabulary Types of film

1 a) Students work on their own and tick the words they know, then check their answers in **V7.1** SB p136.

Check answers with the class and elicit current or well-known films for each type, if possible. Teach the American English word *movie*.

Elicit the singular form of each type of film (*an action film*, a *thriller*, etc). and check the spelling of a *comedy*. Also point out that we use the word *film(s)* in the phrases *action film(s)*, *horror film(s)* and *sci-fi film(s)*, but not with the other types of film.

Model and drill the words. Highlight the pronunciation of *thrillers* /'θrɪləz/, *horror* /'hɒrə/ and *sci-fi* /'saɪfaɪ/.

Note that only the main stress in words/phrases is shown in vocabulary boxes and the Language Summaries.

> **— EXTRA IDEA —**
> • Download some film pictures or posters from the Internet for students to match to the film types.

b) Elicit different ways to talk about likes/dislikes (*I love … , I really/quite like … , … are OK, I don't like … , I hate …*) and write them on the board.

Point out that we usually use plural countable nouns without *the* with these phrases when we are talking generally: *I like action films.* not ~~I like action film.~~ or ~~I like the action films~~.

Use the speech bubbles to remind students of *(Yes,) me too.* to show agreement and *Really?* to show surprise.

Students work in groups and take turns to talk about the films they like and don't like.

Ask each group to tell the class which was the most popular type of film in their group.

Reading and Grammar

2 Focus students on the posters in the article and ask students if they like Bond films.

Students work in groups and think of all the things they know about James Bond, for example, *He's British, he's a spy*, etc.

Students share their ideas with the class. Write the ideas on the board. Note that *007* is pronounced *double oh seven*.

3 a) Pre-teach the vocabulary in the box. Note that the aim of these boxes is to highlight which words you need to pre-teach to help students understand the text that follows. The vocabulary in these boxes is not in the Language Summaries in the Student's Book.

Point out that *kill* must take an object (*They killed him.*), but *die* is intransitive and does not take an object (*He died in 1968.*). Also teach *spy* as a synonym for *secret agent*.

Model and drill the words. Highlight the pronunciation of *climbing* /'klaɪmɪŋ/ and *licence* /'laɪsəns/.

b) Pre-teach *title* and *movie star*, then check students understand the possible titles 1–3.

Students read the article and choose the best title. Set a time limit of two minutes to encourage students to read for gist.

Students compare answers with the whole class and give reasons for their choices.

> 2 From schoolboy to spy

c) Students read the article again and answer questions 1–6. Students check answers in pairs or groups. Check answers with the class.

Point out that Eton and Fettes are British public schools. In the UK 'public schools' are, in fact, private schools and are very expensive. You can tell the class that Prince William from the British Royal family went to Eton.

> 1 Scotland
> 2 His parents died.
> 3 Eton and Fettes.
> 4 He worked as a secret agent for the British navy.
> 5 1950
> 6 one

Help with Grammar Past Simple: negative

4 a)–b) Students do **4a)** on their own, then check their answers in **G7.1** SB p137.

Check answers with the class.

- To make the Past Simple negative of *be*, we use *wasn't* or *weren't*.
- To make the Past Simple negative of all other verbs, we use *didn't* + infinitive.
- Check students understand that *didn't* is the contracted form of *did not*.
- Point out that we use *didn't* for all subjects (*I/you/he/she/it/we/they*) and highlight the word order: subject + *didn't* + infinitive + ...
- Also highlight that we use the infinitive after *didn't*, not the Past Simple form. We say *He didn't study very much.* not ~~He didn't studied very much~~.

c) Students work on their own and find four more Past Simple negatives in the article about James Bond.
Check answers with the class.

> didn't have didn't like didn't get weren't

 Focus on the example sentence and point out that *didn't* is always stressed (all negative auxiliaries are stressed because they carry meaning).
R7.1 **P** Play the recording (SB p152). Ask students to repeat. Check students copy the sentence stress correctly.
You can also ask students to turn to R7.1, SB p152. They can then follow the sentence stress as they listen.

6 a) Focus students on the example. Show how sentence 1 has been made negative.
Students do the exercise on their own, ticking the true sentences and making the other sentences negative.

b) Students work in pairs and compare sentences to find out how many are the same. Encourage them to ask follow-up questions where possible, for example, *What did you have?* for sentence 2.
Ask each pair to share one or two of their sentences that are the same with the class.

7 Tell students they are going to listen to an interview with a writer, Will Forbes. Focus on the two gist questions and check students understand them.
R7.2 Play the recording (SB p152). Students listen and choose the correct answers in 1 and 2.
Check answers with the class. Point out the black and white photo of Ian Fleming in the article on p54.

> 1 Ian Fleming 2 quite similar

Help with Listening Past Simple questions

- This Help with Listening section highlights that *did* is unstressed in Past Simple questions.

8 a) Tell students that they are going to hear six questions from the interview with Will Forbes. Point out that these questions are in the Past Simple.

Elicit that we use *did* to make Past Simple questions.
R7.3 Play the recording. Students listen and fill in the gaps.

> 1 Did ... work ... British 2 Did ... have ... kill
> 3 Did ... work ... war 4 Did ... go ... school
> 5 did ... write 6 Did ... make ... money

b) Play the recording again. Elicit from students that *did* is unstressed in Past Simple questions.

9 a) **R7.4** Focus students on the questions in **8a)** again, then play the recording of the complete interview (SB p152). Students listen and answer the questions.
Check answers with the class.

> 1 Yes, he did. 2 No, he didn't. 3 No, he didn't.
> 4 Yes, they did. 5 In 1952. 6 No, he didn't.

b) Students listen and find four things that are true for Ian Fleming and James Bond. Students can refer to the article if necessary.

> 1 They both went to Eton. 2 They both worked for the British Secret Service. 3 They were both in the navy.
> 4 They were both very good at sports.

Help with Grammar Past Simple: *yes/no* questions and short answers

10 a)–b) Students work on their own and fill in the gaps, then check their answers in **G7.2** SB p137.
Check answers with the class.

- Both questions start with *Did*; the short answers are *Yes, he did./No, he didn't.* and *Yes, they did./No, they didn't.*
- Highlight the word order in Past Simple *yes/no* questions: *Did* + subject + infinitive + ...
- Point out that we don't repeat the infinitive in short answers: *Yes, he did.* not ~~Yes, he did go~~.

11 a) Students do the exercise on their own, then check in pairs. Check answers with the class.

> 1 Did you go to the cinema last week? 2 Did you see a Bond film last year? 3 Did you watch a film on TV last weekend? 4 Did you want to be an actor when you were a child?

b) **R7.5** **P** Play the recording. Ask students to repeat. Encourage students to copy the sentence stress.

c) Students do the activity in pairs and ask follow-up questions (*What did you see?*, etc.) where possible.
While they are working, move around the room and correct where necessary.

- Do a classroom survey. Write the mixed-up questions from **11a)** on separate cards and add more questions of your own so that there is one card for each student. Give the cards to students and ask them to put the words in order. Students then move around the room asking all the other students in the class their question and making notes of the answers. Finally, students report back to the class on the results of their survey (for example, *Five students went to the cinema last week and eight didn't.*)

Get ready ... Get it right!

12 Put students into two groups, group A and group B. Students in group A turn to SB p108 and students in group B turn to SB p116. Check they are all looking at the correct exercise.

a) Focus on the photo of Pierce Brosnan and ask what students know about him.

Give students time to read the text and deal with any vocabulary problems.

Check students understand the information in black is correct, and that some (but not all) of the information in blue is wrong.

b) Put students into pairs with someone from the same group. Focus students on the examples.

Students work in their pairs and write *yes/no* questions to check the information in blue in their version of the text.

While students are working, check their questions for accuracy and help with any problems.

c) Reorganise the class so that each student from group A is working with a student from group B. Students are not allowed to look at each other's text.

Students take turns to ask and answer their questions. Student A asks the first question. Encourage students to use correct short answers (*Yes, he was., No, he wasn't., Yes, he did., No, he didn't.*, etc.).

Students correct the information in blue in their text where necessary.

d) Students work with their partner from the same group from **b)** and check their answers.

Students then read the text again and find three reasons why Pierce Brosnan was 'born to be Bond'.

Check answers with the class.

> 1 He went to live with his mother on the same day that Ian Fleming died. 2 The first film he saw was a Bond film. 3 His wife was a Bond girl.

7B My music

QUICK REVIEW ●●●

This activity reviews Past Simple *yes/no* questions. Students write five *Did you ...* questions about yesterday on their own. Put students into pairs, but do not let them talk to each other yet. Students guess if their partner will answer *yes* or *no* to their five questions. Students then work in pairs and take turns to ask and answer their questions. Ask students how many of their guesses were correct.

Vocabulary Types of music and past time phrases

1 a) R7.6 Focus students on the types of music in the box, then play the recording. Students listen and put the types of music in order.

Play the recording again, pausing after each piece of music to check answers. Check students notice that we say *classical music*, not ~~classic music~~.

Vocabulary types of music; past time phrases with *ago*, *last* and *in*; question words
Grammar question forms
Review Past Simple; Present Simple

Model and drill the words/phrases. Highlight the pronunciation of *reggae* /ˈreɡeɪ/ and point out that *opera* is usually two syllables, not three.

Note that these words are in V7.2 in the Language Summary, SB p136.

> 2 rock music 3 reggae 4 opera 5 rock'n'roll 6 jazz
> 7 dance music 8 classical music 9 pop music

b) Pre-teach *band*, *singer* and *composer*.

If necessary, write the following language on the board: *What type of music do you like?*, *I love ...* , *I (really/quite) like ...* , *... is OK*, *I don't like ...* , *I hate ...* , *My favourite band/singer/composer is ...* .

Also point out that we say *I really like rock music.* not *I really like the rock music*.

Students then do the activity in pairs. Ask students to share their ideas with the class.

┌─ EXTRA IDEA ─────────────────────────────────┐
- Do a classroom survey on musical tastes. Students work on their own and write down their three favourite bands, singers and composers. Students move around the room and ask as many other students as possible if they like their three choices. Students should make notes on the answers. Finally, students report back to the class on how popular their choices were.
└──┘

2 a) Students work on their own and put the past time phrases in order.

Students check answers in pairs. Check answers with the class and highlight the following points.

- We use *ago* with the Past Simple to talk about a time in the past. We say *I went there two years ago.* not *I went there before two years*.
- We use *last* with days, months and with the words *night, week, weekend, month, year, century*.
- We say *last night* but *yesterday morning/afternoon/evening*, not *last morning*, etc.
- We don't use a preposition with *last*. We say *last month* not *in last month*.
- We use *in* with years and months.
- We use *in the* with decades and centuries.

You can refer students to **G7.3** SB p137 to read about *ago*, *last* and *in* during the lesson before checking the above points with the class.

> 2 the day before yesterday 3 last month 4 last year
> 5 in the eighties 6 in February 1964 7 in 1946
> 8 about 80 years ago 9 about 250 years ago
> 10 in the sixteenth century

b) Pre-teach *symphony* /ˈsɪmfəni/ and *guitar* /ɡɪˈtɑː/.

Refer students back to the time phrases in **2a)**. Students do the exercise on their own or in pairs.

c) Students check their answers on p158. Ask how many answers they got right and if they were surprised by any of the answers.

> 1 about 250 years ago 2 about 80 years ago
> 3 in February 1964 4 in the sixteenth century 5 in 1946

3 Write *When did you last go away for the weekend?* on the board. Establish that this question is asking about the last time they did this.

Elicit short answers with *ago*, *last* and *in* (*Six weeks ago.*, *Last month.*, *In June.*, etc.).

Also elicit possible follow-up questions (*Where did you go? What did you do there?*, etc.)

Ask students to suggest a few more questions they could ask with *When did you last ... ?*.

Put students into pairs, student A and student B. Student As turn to SB p110 and student Bs turn to SB p118. Check they are all looking at the correct exercise.

a) Give students a few moments to study the speech bubble examples.

Student A asks student B questions with *When did you last ... ?* using the phrases in the prompts. Student B answers with a phrase with *ago*, *last* or *in*. Encourage student A to ask follow-up questions if possible.

While students are working, correct any mistakes you hear and help with any problems.

b) Students swap roles so that student B is asking student A questions with *When did you last ... ?*.

At the end of the activity, ask students to share any interesting answers with the class.

┌─ EXTRA IDEA ─────────────────────────────────┐
- Students make a list of five free time activities they like doing and another list of past time phrases saying when they last did these activities. Students should not write their two lists in the same order. Students swap lists and try to match their partner's activities to the time phrases. Students then take turns to ask their partner questions to check if their guesses are correct.
└──┘

Help with Vocabulary Question words

4 a)–b) Students do the exercise on their own or in pairs, then check their answers in **V7.3** SB p136. Check answers with the class.

- 1c); 2e); 3b); 4a); 5c); 6j); 7f); 8h); 9g); 10i)
- Point out that we often answer *Why ... ?* questions with *Because ...* and *How long ... ?* questions with *For ...* (*six years, an hour*, etc.). Remind students that we do not say *How long time ... ?*.
- To help students understand the difference between *Which* and *What* give these examples: *Which do you like – the red shirt or the blue shirt?* (a small number of answers), *What's his job?* (many possible answers).
- Note that we can often use *Which* or *What* with no difference in meaning, for example, *Which/What newspaper do you read?*.
- Also check students remember the question words *What time ... ?* and *How much ... ?*.

Reading, Listening and Grammar

5 a) Focus students on the quiz on SB p57 and pre-teach *musical genius, make a record, instrument, trumpet, piano, album, group* (= band), *real name* and *army*.

Ask students if they can name the people and bands in the photos (from the left: Madonna, U2, Sting, Elton John, The Beatles, Shakira, Elvis Presley).

Establish that students have to fill in the gaps in each question with a question word from **4a)**, then answer the question by choosing a), b) or c). Point out that there is one gap for each of the question words in **4a)**.

Students do the quiz in pairs. You can set a time limit of five minutes.

b) Tell students they are going to listen to two people doing the quiz.

R7.7 Play the recording (SB p153). Students listen and check the question words and the answers.

Check answers with the class.

Ask students how many question words and answers they got right. Find out which pair of students are the class's musical geniuses.

> **1** When; a) **2** Where; b) **3** What; a) **4** Which; b)
> **5** How long; b) **6** How old; a) **7** Who; b)
> **8** How many; b) **9** Whose; c) **10** Why; c)

EXTRA IDEAS

- Do the quiz as a competition. Give one point for each correct question word and two points for each correct multiple choice answer.
- If students haven't got all the answers from the first listening, ask students to turn to R7.7, SB p153 and play the recording again. Students listen and check their answers.

Help with Grammar Question forms

6 **a)–d)** Students do the exercises on their own or in pairs, then check their answers in G7.4 SB p137.

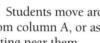 While they are working, draw the table from **6a)** on the board ready for checking.

Check answers with the class.

- Focus students on the table on the board. Establish that the first question in the table is in the past (because of the auxiliary *did*) and the second question is in the present (because of the auxiliary *do*).
- Elicit which words in quiz questions 3 and 4 go in each column and complete the table (see the table in G7.4 SB p137). Check that students understand question 3 is in the past (because of the auxiliary *did*) and question 4 is in the present (because of the auxiliary *does*).
- Use the table to highlight the similarity between questions in the Present Simple and Past Simple. Point out that only the auxiliary verb *do/does/did* is different.
- Establish that the verb in quiz questions 5–9 is *be* and that we don't use *do/does/did* with this verb. Check students remember that the Present Simple of *be* is *am/is/are* and the Past Simple is *was/were*.

Get ready … Get it right!

7 **a)** Focus students on column A in the table and highlight the example question.

Students work on their own and write *yes/no* questions with *you* from the prompts 2–8. Students must decide if the question should be in the present or past.

While students are working, check their questions for accuracy and help with any problems. Early finishers can check questions in pairs.

Check the questions with the class. Students should not ask each other the questions at this stage.

You may like to teach the phrase *go clubbing* as an alternative to *go to a club* in question 4.

> **2** Do you listen to lots of different types of music?
> **3** Were you musical when you were a child? **4** Did you go to a club last month? **5** Do you like classical music? **6** Do you watch music videos on TV? **7** Did you buy any CDs last week? **8** Do you listen to a personal stereo on the train/bus?

b) Focus students on column C in the table and highlight the example question.

Students work on their own and write follow-up questions from the prompts. Again monitor and check questions for accuracy. Check the questions with the class.

> **2** What kind of music do you listen to? **3** Which instrument did you play? **4** Where did you go? **5** Which composers do you like? **6** What's your favourite video? **7** What did you buy? **8** What do you usually listen to?

8 **a)** Students move around the room asking questions from column A, or ask as many people as they can sitting near them.

If students get a *yes* answer, they write the student's name in column B, then ask the follow-up question from column C. Encourage students to ask more follow-up questions if possible.

Students should try to find a different student who answers *yes* for each question in column A.

b) Students work in pairs and tell their partner five things they found out about students in the class.

Finally, ask students to share interesting ideas with the class.

EXTRA PRACTICE AND HOMEWORK

Ph **Vocabulary Plus** 7 Verbs and prepositions p193 (Instructions p184)

Ph **Class Activity** 7B Questions, questions p159 (Instructions p129)

7 Review Exercise 4 SB p61

CD-ROM Lesson 7B

Workbook Lesson 7B p36

QUICK REVIEW ●●●

This activity reviews types of film and music. Students write their list of types of film and music on their own. Set a time limit of three minutes. Students work in pairs and compare their lists, then discuss which types they both like. Ask students to share their answers with the class.

Real World talking about the news
Vocabulary irregular Past Simple forms; verbs and nouns from news stories
Help with Listening stressed words
Review Past Simple

The one o'clock news

1 Pre-teach *the news* and point out that this word looks plural but takes a singular verb: *What time is the news on?* not ~~What time are the news on?~~.

Students then discuss the questions in groups.

Ask students to share interesting answers with the class.

> **EXTRA IDEA**
> * With a strong class, bring in some articles from English newspapers or the Internet. Put students in pairs and give one article to each pair. Students read their article and try to understand the main points of the story. Help students with vocabulary as necessary. Students work in groups or with the whole class and tell one another about their articles.

2 a) Tell students that they are going to listen to some TV news stories.

Pre-teach the vocabulary in the box, which students will need to understand the news stories. Point out that *rain* and *climb* are both regular verbs. Also tell students that *crash*, *rain*, *climb* and *flood* can be nouns or verbs.

Check students know where Mount Everest is (in the Himalayas).

Model and drill the words. Pay particular attention to the pronunciation of *choose* /tʃuːz/, *chose* /tʃəʊz/, *climb* /klaɪm/ and *flood* /flʌd/.

b) Focus students on the photos A–D of some TV new stories. Students work in pairs and try to match the words from **2a)** to the stories.

Check answers with the class.

> A the lottery; choose (past: chose); lucky B a flood; rain C a plane crash D missing (on Mount Everest); climb; a helicopter

3 a) **R7.8** Play the recording (SB p153). Students listen and put photos A–D of the news stories in order.

Check answers with the class.

> 1C 2D 3B 4A

b) Give students time to read the pairs of sentences 1–4. Play the recording again. Students listen and choose the correct answers.

Check answers with the class.

> **1** a) 100 b) China **2** a) married b) missing **3** a) lots of places b) 32 **4** a) £13 b) His dog

Help with Listening Stressed words

* This Help with Listening section reviews sentence stress and highlights that we stress the important words.

4 a) Remind students that in English the important words are usually stressed and the 'grammar' words like *a*, *the*, *with* are usually unstressed.

R7.8 Focus students on the examples and play the first two sentences of the recording. Students listen and notice the stress. Use these examples to illustrate that the words that carry meaning are usually stressed.

b) Students turn to R7.8, SB p153. Play the recording again. Students listen and notice the stressed words.

> **EXTRA IDEA**
> * When you play the recording, ask students to read the news to themselves as they listen.

Read all about it!

5 a) Focus students on the news reports on p59 and use these to teach *headline*. Establish that these two news reports are from the day after the TV news reports. Ask students which news stories they are about (1 = photo D; 2 = photo A). Do not allow students to read the articles yet.

b) Check students understand all the verbs in the infinitive box. Teach any new verbs if necessary.

Students work on their own or in pairs and match the infinitives to their Past Simple forms. Students then check answers in **V7.4** p136. Check answers with the class.

c) **R7.9** **P** Play the recording of the infinitives and their Past Simple forms in **5b)**, and ask students to repeat.

> **EXTRA IDEA**
> * Students work in pairs and take turns to test each other on the Past Simple forms in **5b)**. One student says the infinitive, for example, *find*, and his/her partner says the Past Simple form, for example, *found*.

6 **a)** Put the students into two groups, group A and group B.

Focus students in group A on report 1 and questions 1–5. Focus students in group B on report 2 and questions a)–e). Tell students to cover the report that they are not reading. You can ask the stronger students to read report 1, which contains more new words.

Students read their text and answer the questions, then check their answers with someone from the same group.

b) Put one student from group A with a student from group B. Students ask their partners the questions about each other's report from **6a)**.

Check answers with the class.

> 1 In hospital in Kathmandu. 2 Two days ago. 3 His leg.
> 4 Terry lost the radio. 5 Carla does, but Terry's not sure.
>
> a) At the supermarket where he works. b) The numbers 1 to 49. c) In different places in his house. d) They had a dog biscuit in each one. e) To find him a girlfriend.

— EXTRA IDEAS —

- Note that the following new words appear in the reports. Report 1: *couple, safe, side, hospital, leg, alive, next, (not) sure.* Report 2: *receive, cheque.* With a class of beginners you may want to pre-teach this vocabulary.
- When students have finished the activity, give students time to read the other report.

Talking about the news

7 **a)** Ask students to remind you what the four news stories in photos A-D are about. Tell students they are going to hear four conversations. In each conversation the people are talking about one of these news stories.

[R7.10] Play the recording (SB p153). Students listen and match the conversations to the news stories/photos.

> 1 the lottery winner (A) 2 the flood (B)
> 3 the plane crash (C) 4 the couple on Everest (D)

b) Give students time to read sentences 1–6 and responses a)–f) from the conversations. Establish that a)–f) are typical things that native speakers say in response to news.

Play the recording again. Students listen and match the sentences to the responses.

> 2f) 3a) 4e) 5d) 6c)

Real World Talking about the news

8 **a)–c)** Pre-teach *surprising.* Students do exercises **8a)** and **8b)** on their own or in pairs, then check answers in [RW7.1] SB p137.

Check answers with the class.

- 1 A hear B was; 2 A about B happened
- **good news**: Oh, that's good. **bad news**: Yes, isn't it awful?; Oh, dear. Are they OK?; Oh no, that's terrible. **surprising news**: You're joking!
- Check students understand that *awful* and *terrible* have the same meaning (= very bad).
- Note that we say *What happened?* not ~~What did happen?~~ in this context. This is because *What* is the subject of *happened*, and in subject questions we use the Past Simple form, not *did* + infinitive. However, we suggest you teach this as a lexical phrase and do not draw students' attention to this unless they ask.

9 [R7.11] **P** Play the recording and ask students to repeat the questions in **8a)** and the responses in **8b)**.

Encourage students to copy the intonation patterns in the responses and establish the importance of intonation in sounding interested when responding to news. Also check they pronounce *awful* /'ɔːfəl/ correctly.

10 Pre-teach *desert* /'dezət/, *tourist* /'tʊərɪst/, *jungle* /'dʒʌŋgəl/ and *ate* (Past Simple of *eat*). Model and drill these words.

Put students into pairs, student A and student B. Student As turn to SB p110 and student Bs turn to SB p118. Check they are all looking at the correct exercise.

a) Students work on their own and read about the news stories. They should check any other problem words with you if necessary.

b) Focus students on the phrase box, which reminds them of the language from the Real World box in **8**.

Students work in pairs and take turns to tell each other about their news stories. Students should only give one piece of information about each story at a time. Their partner responds to each piece of information with an appropriate phrase from the box.

Make sure students use full sentences, (for example, *He gave the money to his family., The dog ate his ticket.,* etc.) when talking about the news stories.

While students are working, check students' responses and intonation and help with any problems.

Finally, ask a few pairs to role-play their conversations for the class.

— EXTRA IDEA —

- For homework, students find a news item in an English newspaper or on the Internet that interests them. At the beginning of the next class, put students in groups and ask them to tell their partners about their news stories.

— EXTRA PRACTICE AND HOMEWORK —

Ph **Class Activity** 7C Lost in the Himalayas p161 (Instructions p130)

CD-ROM Lesson 7C

Workbook Lesson 7C p38

7D Do you know any jokes?

QUICK REVIEW ●●●

This activity reviews talking about the news. Students work in pairs and see how much they can remember about the four news stories from lesson 7C, making notes if necessary. Students compare ideas with another pair, then check on p58 and p59. Check answers with the class.

1 Focus students on the title of the lesson and teach *joke* /dʒəʊk/, *funny* and the phrase *It/He/She makes me laugh* /laːf/. Point out that we say *tell a joke* not ~~say a joke~~. Drill this new language with the class.

Students discuss the questions in groups of three or four.

Ask students to share their answers with the class.

2 a) Students work on their own or in pairs and tick the verbs they know.

Teach students any verbs they don't know (*laugh*, *cry* and *wait* are new verbs).

Model and drill the new verbs.

b) Students work on their own or in pairs and write the Past Simple forms of the verbs in the box. Students can check irregular verbs in the Irregular Verb List, SB p159.

 Check answers with the class and write them on the board in two columns with the headings *Regular verbs* and *Irregular verbs*.

Model and drill the verbs and their Past Simple forms. Pay particular attention to the pronunciation of *laughed* /laːft/, *bought* /bɔːt/ and *saw* /sɔː/, and the extra /ɪd/ syllable for the *-ed* ending in *hated*, *waited* and *started*.

> **Regular verbs**
> love/loved; hate/hated; laugh/laughed; cry/cried; wait/waited; start/started; happen/happened
>
> **Irregular verbs**
> come/came; say/said; buy/bought; sit/sat; see/saw

--- EXTRA IDEA ---

- Put students into pairs, student A and student B. Student A looks at **2a)** on SB p60 and student B looks at **5a)** on SB p58. Students take turns to test each other on the Past Simple forms of the verbs in each box. Student A says an infinitive, for example, *buy* and student B responds with the Past Simple, for example, *bought*.

3 a) Pre-teach *front row* and *amazing*. Tell students they are going to read and listen to a joke. Focus students on the text between the pictures.

R7.12 Play the recording. Students read, listen and fill in the two gaps at the end of the joke (*He* **hated** *the* **book**).

Ask students if they think the joke is funny and teach *I don't get it* (= I don't understand the joke).

b) Students read the joke again and match paragraphs 1–4 to pictures A–D.
Check answers with the class.

> 1B 2D 3A 4C

Help with Vocabulary *a, an* and *the*

4 **a)–b)** Focus students on the examples. Students do **4a)** on their own, then check answers in V7.5 SB p136.

- We use *a/an* to talk about things or people for the first time (*An old man ... , ... a long coat, ... a big black dog*).
- We use *the* when we know which thing or person (*The old man ...*).
- We use *the* when there is only one thing or person in a particular place (*... in the front row.*).
- Point out that we also use *the* in some fixed phrases (*go to the cinema, in the evening*, etc.) and elicit other examples from students (*at the weekend, the news*, etc.).

5 Students work on their own and find all the examples of *a, an* and *the* in the joke.

Put students into pairs. Students discuss why *a, an* or *the* is used in each case, referring back the rules in **4a)** where necessary.

Check answers with the class.

> **a/an for the first time**
> paragraph 1: *a film; a drink; an ice-cream*
> paragraph 2: *an old man; a long coat; a big black dog*
> paragraph 3: *a person*
>
> **the when we know which thing or person**
> paragraph 1: *the cinema; the film*
> paragraph 2: *the old man; the dog; the man's feet*
> paragraph 3: *the film; the dog; the film; the dog; the film; the dog; the film*
> paragraph 4: *the film; the old man; the film; the old man; the book*
>
> **the when there is only one**
> paragraph 1: *the front row; the floor*
> paragraph 4: *the end*
>
> **the in fixed phrases**
> paragraph 1: *went to the cinema*
> paragraph 3: *all the way*

6 **a)** Pre-teach the words in the box: *cut down, a tree, an axe, a noise, a chainsaw*.

Check meaning by asking how can you cut down a tree (with an axe or a chainsaw) and which one makes a noise (a chainsaw). Also mime the phrase *start a chainsaw*.

b) Students work on their own and fill in the gaps in the joke with *a, an* or *the*.

Students check answers in pairs. Encourage students to justify their reasons for choosing *a, an* or *the*.

Check answers with the class and ask students if they get the joke (the man hadn't tried to start the chainsaw).

> 1 a 2 a 3 a 4 an 5 The 6 the 7 a 8 The 9 a 10 the
> 11 the 12 The 13 the 14 the 15 the 16 the

7 **a)** Students work on their own and circle the correct words.

Check answers with the class, again asking students to justify their answers if there is any disagreement.

> 1 a 2 a 3 the 4 the; the 5 the 6 the; the

b) Students work in pairs and take turns to ask and answer the questions. Encourage students to ask follow-up questions if possible.

Finally, ask students to share interesting answers with the class (the answer to question 6 is Arnold Schwarzenegger).

EXTRA IDEA

- Write on a piece of paper twelve sentences which include articles. Six of these sentences should be correct and six should include incorrect use of articles, for example, *I listen to radio every morning.*, *John's not in a kitchen, he's in a garden.*, etc. Make one photocopy for each student in the class. Students work in groups and decide which sentences are correct and which are incorrect. Check answers with the class. The group with the most correct sentences wins. Alternatively, you can do this activity as a Grammar Auction, see p22.

EXTRA PRACTICE AND HOMEWORK

7 Review SB p61
CD-ROM Lesson 7D
Workbook Lesson 7D p39
Workbook Reading and Writing Portfolio 7 p76
Progress Test 7 p218

---

7 Review

See p32 for ideas on how to use this section.

1a) 2 science fiction films
3 cartoons
4 love stories
5 thrillers
6 action films
7 comedies
8 historical dramas

2b) Sentences 3 and 7 are correct.

2c) 2 He didn't have any brothers or sisters.
4 He didn't live with this grandparents.
He lived with his aunt.
5 He didn't like studying.
6 He didn't work as a doctor in World War 2.
He worked as a secret agent.

3a) 1 Did 2 Were 3 Was 4 Did 5 Were 6 Did

4a) 1e) 2c) 3f) 4g) 5b) 6d) 7a)

5a)

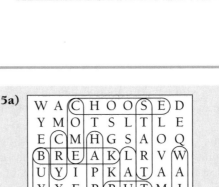

5b) Regular verbs: hated; listened; cried; happened; laughed; started; waited
Irregular verbs: chose; broke; put; saw; won; bought; sat; came

---
Progress Portfolio

See p32 for ideas on how to use this section.

8 Let's go away

8A Holiday USA

Vocabulary holiday activities
Grammar *can/can't* for possibility
Help with Listening *can/can't*
Review Past Simple

QUICK REVIEW ●●●
This activity reviews free time activities. Students do the activity in pairs. If students are having problems remembering how to say free time activities in English, refer them to V3.2 and V4.1 in the Language Summaries. Ask each pair to tell the class one or two activities they both did last week.

Vocabulary Holiday activities

1 Focus students on the context of the lesson and check they remember *tourist*.

Give students a few moments to think of three places tourists go in their country and what they do there.

Students then work in pairs and compare places.

Ask students to share interesting answers with the class. If you have a multilingual class, make sure one student from each country has the opportunity to tell the class about places in his/her country.

2 **a)** Students work on their own and tick the words/ phrases they know, then do the exercise in V8.1 SB p138. They can then check answers in pairs.

Check answers with the class. Highlight that we say *sunbathe* not ~~take the sun~~ and the American English phrase *go on vacation*. Also check students understand *go sightseeing* (visit the famous buildings in a town or city).

Point out the different phrases that follow *go: go **for** walks, go fish**ing**/sightsee**ing**,* etc., *go **to** the beach, go **on** boat trips*.

Model and drill the words. Pay particular attention to the pronunciation of *sightseeing* /ˈsaɪtsiːɪŋ/, *skiing* /ˈskiːɪŋ/, *cycling* /ˈsaɪklɪŋ/ and *sunbathe* /ˈsʌnbeɪð/.

Note that only the main stress in words/phrases is shown in vocabulary boxes and the Language Summaries.

> **V8.1** 1g) 2d) 3j) 4m) 5c) 6i) 7p) 8f) 9r) 10e) 11l)
> 12b) 13h) 14o) 15q) 16a) 17k) 18n)

⌐ **EXTRA IDEA** ─────────────────
● Draw a four-column table on the board with these headings: 1 *go + verb+ing* 2 *go to* 3 *go for* 4 *go on*. Students work in pairs and write down all the phrases they know that can go in each column (1 *go dancing*, 2 *go to the cinema*, 3 *go for a drink*, 4 *go on holiday*, etc.). Check answers and new vocabulary with the class.
└────────────────────────────────

b) Students do the activity in pairs. You can also ask them to discuss things they never do on holiday.

Ask students to share interesting ideas with the class.

3 **a)** Focus students on the example. Students then work on their own and make questions 2–7. They can check their answers in pairs.

Check answers with the class. Check students understand *travel around* (travel to places in the holiday location).

Model and drill the sentences, focusing on sentence stress.

> **2** Where did you go? **3** Who did you go with? **4** Where did you stay? **5** What did you do in the day? **6** How did you travel around? **7** Did you have a good time?

b) Students do the activity in pairs. Encourage students to use natural short answers (*In May.*, *To Mexico.*, *My husband.*, etc.) and to ask follow-up questions if possible.

While students are working, monitor and correct any mistakes you hear.

Ask a few students to tell the class about their partner's last holiday.

Listening and Grammar

4 **a)** Focus students on the photos of San Francisco and ask them what they know about the city. Students share their ideas with the class.

Check students can pronounce all the places in the photos, particularly *Wharf* /wɔːf/ and *Alcatraz* /ælkəˈtræz/.

b) Students work in pairs and try to match the words in the box to things in the photos.

Check answers with the class, using the photos to teach the meaning of any new words.

Model and drill the words. Pay particular attention to the pronunciation of *bridge* /brɪdʒ/ and *island* /ˈaɪlənd/, and point out that the *s* is silent in *island*.

> a prison C a cable car A a bridge D a park D
> an island C tourists B boats B

5 **a)** Tell students they are going to listen to James asking his friend, Rachel, about San Francisco and focus students on photos A–D again.

R8.1 Play the recording (SB p153). Students listen and put photos A–D in order.

Check answers with the class.

> 1D 2A 3B 4C

b) Pre-teach *street musicians*, *seafood* and *relax*.

Students work in pairs and try to match the activities to the places that Rachel talks about. If students can't remember the answers, encourage them to guess by looking at the photos.

c) Play the recording again and ask students to check their answers. You can ask students to shout *Stop!* when they hear one of the activities mentioned. Pause the recording briefly to check which of the three places the activity matches with, then continue the recording.

Check answers with the class.

2N 3F 4N 5F 6N 7G 8F

Help with Grammar *can/can't* for possibility

6 a)–d) Students do the exercises on their own or in pairs, then check their answers in G8.1 SB p139.

Check answers with the class.

- **a)** We use *can* to say that something is possible.
- We use *can't* to say that something isn't possible.
- **b)** For positive sentences, we use subject + *can* + infinitive.
- For negative sentences, we use subject + *can't* + infinitive.
- *Can* and *can't* are the same for all subjects (*I, you, he, they*, etc.).
- **c)** 1 What can you do there? 2 Can you stay on the island? 3 Yes, you can. 4 No, you can't.
- Highlight the word order in questions: (question word) + *can* + subject + infinitive + ...
- Remind students that we also use *can* for ability (*She can speak French.*), requests (*Can you help me?*) and offers (*Can I help you?*). Note that there is more practice of *can* for ability in lesson 9D.

Help with Listening *can/can't*

- This Help with Listening section helps students to hear the weak form of *can* /kən/ and distinguish this from *can't* /kɑːnt/.

7 a) R8.2 Focus on the example sentences, then play the recording. Students listen for the pronunciation of *can* and *can't* and decide which is stressed (*can't*).

Ask students why *can't* is stressed (because it's negative).

Point out that *can* is usually pronounced in its weak form in positive sentences and that the vowel sound is a *schwa* /ə/.

You can also teach students the American English pronunciation of *can't* /kænt/.

b) Check students understand that they will hear both sentences a) and b) and they must decide which sentence they hear first.

R8.3 Play the recording. Students tick the sentence in each pair they hear first. Play the recording again, pausing after each sentence to check students' answers.

1a) 2b) 3b) 4a) 5b)

c) R8.1 Ask students to turn to R8.1, SB p153. Play the recording of James and Rachel's conversation again. Students listen, read and notice the difference between *can* and *can't*, which is shown in phonemics in the recording script.

You can also ask students if *can* is strong/stressed or weak/unstressed in questions (weak/unstressed).

8 R8.4 Focus students on the examples and play the beginning of the recording.

Point out that *can* is weak in questions and is not stressed. Also point out that *can* is pronounced in its strong form /kæn/ in short answers and is stressed. Highlight that *can't* is stressed in short answers.

P Play the whole recording and ask students to repeat. Check students are pronouncing *can* and *can't* correctly and copying the stress patterns.

9 Ask if students know anything about Yellowstone Park in Wyoming, USA (it's a national park that is famous for its scenery, wildlife and spectacular geysers).

Put students into pairs, student A and student B. Student As turn to SB p108 and student Bs turn to SB p116. Check they are all looking at the correct exercise.

a) Focus students on the photo of Yellowstone Park and pictures a)–l) of things that you can and can't do there.

Students work on their own and write questions with *can* about the pictures that don't have ticks or crosses.

While students are working, check their questions for accuracy and help with any problems.

b) Students work with their partners. Student A asks student B his/her questions and puts a tick or a cross next to pictures a)–f). Make sure student B responds with the correct short answers.

c) Student B asks student A his/her questions and puts a tick or a cross next to pictures g)–l).

d) Students discuss whether they would like to go to Yellowstone Park.

Ask students to share their opinions with the class.

Get ready ... Get it right!

10 a) Put students into pairs. Both students choose a holiday place that their partner doesn't know. Encourage students to choose places in countries different to their own if possible.

b) Pre-teach *football matches*.

Students work on their own and decide if they can or can't do the things in the list in the holiday place they chose in **10a)**.

11 Focus students on the speech bubbles, highlighting the extra information in the second speech bubble.

Students work with their partner and take turns to ask and answer questions with *Can you ... ?* to find out what they can and can't do in each other's holiday places. Students should base their questions on the prompts in **10b)** and use the vocabulary in **2a)**. Encourage students to give more information wherever possible.

Finally, ask students to tell the class what they remember about their partner's holiday place.

EXTRA PRACTICE AND HOMEWORK

Ph **Vocabulary Plus** 8 British and American English p194 (Instructions p185)

Ph **Class Activity** 8A Language schools p162 (Instructions p130)

8 Review Exercises 1 and 2 SB p69

CD-ROM Lesson 8A

Workbook Lesson 8A p40

8B A trip to Thailand

QUICK REVIEW ●●●

This activity reviews *can/can't* and holiday activities. Pre-teach *region* (part of a country). Give students a few moments to think of five things people can do in their home town, city or region. Students work in pairs and tell each other their ideas. Ask students to share interesting things they found out about their partner's place with the class.

Vocabulary adjectives to describe places
Grammar comparatives
Review *can* for possibility; holiday activities

Vocabulary Adjectives to describe places

1 Students work on their own and match the opposites in the vocabulary box. They can then check new words in **V8.2** SB p138. The other words are in **V6.1** p134.

Check answers with the class. Check students understand the new words *modern*, *dangerous* and *safe*. Point out that we use *young* for people and animals and *modern* for clothes, buildings and places.

Model and drill the words. Pay particular attention to the pronunciation of *noisy* /ˈnɔɪzi/, *dangerous* /ˈdeɪndʒərəs/, *crowded* /ˈkraʊdɪd/ and *quiet* /ˈkwaɪət/.

> noisy/quiet clean/dirty boring/interesting old/modern
> friendly/unfriendly dangerous/safe crowded/empty

2 a) Students do the exercise on their own. Tell students that they can write the names of places in a town/city as well as countries and towns/cities.

b) Students work in pairs and take turns to tell each other about the places they have chosen, using the adjectives from **1**. Remind students to use *very*, *really* or *quite* in each sentence.

Students can share interesting ideas with the class.

Reading and Grammar

3 a) Focus students on the photos and elicit which country Phuket and Bangkok are in (Thailand).

Ask students to share what they know about Thailand with the class.

b) Students read the texts and decide which they would choose for a holiday. Set a time limit of three minutes to encourage students to read for gist.

Ask students to tell the class which place they chose and why.

Note that these texts contain some new vocabulary items. However, students don't need to know this vocabulary to complete the tasks and it is important that students get used to dealing with texts that contain new words. If you want to use the texts to extend students' vocabulary, see the Extra idea box below.

c) Students read the texts again and find three things you can do in each place. Students compare answers in pairs. Check answers with the class.

> **Phuket:** relax and sunbathe all day; rent a motorbike; eat fresh fish; go for a walk along the beach
>
> **Bangkok:** go sightseeing; visit Buddhist temples and the Royal Palace; take a boat trip; go shopping in the markets; eat traditional Thai food; go dancing in the evening

EXTRA IDEA

● Ask students to choose three or four new words in the texts that they would like to know the meaning of. Students look the words up in their dictionaries. Put students into groups. Students take turns to teach their partners their new words.

4 Students do the activity in pairs by referring back to the texts. Check which sentence is false with the class (e).

Help with Grammar Comparatives

5 a)–c) Check students understand *syllable* by asking how many syllables some of the words in **1** have got. Also check they remember which letters are vowels and which are consonants. Teach the verb *double*.

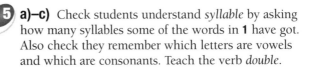

Students do the exercises on their own or in pairs, then check their answers in **G8.2** SB p139.

Check answers with the class.

> • Use the table in **G8.2** SB p139 to check students' answers to the spelling rules.
> • When we compare two things in the same sentence we use *than* after the comparative (*Phuket is hotter than Bangkok.*).
> • Point out that the opposite of *more* is *less* (*The holiday in Bangkok is less expensive.*) and that we can also use *more* with nouns (*There are more rooms in the Sawadee Hotel.*).

6 Students work on their own and write the comparatives, referring to the rules in **5a)** if necessary. Students check answers in pairs. Check answers with the class.

> **1** more boring **2** dirtier **3** more beautiful **4** better
> **5** safer **6** worse **7** bigger **8** more dangerous

7 **a)** Tell students that Luke and Monica are planning a holiday in Thailand and are deciding which place to go to, Phuket or Bangkok.

R8.5 Play the recording (SB p154). Students listen and decide which place each person wants to go to and one reason why they want to go there.

Check answers with the class.

Luke wants to go to Bangkok and Monica wants to go to Phuket. See R8.5, SB p154 for their reasons.

b) Students do the exercise on their own, referring to the rules in **5a)** if necessary. Remind students to use *than* where necessary. Students can check answers in pairs.

Check answers with the class.

> **2** more interesting **3** better than **4** more crowded
> **5** friendlier **6** more expensive **7** more interesting than
> **8** safer **9** quieter

c) Students do the exercise in pairs.

d) Play the recording again. Students listen and check their answers. Check answers with the class.

> **1** Monica **2** Luke **3** Monica **4** Monica **5** Monica
> **6** Luke **7** Luke **8** Monica **9** Monica

— EXTRA IDEA —
• Ask students to turn to R8.5, SB p154. Play the recording and ask students to underline all the comparatives as they listen.

8 Focus students on the sentence stress in the example. Establish that *than* is not stressed after a comparative and is pronounced in its weak form /ðən/. Point out the schwa /ə/.

R8.6 **P** Play the recording and ask students to repeat. Check students copy the sentence stress correctly and don't stress *than*.

9 Elicit from students where they think Luke and Monica went on holiday and why.

R8.7 Play the recording (SB p154). Students listen and check if they were right.

Check the answer with the class (Phuket).

10 **a)** Pre-teach *hair*.

Students work on their own and complete the sentences about their town/city and their life. They should use the comparative form of one of the adjectives in brackets and *than* to complete the sentences.

While they are working, check students' sentences for accuracy and help with any problems.

b) Students write two more sentences about the topics in **10a)**. Help students with new vocabulary if necessary.

c) Put students into pairs. If possible, ask students from different cities or countries to work together. Students compare their sentences, giving reasons for their answers if possible.

Ask students to share interesting sentences with the class.

Get ready … Get it right!

11 Put students into two groups, group A and group B. Students in group A turn to SB p109 and students in group B turn to SB p117. Check they are all looking at the correct exercise.

a) Students work in pairs with someone from the same group. Note that you need an equal number of pairs in each group, so have one or two groups of three if necessary.

Each pair makes sentences using the information and the comparative form of the adjectives in brackets. Draw students' attention to the examples before they start.

While students are working, check their sentences for accuracy and help with any problems.

Make sure that they don't tell students from the other group their sentences.

b) Draw students' attention to the speech bubbles and teach *Yes, I think so.* and *I'm not sure.*

Students stay in the same pairs and discuss the places, people and things using the comparative form of the adjectives in brackets.

They should circle the place, person or thing that they think is smaller, bigger, etc.

While students are working, monitor and help with any problems. Note that students don't have to write sentences at this stage of the activity.

c) Put one pair from group A and one pair from group B together so that students are working in groups of four.

The pair from group A say their sentences from **b)**. The students from group B say if their sentences are right or wrong, referring to the sentences they wrote in **a)** if necessary.

While students are working, monitor and help with any problems.

d) Students continue to work in their groups. The pair from group B say their sentences from **b)**. The students from group A say if their sentences are right or wrong, again referring to the sentences they wrote in **a)** if necessary.

e) Students work out which pair got more sentences right. Finally, each pair can tell the class their score to find out which pair got the most answers right.

> **EXTRA PRACTICE AND HOMEWORK**
>
> **Ph** **Class Activity** 8B Comparative pelmanism p164 (Instructions p131)
> **8 Review** Exercise 3 SB p69
> **CD-ROM** Lesson 8B
> **Workbook** Lesson 8B p41

8C Planning a day out

QUICK REVIEW ●●●
This activity reviews adjectives and comparatives. Students work on their own and write five sentences comparing two holiday places in their country. Put students into pairs. Students take turns to tell their partner their sentences. Encourage students to ask follow-up questions and give more information if possible. Students decide which place is nicer to visit. Ask students to tell the class which place they have chosen and why.

Real World planning a day out; *I'd rather ... /I'd like ... / I want ...*
Help with Listening *I'd* and the schwa /ə/
Review *can/can't*; free time activities

> — **EXTRA IDEA** —
> • Do **2a)** as a jigsaw reading. Divide the class into two groups, group A and group B. Students in group A read about Chessington and answer questions 1–4 and students in group B read about Regent's Park and answer questions 5–8. Put one student from group A with a student from group B. Students work in pairs and swap information.

A day out

 Pre-teach *a day out* (a day away from home to have fun) and check students understand *relaxing*.

Students work in pairs and think of one place for each adjective. Students can discuss places near where they live in their country, or they can discuss places near where they are studying if your students are in an English-speaking country.

Ask students to share their ideas with the class.

2 a) Focus students on the photos and the articles. Establish that these are two places that people in England often go to for a day out.

Use the photos to pre-teach *ride, gorilla* and *zoo*. Also pre-teach *tiger* and *bird*. Point out that you can *go on a ride* at an amusement park and also *go on a bike ride*.

Give students time to read the questions about Chessington and Regent's Park.

Students read the articles and answer the questions. This gives students practice in scanning a text for specific information. Set a time limit of three or four minutes.

Students can check answers in pairs. Check answers with the class.

> **1** Yes, you can. **2** Gorillas and big cats, including a pair of Sumatran tigers. **3** from 10 a.m.–7 p.m./ nine hours **4** the Vampire ride, the Runaway Train ride **5** No, it isn't. **6** No, you can't. **7** 12 miles **8** Everything from rock and jazz to classical.

b) Students read the articles again to find out how many things you can do in each place.

c) Students compare answers in pairs. Check answers with the class.

Note that students choose which place they want to go to in **8a)**, so we suggest you don't ask them which place they prefer at this stage of the lesson.

> **Chessington** You can: go on lots of rides, have lunch in a Mexican restaurant, meet gorillas and see big cats.
>
> **Regent's Park** You can: go to the zoo, listen to music, go to the theatre, go on a bike ride, go on a guided bird walk.

3 a) Set the context of the recording by telling students that the Stevens family are trying to decide where to go for a day out. Focus students on the places a)–e).

R8.8 Play the recording (SB p154). Students listen and put the places a)–e) in order. They should also listen for which place the family decides to go to.

Check answers with the class.

> 1d) 2b) 3e) 4a) 5c)
> They decide to go to Regent's Park.

b) Give students time to read sentences 1–5, then play the recording again. Students decide if the sentences are true or false.

Students check answers in pairs. Ask them to correct the false sentences. Check answers with the class.

> 1T 2F Mrs Stevens thinks there's lots to do in Regent's Park. 3T 4F His friends went to Chessington last week. 5T

Help with Listening *I'd* and the schwa /ə/

- This Help with Listening helps students to hear the contracted form *I'd* and highlights the schwa in weak forms and vocabulary items.

 4 a) Focus students on the example sentences and point out the pronunciation of *do you* /dʒə/ and *I'd* /aɪd/. Remind them that *I'd* is the contracted form of *I would*. Also point out the schwas in the weak forms of *to* /tə/, *the* /ðə/, and in the first syllable of *tomorrow* /təˈmɒrəʊ/.

Point out the stress pattern and ask students if any of the schwas are stressed (they aren't as the schwa is a weak sound and is never stressed).

R8.8 Play the first two sentences of the recording again. Students listen and notice the schwas and the pronunciation of *I'd*.

b) Ask students to turn to R8.8, SB p154. Play the whole recording again. Students listen and notice how we say *I'd* and the schwas in the sentences in bold.

Use the recording to highlight the pronunciation of *would you* /wʊdʒə/.

Real World Planning a day out

5 a)–d) Focus students on the table in **5a)** and point out that *would like* is more polite than *want*.

Pre-teach the phrase *something else* and point out that we say *I want to do something else*, not ~~I want to do another thing~~.

Students do exercises **5b)** and **5c)** on their own or in pairs, then check their answers in RW8.1 SB p139. Check answers with the class.

- We use *I'd rather* to say *I want to do this more than something else*.
- After *would rather* we use the infinitive (*go, do*, etc.).
- After *would like* and *want* we use the infinitive with *to* (*to go, to do*, etc.).
- Use the example in the table to remind students of the word order in questions with *would like*: question word + *would* + subject + *like* + infinitive with *to*.
- Note that throughout **face2face** we refer to *go, do*, etc. as the infinitive and *to go, to do*, etc. as the infinitive with *to*.

 6 Focus students on the examples and use them to remind students of the pronunciation of *Would you* /wʊdʒə/ and *I'd* /aɪd/. Also highlight the sentence stress in the examples.

R8.9 P Play the recording (SB p154) and ask students to repeat. Encourage students to copy the sentence stress and the pronunciation of *would you* and *I'd*.

You can also ask students to turn to R8.9, SB p154. They can then follow the sentence stress as they listen and repeat.

7 a) Tell students to imagine that they have a day off on Friday and want to do something together. Focus students on question 1 and the speech bubbles. Drill the conversation with the class.

Put the students into pairs, student A and student B. Point out that student A speaks first in question 1 and student B speaks first in question 2.

Students work in their pairs and take turns to suggest plans for Friday. Their partners respond as shown.

While they are working, monitor and correct any mistakes you hear.

b) Students work in the same pairs and take turns to make three more suggestions of their own. Students can respond in any way they wish.

Ask students to role-play the conversations for the class.

 8 a) Ask students to choose either Regent's Park or Chessington for a day out. They should not tell the class which place they have chosen at this stage.

Students read the article about the place they have chosen again and find three reasons why they want to go there.

b) Students work in groups of three. If you have extra students, have one or two groups of four.

Focus students on the phrases in the box. Tell students that they should decide on these things during their conversation.

Use the speech bubbles to remind students how we ask for suggestions with *shall we … ?* and make suggestions with *Let's … .*

Students work in their groups and plan a day out together. While students are working, monitor and help with any problems.

c) Each group tells the class where they want to go. Encourage students to use *We'd like to …* when reporting what they have decided.

Finally, find out which place is more popular, Regent's Park or Chessington.

┌─ EXTRA IDEA ─────────────────────────
- Instead of using the Regent's Park and Chessington texts for **8**, you can use the information on Bath, Bournemouth and Stratford-upon-Avon from lesson 8C in the Workbook p43.
└──────────────────────────────────────

┌─ EXTRA PRACTICE AND HOMEWORK ─────────
8 Review Exercises 4 and 5 SB p69
CD-ROM Lesson 8C
Workbook Lesson 8C p43
└──────────────────────────────────────

8D Come to the wedding

Vocabulary verb collocations
Review *can/can't*; question words

QUICK REVIEW ●●●

Elicit the alphabet from students and write it on the board. Students work in pairs and try to write one verb for each letter. Students compare lists in groups of four. Ask which group has the most words. Elicit the group's answers and write them on the board. Ask if other groups have any different words and put them next to the correct letter.

1 a) Focus students on the photos on the page and use them to teach *wedding*.

Students work on their own and answer the questions.

b) Students work in pairs and take turns to answer the questions in **1a)**.

Ask students to tell the class interesting things about the last wedding they (or their partner) went to.

— EXTRA IDEA —

• At the beginning of the lesson, teach some wedding vocabulary (for example, *bride, groom, wedding ring, bridesmaid, best man, wedding reception, go on a honeymoon,* etc.)

2 a) Focus students on email 1. Ask students who wrote it (Phil) and who he wrote it to (Aunt Ellen and Uncle Jeff).

Students read the email and tick the correct sentences.

b) Students check their answers in pairs and correct the false sentences.

Check answers with the class. Also check students know who is getting married (Phil's cousin, Oliver, is getting married to Becky).

1T 2F The wedding is in Canada.
3F He can stay for three weeks. 4T

— EXTRA IDEA —

• Use the information at the top of the email to remind students how we say email addresses.

3 a) Focus students on email 2 and establish that this is Aunt Ellen's reply to Phil.

Students read the email and answer the questions.

b) Students check answers in pairs. Check answers with the class.

1 Two weeks. (He can't stay the first week but he can stay the second and third week.) **2** No, she didn't. (She can send him a list of companies if he wants.)
3 Yes, it is. (It's 2 minutes from the bus stop.)
4 No, he doesn't. (He sometimes works in England.)

Help with Vocabulary Verb collocations

4 a) Write *listen to* and *watch* on the board. Elicit different words and phrases that often go with these verbs, for example, *listen to the radio/the news/music, watch TV/sport on TV/a film,* etc. Tell students that words that often go together are called collocations.

Check students understand the collocations already in the table: *book a flight, rent a motorbike, get to your/our place* and *stay with you/us*. Point out that *get* in this context means *travel*. Tell students that *a flight* is a noun that means *a journey by plane* and elicit the verb (*fly*). Also point out that *place* is often used in informal English to mean *home*.

Students work on their own and read the emails again, then fill in the tables with two more collocations for each verb. Students check answers in **V8.3** SB p138.

Check answers with the class. Point out that *get* in *get a taxi/bus* means *take* and elicit the British English for *an apartment* (*a flat*).

Model and drill the collocations. Pay particular attention to the pronunciation of *flight* /flaɪt/.

book a hotel room; a table (at a restaurant)
rent a car; an apartment
get a taxi; a bus
stay in Canada; in a hotel

b) Draw a five-column table on the board with the headings *play, have, write, go, study*. Elicit one collocation for each verb and write them in the table.

Students work in pairs and think of two more words and phrases that go with each verb. If students are finding it difficult to think of collocations, they can look at Languages Summaries 1–8 in the Student's Book.

Ask students to tell you their ideas and write correct collocations on the board.

Give students time to copy the table into their notebooks.

play tennis, football, the guitar, the piano, etc.
have breakfast, lunch, dinner, coffee with friends, etc.
write a letter, an email, a postcard, etc.
go to bed, to the cinema, shopping, swimming, etc.
study English, French, at university, etc.

— EXTRA IDEA —

• Play Noughts and Crosses (see p21).

5 Focus students on the speech bubbles. Students work in pairs and take turns to test each other on the collocations in **4a)**.

6 a) Check students understand that they must put the verbs in the correct form, for example, the infinitive, Past Simple, etc.

Students do the exercise on their own, then check in pairs. Check answers with the class.

> 2 rent 3 get 4 get 5 stayed 6 book 7 rent 8 book

b) Students do the activity in pairs. Encourage students to ask follow-up questions and give more information if possible.

7 Tell students that two friends from another country want to visit them. Ask them to think of real friends in other countries if possible.

Focus students on the questions that their friends want them to answer. Check students understand them.

Students work on their own and write the email. (Alternatively, students can write their emails for homework). While they are working, check their writing and correct any mistakes.

When they have finished, students can work in pairs and swap emails. Students read their partner's email and answer questions 1–4.

♪ Ask students to turn to SB p102 and look at *Holiday*. This song was Madonna's first hit single and was released in 1983.

1 a) Students work on their own and think of three places they would like to go to on holiday.

b) Students compare their ideas in pairs, giving reasons for their choices.

Ask students to share interesting or unusual choices with the class.

2 a) Focus students on the first two lines of the song. Pre-teach the verb *celebrate* and the noun *celebration*. Also pre-teach the words/phrases *have fun, have a party, nation* and *chorus* /ˈkɔːrəs/.

R8.10 Give students time to read the song, then play the recording (SB p154). Students listen and circle the words they hear. Play the recording again if necessary.

b) Students check answers in pairs. Play the recording again, pausing after each line for students to check answers.

> 2 celebrate 3 day 4 nice 5 word 6 celebration
> 7 nation 8 good 9 bad 10 come 11 need 12 world
> 13 days 14 celebrate 15 find 16 come 17 things
> 18 need

3 a) Students do the exercise on their own, then check in pairs. Check answers with the class.

> great; nice; happy; good; old; bad

b) Students work in pairs and write the comparatives. Check answers with the class.

> greater; nicer; happier; better; older; worse

EXTRA PRACTICE AND HOMEWORK

Ph **Study Skills** 4 Recording vocabulary p205 (Instructions p200)

Ph **Class Activity** 8D Collocation dominoes p165 (Instructions p131)

8 Review SB p69

CD-ROM Lesson 8D

Workbook Lesson 8D p44

Workbook Reading and Writing Portfolio 8 p78

Progress Test 8 p219

---

8 Review

See p32 for ideas on how to use this section.

> **1a)** 3 to 4 on 5 for 6 – 7 in 8 with
>
> **2a)** 2 Can I find a hotel room for under $30? 3 Which museums can I visit for free? 4 Where can I buy some nice presents? 5 Where can I get a really good pizza?
>
> **3a)** 1 smaller 2 bigger 3 more expensive 4 more modern 5 better
>
> **4** 2 to go 3 go 4 do 5 to go 6 go 7 go

Progress Portfolio

See p32 for ideas on how to use this section.

9 All in a day's work

Student's Book p70–p77

9A   The meeting

> **Vocabulary** work
> **Grammar** Present Continuous for 'now'
> **Review** jobs; common verbs

EXTRA IDEA

- Students work in pairs and take turns to test each other on the collocations. One student says the noun or phrase, for example, *letters*, and his/her partner says the whole collocation, for example, *write letters*.

Vocabulary Work

1 a) Students work on their own and tick the words they know, then do the exercise in `V9.1` SB p140. They can then check answers in pairs.

Check answers with the class.

Model and drill the words. Pay particular attention to the pronunciation of *message* /ˈmesɪdʒ/ and the first vowel sound in *company* /ˈkʌmpəni/.

`V9.1` 1f) 2i) 4b) 5h) 6d) 8e) 9c)

b) Check students remember what a collocation is. Pre-teach and drill *sign* /saɪn/.

Focus students on the example to show that we can't use *write* with *customers*, but we can use *write* with *reports* and *letters*.

Students do the exercise on their own, then check their answers in pairs.

Check answers with the class.

Point out that we *take notes* in a meeting or a class and we *write someone a note* when we leave someone a short message. The word *notes* is sometimes confused with *marks*, for example, 16/20 in a test.

Also highlight the prepositions in *work for a company, work in an office, go to meetings, write to a customer/company* and the use of *the* in *answer the phone*.

Point out that we stress the first syllable in *email*, not the second.

Teach the common collocation *have a meeting*.

2 note
3 contract
4 meetings
5 a report
6 contracts
7 contract

2 Give an example by talking about what you, or a member of your family, do at work.

Students do the activity in groups. You can give students a few moments to think of ideas on their own before putting students into groups. While students are working, monitor and help with vocabulary.

Ask students to share interesting information with the whole class.

Listening and Grammar

3 **a)** Focus students on pictures 1 and 2 and ask where the people are (Frank is in the street waiting for a taxi, Liz and Janet are in an office). Ask students what time it is (9.50 a.m.).

🖊 It may be useful to draw a clock on the board at this point in the lesson. You can then change the time for each stage of the story.

b) Establish that Frank is talking to Janet in the pictures.

`R9.1` Play the recording (SB p154). Students listen to find out what Frank's problem is. You can stop the recording at the end of Frank's phone call.

Check the answer with the class (Frank is late for a very important meeting).

c) Give students time to read sentences 1–6.

Play the whole recording again. Students listen and choose the correct answers. Students can then check in pairs.

Check answers with the class.

1 train
2 ten
3 start the meeting
4 Frank's
5 at home
6 finish some reports

4 a) Students work in pairs and decide which person says sentences 1–6.

b) [R9.1] Play the recording again. Students listen and check. Check answers with the class.

> 1 Frank
> 2 Janet
> 3 Janet
> 4 Liz
> 5 Liz
> 6 Liz

Help with Grammar Present Continuous: positive and negative

5 a)–d) Students do the exercises on their own or in pairs, then check their answers in [G9.1] SB p141.

 While they are working, draw the table from **5b)** on the board so that you are ready to check their answers.

Check answers with the class.

- **a)** The sentences in **4a)** are about now. The verbs in these sentences are in the Present Continuous.
- **b)** Check the table with the class (see the table in [G9.1] SB p141).
- Highlight the word order in Present Continuous sentences: subject + *be* + (*not*) + verb+*ing* + … .
- Point out that we can also make negative sentences in two ways for all subjects except for *I*: *you/we/they aren't* or *you're/we're/they're not* + verb+*ing* *he/she/it isn't* or *he's/she's/it's not* + verb+*ing*.
- **c)** smoking; studying; sitting; looking; going; running; writing; living; stopping
- Check students have understood the spelling rules for making verb+*ing* forms (see [G9.1] SB p141).

> ┌─ EXTRA IDEA ─
> - For extra practice of the spelling rules of verb+*ing* forms, choose 20 infinitives of verbs that students know and do a Board Race (see p21).

6 [R9.2] [P] Play the recording (SB p154) and ask students to repeat. Check students copy the contractions and sentence stress correctly.

7 a) Focus students on picture 3. Ask students what time it is now (9.55 a.m.).

Ask students what the people are doing (Danny's playing a computer game, Bob's reading the newspaper and Liz is talking to Danny).

Students do the exercise on their own, then check answers in pairs.

b) [R9.3] Play the recording. Students listen and check their answers.

> 1 'm writing
> 2 's reading
> 3 isn't/'s not reading
> 4 's studying
> 5 'm waiting
> 6 aren't/'re not working
> 7 'm going

8 Tell students it's now 10.05 a.m. Focus students on the names and the speech bubble.

Students work in pairs and discuss what they think these people are doing at this time.

Ask students to share their ideas with the class.

> **Suggested answers**
> 2 Bob's studying the business pages/doing some work.
> 3 The Tamada brothers are having a meeting with Janet.
> 4 Danny is taking notes at the meeting.
> 5 Frank's waiting for a taxi/sitting in a taxi/walking to the office.
> 6 Liz is finishing some reports.

9 Establish that it is now 10.15 a.m. and that Frank is phoning Liz.

[R9.4] Give students time to read the sentences, then play the recording (SB p155). Students listen and answer the questions. Play the recording again if necessary.

Check answers with the class.

> 1 A taxi.
> 2 No, it isn't.
> 3 Janet is talking to/having a meeting with the Tamada brothers. Danny is taking notes in the meeting.
> 4 In Janet's office.
> 5 He's running to the office.

Help with Grammar Present Continuous: questions and short answers

10 a)–c) Students do the exercises on their own or in pairs, then check their answers in [G9.2] SB p141.

 While students are working, draw the table from **10a)** on the board so that you are ready to check their answers.

Check answers with the class.

- **a)** Focus students on the table on the board. Elicit which words in questions 3 and 4 from **9** go in each column and complete the table (see the table in [G9.2] SB p141).
- Highlight the word order in Present Continuous questions: (question word) + auxiliary + subject + verb+*ing* + … .

- **b)** 1 No, you aren't. or No, you're not. 2 Yes, she is./No, she isn't or No, she's not. 3 Yes, they are./No, they aren't. or No, they're not.
- Point out that the short answers are the same as for *yes/no* questions with the verb *be*: *Are you from Italy?*.
- Also point out that there are two possible negative short answers for all subjects except for *I*: *No, we aren't./No, we're not.*; *No, he isn't./No, he's not.*, etc.
- Highlight that we don't contract *are* with question words. We say *What are … ?* not ~~*What're … ?*~~.

 11 Ask students who they think signs the contract, Janet or Frank.

R9.5 Play the recording (SB p155). Students listen and check their answer.

Check the answer with the class (Frank).

12 a) Establish that it is now 6.30 p.m. the same day and that Frank is talking to his wife, Karen, on the phone.

Pre-teach *darling* and check students remember *kids*.

Students work on their own and make questions from the prompts.

Students can check their questions in pairs.

b) R9.6 Play the recording. Students listen and check their answers.

If necessary, play the recording again, pausing after each question and writing it on the board.

> 2 Are you having a nice time?
> 3 What are you doing?
> 4 Are the kids doing their homework?
> 5 What are they doing?

c) R9.7 P Play the recording (SB p155) and ask students to repeat. Encourage students to copy the sentence stress and use the weak forms of *are* /ə/ and *you* /jə/.

You can also ask students to turn to R9.7, SB p155. They can follow the sentence stress as they listen.

EXTRA IDEA
- Students work in pairs and role-play the conversation in **12a)**.

Get ready … Get it right!

13 Put students into two groups, group A and group B. Students in group A turn to SB p110 and students in group B turn to SB p118. Check they are all looking at the correct exercise.

a) Students work in pairs with a partner from the same group and take turns to describe what people are doing in the picture. Draw students' attention to the speech bubbles before they start.

While they are working, check their sentences for accuracy and help with any problems.

b) Tell students that there are eleven differences between picture A and picture B. Focus students on the questions in the speech bubbles and drill these if necessary.

Put one student from group A with a student from group B. Students work in pairs and take turns to ask and answer questions to find the differences. Students are not allowed to look at each other's pictures.

While they are working, monitor and help with any problems.

c) Students work with their original partner from **a)** and tell each other the differences they have found, using the language in the speech bubble.

Check answers with the class.

Finally, find out how many pairs found all the differences.

> 1 A: Kevin's talking on the phone. B: He's sleeping.
> 2 A: Kevin's wearing a jacket. B: He isn't wearing a jacket.
> 3 A: Holly's eating a banana. B: She's eating an apple.
> 4 A: Holly's reading a report. B: She's looking at photos.
> 5 A: Holly's wearing a jumper. B: She's wearing a shirt.
> 6 A: Ashley's writing an email. B: He's playing a computer game.
> 7 A: Angus is reading a newspaper. B: He's reading a (football) magazine.
> 8 A: Angus is smoking a cigarette. B: He's drinking something./He's having a drink.
> 9 A: Angus isn't listening to music/his personal stereo. B: He's listening to music/his personal stereo.
> 10 A: Diana is drinking a cup of tea/coffee. B: She's talking on the phone.
> 11 A: Diana is wearing trousers. B: She's wearing a skirt/a suit.

EXTRA PRACTICE AND HOMEWORK

Ph **Vocabulary Plus** 9 Computer vocabulary p195 (Instructions p185)

Ph **Class Activity** 9A At the park p166 (Instructions p132)

9 Review Exercises 1, 2 and 3 SB p77

CD-ROM Lesson 9A

Workbook Lesson 9A p45

9B Strike!

Vocabulary transport
Grammar Present Simple or Present Continuous?
Help with Listening linking (2)
Review question forms

Vocabulary Transport

1 a) Check students understand the words in the vocabulary box and if necessary teach the new words *tram* and *scooter*. Note that this vocabulary is in **V9.2** in the Language Summary, SB p140.

Students work on their own and draw pictures of six of the types of transport in the vocabulary box. Set a time limit of three minutes.

b) Put students into pairs. Students take turns to show their pictures to their partner and to guess what they are.

2 a) Students do the exercise on their own, then check their answers in **V9.3** SB p140.

Check answers with the class. Establish that each pair of words/phrases has the same meaning. Highlight that we *go by bike/plane/car*, etc. but we *go on foot*, not ~~go by foot~~ or ~~go by walk~~.

Teach students that in British English we can say *the tube* or *the underground*, but *the tube* is more common. Also teach the American English word *subway*. Note that we don't usually use the word *metro* unless we are talking about an underground system in a non-English speaking country, for example, *the Paris metro*.

Model and drill the words/phrases. Highlight the pronunciation of *walk* /wɔːk/ and *cycle* /ˈsaɪkəl/.

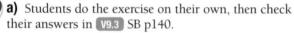

2c) 3b) 4d) 5a) 6f)

b) Use the speech bubbles to remind students of adverbs of frequency (*usually, always*, etc.).

Students work in groups and talk about their travel habits using the prompts 1–5. Encourage students to give reasons for their choices of transport if possible.

Ask students to share any interesting or unusual answers with the class.

Listening and Grammar

3 a) Focus students on the newspaper headline and the photos. Ask students what is happening today and teach *strike*. You can also teach the phrases *go on strike* and *be on strike*.

If appropriate, you can ask students if strikes are common in their country and when the last transport strike was.

b) Tell students that they are going to listen to a radio news report on today's strike. Pre-teach *reporter*.

Give students time to study the table and check they understand that *get to work* means *travel to work*. Note that *get to work* is much more common than *travel to work* in spoken English.

R9.8 Play the recording (SB p155). Students listen and fill in the table, then check answers in pairs.

Check answers with the class.

	how he/she usually gets to work	how he/she is getting to work today
first man	(he goes) by train	he's driving
woman	(she goes) by bike	she's going by bike
second man	(he takes) the tube or the bus	he's walking

c) Pre-teach and drill *journey* /ˈdʒɜːni/ and *normal*.

Give students time to read questions 1–5, then play the recording again. Students listen and answer the questions.

Students compare answers in pairs.

Check answers with the class.

1 About 6.15.
2 About 40 minutes.
3 It's cheaper than the tube.
4 About half an hour.
5 It's quicker than driving.

Help with Listening Linking (2)

● This Help with Listening helps students to understand how consonant-vowel linking makes words 'run together' in normal speech. Students first studied linking in lesson 4A.

4 a) Focus students on sentences 1 and 2 and point out the linking. Ask students why these words are linked (because one word ends with a consonant sound and the next word begins with a vowel sound). Highlight that it is the sound that is important, not the last letter.

Students work on their own or in pairs and find the linking in sentences 3–6.

 While they are working, write the sentences on the board.

Elicit which words are linked in each sentence and draw the links on the board.

b) **R9.9** Play the recording. Students listen and check their answers.

Play the recording again, pausing after each sentence to check the linking in each sentence on the board.

> **3** And_it's taking_a very long time. **4** Here's someone_on_a bike. **5** I'm_in the centre_of the city. **6** The traffic_isn't moving_at_all.

c) Ask students to turn to R9.8, SB p155.

Play the recording again. Students listen and read, noticing the linking.

Note that vowel-vowel links which have an extra linking sound (for example, *to_/w/_our* and *happy_/j/_about*) are not marked in the recording script for R9.8. Extra linking sounds are dealt with in **face2face** Pre-intermediate.

---

5 **R9.10** **P** Focus students on the example, then play the recording (SB p155). Students listen and repeat each section. Check students copy the linking.

If necessary, play the recording again, pausing after each phrase/sentence and drill students individually.

Help with Grammar Present Simple or Present Continuous?

6 **a)–c)** Focus students on the example and ask which verb is in the Present Simple (*go*) and which is in the Present Continuous (*'m driving*).

Students do the exercises on their own or in pairs, then check their answers in **G9.3** SB p141.

Check answers with the class.

> - We usually use the Present Simple to talk about things that happen every day/week/month, etc.
> - We use the Present Continuous to talk about things happening now.
> - We use *am*, *are* and *is* in Present Continuous questions.
> - We use *do* and *does* in Present Simple questions.
> - We usually use the Present Simple with *usually, sometimes, always, often, normally, never, hardly ever, every day*, etc.
> - We usually use the Present Continuous with *now, today* and *at the moment*.

--- **EXTRA IDEA** ---
- Students work on their own and write three true sentences and three false sentences using the words in **6b)**. While they are working, check the sentences for accuracy and correct any mistakes in word order. Students work in pairs and swap sentences. Students guess which of their partner's sentences are false.

7 **a)** Focus students on the photos of Ella, Rose and Albert. Establish that Ella and Rose are talking about what they are doing on the day of the strike.

Students work on their own and put the verbs in brackets in the Present Simple or Present Continuous.

Students can check answers in pairs.

b) **R9.11** Play the recording. Students listen and check their answers.

> **2** work **3** 'm working **4** 'm sitting **5** don't work **6** drive **7** visit **8** 're staying **9** is answering **10** 'm watching **11** don't watch **12** 'm enjoying

8 **a)** Students do the exercise on their own, then check answers in pairs.

Check answers with the class.

> **2** Is … working **3** is … doing **4** Does … work **5** do … do **6** are … doing **7** Does … watch **8** Is … enjoying

b) Students work in pairs and take turns to ask and answer the questions. Students can refer to the speech bubbles in **7a)** if they can't remember the answers.

Encourage students to use correct short answers where appropriate.

> **2** No, she isn't. She's working at home.
> **3** She's sitting in the garden and writing an article.
> **4** No, she doesn't.
> **5** They drive into town and visit some friends.
> **6** Albert is answering his emails and Rose is watching tennis on TV.
> **7** No, she doesn't.
> **8** Yes, she is.

Get ready … Get it right!

9 **a)** Students do the activity on their own.

b) Students continue working on their own and think of what these people are doing at the moment and what they usually do in their free time. Make sure students do not write this information on their paper.

10 Students work in pairs and swap papers. Use the speech bubbles to highlight the three questions students should ask about each person on their partner's paper. Drill these questions with the class if necessary.

Students take turns to ask about the people on their partner's paper. Encourage students to use *I think he's/she's …* or *He/She's probably …* if they aren't sure what the people are doing at the moment. While they are working, monitor and help with any problems.

Finally, ask students to share interesting information about their partner's family and friends with the class.

9C On the phone

QUICK REVIEW ●●●

This activity reviews how to say phone numbers.
Write two or three phone numbers on the board and ask students how we say them in English. Remind students that we say *double five* for 55 and *oh* for 0. Students work on their own and write four phone numbers. Put students into pairs. Students say the phone numbers to their partner once only. Their partner writes the numbers. Students check that their partner has written down the numbers correctly.

Real World phone messages; talking on the phone
Help with Listening phone messages
Review *can* for requests and possibility; suggestions

I'll get back to you

1 Focus students on the photo of Emily. Ask where she is (at work). Focus students on items 1–3 and ask students what they are (1 a 'to do' list, 2 a business card, 3 an advert for a play).

Students work on their own and answer questions a)–h). You can set a time limit of two minutes to encourage students to scan the texts for the correct information.

Students check answers in pairs. Check answers with the class.

a) Business Manager b) a comedy c) M1 7FT
d) September e) four f) cmorris@mc.co.uk
g) Jenny Ross and Brian Winter h) a friend

Help with Listening Phone messages

- This Help with Listening helps students to understand typical phone messages.

2 a) Set the context by asking students if they have answerphones in their homes and when they hear phone messages (when someone isn't at home, when someone's mobile is switched off, etc.). Establish that sentences 1–7 are all common phone messages.

Pre-teach *press* and give students time to read the phone messages.

R9.12 Play the recording. Students listen and fill in the gaps with the words in the box. Play the recording again if necessary, pausing after each sentence to give students time to write.

Check answers with the class. Use the sentences to teach the following words and phrases.

- *Voicemail* is a message recording system at work or on a mobile phone.
- *Get back to someone* is an informal way to say *return someone's call*.
- If someone is *not available* he/she can't answer his/her phone at the moment.
- If you have three *options* you can choose three different things.
- *An enquiry* is a request for information.

2 back 3 person 4 message 5 choose 6 press 7 try

EXTRA IDEA

- Students could try to fill in the gaps in sentences 1–7 before they listen. Then play the recording and ask students to check their answers.

b) Establish that students are going to hear four messages and focus students on the three options. Mime *hang up* to teach this phrase to the class.

R9.13 Play the recording (SB p155). Students listen and decide what they should do for each message. Check answers with the class.

1b) 2b) 3c) 4a)

3 a) Focus students on Emily's 'to do' list (1). Ask students who she wants to phone (Chris Morris, Alan Wick, the theatre, Katrina).

R9.14 Give students time to read the questions, then play the recording (SB p155). Students listen and answer the questions. Students can check answers in pairs.

b) Ask students to turn to R9.14, SB p155. Play the recording again. Students listen, read and check their answers.

> 1a) about 10 a.m. tomorrow b) after work c) on Saturday 2 £27.50 and £22

Can I call you back?

4 **a)** Focus students on conversations 1 and 2 and photos A and B.

Students read the conversations and match them to the photos. Set a time limit of one minute.

Check answers with the class.

> 1B 2A

b) **R9.15** Play the recording. Students listen and choose the words/phrases people say.

c) Play the recording again, pausing after each line for students to check their answers.

> 2 Hold on 3 It's 4 got 5 is that 6 Speaking 7 This is
> 8 back 9 on 10 I'll call

d) Students answer the questions in pairs. Check answers with the class.

> 1 a) conversation 2 b) conversation 1
> 2 a) conversation 1 b) conversation 2
> 3 a) Chris Morris b) Tim

> **Real World** Talking on the phone

5 **a)–b)** Students work on their own and put the headings in the correct places in the table, then check in **RW9.1** SB p141.

Check answers with the class.

- a) asking to speak to people; b) saying who you are; c) calling people back
- Point out that in phone conversations we say *It's (Katrina)*, not *I'm Katrina*.
- Also point out that *This is …* is more formal than *It's … .*
- Check students understand that *Hold on a moment.* means *wait*. A more formal equivalent is *Hold the line, please.*
- Tell students that *I'll (call)* is a contraction of the future form *I will (call)* and point out that *will* is followed by the infinitive.
- Highlight that *get* in *I got your message.* means *receive*, while *get* in *I'll get him/her.* means *find*.

- Teach students that the verbs *call, ring* and *phone* all have the same meaning.
- Encourage students to memorise these fixed phrases, as they are extremely common in all types of phone conversations.

6 **R9.16** **P** Play the recording and ask students to repeat. Encourage students to copy the stress and intonation pattern for each sentence, and remind them of the importance of intonation in sounding polite.

7 **a)** Focus students on photo B again. Ask students who the person is (Katrina). Tell students that Katrina is making some phone calls at work.

Students work on their own and fill in the gaps in the conversations with parts of the phrases from **5a)**. Tell students that they can write one, two or three words in each gap.

b) **R9.17** Play the recording. Students listen and check their answers. Play the recording again if necessary, pausing after each gap to elicit the correct answers.

> 2 This is 3 Can I call 4 Call me on 5 call you 6 It's
> 7 Can I speak 8 Hold on 9 got

8 **a)** Students work in pairs and write a phone conversation including at least five phrases from **5a)**. They can choose whether to write a personal or business conversation.

While they are working, check their conversations for accuracy and help with any problems.

b) Students swap papers with another pair. Students read the other pair's conversation. Allow time for students to check any mistakes they find with the pair who wrote it or with you.

Students practise the new conversation in pairs until they can remember it. While they are working, monitor and help with any problems. Encourage students to use polite intonation.

Students take turns to role-play the conversation for the pair who wrote it. You can ask one or two pairs to role-play their conversation for the class.

> ─ EXTRA IDEA ─
> - Before doing **8a)**, students can practise the conversations in **4b)** and **7a)** in pairs.

9 Put students into pairs, student A and student B. Student As turn to SB p111 and student Bs turn to SB p119. Check they are all looking at the correct exercise.

a) Give students time to read the information for phone conversations 1–4 and help with any problems.

b) Focus students on the prompt box. Students continue working on their own and decide what language they need for conversations 1–4.

Students can make notes at this stage, but they should not write out the whole conversation.

c) Students work with their partners and take turns to role-play phone conversations 1–4. Student A should start conversation 1.

While students are working, monitor and help with any problems.

Finally, ask one or two pairs to role-play conversations for the class.

EXTRA PRACTICE AND HOMEWORK

CD-ROM Lesson 9C

Workbook Lesson 9C p48

9D The Adventure Centre

Vocabulary indoor and outdoor activities; adverbs and adjectives
Review *can/can't*

QUICK REVIEW ●●●

This activity reviews language for talking on the phone. Students work in pairs and write down all the phrases for talking on the phone they can remember. Set a time limit of three minutes. Students compare answers with another pair. Students can check their phrases in RW9.1 p141.

1 a) Students work on their own and tick the words they know, then do the exercise in V9.4 SB p140. They can then check answers in pairs.

Check answers with the class. Point out that we say *play a musical instrument* but *play the guitar/piano*, etc.

Also highlight the irregular verbs *swim, sing, drive, speak* and *ride* and teach their Past Simple forms (*swam, sang, drove, spoke* and *rode*).

Model and drill the words/phrases. Note that only the main stress in words/phrases is shown in vocabulary boxes and the Language Summaries.

> V9.4 1e) 2o) 3g) 4h) 5n) 6i) 7d) 8c) 9f) 10l)
> 11m) 12p) 13j) 14b) 15a) 16k)

— EXTRA IDEAS —
- Students work in pairs and mime the activities for their partner to guess.
- Students categorise the activities into indoor and outdoor activities.

b) Use the speech bubbles to remind students that we use *can* and *can't* to talk about ability. Drill the questions and short answers with the class.

Students work in pairs and ask questions to find four things that they can do but their partner can't do. Encourage students to use the words/phrases in **1a)** and their own ideas.

Ask students to share interesting information with the whole class.

2 Focus students on the job advert for group leaders for the Mayo Adventure Centre.

Students read the job advert quickly to decide if they would like to do the job. Set a time limit of two minutes.

Elicit answers from the class and ask students to give reasons for their answers. Check students understand what a group leader does (looks after groups of people and organises activities for them).

— EXTRA IDEA —
- With a strong class, use the job advert to teach some useful vocabulary for finding jobs: *look for a job, application form, apply for a job, experience, references, qualifications, job interview*, etc.

3 a) Focus students on the photo of Melanie and the letter. Use the letter to teach *reference*.

Students read the letter to find out if they think Melanie is a good person for the job (she is). Set a time limit of three minutes to encourage students to scan the letter for relevant information.

b) Pre-teach *recommend, mountain biking* and *fluently*.

Students read the reference and the job advert again to find six reasons why Melanie can do the job.

Students check their answers in pairs. Check answers with the class.

> She likes working with young people (she played the guitar to the children). She enjoys doing outdoor activities (climbing, mountain biking, etc.). She is good at water sports (she can sail, windsurf and swim). She is good at languages (she speaks French fluently). She has a driving licence (she is an excellent driver). She is friendly and helpful (she makes friends easily and is popular). She has experience.

Help with Vocabulary Adverbs and adjectives

4 a)–d) Focus students on the example and check that students understand that *fluently* is an adverb and *excellent* is an adjective.

Students do the exercises on their own or in pairs, then check their answers in V9.5 SB p140.

Check answers with the class.

- **a)** We use adjectives to describe nouns. They usually come before the noun.
- We use adverbs to describe verbs. They usually come after the verb.
- **b)** Adverbs: made friends **easily**, sail very **well**, play the guitar **beautifully**, speaks French **fluently** Adjectives: **hard** worker, **popular** group leader, **good** windsurfer, **fast** swimmer, **excellent** driver
- **c)** 1 beautifully 2 fluently 3 easily 4 well (irregular)
- Check students understand the spelling rules for adverbs (see the table in V9.5 p140).
- Highlight the irregular adverbs *good/well*, *fast/fast*, *hard/hard*. Point out that the adverb for *bad* is regular (*badly*).

5 Pre-teach *careful*. Students do the exercise on their own. Check answers with the class.

2 happily 3 fast 4 slowly 5 carefully
6 hard 7 quietly 8 badly

6 **a)** Students do the exercise on their own, then check in pairs. Check answers with the class. Point out that *a hard worker* is someone who works or studies a lot.

2 badly 3 hard 4 carefully 5 bad 6 fluently 7 good

b) Students do the exercise on their own. They tick the sentences that are true for them and change the other sentences to make them true, for example, by making the verb negative or changing the adjective or adverb.

c) Students work in pairs and compare sentences to find out how many are the same. Ask students to share interesting information with the class.

7 **a)** Students write three sentences about themselves using adjectives or adverbs from **4c)** or **5** on a piece of paper. Students give their papers to you when they have finished.

b) Shuffle the papers, then read out all three sentences on each paper in turn. Ask students to guess who has written each set of three sentences. Continue until you have read out the sentences on all the papers.

 Ask students to turn to SB p103 and look at *Dancing in the Street*. This song was first recorded by Martha and the Vandellas in 1964 and has been covered by many other artists, including Mick Jagger and David Bowie, Little Richard and Van Halen.

1 Students discuss the questions in groups.
Ask students to share interesting answers with the whole class.

2 **a)** R9.18 Give students time to read the song, then play the recording (SB p155). Students listen and put the lines of the song in order. Play the recording again if necessary.

b) Students check answers in pairs. Play the recording again, pausing after each line for students to check answers.
Note that PA in line q) refers to Pennsylvania (the state that Philadelphia is in) and DC refers to Washington D.C. The motor city referred to in line t) is Detroit.

2b) 3f) 4a) 5c) 6e) 7g) 8j) 9i) 10n) 11l) 12m)
13k) 14h) 15r) 16p) 17o) 18s) 19q) 20t)

3 Focus students on the words in **bold**. Point out that *street* rhymes with *beat* as it has the same final sound.
Students work in pairs and find the rhyming words for the other words in **bold**. Check answers with the class.

world/girl; there/everywhere; playing/swaying; singing/swinging; meet/street; nation/invitation

---

EXTRA PRACTICE AND HOMEWORK

Ph **Class Activity** 9D Blockbuster p169 (Instructions p132)
9 Review SB p77
CD-ROM Lesson 9D
Workbook Lesson 9D p49
Workbook Reading and Writing Portfolio 9 p80
Progress Test 9 p220

---

9 Review

See p32 for ideas on how to use this section.

1a) 2 a report/a message/a contract/a letter/an email
3 a customer/a company 4 a letter/the phone/an email
5 notes/a message 6 for a company/in an office
7 a meeting/a conference

3 2 's … doing 3 's having 4 are … doing 5 're playing
6 isn't/'s not doing 7 'm reading

4a) 2 cycle 3 drive 4 sail 5 walk 6 take the train

4b) 2 go by bike 3 go by car 4 go by boat 5 go on foot
6 go by train

5a) 2 's … doing 3 do … watch 4 are … doing 5 do … go
6 's … doing

Progress Portfolio

See p32 for ideas on how to use this section.

10 Mind and body

10A   A healthy heart

QUICK REVIEW ●●●
This activity reviews adverbs of frequency and the Present Simple. Students do the activity in groups. You can give students a few moments to think of ideas before putting them in groups. Ask students to share interesting answers with the class.

Vocabulary health; *How often … ?* and frequency expressions
Grammar imperatives; *should/shouldn't*
Review Present Simple questions

EXTRA IDEA

- Students work in pairs and take turns to test each other on the collocations. One student says one half of the collocation, for example, *fit*, and his/her partner says the whole collocation, for example, *get fit*.

Vocabulary   Health

1 a) Pre-teach the noun *health*, the adjective *healthy* and its opposite *unhealthy*.

Students work on their own and tick the phrases they know, then do the exercise in **V10.1** SB p142. They can then check answers in pairs.

Check answers with the class. Point out that we *do exercise*, not ~~make exercise~~ and that *exercise* is uncountable in this context (*I do some exercise every day.*).

Also highlight that *get* in the phrases *get stressed* and *get fit* means *become*, and that we usually use the verb *be* with *high/low in fat*. (*This cheese is very high in fat.*).

You can use the phrase *stop smoking* to highlight that *stop* usually takes the verb+*ing* form.

Model and drill the phrases. Pay particular attention to the pronunciation of *lose* /luːz/, *weight* /weɪt/, *stressed* /strest/, *gym* /dʒɪm/, *heart* /hɑːt/, *high* /haɪ/ and *low* /ləʊ/. Point out that *stressed* is one syllable, not two.

Note that only the main stress in words/phrases is shown in vocabulary boxes and the Language Summaries.

> **V10.1**   2c) 3f) 4j) 5b) 6d) 7g) 8i) 9e) 10a)

b) Pre-teach *lifestyle* (the way you live your life). Students work in pairs and decide which of the phrases in **1a)** match a healthy or unhealthy lifestyle.

Check answers with the class.

> Healthy lifestyle: do exercise, lose weight, stop smoking, get fit, go to the gym, low in fat
>
> Unhealthy lifestyle: get stressed, have a heart attack, eat fried food, drink alcohol, high in fat

c) Students work in groups and discuss whether they think they have a healthy or an unhealthy lifestyle. Encourage students to give reasons for their answers using the phrases in **1a)**.

Reading and Grammar

2 a) Ask students to cover the article 'Top Tips for a Healthy Heart!'. Pre-teach *disease* /dɪˈziːz/, *cancer*, *grams* and *portion* /ˈpɔːʃən/. Drill these words with the class.

Students work in pairs and guess the answers to questions 1–7. Students are not allowed to look at the article at this stage.

b) Focus students on the article and teach the phrase *top tips* (the best advice).

Students read the article and check their answers from **2a)**. Check answers with the class.

> 1 heart disease 2 20 (one every three minutes)
> 3 No, they don't. 4 the UK 5 one gram 6 at least five 7 No, it isn't.

c) Students read the article again and find four things that are good for your heart and four that are bad.

Check answers with the class and ask students if anything in the article surprised them. Try to avoid discussing students' own lifestyles in too much detail at this point as they discuss them in **6a)** and **6b)**.

Note that Omega-3 oils are found in oily fish, such as sardines and mackerel, and are thought to be very good for the heart.

> Good for your heart: stopping smoking, regular exercise, fish, fruit and vegetables, losing weight, a glass of red wine every day
>
> Bad for your heart: fried food, too much red meat, too much salt, being overweight, drinking too much alcohol

- With a strong class you can exploit the article for vocabulary. Ask students to read the article again and find three or four new words they would like to know. Students look these words up in their dictionaries. Put students into groups. Students take turns to teach their partners the words they have looked up. While students are working, help with any words they still don't understand.

Help with Grammar Imperatives

3 **a)–b)** Pre-teach *give advice* and point out that in English *advice* is an uncountable noun. We say *Can you give me some advice?* not ~~Can you give me an advice?~~. We use the phrase *a piece of advice* not ~~an advice~~ (*Let me give you a piece of advice.*).

Students do **3a)** on their own, then check their answers in G10.1 SB p143.

- Point out that the positive imperative is the same as the infinitive (*Stop smoking*).
- We make the negative imperative with *don't* + infinitive (*Don't eat a lot of salt.*).
- Highlight that we use the imperative to give very strong advice and only use it when we're giving advice to people we know well.
- We also use the imperative to give orders (*Go home!*) and instructions (*Don't write anything.*).

4 **a)** Students work on their own and write five tips on how to get fit. Focus students on the examples and ask them to identify the imperatives before they start (*Walk …* and *Don't sit and watch …*).

While students are working, check their sentences for accuracy and help with any problems.

b) Put students into groups of three. Students compare their sentences and choose their five best tips.

Ask each group to share their top tips with the class. You can ask the whole class to decide on the top five tips from everyone's lists.

- Students work in groups and make a poster with the heading 'Top Tips for Getting Fit!'. You can display the posters around the class for other students to read.
- Alternatively, give each group a different theme for their poster (for example, getting fit, sleeping well, being happy, avoiding stress, going on a first date, studying English, etc.).

Help with Vocabulary *How often … ?* and frequency expressions

5 **a)–c)** Focus students on the phrases in **bold** in the article. Students do the exercises on their own or in pairs, then check their answers in V10.2 SB p142. While they are working, draw the tables from **5a)** on the board so that you are ready to check their answers. Check answers with the class.

- Check the tables with the class (see the tables in V10.2 SB p142). Point out that we can say *once a day, once a week, once a month*, etc.
- Point out that we don't use the indefinite article *a* with *every*. We say *once a day* but *every day* not ~~every a day~~, etc.
- Elicit other phrases with *once, twice, three times, every*, etc. that are not in the table (*once a minute, every ten years*, etc.).
- Drill *once* /wʌns/ and *twice* /twaɪs/ with the class and highlight that we say *twice*, not *two times*.
- **b)** **1** How often do you go to the theatre? **2** How often does your brother phone you? **3** How often did you visit your grandfather?
- We use *How often … ?* to ask about frequency. Although *How often … ?* is most commonly used with the Present Simple, we also use it with the Past Simple.
- Use questions 1–3 to remind students of the word order in Present Simple and Past Simple questions: question word + auxiliary + subject + infinitive + … .
- Model and drill questions 1–3 with the class.

6 **a)** Students do the activity in pairs. Use the speech bubble examples to illustrate the type of questions and answers students should use before they start.

While students are working, correct any mistakes and help with any problems.

b) Each pair decides which student has the healthier lifestyle. Ask students to share their answers with the class, giving reasons where appropriate.

Listening and Grammar

7 **a)** Focus students on the photo. Ask where My Taylor is (at the doctor's) and if the students think he's healthy.

Pre-teach the phrase *give up* (*smoking*) as a synonym for *stop* (*smoking*).

R10.1 Play the recording (SB p155). Students listen and decide if Mr Taylor is healthy or not, noting down reasons where possible.

Check answers with the class.

> Mr Taylor's not very healthy. He doesn't do much exercise, he eats too much red meat and too many pizzas. However, he gave up smoking two years ago and doesn't drink much alcohol.

b) Give students time to read the questions. Check students understand that *weigh* /weɪ/ in question 1 is a verb and *weight* is a noun.

Play the recording again. Students listen and answer the questions. Students can check answers in pairs.

Check answers with the class.

> 1 93 kilos.
> 2 He goes swimming about once a month.
> 3 Four times a week.
> 4 Two years ago.
> 5 Every day.
> 6 He shouldn't eat so much red meat and so many pizzas. He should eat more chicken and fish. He should do more exercise, maybe three times a week.

— EXTRA IDEA —

• If your students are finding the recording difficult, ask them to turn to R10.1, SB p155. Play the recording again while students listen and read. You can also ask them to find all the frequency expressions in the conversation.

Help with Grammar *should/shouldn't*

8 Focus students on the examples and tell students that we use *should* and *shouldn't* to give advice.

Students work on their own and choose the correct words in the rules. They then check their answers in `G10.2` p143.

Check answers with the class.

• We use *should* to say something is a good thing to do.
• We use *shouldn't* to say something is a bad thing to do.
• After *should* and *shouldn't* we use the infinitive.
• Highlight that *should/shouldn't* is more common than the imperative for giving advice.
• Point out that to ask for advice we often say: *What should I do?*.
• Also tell students that when giving advice we often use *I (don't) think …* to make our advice sound less direct: *I (don't) think you should buy it.*

9 **a)** Focus on the photo of Mr Taylor at the doctor's again. Tell students that the doctor gave Mr Taylor more advice.

Students do the exercise on their own, then check their answers in pairs. Check answers with the class.

> 1 should
> 2 shouldn't
> 3 should
> 4 shouldn't
> 5 should
> 6 should

b) `R10.2` `P` Play the recording and ask students to repeat. Point out that *should* is not stressed, but *shouldn't* is stressed as it is a negative auxiliary. Check students copy the sentence stress correctly.

c) Students do the exercise on their own, then compare sentences in pairs.

While students are working, check their sentences for accuracy and help with any problems.

Ask students to share interesting answers with the class.

Get ready … Get it right!

10 Put students into groups of three, student A, student B and student C. Student As turn to SB p106, student Bs turn to SB p114 and student Cs turn to SB p120. Check they are all looking at the correct exercise.

a) Students work on their own. They read their problems, check they understand them, then write one more problem of their own.

While students are working, check the problems they have written and help with any vocabulary.

b) Use the speech bubbles to remind students how to ask for and give advice.

Students work in their groups of three and take turns to ask for and give advice. Students decide what is the best piece of advice for each problem. Ask students to make a note of this advice so that they can share it with the class at the end of the activity.

While students are working, monitor and help with any problems.

Finally, ask students to share the best piece of advice for each problem with the class.

— EXTRA PRACTICE AND HOMEWORK —

Ph **Class Activity** 10A Something in common p172 (Instructions p133)
10 Review Exercises 1, 2 and 3 SB p85
CD-ROM Lesson 10A
Workbook Lesson 10A p50

10B   What's he like?

Vocabulary describing people's appearance and character
Grammar questions with *like*
Help with Listening sentence stress (3)
Review clothes; free time activities

Vocabulary Appearance

1 a) Focus students on photos 1–4. Students look at the photos for two minutes and try to remember the people and their clothes.

b) Tell students to close their books. Students work in pairs and take turns to describe the people in the photos. Students can then open their books again and check the descriptions.

Ask confident students to describe the four people for the class.

> Jake is wearing a red T-shirt and jeans.
> Lily is wearing a red top and brown trousers.
> Pete is wearing a red shirt and brown trousers.
> Zoë is wearing a red top and a black and white skirt.

2 a) Teach *appearance* and drill this with the class.

Students work in pairs and tick the words they know, then check new words in **V10.3** SB p142.

Check the following points with the class.

- We use *middle-aged* to describe people who are in the middle of their life. Nowadays many people use this phrase to describe people in their late forties and fifties.
- *Overweight* is a more polite word for *fat*. Tell students that calling someone *fat* is quite rude.
- *Thin* usually has a negative connotation (for example, when you're ill) whereas *slim* has a positive connotation and is seen as an attractive quality.
- *Beautiful, attractive* and *good-looking* all have very similar meanings. We usually use *beautiful* for women, *good-looking* for men and *attractive* for both men and women.
- We use *Asian* to describe someone from Asia. In the UK *Asian* usually refers to people of Indian, Pakistani or Bangladeshi origin. In the USA *Asian* usually refers to people of Japanese, Chinese and South Korean origin. British people usually refer to people from these countries by their nationality.
- The word *hair* is uncountable when it refers to all the hair on your head. We say *long hair* not ~~long hairs~~ and *long dark hair* not ~~dark long hair~~.

Model and drill the words. Highlight the pronunciation of *middle-aged* /ˌmɪdlˈeɪdʒd/, *overweight* /ˌəʊvəˈweɪt/, *Asian* /ˈeɪʃən/, *fair hair* /feə heə/, *blonde* /blɒnd/, *beard* /bɪəd/, *moustache* /məˈstɑːʃ/ and *bald* /bɔːld/. Also point out the stress on *middle-aged* and *good-looking*.

b) Students do the exercise on their own or in pairs. Check answers with the class.

> We use the words in group B with *have got*.
> We use the words in group A with *be*.

3 a) Students work on their own and choose one of the people in photos 1–4.

Students write a description of that person on a piece of paper, using vocabulary from **2a)** and their own ideas. They should not write the person's name.

While students are working, check their descriptions for accuracy and help with any problems.

b) Put students into pairs. Students swap papers, read their partner's description and guess who the person is.

Students then try to correct any mistakes in their partner's description. Monitor and help as necessary.

Students give back the descriptions to their partner. Students discuss any mistakes and suggested corrections. Monitor and help students with problems.

4 a) Focus students on the picture of Tina and Leo. Establish that they work for an advertising agency. Ask students what they are doing (trying to choose a person for a poster to advertise a new chocolate bar called *Break*).

Ask students who they think should be on the poster and why.

R10.3 Play the recording (SB p156). Students listen and put the people in photos 1–4 in the order that they are talked about.

Check answers with the class.

> 1 Pete
> 2 Jake
> 3 Zoë
> 4 Lily

b) Check students understand *good points* and *bad points*.

Play the recording again. Students listen and make notes on the people's good points and bad points.

You can pause the recording briefly after each person if your students need more time to make notes.

- Half the class make notes on Pete and Zoë's good and bad points and the other half of the class do the same for Jake and Lily.

c) Students work in pairs and compare answers. Check answers with the class.

Ask the class to predict who they think Tina and Leo will choose and why.

name	good points	bad points
Pete	friendly, the type of person who buys a lot of chocolate	a bit overweight
Jake	tall and good-looking	his hair
Zoë	tall, slim, nice hair, very attractive/beautiful	too beautiful to eat a lot of chocolate
Lily	people her age buy a lot of chocolate, looks very friendly and happy	older

d) **R10.4** Play the recording of the end of Tina and Leo's conversation (SB p156). Students listen to find out who they chose and why.

Check the answer with the class and ask students to explain Tina and Leo's reasons for their choice.

Zoë because:
- women buy more chocolate than men
- she's slim (which is what people want to be)
- she's young (and people always think they're young themselves)

Help with Listening Sentence stress (3)

- This Help with Listening reviews sentence stress, highlighting the fact that we stress the important words in sentences.

 5 a) Focus students on the example from the beginning of Tina and Leo's conversation. Ask students which words are stressed (the important words).

b) Ask students to turn to R10.3, SB p156. Play the recording again. Students listen, read and notice the sentence stress.

Vocabulary Character

6 a) Teach *character* /ˈkærɪktə/ and *promise*, and check students remember *present*. Drill these words with the class and contrast *character* with *appearance*.

Students work on their own and tick the sentences that are true for them.

b) Students compare answers in pairs and find out how many of their answers are the same.

 7 Students work on their own or in pairs and match the words in the vocabulary box to the sentences in **6a)**. Students check their answers in **V10.4** SB p142.

Check answers with the class. Tell students we use the verb *be* with these adjectives, not ~~have~~: *I'm a bit shy.* not ~~I have a bit shy~~.

Highlight that we can use *funny* to describe a book, TV programme, etc. You can point out that *funny* also means strange or unusual (*Can you hear a funny noise?*).

Model and drill the words. Pay particular attention to the pronunciation of *generous* /ˈdʒenərəs/, *kind* /kaɪnd/ and *reliable* /rɪˈlaɪəbəl/.

2 shy
3 lazy
4 kind
5 funny
6 selfish
7 outgoing
8 reliable

- If you have a strong class, teach the opposites to some of the adjectives in **7**: *generous/mean*, *shy/outgoing* or *self-confident*, *lazy/hard-working*, *kind/unkind*, *selfish/unselfish*, *reliable/unreliable*. Point out the prefix *un-* on these last three opposites, and that *funny* doesn't have an opposite (we say *He's not very funny.*).

 8 Students do the activity in groups. You can give students a minute or two to think of ideas on their own before putting them in groups.

Ask students to share interesting information about their family with the class.

Listening and Grammar

 9 Refer students back to the picture of Tina and Leo. Tell students that Tina is asking Leo about his new girlfriend.

Give students time to read questions 1–3 and answers a)–c) before they listen.

R10.5 Play the recording (SB p156). Students listen and match the questions to the answers.

Check answers with the class and ask students who Leo's new girlfriend is.

1c) 2b) 3a)
Leo's new girlfriend is Zoë.

- Ask students to try and match up the questions and answers before they listen. Then play the recording for students to listen and check.

Help with Grammar Questions with *like*

10 **a)–b)** Students do **10a)** on their own, then check their answers in **G10.3** SB p143.

Check answers with the class.

- We use *What's he/she like?* to ask for a general description of a person. We often use this question when we don't know the person. The answer can include character and physical appearance.
- Point out that the *What's* in this question is a contraction of *What is*.
- We use *What does he/she look like?* to ask about physical appearance only.
- We use *What does he/she like doing?* to ask about people's likes and free time interests.
- Highlight that we don't use *like* in answers to these questions: *What's he like? He's very kind.* not ~~He's like very kind~~.
- Point out that the question *How is he/she?* asks about health, not personality: *How's Buffy? She's fine, thanks.*
- You can also teach students that we can ask *What … like?* questions about places: *What's Venice like? It's very beautiful.*

11 **a)** Students do the exercise on their own, then check their answers in pairs.

b) **R10.6** Play the recording (SB p156). Students listen and check their answers. Check answers with the class.

P Play the recording again. Ask students to repeat. Check students copy the sentence stress and weak forms correctly.

2 What does she look like? 3 What's he like?
4 What does she like doing? 5 What does he look like? 6 What are they like?

Get ready … Get it right!

12 Students work on their own and write the names of four friends on a piece of paper.

Give students a few minutes to plan how they can describe these people's character, appearance and things they like doing in their free time. Students should not write this information on their paper.

13 **a)** Students work in pairs and swap papers. Students take turns to ask and answer the questions in **9** about the people on their partner's paper. Encourage students to ask follow-up questions where possible.

While students are working, monitor and help with any problems.

b) Students choose one of their partner's friends they would like to meet.

Finally, ask students to share their choices with the whole class. Encourage students to give reasons for their choices.

— EXTRA IDEA —
- You can demonstrate the Get ready … Get it right! activity yourself first by writing the names of four of your friends on the board and inviting students to ask you about them.

— EXTRA PRACTICE AND HOMEWORK —
Ph **Class Activity** 10B Who's Alex? p173 (Instructions p133)
10 Review Exercises 4 and 5 SB p85
CD-ROM Lesson 10B
Workbook Lesson 10B p52

10C I feel terrible!

QUICK REVIEW ●●●
This activity reviews ways of describing people's appearance and character. Give students two minutes to think of three famous people and what they know about them (appearance, character, job, age, nationality, etc.) Put students into pairs. Students take turns to describe their famous people. Their partner must guess who they are.

What's the matter?

1 **a)** Focus students on the picture. Ask students where the people are (in a doctor's waiting room) and why they're there (they're ill).

Real World talking about health; giving advice with *Why don't you … ?*
Vocabulary health problems and treatment
Help with Listening being sympathetic
Review *have got*; imperatives; *should/shouldn't*

Students work on their own and try and match sentences 1–6 to the people A–F.

b) **R10.7** Play the recording. Students listen and check their answers. Check answers with the class.

2A 3D 4C 5E 6F

— EXTRA IDEA —

- If you have a class of beginners and you don't think they know the parts of the body, do the Vocabulary Plus worksheet, 10 Parts of the body p196 (Instructions p186) before starting the lesson.

 a) Focus students on the table and the examples.

Students do the exercise in pairs, then check in **V10.5** SB p142. Check answers with the class.

Highlight the following points with the class.

- We always use the indefinite article *a* with *headache* (*I've got a headache.*), but we can say *I've got a stomach ache/a toothache.* or *I've got stomach ache/toothache.* You can also teach *I've got backache.* (not *I've got a backache.*).
- *I've got a temperature.* means *I've got a high temperature.*
- *I've got a cold.* means *I'm ill.*, while *I'm cold.* means *I'm not warm.*
- We can say *I feel ill/sick/better.* or *I'm ill/sick/better.*, but not *I'm terrible.*
- In British English *I'm sick.* usually means *I'm ill.*, while *I feel sick.* usually means *I want to be sick.*

> **I've got** a temperature, a headache, a toothache, a sore throat, a cold, a cough. **I feel** terrible, sick, better
> **My arm, foot, leg hurts.**

b) **R10.8** **P** Play the recording (SB p156). Ask students to repeat. Check students are pronouncing the following words correctly: *stomach ache* /ˈstʌmək-eɪk/, *temperature* /ˈtemprətʃə/, *headache* /ˈhedeɪk/, *toothache* /ˈtuːθ-eɪk/, *sore throat* /sɔːˈθrəʊt/ and *cough* /kɒf/. Point out that *temperature* is three syllables, not four.

c) Use the speech bubbles to illustrate the activity.

Students work in pairs and test each other on the phrases in **2a)**. While students are working, monitor and check their pronunciation.

Get better soon!

3 **a)** Students do the exercise on their own or in pairs, then check in **V10.6** SB p143. Check answers with the class.

Check students understand the following new words/phrases: *take the day off, the dentist, painkillers, cough medicine, antibiotics.* Highlight that we usually use *medicine* to describe a liquid, and use *pills* or *tablets* to describe painkillers, antibiotics, etc.

Also point out that we say *go home*, not *go to home*.

Model and drill the phrases. Pay particular attention to the pronunciation of *cough medicine* /ˈkɒf ˌmedsən/ and *antibiotics* /ˌæntɪbaɪˈɒtɪks/, and the stress on *painkillers*.

> **go:** home, to the doctor, to the dentist **stay:** in bed
> **take:** some painkillers, some cough medicine, some antibiotics

b) Drill the sentences in the speech bubbles to highlight the language students need to do the exercise.

Students do the activity in groups. Encourage them to use phrases from **2a)** and **3a)** in their conversations.

While students are working, check for accuracy and help with any problems.

Ask students to share interesting answers with the class.

4 **a)** Give students one minute to read the conversations and match them to the photos (1A, 2B).

Students then work on their own and fill in the gaps with the words in the boxes.

Students can check answers in pairs.

b) **R10.9** Play the recording. Students listen and check their answers. Check answers with the class.

> 1 how 2 wrong 3 stomach 4 can't 5 dear 6 terrible
> 7 headache 8 throat 9 should 10 drink

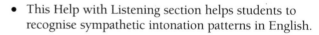

Real World Talking about health

5 **a)–b)** Focus students on the table and check they understand the headings. Teach and drill *sympathy* /ˈsɪmpəθi/.

Students do **5a)** on their own, then check their answers in **RW10.1** SB p143.

Check answers with the class.

- asking about someone's health: *What's the matter?*.
- expressing sympathy: *I hope you get better soon.*
- giving advice: *Why don't you go home?*.
- Point out that *Why don't you … ?* is followed by the infinitive. This phrase is a less direct way to give advice than *should/shouldn't* or the imperative.
- You can also teach the expression *Get well soon!*.

Help with Listening Being sympathetic

- This Help with Listening section helps students to recognise sympathetic intonation patterns in English.

6 Check students understand *sympathetic*, which is a false friend in some European languages. In English it can only be used to describe someone who is being kind to a person who is ill or has a problem. We usually use *nice* to describe friendly/kind people in general.

R10.10 Establish that intonation is very important if we want to sound sympathetic. Play question 1 on the recording to show students that a) sounds sympathetic, but b) does not.

Play the rest of the recording. Students listen and circle the sentence that sounds sympathetic, a) or b).

Play the recording again, pausing after each pair of phrases to check students' answers.

2b)
3b)
4a)
5a)
6b)

7 R10.11 P Play the recording and ask students to repeat. Check students are copying the intonation patterns correctly. Repeat the drill if necessary.

8 **a)** Students work in pairs and practise one of the conversations in **4a)** until they can remember it.

b) Students close their books and then practise the conversation again. You can ask one or two pairs to role-play the conversation for the class.

— EXTRA IDEA —

• Do one of these conversations as a Dialogue Build (see p22).

9 **a)** Check students understand *illness*, then use the speech bubbles to remind students of a typical conversation pattern with someone who is ill.

Give students a few moments to choose an illness from **2a)**.

Students move around the room and have conversations with other students, or talk to students sitting near them. Remind students to use all the phrases from **5a)** in their conversations.

While students are working, monitor for accuracy and help with any problems.

b) Finally, students take turns to tell the class their illnesses and the advice other students gave them. Each students can decide what the best advice was.

— EXTRA PRACTICE AND HOMEWORK —

Ph **Vocabulary Plus** 10 Parts of the body p196 (Instructions p186)

Ph **Class Activity** 10C Get well soon! p175 (Instructions p134)

CD-ROM Lesson 10C

Workbook Lesson 10C p53

10D Are you SAD in winter?

QUICK REVIEW ●●●

This activity reviews health problems and giving advice. Give students a few moments to think of some illnesses, referring to lesson 10C if necessary. Put students into pairs. Students take turns to mime the illnesses. Their partner guesses what's wrong and gives advice. You can demonstrate this activity by miming one or two illnesses for the class before they start.

1 **a)** Students do the exercise on their own, then check in V10.7 SB p143.

Check answers with the class and highlight the American English word *fall*.

Also point out that we use *in* with seasons: *in (the) winter*.

Note that for some countries we talk about *the monsoon/ rainy/dry season*.

Model and drill the words. Highlight the pronunciation of *autumn* /'ɔːtəm/. Also drill *season* with the class.

2 summer 3 autumn [US: fall] 4 winter

b) Students do the exercise on their own. Check answers with the class.

1 winter 2 summer

Vocabulary seasons; weather; word building
Review *What's ... like?*

2 **a)** Focus students on the title of the article and photo 1. Ask students what *sad* usually means (the opposite of *happy*) and check they know the meaning of *light*.

Give students two minutes to skim the first paragraph of article and find out why the woman in photo 1 has a light on her desk. Check the answer with the class (because she has an illness called SAD, or Seasonal Affective Disorder, which makes her depressed in the winter).

b) Pre-teach *depressed* /dɪ'prest/, *scientist* /'saɪəntɪst/ and *bright* /braɪt/. Drill these words with the class.

Students read the whole article and answer the questions.

c) Students check answers in pairs. Check answers with the class.

1 In summer he felt happy and he had a lot of energy. In winter he became depressed and lazy. 2 A 'light box'.
3 The USA, the UK and Sweden. 4 Because the days are shorter and there is less daylight in autumn and winter.
5 No, they don't. SAD is more common in women.
6 They sleep a lot, feel tired all the time, eat a lot of sweet food and feel depressed. 7 For half an hour.

3 Students discuss the questions in groups.

Ask students to share interesting answers with the class.

4 **a)** Use the speech bubbles to teach the question *What's the weather like?*. Point out that the answer is *It's (hot)* not ~~Is hot~~. or ~~It's like hot~~.

Students work on their own and tick the words they know, then do the exercise in **V10.8** SB p143. They can then check answers in pairs.

Check answers with the class. Point out that *It's wet.* is more general than *It's raining*.

Model and drill the words. Highlight the pronunciation of *warm* /wɔːm/, *windy* /ˈwɪndi/ and *cloudy* /ˈklaʊdi/.

> **V10.8** 3c) 4f) 5b) 6k) 7i) 8a) 9h) 10j) 11g)

b) Ask the students what the weather is like today. Discuss the answer with the class.

> ── EXTRA IDEA ──
> • With a strong class, teach more weather words: *cool, foggy, freezing, icy, humid, changeable*, etc.

5 Put students into pairs, student A and student B. Student As turn to SB p109 and student Bs turn to SB p117. Check they are all looking at the correct exercise.

a) Check students know the cities in the table. Drill any difficult names.

Use the speech bubbles to remind students of the questions and answers they need to do the activity.

Students work in their pairs and take turns to ask and answer questions about the places, then fill in the gaps in their table. Students are not allowed to look at their partner's table.

b) Students work in the same pairs and decide which places in the list are hot, warm, cold, wet and dry.

> hot: Bangkok, Paris
> warm: Athens, Buenos Aires, Chicago, Munich, Rome
> cold: Helsinki, Moscow, Stockholm
> wet: Athens, Stockholm
> dry: Buenos Aires, Bangkok, Chicago, Munich, Paris, Rome

c) Each pair decides on the best place to go today and reasons for choosing this place.

Ask students to share their ideas with the class.

Help with Vocabulary Word building

6 **a)–b)** Focus students on the table and check students understand the headings *noun*, *adjective* and *verb*. Elicit examples of these parts of speech if necessary.

Students complete the table on their own or in pairs, then check their answers in **V10.9** SB p143. Check answers with the class.

> • Check the table with the class (see the table in **V10.9** SB p143).
> • Highlight that we add *-y* to the noun to make the adjective.
> • Point out that *sun* ends in consonant + vowel + consonant, so we double the finally consonant to make the adjective *sunny*.
> • Point out that there is no verb for *wind*, *cloud* or *sun* (we don't say ~~It's winding.~~, ~~It's clouding.~~ or ~~It's sunning.~~). You can teach the verbs *blow* (for *wind*) and *shine* (for *sun*), and the phrase *The sun is shining*.

7 **a)** Students do the exercise on their own, then check in pairs. Check answers with the class.

> 2 sunny 3 snow 4 windy 5 cloudy 6 raining

b) Students do the exercise on their own, then compare sentences in pairs.

Finally, ask students to share their sentences with the class.

> ── EXTRA PRACTICE AND HOMEWORK ──
> **Ph** **Study Skills 5** Wordbuilding p206 (Instructions p201)
> **10 Review** SB p85
> **CD-ROM** Lesson 10D
> **Workbook** Lesson 10D p54
> **Workbook** Reading and Writing Portfolio 10 p82
> **Progress Test 10** p221

10 Review

See p32 for ideas on how to use this section.

1a) eat fried food; drink alcohol; get stressed; lose weight; stop smoking; get fit; go to the gym

4a)–b) overweight A; good-looking A; attractive A; funny C; selfish C; lazy C; reliable C; slim A; outgoing C; bald A; short A

5a) 2 What does he look like? 3 What does he like doing? 4 What's he like?

5b) a)3 b)4 c)1 d)2

6a) See **V10.5** SB p142, **V10.7** and **V10.8** SB p143.

Progress Portfolio

See p32 for ideas on how to use this section.

11 Future plans

11A New Year's resolutions

Vocabulary verb collocations
Grammar *be going to* (1): positive, negative
and *Wh-* questions
Review weather

QUICK REVIEW ●●●
This activity reviews the weather. Give students a few
moments to think of a country they know, but not their
own. Students do the activity in groups. Ask students to
share interesting information with the class.

Vocabulary Verb collocations

1 Ask students when *New Year* is, then teach *celebrate* and
New Year's resolution (a promise you make at New Year to
improve your life in some way). Drill these words/phrases
with the class.

Students discuss the questions in pairs.

Ask students to share interesting answers with the class.

2 Focus students on box A and establish that the phrases in
the box are typical New Year's resolutions.

Students work on their own and tick the phrases they
know in box A.

Focus students on box B. Students match the verbs in
bold in box A with the phrases in box B.

Students can check their answers in pairs, then in V11.1
SB p144.

Check answers with the class.

Check students understand the new phrases *eating sweet
things* (chocolate, cake, etc.), *have fun* (enjoy yourself) and
move house (go to live in a new house or flat).

Point out that we *move to another country* but we *move
house*, not ~~move to house~~ or ~~move my house~~.

Also highlight that we can *do a course* or *take a course* but
not ~~study a course~~. However, we can *study a subject*, for
example, English, history, computing, etc.

Model and drill the collocations with the class.

work harder; lose three kilos;
stop eating sweet things;
do a computer course;
have fun; move house

─── **EXTRA IDEA** ───
* With a strong class, put students into pairs or
groups and ask them to think of as many
collocations as they can with the verbs in bold
in **2**. While students are working, draw the
wordmaps from V11.1 SB p144 on the board.
Elicit students' ideas and write them on the board.
Give students time to copy the wordmaps into
their notebooks.

Listening and Grammar

3 Focus students on the picture and ask where the people
are (at a New Year's Eve party). Then focus students on
pictures A–E and tell them that these are the people's
New Year's resolutions.

R11.1 Play the recording (SB p156). Students listen and
match the people to their New Year's resolutions A–E.

Check answers with the class.

A Jack B Meg C David D Ed E Val

4 a) Students work on their own and fill in the gaps in
the sentences with words from **2**. Students can compare
answers in pairs.

b) R11.1 Play the recording again. Students listen and
check their answers.

Check answers with the class.

2 holiday 3 move 4 computer course 5 fit; smoking
6 lose 7 exercise 8 sweet things

─── **EXTRA IDEA** ───
* Ask students to turn to R11.1, SB p156. Play
the recording again. Students listen, read and
underline the New Year's resolutions when they
hear them.

Help with Grammar *be going to*: positive and negative

5 a)–c) Ask students to look at the sentences in **4a)**.
Students do the exercises on their own or in pairs, then
check their answers in G11.1 SB p145.

While they are working, draw the table from **5b)** on
the board so that you are ready to check their answers.

Check answers with the class.

* The sentences in **4a)** talk about the future.
* The people decided to do these things before they
said them.
* We use *be going to* + infinitive for future plans.

- Focus students on the table on the board. Elicit which words in questions 7 and 8 from **4a)** go in each column and complete the table (see the table in G11.1 SB p145).
- Highlight the word order in positive and negative sentences with *be going to*: subject + auxiliary (+ *not*) + *going to* + infinitive + … .
- Point out that the auxiliary *be* changes according to the subject: *I'm (not), you/we/they're* or *you/we/they aren't, he/she/it's* or *he/she/it isn't*.
- Also highlight that with the verb *go* we usually say *I'm going to Spain.* not *I'm going to go to Spain.* But both forms are correct.

6 R11.2 Point out the stress pattern and the pronunciation of *going to* /ɡəʊɪŋtə/ in the example.

P Play the recording (SB p156). Ask students to repeat. Check students copy the stress pattern and pronunciation of *going to* correctly.

You can also ask students to turn to R11.2, SB p156. They can then follow the sentence stress as they listen.

7 **a)** Students do the exercise on their own, then check in pairs. Check answers with the class.

> 2 isn't/'s not going to eat 3 's going to sell 4 're going (to go) 5 'm not going to buy 6 's going to study

b) Students do the exercise in pairs by referring back to the pictures and the sentences in **7a)**.
Check answers with the class.

> 1 Ed 2 David 3 Meg 4 David and Val 5 Val 6 Ed

8 **a)** Ask students what Jack's New Year's resolution was (to have a holiday). Focus students on email 1 and give students a few moments to read it.

Ask students who wrote it (Jack) and who he wrote it to (Meg). Also ask why he is sending her the photo (because he's going on holiday there).

b) Students read email 2 and find three questions with *be going to*.
Check answers with the class. Ask if Meg thinks the place in the photo is a good place to go on holiday (she doesn't).

> 1 But what are you going to do all day?
> 2 And where are you going to stay?
> 3 And what are you going to eat?!

c) Students read email 3 and find Jack's answers.
Check answers with the class.

> 1 I'm going to sit on the beach and read lots of books.
> 2 I'm going to stay in a small house by the beach.
> 3 Fish.

Help with Grammar *be going to: Wh-* questions

9 **a)–b)** Students complete the table on their own, then check answers in G11.2 SB p145.

 While students are working, draw the table from **9a)** on the board so that you are ready to check their answers. Check answers with the class.

- Focus students on the table on the board. Elicit which words in the other two questions from email 2 go in each column and complete the table (see the table in G11.2 SB p145).
- Highlight the word order of *Wh-* questions with *be going to*: question word + auxiliary + subject + *going to* + infinitive + … .

10 **a)** Students do the exercise on their own, then check in pairs. Check answers with the class.

> 2 How are you going to get home today? 3 What are you going to do next weekend? 4 What are you going to have for dinner tonight? 5 Where are you going to have lunch tomorrow? 6 When are you going to do your English homework?

b) R11.3 P Play the recording of the questions in **10a)** and ask students to repeat. Encourage them to copy the sentence stress and the weak forms of *are you* /əjə/ and *to* /tə/. Repeat the drill if necessary.

c) Teach *I'm not sure.*, *I've no idea.* and *I don't know.* as possible answers to *be going to* questions when you haven't made any plans.

Students then do the exercise in groups. While they are working, check their questions for accuracy and help with any problems.

Ask students to share interesting answers with the class.

Get ready … Get it right!

11 Give students a few moments to think of at least three plans they have already made for next week, next month and next year. Encourage them to use phrases in **2** or their own ideas.

While they are working, help students with any vocabulary they need.

12 **a)** Use the speech bubble to remind students of the type of question they need to ask. Drill the question if necessary, and also drill similar questions with *next month* and *next year*.

Put students into groups of four. Students take turns to ask and answer questions about their plans and find out if they are the same or different.

b) Finally, ask students to tell the class about people with the same plans as them.

— EXTRA IDEA —
- Students work on their own and make notes on the future plans of their family and friends. Put students into groups. Students take turns telling their partners about the future plans of their family and friends.

— EXTRA PRACTICE AND HOMEWORK —
Ph **Class Activity** 11A New Year's Day p176 (Instructions p134)
11 Review Exercises 1 and 2 SB p93
CD-ROM Lesson 11A
Workbook Lesson 11A p55

 ## 11B No more exams!

QUICK REVIEW ●●●
This activity reviews future plans with *be going to*. Give students a few moments to think of three things they are going to do tomorrow evening and three things they aren't going to do. Students do the activity in pairs. Ask each pair to share any plans they both have with the class.

Vocabulary studying
Grammar *might; be going to* (2): *yes/no* questions and short answers
Help with Listening *going to*
Review *be going to*: positive, negative and *Wh-* questions

Vocabulary Studying

1 Focus students on the vocabulary box and establish that all the words are connected with studying.

Students work on their own or in pairs and fill in the gaps in the diagram with the words/phrases in the box, then check their answers in **V11.2** SB p144.

Check answers with the class.

Tell students that *college* is any place you go when you are over 16 to get qualifications and training, for example, *teacher training college, art college*, etc.

Also point out that we can only *get a degree* when we finish university. We *get a qualification* when we pass any official exam (for example, when you leave school, finish a training course, etc.).

Model and drill the phrases. Pay particular attention to the pronunciation of *college* /'kɒlɪdʒ/ and *qualification* /ˌkwɒlɪfɪ'keɪʃən/.

> start; go to; leave school/college/university
> revise for; take; pass; fail an exam
> get a qualification; a degree; a job

2 Check students remember *celebrate*.

Students discuss the questions in groups.

Ask students to share interesting answers with the class.

Listening and Grammar

3 a) Focus students on the photos. Establish that Tim, Debbie, Sid and Clare have just finished their final university exams.

Note that in British universities, students generally study full-time for three or four years and have very important exams (called 'finals') at the end of the course. The results of these exams determine what class of degree they get.

R11.4 Focus students on the words in the box, then play the recording (SB p156). Students listen and tick the things that the people talk about.

Check answers with the class.

> a drink; a party; a club; a video; a film

b) Give students time to read sentences 1–6. Check students understand *sure*.

Play the recording again. Students listen and tick the true sentences. Students check answers in pairs.

Check answers with the class.

> 1F 2F 3T 4T 5F 6F

Help with Grammar *might* or *be going to*

4 a)–b) Focus students on the examples. Students choose the correct words on their own, then check answers in **G11.3** SB p145. Check answers with the class.

- We use *be going to* to say that a future plan is decided.
- We use *might* to say something in the future is possible, but not decided.
- After *might* we use the infinitive: *We might go and see a film*. not ~~We might to go and see a film~~.
- Point out that *might* is the same for all subjects (*I, you, he, they*, etc.).
- Also teach students that to make questions with *might* we usually use *Do you think … ?*: *Do you think he might come to the party?*. We can also say *Might he come to the party?*, but this question form is not very common.
- You can also point out that *might* is similar grammatically to *can*, as they are both modal auxiliary verbs.

EXTRA IDEA

- Ask students to turn to R11.4, SB p156. Play the recording again. Students listen, read and underline all the examples of *be going to* and *might*.

 Focus students on the example and highlight that *might* is always stressed.

R11.5 **P** Play the recording (SB p157). Ask students to repeat. Check students copy the sentence stress correctly.

You can also ask students to turn to R11.5, SB p157. They can then follow the sentence stress as they listen.

 Focus students on sentences 1–6. Tell students that sentences 1–3 are about Tim and that sentences 4–6 are about Debbie.

Check students understand that a tick (✓) means this is decided, and a tick and cross (✓✗) means that this thing is not decided.

Students do the exercise on their own, then check their answers in pairs.

Check answers with the class.

> **1** 'm not going to do **2** might go **3** 'm not going to work
> **4** might get **5** 'm going to do **6** might get

7 **a)** Students do the exercise on their own.

While they are working, check their sentences for accuracy and help with any problems.

b) Students work in pairs and take turns to say their sentences. Students should tick any sentences that are the same.

Ask students to share similar sentences or any other interesting ideas with the class.

EXTRA IDEA

- Students make two of their sentences false. Their partner has to guess which sentences are true and which are false.

Help with Listening *going to*

- This Help with Listening section helps students to understand two different ways native speakers say *going to* in everyday speech.

 a) **R11.6** Focus students on the examples and play the recording. Check students can hear the difference between the two ways we say *going to*. Point out that both are correct. Play the recording several times if necessary.

b) Give students time to read sentences 1–6 and check they understand which version of *going to* is above the two columns.

R11.7 Play the recording. Students listen and decide which pronunciation of *going to* they hear, a) or b).

Play the recording again, pausing after each sentence for students to check their answers.

You can also point out that in songs and very informal writing such as comics, *going to* is often written *gonna*. Do not encourage students to write this themselves, however.

> **2a)** **3a)** **4b)** **5b)** **6b)**

 Focus students on the photo again to remind students of Tim, Sid and Clare. Tell students that Tim is talking to Sid and Clare about their plans.

Give students time to read questions 1–5.

R11.8 Play the recording (SB p157). Students listen and answer the questions. Play the recording again if necessary. Check answers with the class.

> **1** No, they aren't.
> **2** No, they aren't.
> **3** Yes, he is.
> **4** No, he isn't.
> **5** Yes, he is.

Help with Grammar *be going to: yes/no questions and short answers*

10 **a)–b)** Students fill in the gaps with part of the verb *be*, referring to the questions in **9** if necessary. Students check their answers in **G11.4** SB p145.

Check answers with the class.

- **1** A Are B am; 'm **2** A Is B is; isn't or 's not
  3 A Are B are; aren't or 're not
- Point out that the short answers are the same as for *yes/no* questions with the verb *be* (*Are you from Italy?*) and the Present Continuous (*Is he watching TV now?*).
- Also tell students that we can use *might* in short answers to *yes/no* questions with *be going to*: *(Yes), I might.*

11 Put students into pairs, student A and student B. Student As turn to SB p107 and student Bs turn to SB p115. Check they are all looking at the correct exercise.

a) Focus students on the photos of the people and the table of their plans for next weekend.

Use the speech bubbles to highlight the *yes/no* question, the possible short answers and the meaning of the symbols in the table.

Students work in their pairs and take turns to ask and answer questions about the people. They fill in the gaps in the table after each answer they hear.

While students are working, check their questions and short answers for accuracy and help with any problems.

b) Check students remember *lazy, busy* and *active*.

Students do the exercise in their pairs. Check answers with the class.

> a lazy weekend: Debbie a busy weekend: Sid and Clare
> an active weekend: Tim

Get ready … Get it right!

12 Students work on their own and make *yes/no* questions for the prompts in the box.

Check answers with the class. Drill the questions if necessary.

13 a) Students move around the room and ask other students their questions, or ask students who are sitting near them.

Students should try to find one person who is going to do each thing. They should make a note of the students' name, then ask two follow-up questions (for example, *Where are you going to meet?* and *What are you going to do?* for the first prompt in the box).

While students are working, monitor and help with any problems. Encourage students to talk to as many people as possible and to move on when the student they are talking to has answered *yes* to one of their questions.

If necessary, demonstrate this activity to the whole class before they begin.

b) Ask each student to tell the class about another student's plans.

Finally, ask students to decide who has the most interesting plans.

EXTRA IDEA
- With a large class, ask students to work in pairs and take turns to tell their partner about other students' plans.

EXTRA PRACTICE AND HOMEWORK
11 Review Exercise 3 SB p93
CD-ROM Lesson 11B
Workbook Lesson 11B p56

11C Finding your way

QUICK REVIEW ●●●
This activity reviews places in a town/city. Students work on their own and write a list of places in a town/city. Set a time limit of three minutes. Put students into pairs to compare lists and discuss how many of the places are near where they are now. Find out which pair has the most words. Elicit the pair's words and write them on the board. Ask if other pairs have any different words and add them to the list. Ask students to tell you which of these places are near where you are now.

Real World asking for and giving directions
Vocabulary prepositions of place and movement
Review rooms in a house; places in a town; imperatives

Choosing a holiday home

1 a) Focus students on the photo of Sue Daniels and her family and elicit the family members (grandfather, father, mother, son and daughter).

Also focus students on the advert and elicit the name of the company (Craven Holiday Homes).

Establish that Sue wants to rent a holiday home for her family. Point out that a 'holiday home' is a house/flat you can rent and live in as though it was your own house during your holiday.

If necessary, pre-teach *fully equipped, dining area, large, separate (room)*.

Students read the adverts and decide which is the best holiday home for Sue's family and why.

b) Students do the exercise in groups. Encourage students to give reasons for their choices.

Ask students to share answers with the class.

Do not tell students which holiday home Sue chose at this stage.

2 Tell students that they are going to listen to Sue phone Craven Holiday Homes.

R11.9 Play the recording (SB p157). Students listen and answer the questions.

Check answers with the class.

> The family's holiday is from September 12th for two weeks.
> Sue chooses Benton House because Hill Place is not available in the second week.

EXTRA IDEA
- R11.9 Ask students to turn to R11.9, SB p157. Play the recording. Students listen again and check their answers.

Directions

3 Check students understand *directions* and *pub*.

Students work on their own and tick the phrases they know, then do the exercise in SB p145. They can then check answers in pairs.

Check answers with the class.

Highlight the different prepositions in the phrases and point out that we can say *it's on the left/right* or *it's on your left/right*.

Check students understand the difference between *opposite* (on the other side of the road) and *in front of* (on the same side of the road). Draw pictures to illustrate this difference if necessary.

Model and drill the phrases. Pay particular attention to the pronunciation of *bridge* /brɪdʒ/ and *opposite* /ˈɒpəzɪt/.

RW11.1 1d) 2i) 3a) 4g) 5c) 6f) 7b) 8h) 9e)

4 a) Focus students on the map of Seaton on SB p91 and check they understand the names of the places. Teach the new words *hospital*, *church*, *Internet café* and *car park*. Point out the *You are here* circle.

Focus students on the email and ask who it is from (Angela Craven from Craven Holiday Homes).

Students read the email and draw the route from *You are here* to the holiday home.

b) Students check their routes in pairs.

Check the route with the class (Benton House is number 14 on the map).

5 Focus students on the map and tell them that they are standing in the *You are here* circle. Establish that students are going to hear directions to four different places that are already marked on the map (not the places that are numbered 1–14).

R11.10 Play the recording (SB p157). Students listen and follow the directions on the map to find out where they take them to.

Play the recording again, pausing after each set of directions to check students' answers.

> 1 the bookshop
> 2 the restaurant
> 3 the hospital
> 4 the car park

6 a) Ask students to find the bus station on the map. Establish that Sue is now at the bus station (not at *You are here*) and is asking for directions.

Students work on their own and put each of the three conversations in order.

Students can check their answers in pairs.

b) R11.11 Play the recording. Students listen, check their answers and find the places on the map.

Check answers with the class.

> 1 3; 2; 5; 1; 4
> 2 3; 1; 4; 2
> 3 2; 5; 3; 4; 1
> newsagent's = 3, police station = 5, Park Hotel = 9

Real World Asking for and giving directions

7 a)–b) Students do **7a)** on their own by referring back to conversations 1–3 in **6a)**, then check their answers in RW11.2 SB p145.

Check answers with the class.

- Check students' answers with the sentences in RW11.2 SB p145.
- Tell students that we can say a place is *in Berry Street*, etc. or *on Berry Street*, etc.
- Establish that we say *It's over there.* when we can see and point to the place.
- Teach students the following expressions we use if we can't give directions: *Sorry, I don't know.* and *Sorry, I don't live around here.*

8 R11.12 P Play the recording. Ask students to repeat. Check students copy the stress pattern and polite intonation. Stress the importance of polite intonation when asking strangers for information.

— **EXTRA IDEA** —
- Ask students to practise the conversations in **6a)** in pairs before moving on to the pairwork practice in **9**.

9 Put students into pairs, student A and student B. Student As turn to SB p104 and student Bs turn to SB p112. Check they are all looking at the correct exercise.

a) Students work on their own and find the places on the map of Seaton on p91. Students should not show their partner where the places are.

b) Students work in their pairs. Tell students to hold their books so that they can't see each other's maps.

Students take turns to ask for directions to the places listed. Make sure students start from *You are here* each time.

When students have found a place, they should say the number to their partner to check they have found the correct place. Students are not allowed to check by looking at each other's maps.

While students are working, monitor and help with any problems.

Finally, ask students to compare maps and check they have found all the places.

11D The grass is always greener

QUICK REVIEW ●●●

This activity reviews ways to ask for and give directions. Students do the activity in pairs. Check students understand *Go out of the building and ...* before they start.

Vocabulary verb patterns
Review comparatives; things you like and don't like

1 Focus on the title of the lesson and establish that we say this when we aren't happy with what we have and think that something else would be better. It is short for 'the grass is always greener on the other side of the fence'. Ask students if they have a similar expression in their own language.

Check students understand *in the country* means in the countryside outside cities and towns (not England, Spain, Germany, etc.).

Students discuss the questions in groups.

Ask students to share interesting answers with the class.

2 Pre-teach *the cost of living* (the amount of money we need to live in a place) and point out that we don't say ~~the cost of life~~.

Students work in the same groups and discuss which sentences they agree with, giving reasons if possible.

Ask students to share interesting ideas with the class. Encourage students to give reasons for their answers. Find out how many students would prefer to live in the city or the country.

EXTRA IDEA

- Before students work in groups, write these expressions for agreeing and disagreeing on the board: *I think (that's true). Me too. I'm not sure. Oh, I don't. I don't think (that's true). Me neither. Oh, I do.* Encourage students to use them when discussing the sentences in **2**.

3 **a)** Focus students on the photos of Matthew Lane and his family, and Stuart Reed.

Students work on their own and decide which person, Matthew or Stuart, agrees with the sentences in **2**. Students check answers in pairs or groups.

b) Students read the article and check their answers.

Matthew agrees with sentences 1, 3 and 4. Stuart agrees with sentences 2, 5 and 6.

4 Pre-teach *teenager* and point out that the stress is on the first syllable, not the second. Students read the article again and answer questions 1–7. Students can check answers in pairs.

Check answers with the class.

1 To a beautiful village in the mountains. 2 Only one day a week (Sunday). 3 No, they don't. The children want to stay in the city. 4 Yes, he did. He found one in the first week. 5 No, he hasn't. 6 No, he doesn't. The city is really noisy at night. 7 He wants to live in a little place by the sea where it's really quiet.

Help with Vocabulary Verb patterns

5 **a)** Focus students on the examples. Elicit that *want* is followed by the infinitive with *to* and *love* is followed by verb+*ing*. Use these examples to establish that some verbs are often followed by a particular verb form.

b)–c) Students do the exercise on their own by referring back to the article, then check in **V11.3** SB p144. Check answers with the class.

- *want, need, would like* and *would love* are followed by the infinitive with *to*.
- *love, hate, enjoy* and *like* are followed by verb+*ing*.

- Highlight the difference between *would like/love*, which are followed by the infinitive with *to*, and *like/love*, which are followed by verb+*ing*.
- Point out that all these verbs can also be followed by a noun (*You don't need a car.*) or a pronoun (*He hates it.*).
- Tell students that we can also use the infinitive with *to* after *like*, *love* and *hate* (*Teenagers like to go out.*, etc.), and that this form is common in American English. In British English these verbs are usually followed by verb+*ing*.

6 a) Students do the exercise on their own, then check in pairs.

Check answers with the class.

> 2 reading 3 watching
> 4 to find 5 studying
> 6 going 7 to be

b) Focus students on the example and show how this is the question form of sentence 1 in **6a)**.

Students work on their own and make questions with *you* for the other sentences in **6a)**, then add two more questions of their own.

While students are working, check their questions for accuracy and help with any problems.

Check answers with the class.

Drill the questions, focusing on the weak forms of *do you* /dʒə/ and *would you* /wʊdʒə/.

> 2 Do you like reading newspapers? 3 Do you hate watching football on TV? 4 Do you want to find a new job? 5 Do you enjoy learning languages? 6 Do you love going to the cinema? 7 Would you like to be famous?

c) Students work in pairs and take turns to answer the questions. Encourage students to ask follow-up questions where possible.

Finally, ask students to share interesting answers with the class.

♪ Ask students to turn to SB p103 and look at *Chapel of Love*. This song was originally recorded by the American group The Dixie Cups in 1958 and has been covered by many other artists, including the Beach Boys and Elton John (who recorded it for the film *Four Weddings and Funeral*).

1 Students do the exercise in pairs or on their own.

Check answers with the class. Check students understand these new words/phrases: *chapel, lonely, the sky, the sun shines, bells ring*. Drill these words/phrases with the class.

> 2e) 3f) 4a) 5c) 6d)

2 a) R11.13 Give students time to read the song, then play the recording (SB p157). Students listen and match 1–8 to a)–h) to complete the verses. Play the recording again if necessary.

b) Students check answers in pairs. Play the recording again, pausing after each line for students to check answers.

> 1c) 2a) 3d) 4b) 5g) 6e) 7h) 8f)

3 Students discuss the questions in groups.

Ask students to share interesting answers with the whole class. Encourage students to give reasons for their answers.

EXTRA PRACTICE AND HOMEWORK

[Ph] **Class Activity** 11D Thought bubbles p179 (Instructions p135)
11 Review SB p93
CD-ROM Lesson 11D
Workbook Lesson 11D p59
Workbook Reading and Writing Portfolio 11 p84
Progress Test 11 p222

---

11 Review

See p32 for ideas on how to use this section.

1a) 2 get 3 move 4 have 5 work 6 stop 7 lose

2a) 2 Are you going to have a holiday next year? 3 Where are you going to be tomorrow afternoon? 4 What are you going to do after class? 5 Are you going to study English next year?

5a) 2 eating 3 taking 4 to live 5 driving 6 to get up 7 to be 8 studying

Progress Portfolio

See p32 for ideas on how to use this section.

12 Life experiences

12A World records

Vocabulary big and small numbers
Grammar superlatives
Review comparatives; Past Simple

QUICK REVIEW ●●●
This activity reviews verb patterns. Students work on their own and write something they love doing, want to do tomorrow, etc. Students then compare answers in pairs to find out how many of the things on their lists are the same. Ask students to share their answers with the class.

Vocabulary Big and small numbers

 1 Students do the exercise on their own or in pairs, then check their answers in **V12.1** SB p146.

Check answers with the class. Highlight these points.
- For 0 we usually say *nought* or *zero* (or *oh* in phone numbers).
- For numbers with a decimal point (.), we say *point* (*0·6 = nought point six*, etc.). Note that in English we use a decimal point, not a comma (,). We write 7.5 not 7̶,̶5̶.
- We can use *one* or *a* with *hundred*, *thousand* or *million* (*a hundred = one hundred*). Using *a* is more common.
- For long numbers we use *and* after *hundred*, but not after *thousand* or *million*. We say *a hundred and fifty six*, but *two thousand, three hundred*, not t̶w̶o̶ ̶t̶h̶o̶u̶s̶a̶n̶d̶ ̶a̶n̶d̶ t̶h̶r̶e̶e̶ ̶h̶u̶n̶d̶r̶e̶d̶, etc.
- We don't add a plural -s to *hundred*, *thousand* or *million*. We say *seven hundred*, not s̶e̶v̶e̶n̶ ̶h̶u̶n̶d̶r̶e̶d̶s̶, etc.

Model and drill the numbers with the class, focusing on natural rhythm and stress. Pay particular attention to the pronunciation of *nought* /nɔːt/ and *thousand* /'θaʊzənd/.

> 2 3.25 3 156 4 2,300 5 45,270 6 650,000 7 1,000,000
> 8 70,000,000

 2 **R12.1** Play the recording (SB p157). Students listen and write down the numbers they hear. Play the recording again if necessary.

Students compare numbers in pairs.

Play the recording again, pausing after each number to check answers with the class. You can ask individual students to come to the board and write each answer.

> 1 16,000,000 2 4.23 3 500,000 4 7,650 5 390 6 0.1
> 7 172 8 98,500

— EXTRA IDEAS —
- Students work on their own and write eight big and small numbers. Students work in pairs and take turns to dictate their numbers to their partner. When they have finished, students check that their partners have written the numbers correctly.
- Play Bingo! (see p21).

Reading and Grammar

 3 Focus students on the article and teach *Record breakers*. Also teach the phrases *world record* and *break a record*.

You can ask the students if they know of anyone who holds a world record (for example, athletes, etc.).

Pre-teach *engagement, get engaged, average, a cure for insomnia*.

Students read the article and match the word records to the pictures. Set a time limit of two or three minutes to encourage students to skim the article for the main points in each paragraph.

Check answers with the class.

> 1C 2B 3D 4E 5A

 4 **a)** Students read the article again and fill in the gaps with the prices and numbers in the vocabulary box. Students can check their answers in pairs.

b) **R12.2** Play the recording. Students listen and check their answers.

> a) 82 b) 335 c) 11.68 d) 0.01 e) $120,000 f) 85
> g) £44,007 h) £12,300

c) Ask students which record they think is the most interesting and surprising. Encourage students to give reasons for their answers.

Help with Grammar Superlatives

5 **a)–d)** Focus students on the table in **5a)** and check students remember the comparatives in the second column. Highlight the examples of superlatives in the third column.

Students then do the exercises on their own or in pairs, then check their answers in **G12.1** SB p146.

Check answers with the class.

- The missing superlatives in the third column of the table are: *wettest, earliest, most boring, most expensive, best*.
- We use superlatives to compare three or more things.
- We use comparatives to compare two things.

- Use the table in **G12.1** SB p146 to check students understand the spelling rules for making superlatives. Point out that the rules are similar to those for making comparatives in **G8.2** SB p139.
- Point out that we often use *the* with superlatives: *The best bottle of wine cost £12,300.* However, we don't use *the* when the superlative is preceded by the possessive *'s* or a possessive adjective. We say *He's my sister's oldest relative.* not *He's my sister's the oldest relative.* and *Mat's my best friend.* Not *Mat's my the best friend*.
- Also point out that we say *the best in the world*, not *the best of the world*.

6 **a)** Students do the exercise on their own, then check in pairs. Check answers with the class.

2 most difficult
3 thinnest
4 happiest
5 hottest
6 most modern
7 safest
8 most crowded
9 friendliest
10 most beautiful
11 worst
12 best

─ EXTRA IDEA ─

- ✐ Write these adjectives on the board: *crowded, beautiful, safe, dangerous, good, bad, old, boring, interesting, expensive, cheap*. Students work on their own and write the place in their town, city or country that corresponds to the superlative of each adjective on the board. They should not write the places in the same order as the adjectives. Students work in pairs and either guess why their partner has written the things on his/her paper (if they are from the same country/city), or tell their partner about the places they have written (if they are from different countries/cities).

b) Focus students on the example and highlight that *-est* endings are pronounced /ɪst/.

R12.3 **P** Play the recording and ask students to repeat. Check students copy the word stress and the *-est* endings correctly.

7 **a)** Focus students on the quiz. Pre-teach *population, score a goal* and *the Equator*.

Put students into teams of three or four. Students read the quiz, put the adjective in the correct superlative form, then choose an answer for each question. If students don't know the answers, encourage them to guess.

1 largest
2 oldest
3 most crowded
4 biggest
5 most expensive
6 youngest
7 most common
8 nearest

b) Students check their answers on SB p158 and work out how many points they got.

Note that students get one point for each correct superlative and two points for each correct answer.

If necessary, check answers with the class and find out which team got the most points.

Ask students which of the answers they found surprising.

Get ready … Get it right!

8 Students work on their own and write six of these things on a piece of paper.

Make sure students only write one or two words for each point, not complete sentences, and that they write them in random order (*Eva, cinema, car, jumper, 4.30*, etc.). Point out that students should write only one thing for each prompt, not two.

✐ You can demonstrate this activity by writing your ideas on the board before they begin.

9 **a)** Students work in pairs and swap papers. Students take turns to ask questions about their partner's words. Encourage students to ask follow-up questions if possible.

Use the speech bubbles to show a typical conversation before they start. Alternatively, tell students to ask you about the words you have written on the board.

While students are working, monitor and help with any problems.

b) Finally, students share one or two things about their partner with the class.

─ EXTRA IDEA ─

- Students write a paragraph about their family, using at least six superlatives.

─ EXTRA PRACTICE AND HOMEWORK ─

Ph **Class Activity** 12A Four restaurants p180 (Instructions p135)
12 Review Exercise 1 SB p100
CD-ROM Lesson 12A
Workbook Lesson 12A p60

Vocabulary past participles
Grammar Present Perfect for life experiences:
positive and negative, *Have you ever ... ?* questions
and short answers
Review Past Simple

Listening, Reading and Grammar

1 Pre-teach *self-employed*. Students then discuss the
questions in groups.
Ask students to share interesting answers with the class.

2 a) Focus students on the photos and the captions. Check
students understand the people's jobs (travel writer and
restaurant owners) and *Prime Minister*.

R12.4 Play the recording. Students listen, read and find
out if the people like being self-employed.
Check the answer with the class (Yes, they do.).

b) Students do the exercise on their own, then check
their answers in pairs.
Check answers with the class.

> 1T 2F He went last month. 3T 4F Three years ago
> Guy was a teacher and Lucy worked in an office.
> 5F He came to their restaurant last year. 6T

— **EXTRA IDEA** —
- After **2b)**, students close their books. Ask students
  to work in pairs to tell each other everything they
  can remember about the three people.

Help with Grammar Present Perfect: positive and negative

3 a)–d) Focus students on sentences 1 and 2. Point out
that the verb in sentence 1 is in the Present Perfect
(*'ve been*) and the verb in sentence 2 is in the Past
Simple (*went*).
Students do the exercises in pairs, then check in **G12.2**
SB p147. Check answers with the class.

- **a)** a) In sentence 1, we don't know when Steve
  went to these countries. b) In sentence 2, we
  know when he went to Mexico (two weeks ago).
- **b)** We use the Present Perfect to talk about
  experiences in life until now. We don't say when
  they happened.
- We use the Past Simple if we say when something
  happened.

- Point out that we can't use the Present Perfect if
  we say a time. We say *I went to England in 2003*,
  not *I've been to England in 2003*.
- **c)** The other examples of the Present Perfect in
  the texts are as follows. Steve: *I've stayed; I've
  written, I've never been*. Guy and Lucy: *We've had;
  We've met; Guy and I have never had; Guy hasn't been*.
- Check the table with the class (see the tables
  in **G12.2** SB p147) and point out the new
  grammatical term *past participle*.
- Point out that we often make negative Present
  Perfect sentences with *never*: *I've never been to
  Australia*.
- Highlight that we make past participles for regular
  verbs by adding *-ed* or *-d* to the infinitive (*work* →
  worked, live → *lived*, etc.). The past participle for
  regular verbs is the same as the Past Simple.
- There are no rules for irregular verbs. Remind
  students of the Irregular Verb List, SB p159.
- Point out that *go* has two past participles, *been*
  and *gone*. We usually use *been* to talk about life
  experiences: *I've been to Italy*. (I'm back in my
  country now), and *gone* when the person is still
  in the place: *She's gone to Italy*. (She's in Italy now).

4 a) Students do the exercise on their own, then check in
pairs. Check answers with the class. Make sure they have
spelt the words correctly.
Point out that *been* could be the past participle of *be* or *go*.
When *been* is the past participle of *go*, it is often followed
by the preposition *to*: *I've been **to** Germany*. Compare this
with *I've been married twice*.

> 2 stayed 3 been 4 had 5 worked 6 lost 7 met
> 8 studied 9 seen 10 been or gone

— **EXTRA IDEA** —
- Ask students to write the Past Simple of the verbs
  in **4a)** as well (for example, *write, wrote, written*) in
  preparation for the drill in **4b)**.

b) **R12.5** **P** Play the recording of all three parts of the
verbs in **4a)**. Students listen and repeat. Repeat the drill
if necessary. Check students say *worked* /wɜːkt/ as one
syllable, not two.

- Students work in pairs and take turns to test each other on the verbs. One student says the infinitive and his/her partner says the Past Simple and past participle.

5 **a)** Focus students on the examples to show that the sentences can be positive or negative. Remind students that we can say *I haven't been to the UK* or *I've never been to the UK.*

Students choose six of the prompts and write sentences on their own. While they are working, check their sentences for accuracy and help with any problems.

b) Students work in groups and tell each other their sentences. Students should tick any of their sentences that are the same as other students' sentences.

Ask students to share these sentences with the class.

- Students write six sentences about their life. Three should be true and three should be false. Students work in pairs, swap sentences and guess which of their partner's sentences are false.

- Students write three sentences about their experiences on a piece of paper. Collect all the students' papers. Read out all three sentences on each paper and invite the class to guess which student wrote them. Continue until you have read out all the sentences.

6 **a)** Focus students on the photos again and ask them what they know about the people.

Tell students that they are going to listen to Steve and Lucy talking to each other.

R12.6 Play the recording (SB p157). Students listen and answer the two questions.

Check answers with the class.

> Steve and Lucy are in Guy and Lucy's restaurant. They talk about places they would like to go on holiday.

b) Give students time to read sentences 1–6.

Play the recording again. Students listen and decide if the sentences are true or false.

Check answers with the class. Encourage students to explain why sentences 2 and 5 are false.

> 1T 2F He went there four or five years ago. 3T 4T
> 5F She travelled around in an old car. 6T

- Ask students to turn to R12.6, SB p157. Play the recording again. Students listen, read and underline all the examples of the Present Perfect. This activity would be useful to prepare students for the Help with Grammar section that follows.

Help with Grammar Present Perfect: *Have you ever … ?* questions and short answers

7 **a)–c)** Students do the exercises on their own or in pairs, referring to R12.6, SB p157 if necessary. Students then check their answers in **G12.3** SB p147.

Check answers with the class.

- *Have you ever been to Australia? Yes, I have.; Did you have a good time? Yes, I did.*
- We use the Present Perfect to ask about people's experiences. If the answer is *yes*, we use the Past Simple to ask for (or give) more information.
- Point out that we often use *ever* in questions with the Present Perfect. It means 'any time in your life until now'. It is often useful for students to learn *Have you ever …* as a 'chunk' of language.
- Note that this lesson only introduces and practises Present Perfect questions with *you*, as these are the most common. The form of Present Perfect questions with other subjects (*He, they,* etc.) is shown in the Language Summary.

8 Focus students on the examples and point out that *have* is not stressed in questions, but is stressed in short answers.

R12.7 **P** Play the recording (SB p157) and ask students to repeat. Check students copy the stress pattern correctly.

You can also ask students to turn to R12.7, SB p157. They can then follow the sentence stress as they listen.

9 **a)** Check students remember *diary* and *teenager*.

Students do the exercise on their own, then check in pairs.

b) **R12.8** Play the recording. Students listen and check their answers.

Check answers with the class.

> 1 Have … been 2 have 3 went 4 did … stay
> 5 rented 6 Have … written 7 have 8 wrote
> 9 Did … write 10 didn't 11 was

Get ready … Get it right!

10 Put students into two groups, group A and group B. Students in group A turn to SB p111 and students in group B turn to SB p119. Check they are all looking at the correct exercise.

a) Focus students on the examples and highlight that the first question is in the Present Perfect and the follow-up question is in the Past Simple.

Students work in pairs with someone from the same group and write the questions for prompts 2–5.

While students are working, check their questions for accuracy and help with any problems.

b) Put one student from group A with a student from group B. Students take turns to ask and answer their *Have you ever … ?* questions.

If the answer is *yes*, they should ask the follow-up question in the Past Simple. Encourage students to ask two more follow-up questions if possible and to make brief notes on their partner's answers.

c) Students work again with their partner from the same group who they worked with in **a)**.

Students tell their partner about the life experiences of the person they talked to in **b)**.

Again monitor and help with any problems.

Finally, ask students to share any interesting experiences with the class.

---- EXTRA IDEA ----

- Students write a paragraph about their experiences, using both the Present Perfect and the Past Simple. You can put the paragraphs around the room for other students to read.

---- EXTRA PRACTICE AND HOMEWORK ----

Ph **Vocabulary Plus** 12 Past participles p198 (Instructions p186)

Ph **Class Activity** 12B Life experiences p181 (Instructions p136)

12 Review Exercises 2 and 3 SB p100

CD-ROM Lesson 12B

Workbook Lesson 12B p61

12C Have a good trip!

QUICK REVIEW ●●●
This activity reviews *Have you ever … ?* questions and short answers. Focus students on the prompts. Elicit some more past participles they could use. Students then do the activity in pairs to find three things they have both done. Ask students to share interesting ideas with the class.

Real World at the airport; saying goodbye
Vocabulary things and places at an airport
Help with Listening questions on the phone
Review prices; times; requests

Buying a plane ticket

1 Students discuss the questions in pairs or groups.

Ask students to share interesting answers with the class. When students are sharing their answers to question 3, elicit *on the Internet, on the phone, at a travel agent's* and highlight the prepositions in these phrases.

2 a) Focus students on the two adverts and ask students what the companies sell (flights and holidays).

Pre-teach *a (return) flight, car hire* and *city break* (a short holiday in a famous city). If you think your students won't know the places in the adverts, check them with the class.

Students answer questions 1–8 on their own. Set a time limit of three minutes to encourage students to scan for specific information.

Students can check answers in pairs. Check answers with the class.

> 1 Call-a-Flight 2 Istanbul 3 seven 4 £199 5 Lisbon
> 6 the round the world ticket 7 Yes, it does. 8 Yes, they do. Call-a-Flight is cheaper.

b) Give students a minute or two to choose a flight or holiday for £500 or less. Students can discuss their ideas in pairs or groups, giving reasons for their choices.

Ask students to share their ideas with the class. Find out which is the most popular destination.

Help with Listening Questions on the phone

- This Help with Listening helps students to recognise typical questions they will be asked if they want to buy a flight by phone.

3 a) Establish that a man named Joe Hunter wants to buy a ticket to Boston, in the USA. He phones one of the travel companies in the adverts.

Students work on their own and match the travel agent's questions a)–g) to the things she asks about 1–7.

Students compare answers in pairs. Check answers with the class.

> b)4 c)2 d)7 e)1 f)3 g)5

b) **R12.9** Play the recording. Students listen and put questions a)–g) in the order they hear them.

Play the recording again, pausing after each question to check students' answers.

> 1b) 2c) 3f) 4a) 5g) 6d) 7e)

4 Focus students on Joe's notepad. Check students know Heathrow is an airport near London.

Tell students that they are going to hear the whole phone conversation between Joe and the travel agent.

R12.10 Play the recording (SB p157). Students listen and fill in the gaps 1–7 in Joe's notes. Play the recording again if necessary.

Check answers with the class.

> **1** 24th **2** 13.20 **3** 18.45 **4** 11th **5** 5.15 **6** 8.20 **7** 259

EXTRA IDEAS

- Ask students to turn to R12.10, SB p157. Play the recording again. Students listen, read and underline all the travel agent's questions.
- Students work in pairs and role-play the conversation between Joe and the travel agent. Students can use the questions in **3a)** and Joe's notes on his notepad as prompts. Alternatively, use authentic adverts from travel companies or the Internet as the basis for the role-plays.

At the airport

5 Students work in pairs and tick the words/phrases they know, then do the exercise in **V12.2** SB p146.

Check answers with the class.

Establish that *hand luggage* is the bag that you take on the plane, and point out that *luggage* is uncountable and takes a singular verb. Teach students that they can use the word *luggage* on its own to refer to all their bags (*I've got a lot of luggage.*).

You can also teach *rucksack* /ˈrʌksæk/ (US: *backpack*) and revise *suitcase*.

Check the meaning of *sharp* and ask students what kind of things are *sharp items* (penknives, scissors, etc.).

You can ask what other places have *aisles* (cinemas, theatres, supermarkets, etc.).

Model and drill the words/phrases. Pay particular attention to the pronunciation of *boarding* /ˈbɔːrdɪŋ/, *luggage* /ˈlʌɡɪdʒ/, *flight* /flaɪt/ and *aisle* /aɪl/.

> **V12.2** 1b) 2c) 3g) 4d) 5f) 6a) 7j) 8h) 9i) 10e)
> 11m) 12l) 13k)

EXTRA IDEA

- Introduce the vocabulary through a Know, Might Know, Don't Know activity (see p21).

---

6 **a)** Focus students on the photo and ask where Joe is now (at the check-in desk).

Students work in pairs and look at the woman's sentences in the conversation. Students work out what the woman says to Joe from the pictures.

Note that students should not try to fill in Joe's part of the conversation at this stage.

Students will check their answers to this exercise in **6c)**.

b) Pre-teach *on time* (= at the time planned). Students do the exercise in their pairs.

c) **R12.11** Play the recording (SB p158). Students listen and check their answers to **6a)** and **6b)**.

Play the recording again, pausing after each sentence to check student's answers. Point out to students that this language is in **RW12.1** SB p147.

> For answers see R12.11, SB p158.

7 **a)** Students work in the same pairs and practise the conversation in **6a)**, taking turns to be Joe.

b) Put the students in new pairs if possible. Students practise the conversation with their new partner. When a student is Joe, he/she should close his/her book and role-play the conversation from memory.

Real World Saying goodbye

8 **a)–b)** Students do **8a)** on their own or in pairs, then check their answers in **RW12.2** SB p147. Check answers with the class.

- Check the table with the class (see the table in **RW12.2** SB p147).
- Teach students that *a trip* is when you travel to a place and come back again. You can compare this to *a journey*, which is in one direction only.
- Also check students understand that *in two weeks* refers to the future.

9 **R12.12** **P** Play the recording and ask students to repeat. Check students copy the stress and intonation correctly. Repeat the drill if necessary.

10 **a)** Tell students that Joe is now saying goodbye to his friends before getting on his flight to Boston.

R12.13 Focus students on the table in **8a)**, then play the recording (SB p158). Students listen and tick the sentences they hear. Play the recording again if necessary. Check answers with the class.

> Have a good trip.; Thanks, I will.; Have a nice holiday.; See you in two weeks.; Yes, see you.; Send me a postcard.

b) Tell students to imagine they are at an airport. Students move around the room and say goodbye to other students in the class, or talk to people sitting near them. Encourage students to use phrases from **8a)** in their conversations.

Finally, you can ask a few students to role-play similar conversations for the class.

EXTRA PRACTICE AND HOMEWORK

12 Review SB p100
CD-ROM Lesson 12C
Workbook Lesson 12C p63
Workbook Reading and Writing Portfolio 12 p86
Progress Test 12 p223–p224

---

12 Review

See p32 for ideas on how to use this section.

1a) 2 the youngest 3 the nearest 4 the most interesting
5 the happiest 6 the biggest 7 the best

2a) 3 haven't been 4 went 5 stayed in 6 've never worked
7 've been

4 2 aisle 3 arrive 4 passenger 5 bags 6 luggage 7 book
8 window 9 boarding 10 gate 11 sharp 12 check-in
13 pack. The message is: Have a good trip!

Progress Portfolio

See p32 for ideas on how to use this section.

End of Course Review

- The aim of this activity is to review language that students have learned throughout the course in a fun, student-centred way. The activity takes about 30–45 minutes.

Pre-teach *a counter, throw a dice, land on a square, move forward/back* and *have a rest*.

Give students time to read the rules on SB p100 and answer any questions they may have.

Check students have understood that when a student lands on a Grammar or Vocabulary square, they only need to answer question 1.

Ask what happens when a second student lands on the same square (they answer question 2).

Also check what happens when a third students lands on the square (they can stay there without answering a question).

Put students into groups of four and give a dice and counters to each group (or students can make their own counters).

Ask a student with a watch in each group to be the time-keeper for the group. He/She should time students when they land on a Keep Talking square and have to talk about a topic for 20 seconds.

Students take turns to throw the dice and move around the board.

If a student thinks another student's answer to a question on a Grammar or Vocabulary square is wrong, they can check in the Language Summaries in the Student's Book, or ask you to adjudicate.

While students are working, monitor and help with any problems.

The first student to get to *FINISH* is the winner. Students can continue playing until three students have finished if you wish.

If one group finishes early, ask them to look at all squares they didn't land on and answer the questions.

1 1 some cheese; a book; some money; some toast
2 some water; some rice; a sandwich; an apple

8 1 became; found; chose; met 2 left; took; wrote; put

11 1 Where was her mother born? 2 Where does Tom's sister live?

12 1 two hundred and thirty nine; four thousand, five hundred; nought point three; seven hundred and fifty thousand dollars 2 two hundred and fifty thousand pounds; three point four; seven hundred and sixty; twenty two thousand, six hundred and fifty

14 1 I usually get up at about nine. 2 We bought our house a year ago.

15 1 Spanish; Chinese; American; Polish
2 French; Turkish; Italian; Brazilian

17 1 fall; win; lose 2 break; forget; tell

18 1 sometimes: Present Simple; at the moment, now: Present Continuous 2 never, often: Present Simple; today: Present Continuous

19 1 What did you do last weekend?
2 Who are you going to meet tonight?

22 1 more boring; better; longer; easier
2 more expensive; worse; happier; wetter

26 1 beautifully; fast; badly 2 happily; hard; well

29 1 expensive; friendly; slow; dirty
2 interesting; rich; unhappy/sad/depressed; quiet

31 1 I'm not going to meet my sister tonight.
2 We might go to the theatre next weekend.

34 1 most beautiful; shortest; worst; dirtiest
2 best; fastest; friendliest; most modern

38 1 We didn't go on holiday last year.
2 They haven't got a car.

Photocopiable Materials

Class Activities

Instructions

There are 35 Class Activities worksheets (p137–p181). These worksheets give extra communicative speaking practice of the key language taught in the Student's Book. Each activity matches a lesson in the Student's Book, for example, *1A At the conference* matches lesson 1A and *1C At the car hire office* matches lesson 1C, etc. There are three activities for each unit in units 1–11 and two activities for unit 12.

The Class Activities can be used as extra practice when you have finished the relevant lesson or as review activities in the next class or later in the course.

Many of the activities involve students working in pairs or groups. When you have an odd number of students, you can:

- ask two weaker students to share a role card or set of information.
- give two role cards or two sets of information to a stronger student.
- vary the size of the groups.

1A At the conference p137

Language

be: positive and *Wh*- questions; countries

Activity type, when to use and time

Information gap. Use any time after lesson 1A. 10–20 minutes.

Preparation

Photocopy one worksheet for each pair of students. Cut into two separate worksheets.

Procedure

- Put students into pairs. Give a copy of the student A worksheet to one student in each pair and a copy of the student B worksheet to his/her partner. Students are not allowed to look at each other's worksheets. Ask students where the people are (at the conference) and remind them of the conference setting from lesson 1A in the Student's Book if necessary.

- Students take it in turns to say a letter A–F and then ask questions to fill in the gaps on their worksheet. For example, student A says *Letter A. Where's she from?*. When student B gives the answer, student A writes it on his/her worksheet. If necessary, remind students of the questions: *What's his/her first name/surname? Where's he/she from? Where are they from? What are their first names/ surnames?* and *How do you spell that?* before they start.

- When students have finished, they compare answers and check spelling.

1B Short answer dominoes p138

Language

be: yes/no questions and short answers

Activity type, when to use and time

Dominoes. Use any time after lesson 1B. 15–20 minutes.

Preparation

Photocopy one set of dominoes for each pair of students. Cut into sets and shuffle each set.

Procedure

- Put students into pairs. Give one set of dominoes to each pair. Students share out the dominoes equally. Students are not allowed to look at each other's dominoes.

- One student puts a domino on the table. His/Her partner puts another domino at either end of the first domino so that the question and short answer match. Students continue taking turns to put dominoes at either end of the domino chain.

- If a student thinks that the question and answer don't match, he/she can challenge his/her partner. If the short answer is incorrect, the student must take back the domino and the turn passes to his/her partner. If students can't agree, they should ask you to adjudicate.

- When a student can't put down a domino, the turn automatically passes to his/her partner. The game continues until one student has put down all his/her dominoes, or until neither student can make a correct match. The student who finishes first, or who has the fewer dominoes remaining, is the winner.

- As a follow-up activity, students can place the dominoes face-down in a pile in the centre of the table. They take turns to turn over a domino and read out the question. The other student responds with an appropriate *yes/no* short answer.

1C At the car hire office p139

Language

asking for and giving personal details

Activity type, when to use and time

Information gap. Procedure A: use any time after lesson 1C. Procedure B: use any time after lesson 1C exercise 10a). 15–25 minutes.

Preparation

Procedure A: photocopy one worksheet for each pair of students. Cut into two separate worksheets.

Procedure B: photocopy one worksheet for every two pairs of students. Cut up the completed forms. Discard the blank forms.

Procedure A

This procedure provides practice of personal details questions with *his* and *her*.

- ✏️ Draw a blank car hire form on the board. Elicit these *he/she* questions for the prompts on the form: *What's his/her surname?*, *What's his/her first name?*, *What's his/her nationality?*, *What's his/her address?*, *What's his/her home phone number?*, *What's his/her mobile phone number?*, *What's his/her email address?*. Drill these questions with the class if necessary.

- Put students into pairs. Give a copy of the student A worksheet to one student in each pair and a copy of the student B worksheet to his/her partner. Students are not allowed to look at each other's worksheets.

- Students take turns to ask their partner questions and fill in the information on their worksheets. Tell students to start each conversation by saying the customer reference number at the top of the form. They should also look at the *Mr* and *Mrs* tick boxes on each card to decide if they should use *his* or *her* in their questions. For example, student A starts by saying *Number 239. What's her name?*.

- Before students start, remind them of the questions: *How do you spell that?*, *Could you say that again, please?*, *I'm sorry?* and *Sorry, could you repeat that, please?*.

- When students have finished, they compare answers and check spelling.

Procedure B

This procedure is suitable for classes where the students know each other well, or classes where you feel it is inappropriate for students to reveal their personal details to each other.

- After students have done exercise 10a) on SB p11, put students into pairs and give one completed car hire form to each student. Tell students that this is their new identity. Note that there are two different forms for women (Raquel and Kumiko) and two forms for men (Jacques and Salvatore). Students are not allowed to look at each other's forms.

- Students take turns to ask questions with *you* and complete the form on SB p11. Students should answer using the information on the form you gave them. Before students start, remind them of the questions: *How do you spell that? Could you say that again, please?, I'm sorry?* and *Sorry, could you repeat that, please?*.

- When students have finished, they compare answers and check spelling.

2A Harry and Harriet p140

Language

have got; personal possessions

Activity type, when to use and time

Information gap. Use any time after lesson 2A. 15–20 minutes.

Preparation

Photocopy one worksheet for each pair of students. Cut into two separate worksheets.

Procedure

- Put students into pairs. Give a copy of the student A worksheet to one student in each pair and a copy of the student B worksheet to his/her partner. Students are not allowed to look at each other's worksheets.

- Tell students that Harry and Harriet are twins and that they have different possessions. Students must find <u>eight</u> things that the person in his/her picture has got that the other person hasn't got. With a low-level class you can revise the vocabulary in the activity with the whole class before handing out the worksheets.

- Students take turns to ask and answer questions with *has got*. For example, student A asks *Has Harriet got a bike?* and student B answers *No, she hasn't*. Before students start, remind them to use *any* for plural questions, for example, *Has he/she got any CDs?*. Students can check any vocabulary they can't remember in V1.6 SB p122 or V2.3 SB p124.

- When students have found all the different possessions, check answers with the whole class. Students can take it in turns to say one of the differences they found, for example, *Harry's got a bike but Harriet hasn't*.

- When students have finished, ask them to find five possessions that both Harry and Harriet have got. If students finish early, ask them to check the differences by looking at each other's pictures and then memorise the differences ready to tell the class.

> **Harry's got:** a personal stereo; a wallet; a suitcase; a DVD player; DVDs; a digital camera; a bike; a dog
> **Harriet's got:** a diary; books; a watch; a video recorder; videos; a radio; a bag; a coat
> **They've both got:** a TV; a computer; a CD player; CDs; a mobile phone

2C Time and money p141

Language

times and prices

Activity type, when to use and time

Hear/Say activity. Use any time after lesson 2C. 10–15 minutes.

Preparation

Photocopy one worksheet for every three students. Cut into three separate worksheets.

Procedure

- Check students can pronounce these currencies correctly: *dollars, cents* /sents/, *euros* /ˈjʊərəʊz/, *pounds* and *p* /piː/, for example, *40p*.

- Put the students into groups of three. Give a copy of the student A worksheet to one student in each group, a copy of the student B worksheet to the second student and a copy of the student C worksheet to the third student. If you have one or two extra students, put two students together to share one worksheet.

- Explain that students listen to the times and prices other students say. If the time or price is in their *Hear* column, students then say the time or price next to it in their *Say* column.

- Student A in each group starts by saying *ten o'clock*. The activity continues until the students reach *Finish*. Students can tick the prices and times on their worksheets when they hear or say them.

- If necessary, demonstrate the activity with the whole class before students work in their groups.

2D Where is it? p142

Language

prepositions of place

Activity type, when to use and time

Information gap. Use any time after lesson 2D. 15–20 minutes.

Preparation

Photocopy one worksheet for each pair of students. Cut into two separate worksheets.

Procedure

- Put students into pairs. Give a copy of the student A worksheet to one student in each pair and a copy of the student B worksheet to his/her partner. Students are not allowed to look at each other's worksheets. Tell students that they both have pictures of the same room, but they can't find the six things in the small pictures and have to ask their partners where they are.

- Students take turns to ask their partners where the things in the small pictures are, using questions with *Where's … ?* or *Where are … ?*. For example, student A asks *Where's the coat?* and student B answers *It's on the chair by the desk*. When students are told the location of an item, they should draw the items on the picture.

- If necessary, demonstrate the activity with a strong student before students begin.

- When students have finished, they can compare pictures and check they have drawn the missing items in the correct places.

- If students finish early, ask them to work with their partner and describe where all the things are in the picture.

3A World routines p143

Language

daily routines; Present Simple: positive and *Wh-* questions

Activity type, when to use and time

Information gap. Use any time after lesson 3A. 15–25 minutes.

Preparation

Photocopy one worksheet for each pair of students. Cut into two separate worksheets.

Procedure

- Pre-teach *hospital* and *office*.

- Put students into pairs. Give a copy of the student A worksheet to one student in each pair and a copy of the student B worksheet to his/her partner. Students are not allowed to look at each other's worksheets.

- Ask students where the three married couples on the worksheets are from and where they work (in a shop, in a hospital, in an office). Tell students that the husband and wife in each couple work together and have the same daily routine.

- Students take it in turns to ask questions to complete their worksheet. For example, student A asks *What time do Alfonso and Barbara get up?* and student B answers *At 8 o'clock*. With a low-level class, check students can make questions for the prompts at the top of their worksheets before they start.

- When students have finished, they compare answers with their partner.

3B Time phrase snap p144

Language

time phrases with *on, in, at, every*

Activity type, when to use and time

'Snap' card game. Use any time after lesson 3B. 10–20 minutes.

Preparation

Photocopy one worksheet for each pair of students. Cut into two separate sets and shuffle each set.

Procedure

- Put students into pairs. Give a student A set to one student in each pair and a student B set to his/her partner. It is helpful if student A sits on the left of student B. Students need a pen and paper to keep score.

- Both students put down a card on the table in front of them at the same time. If the cards match, the first student to say *Snap!* gets a point. (Note: students do not pick up any cards at this point.) If the cards don't match, students continue putting down cards at the same time until someone says *Snap!*.

- Students put down cards until the piles of cards are finished. Students then pick up their own cards only (<u>not</u> their partner's cards) and shuffle them before playing again. The first student to get 10 points wins.

- If a student says *Snap!* and the cards don't match, then his/her partner gets a bonus point. If students can't agree if the cards match, they can check in **V3.3** SB p126, or ask you to adjudicate.

- If possible, demonstrate the activity with a strong student in front of the whole class before students begin.

3D Snakes and ladders p145

Language
Review of lessons 1A–3D

Activity type, when to use and time
Board game. Use any time after lesson 3D. 20–35 minutes.

Preparation
Photocopy one worksheet for each group of three students. You also need a dice for each group and a counter for each student.

Procedure

- Put students into groups of three. Give each group a copy of the snakes and ladders board, a dice and three counters (or students can make their own counters). Ask a student with a watch in each group to be the time-keeper and time students when they have to talk about a topic for 20 seconds.

- Students take turns to throw the dice and move around the board. When they land on a square, they must answer the question correctly in order to stay on the square. If a student can't answer the question correctly, he/she must move back to his/her previous square.

- If a student lands at the bottom of a ladder, he/she must answer the question correctly before he/she is allowed to go up it. He/She doesn't have to answer the question at the top of the ladder. If he/she lands on the head of a snake, he/she must always go down the snake to its tail.

- If a student thinks another student's answer is wrong, they can check in the Language Summaries in the Student's Book, or ask you to adjudicate.

- The first student to reach the *Finish* square is the winner. If some groups finish early, students can go through the squares in number order and discuss the answers in their groups.

2 Bill is Lisa's father. Is he a musician? 5 first; second; third; fourth; fifth 6 on Monday; at 9 p.m.; in the morning; at night 7 Happy birthday! Congratulations! Happy New Year! 9 January; February; March; April; May; June; July; August; September; October; November; December 11 go to concerts; do sport; go shopping; stay in 13 No, he isn't./No, he's not. Yes, they have. 17 twenty past ten/ten twenty; quarter to four/three forty-five; quarter past six/six fifteen; half past seven/seven thirty 19 watches; women; people; diaries

20 My father hasn't got a dog. Where do you live? 22 They haven't got a car. I don't work at home. 24 seven pounds fifty; fifty cents; twenty-nine (dollars) ninety-nine (cents); twenty-one pounds fifty 28 old; difficult; expensive; fast 29 always; usually; often; sometimes; never 30 Where do you have dinner on Sunday? 31 It's a very old bag. I don't go out in the week.

4A Verb-noun collocations p146

Language
free time activities

Activity type, when to use and time
Pelmanism. Use any time after lesson 4A. 10–20 minutes.

Preparation
Photocopy one worksheet for each group of three students. Cut into sets. Shuffle each set.

Procedure

- Put the class into groups of three. Give each group a set of cards. Ask them to put the cards face-down in front of them, with the smaller verb cards on one side and the bigger picture cards on the other.

- Students take it in turns to turn over one verb card and one picture card. If a student thinks that the verb matches the picture, he/she says the appropriate phrase, for example, *read a book*, *watch DVDs*, etc. If the phrase is correct, the student keeps the pair of cards and has another turn. If the two cards don't match, the student puts them back on the table face-down in exactly the same place.

- The activity continues until all the cards are matched up. The student with the most cards is the winner.

- If a group finishes early, students can take turns to say sentences using the phrases on their cards, for example, *I don't often read books. I usually watch DVDs at the weekend.*

read books; do sports; watch DVDs; go dancing; play tennis; read magazines; take photos; watch TV; go swimming; listen to the radio; listen to music; go to concerts; go for a drink; have coffee with friends; go to the cinema; go running

4B A TV presenter's weekend p147–p148

Language
Present Simple: *Wh-* questions with *he*

Activity type, when to use and time
Information gap. Use any time after lesson 4B. 20–35 minutes.

Preparation
Photocopy one student A worksheet and one student B worksheet for each pair of students.

Procedure

- Set the context of the activity by asking students what they remember about the TV game show *First Date!* from lesson 4B. Use the photo on SB p32 to review/pre-teach: *a TV programme, a presenter, a contestant, a studio, a director.*

- Put the students into two groups, A and B. Give a copy of the student A worksheet to each student in group A and a copy of the student B worksheet to each student in group B.

- Students work in pairs with another student from the same group. They read their text about Max's weekend and then complete the questions, as in the example on each worksheet. Tell students that there is one gap for each word in the questions. Check answers with the class (see answer key).

- Put students into pairs, student A and student B. Students are not allowed to look at their partner's worksheets. Students take turns to ask their questions and fill in the gaps in their text. Tell student A to ask the first question.

- When students have finished, they look at each other's worksheets and compare answers. Finish the activity by asking students to suggest how Max can find a girlfriend, for example, be a contestant on *First Date!*.

> **STUDENT A** 2 does … get up 3 does he have 4 does he do 5 does he have 6 does … finish 7 does he watch … in 8 does he do on 9 does he go … the
>
> **STUDENT B** b) does … do c) does he have d) does he meet e) does … start f) does he do … finishes g) does he go h) does he do on i) does he like

4D Food habits p149

Language

food and drink; Present Simple: *yes/no* questions with *you*

Activity type, when to use and time

'Find someone who' activity. Use any time after lesson 4D. 15–25 minutes.

Preparation

Photocopy one worksheet for each student.

Procedure

- Give a copy of the worksheet to each student. Tell students that they must complete sentences 1–10 with the name of a student in the class who does or has these things.

- Go through the example question for sentence 1 with the whole class. Check students understand that this is the question they will need to ask in order to complete sentence 1 on their worksheets. Students then work on their own or in pairs and write questions with *you* for sentences 2–10. If students can't remember any of the vocabulary, they can check in V4.6 on SB p129.

- Check the questions with the whole class and drill them if necessary (see answer key).

- Students move around the room asking the questions they have prepared. If students aren't able to leave their seats, they should ask as many students as they can sitting near them. Before they begin, remind students to use the appropriate short answers: *Yes, I do./No, I don't.*, etc.

- When a student gets a positive answer to a question, he/she should write the other student's name in the space provided. He/She should then move on to talk to a different student. Encourage students to collect as many different names as possible on their worksheet. Students only need to find one name to complete each sentence.

- When students have finished, they can work in pairs and tell their partners what they have found out about their classmates. Finish the activity by asking students to share interesting information with the class.

> 2 Do you drink a lot of tea? 3 Do you usually have toast and jam for breakfast? 4 Have you got an apple or a banana in your bag? 5 Do you eat a lot of biscuits? 6 Do you hate cheese or fish? 7 Do you have cereal with milk for breakfast? 8 Do you like sausages and eggs? 9 Do you often have soup and bread for lunch? 10 Do you eat a lot of vegetables?

5A Places bingo p150

Language

places in a town/the country

Activity type, when to use and time

Bingo game. Use any time after lesson 5A. 10–15 minutes.

Preparation

Photocopy one worksheet for every four students in the class. Cut into four separate worksheets.

Procedure

- Give one bingo card to each student. Allow students a few minutes to check they know the words for all the places on their card. Students can check in V5.1 SB p131. Students are not allowed to write the words on their cards.

- Read out the places in this order to the whole class: *a market, mountains, a bus station, a museum, a square, a beach, the sea, an airport, a house, a lake, a station, a hotel, a bar, a shop, a park, a road, a café, a bed and breakfast* (student D card is completed), *a river* (student A card is completed), *a flat* (student B and student C cards are completed).

- When students hear a place that they have on their cards they put a cross through it.

- When a student has crossed out all the places on his/her card, he/she shouts *Bingo!*. The first student to shout *Bingo!* wins the game.

- If you want to play the game again, distribute new cards and read out the places in a random order.

5B A place to rent p151–p152

Language

rooms and things in the house; *there is/there are; some, any, a*

Activity type, when to use and time

Information gap. Use any time after lesson 5B. 20–30 minutes.

Preparation

Photocopy one Flat questionnaire for each student, and one copy of Flat A, Flat B and Flat C cards for each group of three students. Cut into separate questionnaires and cards. Discard the extra Flat A cards.

Procedure

- Put students into groups of three. Tell the students that each group wants to share a flat together and that each student is going to look at a different flat.

- Give each student a copy of the Flat questionnaire. Elicit the questions for prompts 1 and 2 (*How much is the rent?* and *How many rooms are there?*). Students then work in their groups and write questions with *there is/there are* for prompts 3–12. Check these questions with the whole class (see answer key). Drill them with the class if necessary. You can also point out that questions with *have got/has got* (*How many rooms has it got?*, etc.) are also correct in this situation.

- Give a copy of the Flat A card to one student in each group, a copy of the Flat B card to the second student and a copy of the Flat C card to the third student. Point out that F = *fridge* and WM = *washing machine*. Students are not allowed to look at each other's cards. Students work on their own and fill in the column for their flat on their Flat questionnaire.

- Students work in their groups and take turns to ask the questions they have prepared. Students write the answers on the Flat questionnaire so that they have the information about all three flats.

- Students then decide as a group which flat they want to live in. They must all agree on one flat and decide on the reasons why they have chosen it.

- Finally, each group tells the class which flat they have chosen and their reasons for choosing it.

> 1 How much is the rent?
> 2 How many rooms are there?
> 3 Are there any beds?
> 4 Is there any furniture in the living room?
> 5 Is there a shower and a bath?
> 6 Is there a washing machine?
> 7 Is there a fridge?
> 8 Is there a garden?
> 9 Is there a balcony?
> 10 Is there a station near the flat?
> 11 Are there any shops near the flat?
> 12 Is there a park near the flat?

5D Shopping crossword p153

Language

clothes and shops

Activity type, when to use and time

Paired crossword. Use any time after lesson 5D. 15–25 minutes.

Preparation

Photocopy one worksheet for each pair of students. Cut into two separate worksheets.

Procedure

- Put the class into two groups, group A and group B. Give a copy of the student A crossword to each student in group A and a copy of the student B crossword to each student in group B.

- Students work in pairs with a partner from the same group and check they know the meanings of all the words on their worksheet. Students can check any words they don't know in **V5.3** SB p131 and **V5.6** SB p132.

- Put students into pairs so that one student from group A is working with a student from group B. Students are not allowed to look at each other's worksheets. Check that students understand how to refer to words in a crossword, for example, *1 down* and *7 across*. Students then take it in turns to give their clues for the words on their crossword. These clues can be a sentence (*You buy meat there.*) or visual (students can point to articles of their own clothing or draw a picture on a piece of paper). Students are not allowed to use the words themselves or to give letters as clues. Students should also tell their partner if the answer is two words.

- When students have finished, they check their completed crosswords and their spelling.

6A Famous people quiz p154

Language

Wh- questions with *was/were*

Activity type, when to use and time

Pairwork quiz. Use any time after lesson 6A. 15–25 minutes.

Preparation

Photocopy one worksheet for each pair of students. Cut into two separate worksheets.

Procedure

- Put students into groups of four. Divide each group into two pairs, pair A and pair B. Give a copy of Quiz A to each student in pair A and a copy of Quiz B to each student in pair B. Students are not allowed to show their quizzes to the other pair in their group.

- Students work in their pairs and choose *was* or *were* for questions 1–8 on their quiz. Check answers with the class and note that the answers are the same for both Quiz A and Quiz B (see answer key). Each pair gets one point for each correct answer and a bonus point if all eight answers are correct.

- Students work in their groups of four. Each pair takes it in turns to ask the other pair a question from their quiz. Students read out the question and the three possible answers. If the other pair gets an answer correct, they get two points. Before they begin, tell students that the words/phrases in bold on their worksheets are the correct answers.

- When both pairs have asked all their questions students in each pair add up their points from both parts of the quiz. The pair with the most points wins.

> 1 was 2 was 3 were 4 was 5 were 6 was 7 were 8 was

6B Antonio's honeymoon p155

Language
Past Simple: positive and *Wh-* questions

Activity type, when to use and time
Information gap/whole class mingle. Use any time after lesson 6B. 20–30 minutes.

Preparation
Photocopy one worksheet for each student. Cut into one Antonio's honeymoon worksheet for each student. Cut into one set of information cards for every ten students in the class. Discard the other information cards.

Procedure
- Pre-teach *eat*, *buy* and *miss*, for example, *miss a train* and their Past Simple forms *ate*, *bought* and *missed*. Drill these with the class.

- Give each student a copy of the Antonio's honeymoon worksheet. Focus students on the photo and use this to teach *wedding* and *honeymoon*.

- Students work on their own or in pairs and complete gaps 1–10 with the Past Simple form of the verbs in the box on their worksheets. Do the first one together as an example (*met*). Check answers with the whole class.

- Students work in pairs and decide what questions they need to ask to find out the missing information for gaps 11–20. 🖊 With low-level classes, you can write the question words for each sentence 11–20 on the board. Do the first question on the board as an example. Check the questions with the whole class and drill if necessary (see answer key).

- Give each student in the class one information card. If you have less than ten students, give two cards to some students. If you have more than ten students, give out duplicate cards (it doesn't matter if two or three students have the same information card). Point out that students are not allowed to look at each other's cards.

- Tell students to write the information on their card in the correct gap 11–20 on their Antonio's honeymoon worksheet.

- Students then move around the room asking each other questions in order to complete their worksheet. Remind them of the answer *I'm sorry, I don't know.* before they start. When students have completed their worksheets, they should continue mingling to help other students.

- Finally, students can compare answers in pairs or groups before you check answers with the whole class.

> a) 1 met; Who did Antonio meet in Paris in 2003? 11 Veronica b) 2 got; When did they get married? 12 June 2005 c) 3 went; Where did they go on their honeymoon? 13 Egypt d) 4 stayed; Where did they stay? 14 a 5-star hotel in Luxor e) 5 bought; What did they buy on their first day? 15 some beautiful carpets f) 6 went; Where did they go swimming on the second day of their honeymoon? 16 the Red Sea g) 7 went; What did they go to see on the third day? 17 the Pyramids h) 8 ate; What did they eat on their last night? 18 fish i) 9 left; What time did they leave the hotel the next day? 19 5.30 j) 10 missed; Why did they miss the plane? 20 Antonio forgot his passport

6D Money, money, money! p156–p157

Language
Review of lessons 4A–6D

Activity type, when to use and time
Board game. Use any time after lesson 6D. 25–40 minutes.

Preparation
Photocopy one board, one set of Vocabulary cards and one set of Grammar cards for each group of three or four students. Cut the Vocabulary cards and Grammar cards into two separate sets. Shuffle each set. You also need a dice for each group and a counter for each student.

Procedure
- Pre-teach *on your right*, *on your left*, *a thousand* and how to say numbers ending in 50, for example, 150 (*a hundred and fifty*), 350 (*three hundred and fifty*), etc.

- Put the class into groups of three or four. Give each group a copy of the board, a dice and counters (or students can make their own counters). Ask a student with a watch in each group to be the time-keeper.

- Give each group a set of Vocabulary cards and a set of Grammar cards. Students should put these face-down on the table in front of them.

- The aim of the game is to win the most money. Tell students that they all start with £1,000 in the bank. Students need a pen and paper to keep a record of their winnings, and should adjust their total each time they win or lose some money.

- Students take turns to throw the dice and move around the board. When a student lands on a *Talk about* square, he/she must talk about the topic for 20 seconds. If he/she does this, he/she wins the amount of money shown on the square. If he/she stops talking before 20 seconds are up, he/she loses the amount of money shown on the square.

- When a student lands on a square that says Vocabulary card or Grammar card, he/she turns over the top card on the appropriate pile and reads out the question to the group. He/She must then answer the question. Again, if the student answers the question correctly, he/she wins the amount of money on the square. If he/she doesn't answer the question correctly, he/she loses the amount of money on the square. Students then put the card back at the bottom of the appropriate pile.

- If a student thinks another student's answer is wrong, they can check in the Language Summaries in the Student's Book, or ask you to adjudicate.

- Students always stay on the square they landed on, whether they win or lose.

- The game finishes when one student reaches the *FINISH* square and wins £500. The winner of the game is the person who has the most money.

- If one group finishes early, students can discuss the answers to the questions on the Vocabulary cards and Grammar cards in their groups.

V1 go swimming; take photos; read books **V3** countable: egg; uncountable: furniture, meat, toast **V5** become a lawyer; study law; get divorced **V6** nineteen fifty-three; two thousand and five; eighteen forty-two; ninteen ninety **V8** boring; well; poor; short **V10** countable: vegetable, biscuit; uncountable: milk, rice **V11** watch sport on TV; listen to the radio; go skiing **V13** unfriendly; intelligent; quiet; dirty **V15** usually plural: shoes, boots, trainers; always plural: jeans, trousers, shorts **V16** the kitchen: a fridge, a sink; the living room: a sofa; the bathroom: a shower, a toilet; the bedroom: a bed

G1 How many rooms are there in your flat? **G2** went; had; started; wrote **G3** There isn't any furniture. He doesn't work in New York. **G4** Yes, they do./No, they don't.; Yes, there is./No, there isn't. **G5** left; met; slept; wanted **G6** My sister lives in Italy. John wasn't at home. **G7** some; any **G8** How much; How many **G9** any; a **G10** What does he do in his free time? **G11** There are some chairs. She likes cats. **G12** finished; became; got; stayed **G13** Yes, there are./No, there aren't.; Yes, she does./No, she doesn't. **G14**; watches; studies; does; has **G15** How many; How much **G16** What did you do on Sunday evening?

7A My partner's past p158

Language

Past Simple: *yes/no* questions

Activity type, when to use and time

Personalised information gap. Use any time after lesson 7A. 15–25 minutes.

Preparation

Photocopy one worksheet for each pair of students. Cut into two separate worksheets.

Procedure

- Put students into pairs. If possible, put students with someone they don't know very well. Give a copy of the student A worksheet to one student in each pair and a copy of the student B worksheet to his/her partner. Students are not allowed to look at each other's worksheets.

- Students work on their own and make sentences they think are true about their partner by choosing one of the alternatives in each sentence, for example, *He/She (went out)/stayed in last Saturday night*. Students are not allowed to speak to their partner at this stage of the activity.

- Students prepare *yes/no* questions with *you* to ask their partner for each sentence on their worksheet. Do the first question from each worksheet on the board as examples: *Did you go out (or stay in) last Saturday night/ last night? Did you watch some sport on TV/a DVD last weekend?*. Remind students of the short answers *Yes, I did.* and *No, I didn't.*

- Students work in their pairs and take turns to ask and answer their questions. For each sentence they put a tick in the second column if their prediction was correct and a cross if their prediction was incorrect. The student with the most ticks wins.

- Students can then work in new pairs and tell their new partners about the person they have just talked to.

7B Questions, questions p159–p160

Language

question forms; question words

Activity type, when to use and time

'Find someone who' activity with role cards. Use any time after lesson 7B. 20–30 minutes.

Preparation

Photocopy one worksheet for each student and one set of role cards for every ten students in the class. Cut the role cards into ten separate cards.

Procedure

- Pre-teach *film director, babysitter, look after (children), journalist, interview, castle, footballer*. Check students know the Past Simple of *buy (bought)* and what *an Oscar* is.

- Tell the class they are going to a party. Give each student a copy of the worksheet. Students work in pairs and write the questions they will need to ask to complete the information about each party guest. Tell students to make questions with *you* and to use each question word in the box once only. ✎ Do the first question with the class as an example: *Which instrument do you play?*. Check the questions with the whole class (see answer key).

- Give each student a role card. If you have more than ten students in the class, distribute extra role cards. (This will not affect the outcome of the activity.) If you have less than ten students in the class, don't give extra role cards to each student. Students are not allowed to look at each other's role cards or say who they are. Give students a few minutes to read the role cards and ask you any questions.

- Students move around the room and talk to the other guests at the party. Tell students to start the conversations by asking 'getting to know you' questions, for example, *Where are you from?, What do you do?*, etc. When students find out who someone is, they write his/her name in the second column on the Party guests worksheet. They then ask the question needed to complete the information about the person and fill in the gap on the worksheet. Encourage students to continue the conversation if possible. The aim of the activity is to fill in all the gaps on the worksheet.

- When students have finished, they can compare what they have found out about each person. Finally, check answers with the whole class.

> 1 Which instrument do you play? (guitar) 2 When did you make your first album? (three) 3 How many Oscars have you got? (five) 4 How long did you work in Hollywood? (29) 5 Whose children do you look after? (David and Victoria Beckham) 6 Who did you interview last month? (Brad Pitt) 7 Why did you leave your job last week? (he/she won the lottery.) 8 How old is your castle? (900) 9 What did you buy last week? (a new red Ferrari) 10 Where did you go last month? (Brazil)

7C Lost in the Himalayas p161

Language

Past Simple review

Activity type, when to use and time

Role play. Use any time after lesson 7C. 25–40 minutes.

Preparation

Photocopy one worksheet for each pair of students. Cut into two separate role cards.

Procedure

- Pre-teach *journalist, interview, across the Himalayas, border, get lost* and the Past Simple of *eat (ate), drink (drank)* and *see (saw)*.

- Put the class into two groups, journalists and tourists. Give a copy of the Journalist role card to each student in the journalist group and a copy of the Tourist role card to each student in the tourist group. If you have an odd number of students, have an extra journalist.

- Students read the news item at the top of their role cards. Check students have understood the situation by asking questions, for example, *When did they find the tourists? When did the tourists leave Kathmandu?*, etc.

- Divide each group into pairs of journalists and pairs of tourists. You need to have the same number of pairs of journalists as pairs of tourists, so if you have extra students have one or two groups of three journalists.

- Students prepare questions and answers in their pairs, following the guidelines on the role card. Help students with new vocabulary as necessary.

- Reorganise the class so that a pair of journalists sits next to a pair of tourists. The journalists then interview the tourists and make brief notes on their answers. With a strong class, you may wish the journalists to interview tourists on their own. If so, make sure all students have written questions or made notes during the preparation stage of the activity.

- At the end of the interviews, journalists can tell the class the most interesting things they found out during the interview.

- As a follow-up activity, put one journalist and one tourist together to write the report for the News365 website. The report can be started in class and finished for homework. You can display the reports in the classroom for other students to read.

8A Language schools p162–p163

Language

can/can't for possibility; holiday activities

Activity type, when to use and time

Information gap. Use any time after lesson 8A. 20–35 minutes.

Preparation

Photocopy one set of Language school cards for every four students. Cut into four separate worksheets.

Procedure

- Pre-teach *library, study centre, accommodation, art gallery, traditional English pub, cathedral, go sailing*.

- Tell the class they are going to study English in England for a month and that they must decide which school to go to.

- Put the class into four groups, A, B, C and D. Give a copy of The City Language School worksheet to every student in group A, a copy of the English World Language School worksheet to every student in group B, a copy of the Sea View Language School worksheet to every student in group C and a copy of the Lakeside Language School worksheet to every student in group D. Tell students that all the schools cost the same.

- Students work together in pairs with a student from the same group. They discuss what you can and can't do at the language schools and the places where they are located. For example, a student from group A could say *You can do a general English course at this school, but you can't do a course in the evening.* Students can make notes at this stage, but they shouldn't write complete sentences.

- Reorganise the class into groups of four with one student from each of the four groups. If you have extra students, make some groups of five. Students take it in turns to tell the group what they can and can't do at their language school and the place where it is located. The whole group must then discuss and decide which school they want to go to. Students must all decide on the same school.

- Finally, each group tells the class which school they have decided to go to and their reasons for choosing this school.

8B Comparative pelmanism p164

Language
comparatives

Activity type, when to use and time
Pelmanism. Use any time after lesson 8B. 15-25 minutes.

Preparation
Photocopy one worksheet for each group of three students. Cut into sets. Shuffle each set.

Procedure
- If necessary, check that students know all the famous people and places on the cards. Pre-teach *continent*.

- Put the class into groups of three students. Give each group a set of cards. Ask them to put the cards face-down in front of them, with the smaller cards on one side and the bigger cards on the other.

- Students take it in turns to turn over one small card and one big card. If a student thinks that the two words/phrases on the cards match, for example, *The USA* and *Spain*, he/she says what type they are, for example, *They're both countries.* He/She then makes a comparative sentence using the words/phrases on the cards, for example, *The USA is bigger than Spain.* or *Spain is smaller than the USA.* If the sentence is correct, the student keeps the pair of cards and has another turn. If the two cards don't match, the student puts them back on the table face-down in exactly the same place.

- If a student thinks that one of his/her partner's sentences isn't correct, he/she can challenge him/her. If it is incorrect, the student must put back the cards and the turn passes to the next student. If students can't agree, they should ask you to adjudicate.

- The activity continues until all the cards are matched up. The student with the most cards is the winner.

- If a group finishes early, students can take turns to say sentences using the words/phrases on their cards, for example, *I really like cats. I've got a new CD player. I'd like to go to the Pyramids.*

8D Collocation dominoes p165

Language
collocations review

Activity type, when to use and time
Dominoes. Use any time after lesson 8D. 15–25 minutes.

Preparation
Photocopy one set of dominoes for each pair of students. Cut into sets and shuffle each set.

Procedure
- Put students into pairs. Give one set of dominoes to each pair. Students share out the dominoes equally. Students are not allowed to look at each other's dominoes.

- One student puts a domino on the table. His/Her partner puts another domino at either end of the first domino so that they make a sentence. Encourage students to look at the words in **bold** to make sure that they form a collocation. Students then continue taking turns to put dominoes at either end of the domino chain.

- If a student thinks that one of his/her partner's sentences isn't correct, he/she can challenge him/her. If it is incorrect, the student must take back the domino and the turn passes to his/her partner. If students can't agree, they should ask you to adjudicate.

- When a student can't put down a domino, the turn automatically passes to his/her partner. The game continues until one student has put down all his/her dominoes, or until neither student can make a correct sentence. The student who finishes first, or who has the fewer dominoes remaining, is the winner.

9A At the park p166–p167

Language
Present Continuous for 'now'

Activity type, when to use and time
Information gap/mingle. Use any time after lesson 9A. 15–25 minutes.

Preparation
Photocopy one picture of the park for each student. Photocopy one set of Activity cards for every 16 students in the class. Cut into 16 separate cards.

Procedure
- Give each student a copy of the picture of the park and an Activity card. If you have less than sixteen students in the class, give two Activity cards to some students. If you have more than 16 students you can give duplicate cards to students without affecting the outcome of the activity. Students are not allowed to look at each other's Activity cards. Tell students to read the cards, write the person's name or the people's names in the correct gap on the picture and cross out the name(s) in the box above the picture.

- Students then move around the room and ask questions about the people in the box above the picture to find out what they are doing. For example, student A says *What's Anna doing?* and student B replies *She's going into the café.* or *I don't know.*

- When students find out what people are doing they write their names in the correct gap on the picture and cross off the names in the box above the picture. Students are only allowed to find out which name(s) to write in one gap from each person they speak to. When they have finished writing the name(s) in the gap they find another partner.

- When students have finished, they can compare their answers in pairs or groups before you check answers with the whole class.

- As a follow-up activity, tell students to look at the completed picture for two minutes and remember what everyone is doing. Put the students in pairs: student A and student B. Student A turns over his/her picture and student B asks him/her what ten people are doing. Student A gets one point for each correct answer. Students then swap roles so that student A asks student B ten questions. The student with the most points wins.

9B Stuck in traffic p168

Language
Present Simple and Present Continuous

Activity type, when to use and time
Information gap. Use any time after lesson 9B. 20–30 minutes.

Preparation
Photocopy one worksheet for each pair of students. Cut into two separate worksheets.

Procedure
- Put students into two groups, group A and group B. Give a copy of the student A worksheet to each student in group A and a copy of the student B worksheet to each student in group B. Allow students a couple of minutes to read the email. Check they understand that Olivia and Robert are in a taxi during the strike that was discussed in lesson 9B in the Student's Book.

- Students work in pairs with people from the same group. They write the questions they need to ask to complete the email using the question words in brackets. Tell students the questions should be in the Present Simple or the Present Continuous. You can do the first one on each worksheet on the board as an example (see answer key).

- Reorganise the class into pairs with one student from group A and one student from group B. Students are not allowed to look at each other's worksheets. Students work in their pairs and take turns to ask their questions. They write the answers on their worksheets in the gaps. Tell Student As to ask the first question.

- When students have finished, they can check answers by comparing emails.

Student A questions
1 Where are Robert and Olivia sitting (at the moment)? 2 What is Robert reading? 3 What does Olivia like? 4 What time does she/Olivia start work? 5 Why is she/Olivia having a day off (today)? 6 Who is Robert talking to (on his mobile)? 7 What does Tom have every week? 8 What do Tom and Sally (both) like?

Student B questions
a) Where are Robert and Olivia going? b) What is Olivia eating? c) What does she/Olivia hate? d) What time does she/Olivia finish work? e) Where do Lucas and Karen live? f) What is the taxi driver doing (now)? g) What does Sally want to be (when she's older)? h) Where are Tom and Sally/the children staying (at the moment)?

9D Blockbuster p169–p171

Language
Review of lessons 7A–9D

Activity type, when to use and time
Board game. Use any time after lesson 9D. 25–40 minutes.

Preparation
Photocopy one board for every four or six students in your class. Photocopy one Team A question sheet for half the number of students in your class and one Team B question sheet for the other half. You also need a counter for each team.

Procedure

- Put students into groups of four or six. Divide each group into two teams: team A and team B. Give each student in each team A a copy of the Team A question sheet and each student in each team B a copy of the Team B question sheet. Students are not allowed to look at the other team's question sheet.

- Each team puts a counter on their 'home square', which is marked with A or B. The object of the game is to move your team's counter to the other team's home square. Each team can only move one square at a time, and can only move to a square which has a side that is touching the square they are on.

- Tell students that G = grammar, V = vocabulary, M = mystery question and T = talk about. When a team lands on a G, V or M square, the other team reads out a grammar question, a vocabulary question or mystery question from their question sheet. Students read out the questions on their question sheet in number order. The other team must answer the question correctly in order to stay on the square. (Note that the answers are in brackets on the question sheet.) If a team gets the answer wrong, they must move back to their original square and they must move to a <u>different</u> square for their next go.

- If a team lands on a T square, they must nominate a member of their team to talk about the topic <u>before</u> the other team tells them the topic. The student must then talk about the topic for 20 seconds without stopping. When the team lands on another T square, they must nominate a different student each time until all the students in their team have talked about a topic.

- The team that gets to the other team's home square first is the winner. It is advisable to demonstrate this game on the board or in front of the class before students start playing in their groups.

- If one group finishes early students can take turns to ask and answer the remaining questions on their question sheets.

10A Something in common p172

Language

How often … ? and frequency expressions; prepositions

Activity type, when to use and time

'Find someone who' activity. Use any time after lesson 10A. 15–25 minutes.

Preparation

Photocopy one worksheet for each student.

Procedure

- Give a copy of the worksheet to each student. Students work on their own and choose the correct preposition (or no preposition) in the phrases 1–12 on the worksheet. They can check in pairs or groups before you check answers with the whole class (see answer key).

- Students work on their own and write how often they do these things in the *Me* column. Tell students to write short phrases only, for example, *once a week, twice a month, three or four times a year, every day, every week,* etc., not whole sentences.

- Students move around the room and ask questions with *How often do you … ?*. When a student finds another student who does one of these things with the same frequency as him/her, he/she says *Me too.* and writes the student's name in the *Name* column on the worksheet. Students should then ask one or two follow-up questions about the topic, for example, *When did you last … ?, Where do you usually … ?,* etc.

- When students have found something in common with each other, they move on and talk to a new person. Students should try to collect twelve different names on their worksheet if possible.

- When students have finished, they can compare answers in pairs or groups. Finally, students tell the whole class one thing they have found out, for example, *Giada and I both go to the cinema every weekend.*

> 1 to 2 up 3 for 4 – 5 out 6 – 7 on 8 to 9 for 10 to 11 – 12 to

10B Who's Alex? p173–p174

Language

describing people's appearance

Activity type, when to use and time

Information gap. Use any time after lesson 10B. 15–25 minutes.

Preparation

Photocopy one Student A worksheet and one Student B worksheet for each pair of students.

Procedure

- Pre-teach *He/She's wearing glasses.*

- Put students into pairs. Give a copy of the student A worksheet to one student and a copy of the student B worksheet to his/her partner. Students are not allowed to look at each other's worksheets.

- Students work in pairs and take turns to describe one of the people on their picture who <u>hasn't</u> got a name, i.e. student A describes the men and student B describes the women. Students must describe the people's appearance and their clothes, not where they are in the picture or who they are talking to. The aim of the activity is for students to find out which person is Alex. This is the only person at the party without a name on either worksheet.

- When a student has finished describing a person, his/her partner says the name of that person. If a student is unsure which person is being described, he/she should ask questions to clarify any problems, for example, *Has he got long or short hair?, What is she wearing?,* etc. Students write the names on their worksheets when they are sure who their partner has described.

- When students have finished they decide which person is Alex. She is the only person without a name on either worksheet. She has short dark hair, is wearing glasses and is talking to Jean, Tim and Max. Check this with the whole class.

- Finally, students can look at each other's pictures and compare their answers for the other people.

10C Get well soon! p175

Language
health problems and treatments

Activity type, when to use and time
Paired crossword. Use any time after lesson 10C. 15–25 minutes.

Preparation
Photocopy one worksheet for each pair of students. Cut into two separate worksheets.

Procedure

- Put the class into two groups, group A and group B. Give a copy of the student A crossword to each student in group A and a copy of the student B crossword to each student in group B.

- Students work in pairs with a partner from the same group and check they know the meanings of all the words on their worksheet.

- Put students into pairs so that one student from group A is working with a student from group B. Students are not allowed to look at each other's worksheets. Check that students understand how to refer to words in a crossword, for example, *1 down* and *4 across*. Students then take it in turns to give clues for the words on their crossword. These clues can be a sentence (*You take these when you've got a headache.*) or visual (students can mime an illness or point to a part of the body). Students are not allowed to use the words themselves or to give letters as clues. Students should also tell their partner if the answer is two, three or four words.

- When students have finished, they check their completed crosswords and their spelling.

11A New Year's Day p176

Language
Wh- questions with *be going to*

Activity type, when to use and time
Information gap. Use any time after lesson 11A. 15–25 minutes.

Preparation
Photocopy one worksheet for each pair of students. Cut into two separate worksheets.

Procedure

- Tell students they are going to find out how the members of one family are going to spend New Year's Day. Put the students into two groups, group A and group B. Give a copy of the student A worksheet to each student in group A and a copy of the student B worksheet to each student in group B.

- Students work in pairs with someone from the same group and write *Wh-* questions with *be going to* that they need to ask in order to fill in the gaps on their worksheets. ✎ If necessary, do the first one for each worksheet on the board (see answer key).

- Reorganise the class into pairs, with one student from group A and one student from group B in each pair. Students are not allowed to look at each other's worksheets. Students work in their pairs and take turns to ask and answer their questions. They write the answers on their worksheets in the gaps. Tell student As to ask the first question.

- When students have finished, they can check their answers by looking at their partner's worksheet.

- Students stay in their pairs and draw a family tree for the people on the worksheet. ✎ Check with the students by drawing the family tree on the board.

Student A questions
1 What are Tom and Katrina going to buy? 2 Where are they going to have dinner? 3 Who are Rebecca and Gary going to meet for lunch? 4 What is Daniel going to do in the afternoon? 5 What are Daniel and Freddy going to buy (in town)? 6 Who is going to visit Harold in the afternoon?

Student B questions
a) Who are Tom and Katrina going to visit in the afternoon? b) What are Rebecca and Gary going to do in the morning? c) What is Rebecca going to cook (for dinner)? d) Who is Daniel going to meet in town? e) What is Harold going to play in the morning? f) Where is Harold going to have dinner in the evening?

Family tree

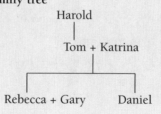

11C The missing lottery ticket p177–p178

Language

asking for and giving directions

Activity type, when to use and time

Maze activity. Use any time after lesson 11C. 15–30 minutes.

Preparation

Photocopy one map and one set of Directions cards for each pair of students. Cut the Directions cards into separate cards and organise them so that you have one class set of card 1, one class set of card 2, etc.

Procedure

- Tell the students that you won the lottery last week, but you lost your lottery ticket! You want the students to help you find the ticket and the first pair of students to find it can share your prize.

- Put the students into pairs. Give each pair a copy of the map and allow them a minute or two to study it. Tell the students that you left your bag and your lottery ticket in one of the places on the map, but you can't remember where. Tell students that they will start their search at the station.

- Give each pair a copy of Directions card 1. Students read the directions and write the name of the place at the bottom of the card. When they have done this, one of the students in each pair comes up to the front of the class and gives you the card.

- If the place written on the card is correct, give the student Directions card 2. The student then goes back to his/her partner and they follow the directions on their new card, again writing the name of the place on the card when they have found it. If the place written on a card is not correct, you should send the student back to his/her partner with the same card to try again.

- Continue this procedure with the rest of the Directions cards until a student gives you the final card with the correct answer written on it. The first pair to finish the activity wins. You can choose to stop the activity at this point or allow it to continue until most of the pairs have finished.

- At the end of the activity you can take out a lottery ticket from your bag, study the numbers closely, then say that you have got the numbers wrong and haven't won anything at all – or, alternatively, give the winning pair a prize!

- As a follow-up activity, students can work in new pairs and give each other directions to places on the map from the station.

1 Harmony's Bar 2 newsagent's 3 Park Hotel 4 shoe shop 5 City Hospital 6 department store 7 Cordy's Café 8 City Museum 9 bookshop 10 Station Café

11D Thought bubbles p179

Language

verb patterns; *be going to*

Activity type, when to use and time

Personalised guessing game. Use any time after lesson 11D. 15–30 minutes.

Preparation

Photocopy one worksheet for each student.

Procedure

- Give a copy of the worksheet to each student. Tell students to read the points in the box and then write the things, people and places in the thought bubbles. Students should write single words or short phrases, for example, *getting up early, my sister, go to the USA, a car*, etc., not complete sentences. They can write them in any bubble they want, but <u>not</u> in the same order as the points. 🖉 You can demonstrate this before they begin by drawing some thought bubbles on the board and writing in your own ideas in random order.

- Students work in pairs and swap worksheets with their partner. Students then take it turns to ask yes/no questions to guess why their partners have written the things in the thought bubbles. For example, if a student has written *go to the theatre*, his/her partner might ask *Are you going to (go to) the theatre next weekend?* or *Do you want to go to the theatre next month?*. Students should ask one or two follow-up questions for each point, for example, *What are you going to see?*.

- When students have finished, each student can tell the class two or three things that they have found out about their partner.

12A Four restaurants p180

Language

superlatives

Activity type, when to use and time

Information gap and discussion. Use any time after lesson 12A. 20–30 minutes.

Preparation

Photocopy one worksheet for each student. Cut out the *Which restaurant …* worksheet. Cut the Restaurant reviews into four separate cards.

Procedure

- Put the students into groups of four. Tell students that each group is planning to go out for a celebration meal at the end of their English course and they are going to choose which restaurant to go to. Pre-teach *main course, chef* and *traditional (restaurant/food)*.

- Give each student a copy of the *Which restaurant …* worksheet. Students work on their own and fill in the gaps with the superlative forms of the adjective. Check answers with the whole class (see answer key).

- Give a different Restaurant review card to each student in each group. If you have extra students, have one or two groups of five and ask two students to work together with one Restaurant review card. Discard the extra Restaurant review cards. Allow students a few minutes to read the information on their card. Students are not allowed to look at each other's cards.

- Students work in their groups and share information about their restaurants in order to complete their *Which restaurant …* worksheet. For example, to find out which restaurant opens the earliest, each student in the group has to tell their partners the name of their restaurant and what time it opens. Students work down the list on the *Which restaurant …* worksheet and write the name of the appropriate restaurant in the right-hand column.

- When students get to question 12 they must decide which they think is the best restaurant for their group to go to, based on the information they have on their worksheet. Students must all agree on one restaurant.

- Finally, ask each group to tell the class which restaurant they have chosen and their reasons for choosing it.

Superlatives
1 most modern 2 oldest 3 smallest 4 biggest 5 cheapest
6 most expensive 7 nearest 8 furthest/farthest 9 earliest
10 latest 11 most interesting 12 best

Restaurants
1 Asia Garden 2 The Golden Palace 3 Asia Garden
4 The World Food Café 5 Food: Asia Garden;
Wine: La Trattoria 6 Food and wine: The Golden Palace
7 La Trattoria 8 The World Food Café 9 The World
Food Café 10 La Trattoria 11 The World Food Café
12 Students' answer

12B Life experiences p181

Language
Present Perfect and Past Simple

Activity type, when to use and time
'Find someone who' activity. Use any time after lesson 12B. 20–30 minutes.

Preparation
Photocopy one worksheet for each student.

Procedure
- Give a copy of the worksheet to each student. Tell students that they must find one student in the class who has done the things in **bold** on the worksheet.

- Elicit the questions for 1a), 1b) and 1c) on the worksheet and write them on the board. Check students understand that question a) should be in the Present Perfect and should begin with *Have you ever … ?* and that the follow-up questions 1b) and 1c) should be in the Past Simple.

- Students work on their own or in pairs and prepare the rest of the questions on the worksheet. With a low-level class students can write the questions on the worksheet. If you have a stronger class, you may wish to ask them to prepare the questions orally, but not write anything on the worksheet. This will make the communicative stage of the activity more challenging. Check the questions with the whole class if necessary (see answer key).

- Students move around the room asking the questions they have prepared. If students are not able to leave their seats, they should ask as many students as they can sitting near them. Before they begin, remind students to use the appropriate short answers to *Have you ever … ?* questions (*Yes, I have./No, I haven't.*).

- If a student answers *yes* to a *Have you ever … ?* question, the student asking the question writes the person's name in the *Name* column on the worksheet. He/She then asks the two follow-up questions b) and c) and writes brief answers in the *Extra information* column. He/She then moves on to talk to a different student. Encourage students to talk to as many different people as possible. Students only need to find one person who has done each thing.

- When students have finished, they can work in pairs and tell their partners what they have found out about their classmates. Finish the activity by asking each student to tell the class one or two interesting things they have found out.

1 a) Have you ever been skiing? b) Where did you go? c) Did you have a good time? 2 a) Have you ever worked or studied in another country? b) Which country was it? c) What did you do there? 3 a) Have you ever met someone famous? b) Who did you meet? c) What did you say to him or her? 4 a) Have you ever been to an important football match? b) Which teams did you see? c) Did you enjoy it? 5 a) Have you ever lost your mobile phone? b) How did you lose it? c) Did you find it? 6 a) Have you ever wanted to be in a band? b) What type of music did you want to play? c) Which instrument did you play? 7 a) Have you ever been to the cinema in another country? b) Which country was it? c) Which film did you see? 8 a) Have you ever worked in a shop? b) What did you do there? c) How old were you? 9 a) Have you ever written a diary? b) How old were you when you started it? c) Did you write it every day? 10 a) Have you ever walked more than 20 km in one day? b) Why did you walk so far? c) What did you do the next day?

Student A

A Name: Anita Timpson
Country: ....

B Names: Hiroki Matsui
         Yoshi Kitamura
Country: ....

C Name: ....
Country: Russia

D Name: ....
Country: Spain

E Name: Yao Zhang Jiang
Country: ....

F Names: ....
         ....
Country: Brazil

Student B

A Name: ....
Country: Australia

B Names: ....
         ....
Country: Japan

C Name: Leonid Kyznetsov
Country: ....

D Name: Catalina Lorano
Country: ....

E Name: ....
Country: China

F Names: Marcello Lindoso
         Marta Beterman
Country: ....

© Cambridge University Press 2005   **face2face** Elementary Photocopiable

No, we aren't.	Are Susannah and Ari in class 3A?	No, they aren't.	Is Peter a lawyer?
Yes, he is.	Are we in room 17?	No, you aren't.	Are Bob and Mary doctors?
Yes, they are.	Are you from China?	No, I'm not.	Is your teacher Australian?
Yes, she is.	Am I late?	Yes, you are.	Is he a musician?
No, he isn't.	Is she from Brazil?	No, she isn't.	Are you Spanish?
Yes, I am.	Are you and Sergei from Moscow?	Yes, we are.	Is our class in room 19?
Yes, it is.	Is it on page 12?	No, it isn't.	Am I in your English class?
No, you aren't.	Are you a waitress?	Yes, I am.	Are you and Gabi from Germany?
Yes, we are.	Are they engineers?	No, they aren't.	Is Patricia retired?
No, she isn't.	Is Mr Walker in Poland?	Yes, he is.	Are you Mr and Mrs Kramer?

1C At the car hire office asking for and giving personal details

Student A

Student B

Mr ☐ Mrs ✔
Car Hire Form
Customer ref. **000239**
CITY CAR HIRE

Surname	Moreno
First name	Raquel
Nationality	Mexican
Address	15 Grove Road
	London SW7 4FL
Home phone number	020 7782 4690
Mobile phone number	07799 354981
email address	moreno23@ibana.com

Mr ☐ Mrs ✔
Car Hire Form
Customer ref. **000239**
CITY CAR HIRE

Surname	
First name	
Nationality	
Address	
Home phone number	
Mobile phone number	
email address	

Mr ✔ Mrs ☐
Car Hire Form
Customer ref. **000240**
CITY CAR HIRE

Surname	
First name	
Nationality	
Address	
Home phone number	
Mobile phone number	
email address	

Mr ✔ Mrs ☐
Car Hire Form
Customer ref. **000240**
CITY CAR HIRE

Surname	Amato
First name	Salvatore
Nationality	Italian
Address	33 Lissen Road
	London W18 8HT
Home phone number	020 8244 7941
Mobile phone number	07930 239982
email address	salvamato@globenet.co.uk

Mr ✔ Mrs ☐
Car Hire Form
Customer ref. **000241**
CITY CAR HIRE

Surname	Langlet
First name	Jacques
Nationality	French
Address	48 Porthall Street
	London EC16 7DQ
Home phone number	020 8788 3286
Mobile phone number	07344 126544
email address	jlanglet@freeweb.com

Mr ✔ Mrs ☐
Car Hire Form
Customer ref. **000241**
CITY CAR HIRE

Surname	
First name	
Nationality	
Address	
Home phone number	
Mobile phone number	
email address	

Mr ☐ Mrs ✔
Car Hire Form
Customer ref. **000242**
CITY CAR HIRE

Surname	
First name	
Nationality	
Address	
Home phone number	
Mobile phone number	
email address	

Mr ☐ Mrs ✔
Car Hire Form
Customer ref. **000242**
CITY CAR HIRE

Surname	Yamazaki
First name	Kumiko
Nationality	Japanese
Address	11 Denzel Street
	London E4 5RF
Home phone number	020 7922 3211
Mobile phone number	07883 233451
email address	kumiko37@webmail.com

© Cambridge University Press 2005   face2face Elementary Photocopiable

2A Harry and Harriet *have got*; personal possessions

Student A: Harry's room

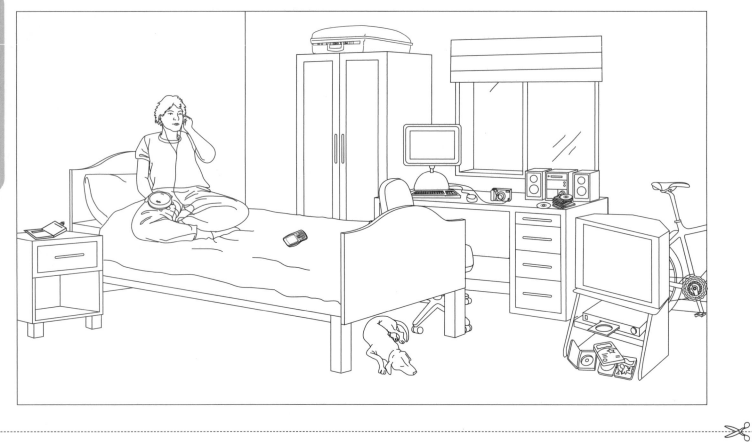

Student B: Harriet's room

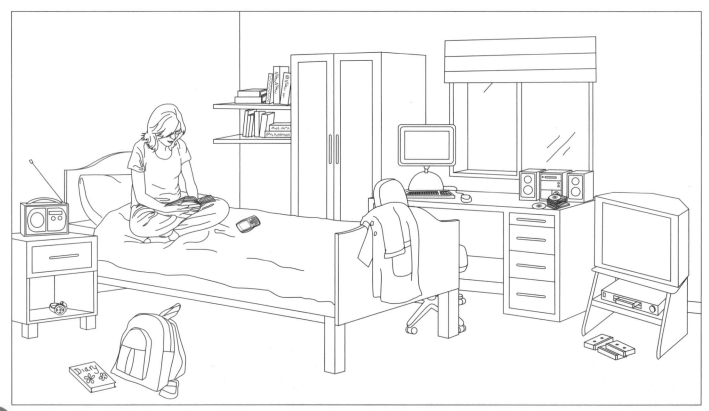

Instructions p123

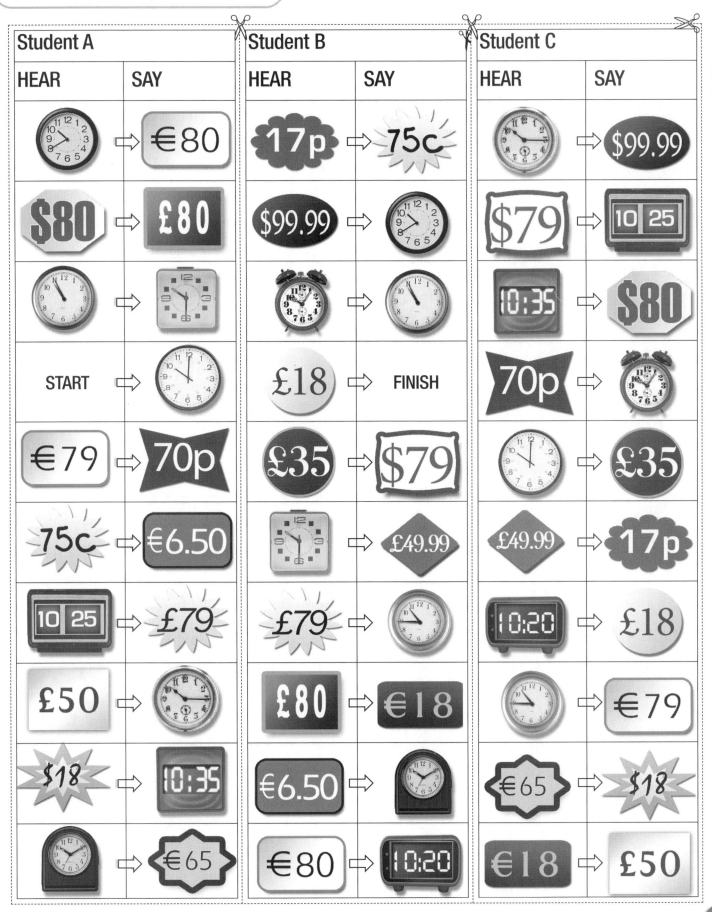

2D Where is it? prepositions of place

Student A

Student B

3A World routines daily routines; Present Simple: positive and *Wh-* questions

Student A

	What time / get up?	When / start work?	Where / have lunch?	When / finish work?	Where / have dinner?	What time / go to bed?
Alfonso and Barbara, Italy		8.45			at home	
Omar and Layla, Egypt	6.30		at the hospital	5.30		10.30
Satoshi and Tomoko, Japan		8.45	at the office			12.30

✂ -

Student B

	What time / get up?	When / start work?	Where / have lunch?	When / finish work?	Where / have dinner?	What time / go to bed?
Alfonso and Barbara, Italy	8.00		at home	7.45		12.15
Omar and Layla, Egypt		8.00			at a restaurant	
Satoshi and Tomoko, Japan	7.15			6.30	at home	

Instructions p124 © Cambridge University Press 2005 face2face Elementary Photocopiable

3B Time phrase snap time phrases with *on, in, at, every*

Student A

ON	ON	ON	ON
IN	IN	IN	IN
AT	AT	AT	AT
EVERY	EVERY	EVERY	EVERY

Student B

SATURDAY	DAY	EIGHT O'CLOCK	THE WEEK
WEEK	HALF PAST TEN	THE MORNING	THURSDAY EVENING
THE AFTERNOON	MONDAY MORNINGS	THE WEEKEND	THE EVENING
SUNDAY AFTERNOONS	NIGHT	FRIDAYS	AFTERNOON

Instructions p124

3D Snakes and ladders Review of lessons 1A–3D

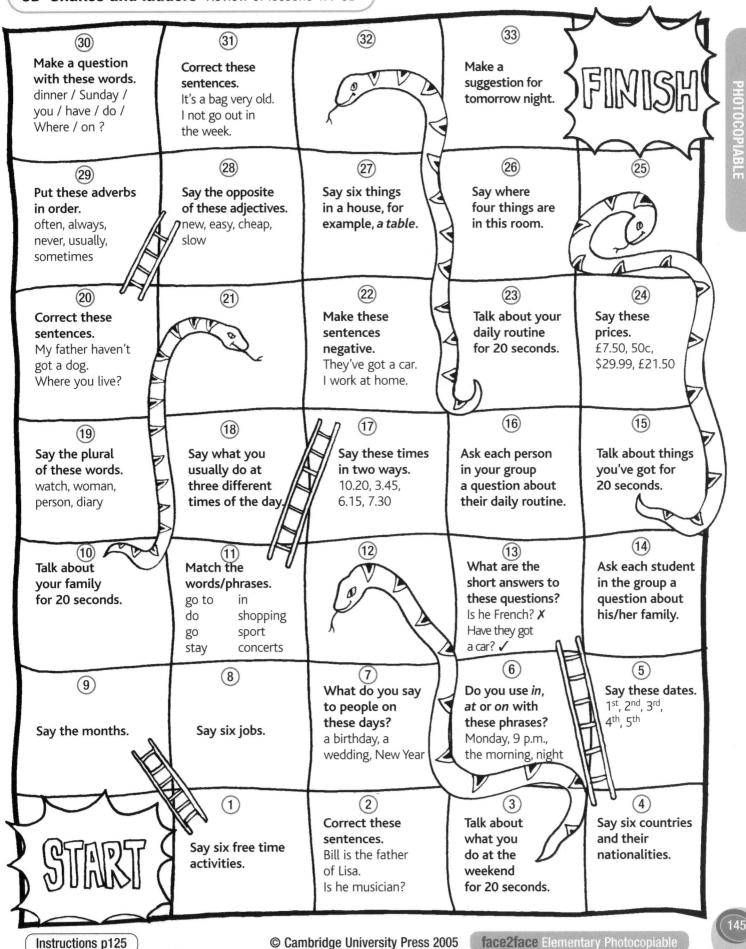

30 Make a question with these words.
dinner / Sunday / you / have / do / Where / on ?

31 Correct these sentences.
It's a bag very old.
I not go out in the week.

32

33 Make a suggestion for tomorrow night.

FINISH

29 Put these adverbs in order.
often, always, never, usually, sometimes

28 Say the opposite of these adjectives.
new, easy, cheap, slow

27 Say six things in a house, for example, *a table*.

26 Say where four things are in this room.

25

20 Correct these sentences.
My father haven't got a dog.
Where you live?

21

22 Make these sentences negative.
They've got a car.
I work at home.

23 Talk about your daily routine for 20 seconds.

24 Say these prices.
£7.50, 50c, $29.99, £21.50

19 Say the plural of these words.
watch, woman, person, diary

18 Say what you usually do at three different times of the day.

17 Say these times in two ways.
10.20, 3.45, 6.15, 7.30

16 Ask each person in your group a question about their daily routine.

15 Talk about things you've got for 20 seconds.

10 Talk about your family for 20 seconds.

11 Match the words/phrases.
go to   in
do   shopping
go   sport
stay   concerts

12

13 What are the short answers to these questions?
Is he French? ✗
Have they got a car? ✓

14 Ask each student in the group a question about his/her family.

9 Say the months.

8 Say six jobs.

7 What do you say to people on these days?
a birthday, a wedding, New Year

6 Do you use *in*, *at* or *on* with these phrases?
Monday, 9 p.m., the morning, night

5 Say these dates.
1st, 2nd, 3rd, 4th, 5th

START

1 Say six free time activities.

2 Correct these sentences.
Bill is the father of Lisa.
Is he musician?

3 Talk about what you do at the weekend for 20 seconds.

4 Say six countries and their nationalities.

read		do	
watch		go	
play		read	
take		watch	
go		listen to	
listen to		go to	
go for		have	
go to		go	

face2face Elementary Photocopiable   © Cambridge University Press 2005

Instructions p125

4B A TV presenter's weekend Present Simple: Wh- questions with *he*

Student A

Max Williams is a famous TV presenter in the UK. He's 34 years old and he lives in ¹_____ with his brother. He presents a TV game show called *First Date!*. It's on TV every Saturday evening and about 15 million people watch it every week.

On Saturdays Max always gets up at ²_____ and before breakfast he goes running for about half an hour. He has breakfast ³_____ at about 10.00. Then after breakfast he ⁴_____ . At 12.30 he meets Julie Richards, the director of *First Date!*, and they talk about the day's programme. He has lunch ⁵_____ at about 2.00, then he meets the contestants.

The programme starts at 6.15 and finishes at ⁶_____ . After the programme finishes he has dinner with Julie and then he goes home. In the evening he watches ⁷_____ on TV – he always records it on his DVD player – and then goes to bed at about midnight.

On Sunday morning Max ⁸_____ and in the afternoon he watches football on TV. In the evening he goes ⁹_____ with his friends – he likes Chinese food. Max is very happy with his life, except for one thing – he doesn't have a girlfriend!

1 Where _does_ Max _live_ ?

2 What time _____ he _____ _____ on Saturdays?

3 Where _____ _____ _____ breakfast?

4 What _____ _____ _____ after breakfast?

5 Where _____ _____ _____ lunch?

6 What time _____ the programme _____ ?

7 What _____ _____ _____ on TV _____ the evening?

8 What _____ _____ _____ Sunday morning?

9 Where _____ _____ in _____ evening?

Student B

Max Williams is a famous TV presenter in the UK. He's 34 years old and he lives in London with a) _____ . He presents a TV game show called *First Date!*. It's on TV every Saturday evening and about 15 million people watch it every week.

On Saturdays Max always gets up at 8.30 and before breakfast he b) _____ for about half an hour. He has breakfast in a café at c) _____ . Then after breakfast he goes to the TV studio. At 12.30 he meets d) _____ , the director of *First Date!*, and they talk about the day's programme. He has lunch at the studio at about 2.00, then he meets the contestants.

The programme starts at e) _____ and finishes at 7.15. After the programme finishes he f) _____ and then he goes home. In the evening he watches *First Date!* on TV – he always records it on his DVD player – and then goes to bed at g) _____ .

On Sunday morning Max usually plays tennis and in the afternoon he h) _____ . In the evening he goes to a restaurant with his friends – he likes i) _____ food. Max is very happy with his life, except for one thing – he doesn't have a girlfriend!

a) Who _does_ does Max _live_ with?

b) What _____ he _____ before breakfast?

c) What time _____ _____ _____ breakfast?

d) Who _____ _____ _____ at 12.30?

e) What time _____ the programme _____ ?

f) What _____ _____ _____ after the programme _____ ?

g) When _____ _____ _____ to bed?

h) What _____ _____ _____ _____ Sunday afternoon?

i) What food _____ _____ _____ ?

Instructions p125

4D Food habits food and drink; Present Simple: *yes*/*no* questions with *you*

1 _____ eats every day.

   Question: *Do you eat fruit every day?*

2 _____ drinks a lot of .

   Question: _____

3 _____ usually has and for breakfast.

   Question: _____

4 _____ has got or in his/her bag.

   Question: _____

5 _____ eats a lot of .

   Question: _____

6 _____ hates or .

   Question: _____

7 _____ has with for breakfast.

   Question: _____

8 _____ likes and .

   Question: _____

9 _____ often has and for lunch.

   Question: _____

10 _____ eats a lot of .

   Question: _____

Instructions p126 | © Cambridge University Press 2005 | face2face Elementary Photocopiable

5A Places bingo places in a town/the country

Student A

Student B

Student C

Student D

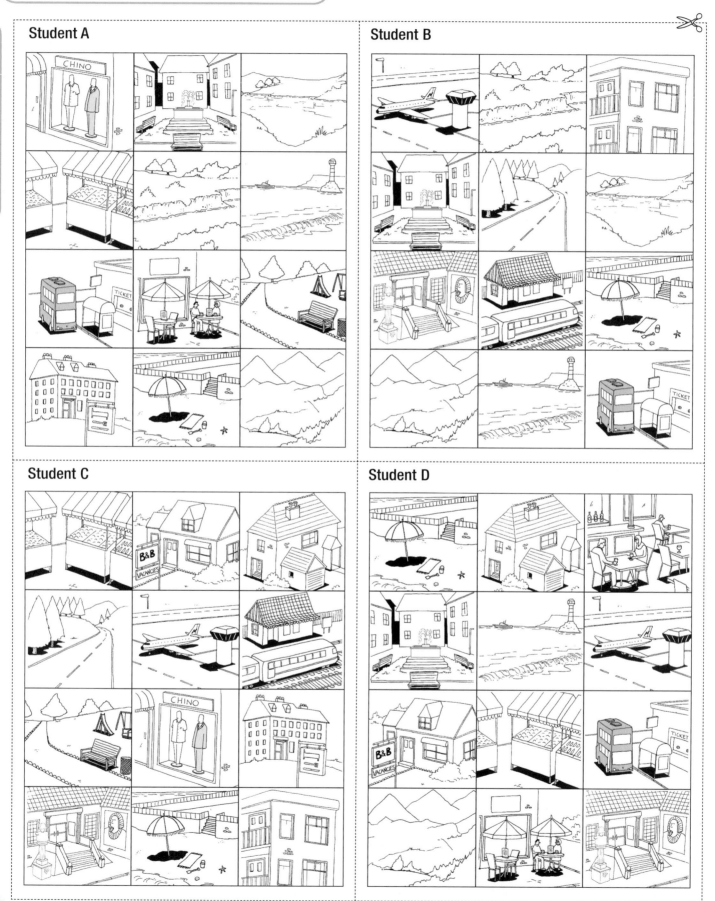

Flat questionnaire

		Flat A	Flat B	Flat C
1	rent?			
2	rooms?			
3	beds?			
4	furniture in the living room?			
5	shower and a bath?			
6	washing machine?			
7	fridge?			
8	garden?			
9	balcony?			
10	station near the flat?			
11	shops near the flat?			
12	park near the flat?			

Flat A

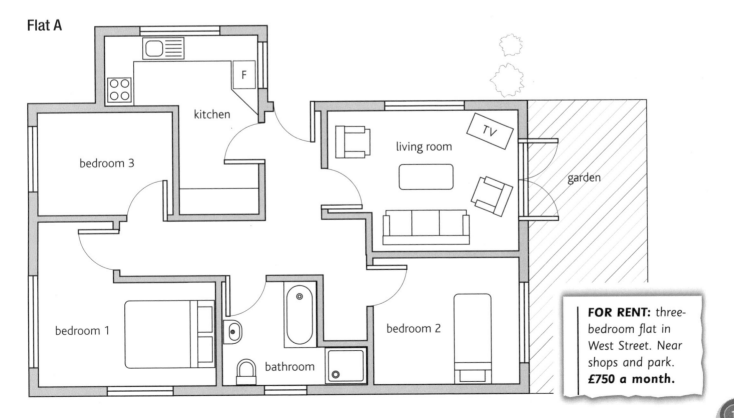

kitchen

bedroom 3

bedroom 1

bathroom

living room

TV

garden

bedroom 2

FOR RENT: three-bedroom flat in West Street. Near shops and park. **£750 a month.**

© Cambridge University Press 2005   face2face Elementary Photocopiable

Flat B

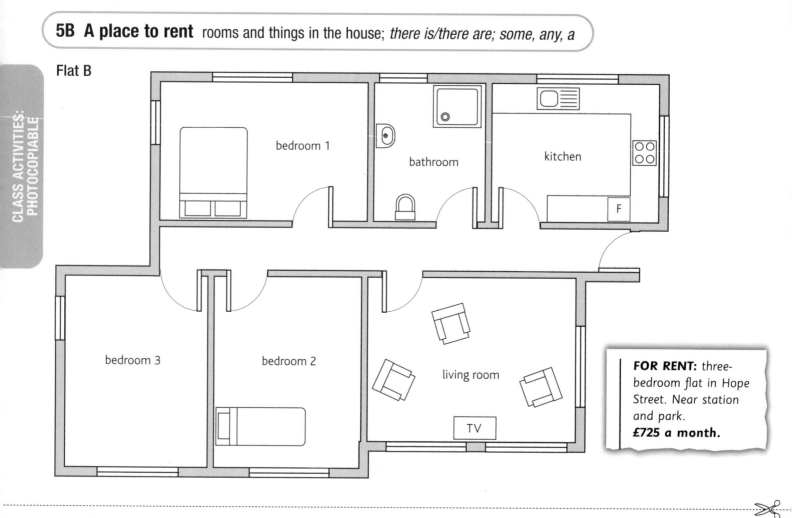

FOR RENT: three-bedroom flat in Hope Street. Near station and park.
£725 a month.

Flat C

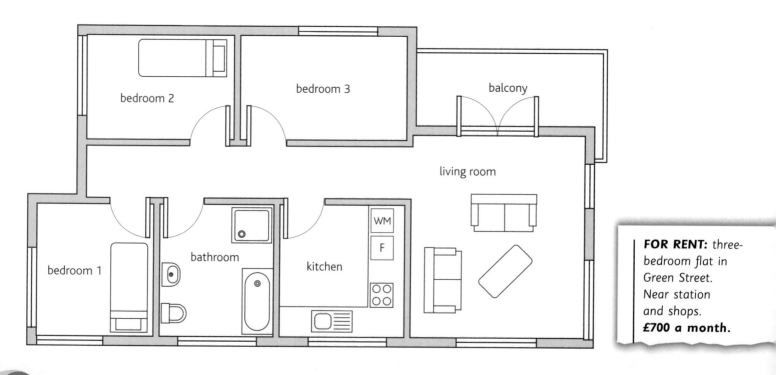

FOR RENT: three-bedroom flat in Green Street. Near station and shops.
£700 a month.

Instructions p127

5D Shopping crossword — clothes and shops

Student A

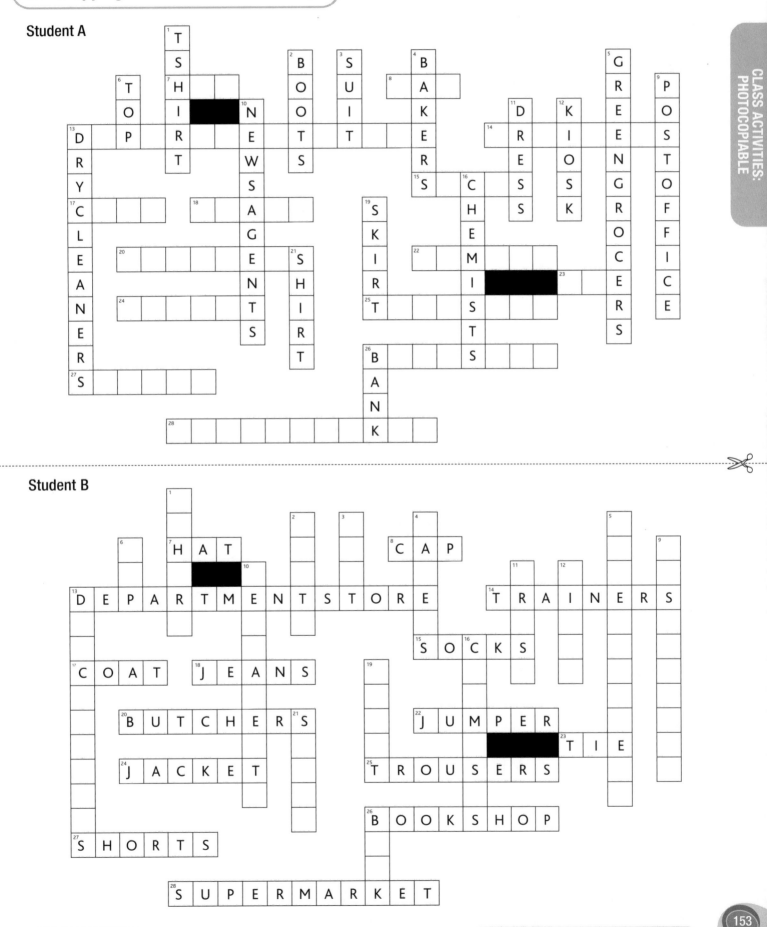

Student B

© Cambridge University Press 2005   face2face Elementary Photocopiable

6A Famous people quiz *Wh-* questions with *was/were*

Quiz A

1 Who *was/were* the director of the film *Titanic*?

a) Steven Spielberg
b) Peter Jackson
c) **James Cameron**

2 Who *was/were* the President of the USA before George W. Bush?

a) His father, George Bush
b) Ronald Reagan
c) **Bill Clinton**

3 Who *was/were* Laurel and Hardy?

a) musicians
b) doctors
c) **actors**

4 Where *was/were* Charlie Chaplin born?

a) New York
b) Paris
c) **London**

5 Where *was/were* David Beckham and Victoria Adams married?

a) England
b) Spain
c) **Ireland**

6 Who *was/were* the first man on the moon?

a) John Glenn
b) **Neil Armstrong**
c) Yuri Gagarin

7 Who *was/were* the two stars of the film *Pretty Woman*?

a) Nicole Kidman and Richard Gere
b) Julia Roberts and Brad Pitt
c) **Julia Roberts and Richard Gere**

8 When *was/were* the British singer David Bowie born?

a) **1947**
b) 1957
c) 1967

Quiz B

1 Who *was/were* Nicole Kidman married to?

a) Mel Gibson
b) Tom Hanks
c) **Tom Cruise**

2 What *was/were* John F Kennedy's middle name?

a) **Fitzgerald**
b) Frank
c) Frederick

3 Where *was/were* Madonna and Guy Ritchie married?

a) The USA
b) **Scotland**
c) England

4 Where *was/were* William Shakespeare born?

a) London
b) Oxford
c) **Stratford-upon-Avon**

5 Which film *was/were* Sean Connery and Harrison Ford in together?

a) Star Wars
b) **Indiana Jones and the Last Crusade**
c) Jurassic Park

6 Who *was/were* the British Prime Minister in 1998?

a) Margaret Thatcher
b) **Tony Blair**
c) John Major

7 Who *was/were* the Jackson Five?

a) **singers**
b) actors
c) footballers

8 What *was/were* the name of Paul McCartney's first wife?

a) **Linda McCartney**
b) Yoko Ono
c) Stella McCartney

face2face Elementary Photocopiable © Cambridge University Press 2005

Instructions p127

6B Antonio's honeymoon Past Simple: positive and *Wh-* questions

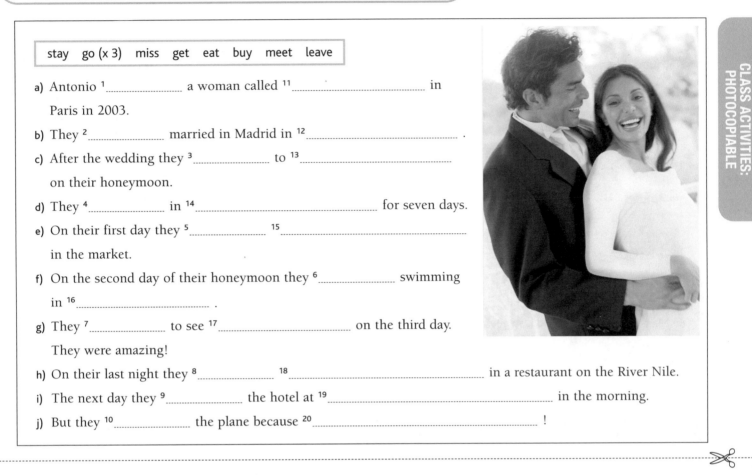

| stay | go (x 3) | miss | get | eat | buy | meet | leave |

a) Antonio [1]_____ a woman called [11]_____ in Paris in 2003.

b) They [2]_____ married in Madrid in [12]_____ .

c) After the wedding they [3]_____ to [13]_____ on their honeymoon.

d) They [4]_____ in [14]_____ for seven days.

e) On their first day they [5]_____ [15]_____ in the market.

f) On the second day of their honeymoon they [6]_____ swimming in [16]_____ .

g) They [7]_____ to see [17]_____ on the third day. They were amazing!

h) On their last night they [8]_____ [18]_____ in a restaurant on the River Nile.

i) The next day they [9]_____ the hotel at [19]_____ in the morning.

j) But they [10]_____ the plane because [20]_____ !

Information cards

Egypt	the Pyramids
a 5-star hotel in Luxor	June 2005
some beautiful carpets	fish and salad
Veronica	5.30
the Red Sea	Antonio forgot his passport

Instructions p128

© Cambridge University Press 2005   face2face Elementary Photocopiable

6D Money, money, money! Review of lessons 4A–6D

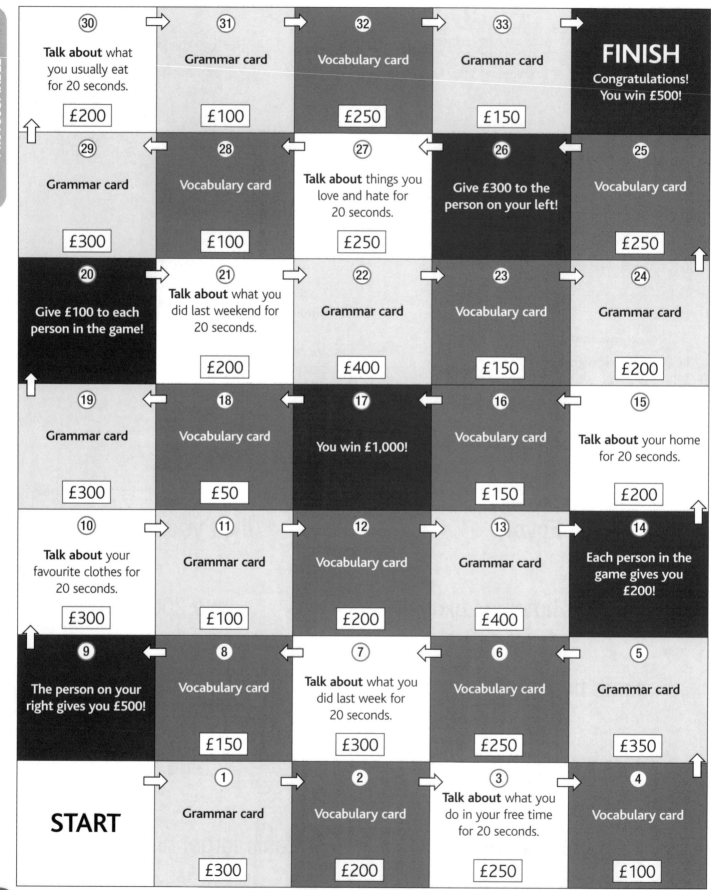

30 Talk about what you usually eat for 20 seconds. £200

31 Grammar card £100

32 Vocabulary card £250

33 Grammar card £150

FINISH Congratulations! You win £500!

29 Grammar card £300

28 Vocabulary card £100

27 Talk about things you love and hate for 20 seconds. £250

26 Give £300 to the person on your left!

25 Vocabulary card £250

20 Give £100 to each person in the game!

21 Talk about what you did last weekend for 20 seconds. £200

22 Grammar card £400

23 Vocabulary card £150

24 Grammar card £200

19 Grammar card £300

18 Vocabulary card £50

17 You win £1,000!

16 Vocabulary card £150

15 Talk about your home for 20 seconds. £200

10 Talk about your favourite clothes for 20 seconds. £300

11 Grammar card £100

12 Vocabulary card £200

13 Grammar card £400

14 Each person in the game gives you £200!

9 The person on your right gives you £500!

8 Vocabulary card £150

7 Talk about what you did last week for 20 seconds. £300

6 Vocabulary card £250

5 Grammar card £350

START

1 Grammar card £300

2 Vocabulary card £200

3 Talk about what you do in your free time for 20 seconds. £250

4 Vocabulary card £100

Instructions p128

6D Money, money, money! Review of lessons 4A–6D

Vocabulary cards

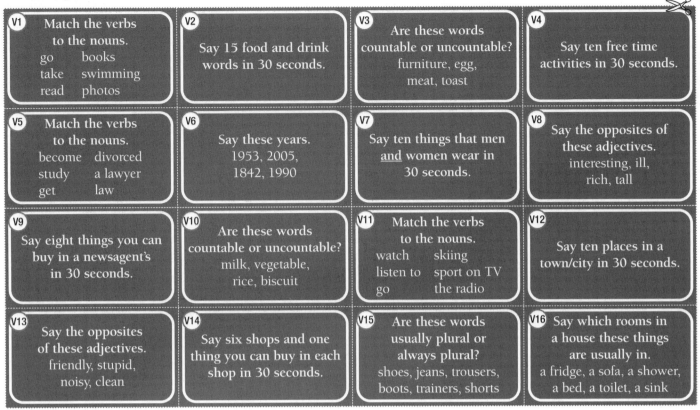

V1 Match the verbs to the nouns.
go   books
take   swimming
read   photos

V2 Say 15 food and drink words in 30 seconds.

V3 Are these words countable or uncountable?
furniture, egg, meat, toast

V4 Say ten free time activities in 30 seconds.

V5 Match the verbs to the nouns.
become   divorced
study   a lawyer
get   law

V6 Say these years.
1953, 2005, 1842, 1990

V7 Say ten things that men _and_ women wear in 30 seconds.

V8 Say the opposites of these adjectives.
interesting, ill, rich, tall

V9 Say eight things you can buy in a newsagent's in 30 seconds.

V10 Are these words countable or uncountable?
milk, vegetable, rice, biscuit

V11 Match the verbs to the nouns.
watch   skiing
listen to   sport on TV
go   the radio

V12 Say ten places in a town/city in 30 seconds.

V13 Say the opposites of these adjectives.
friendly, stupid, noisy, clean

V14 Say six shops and one thing you can buy in each shop in 30 seconds.

V15 Are these words usually plural or always plural?
shoes, jeans, trousers, boots, trainers, shorts

V16 Say which rooms in a house these things are usually in.
a fridge, a sofa, a shower, a bed, a toilet, a sink

Grammar cards

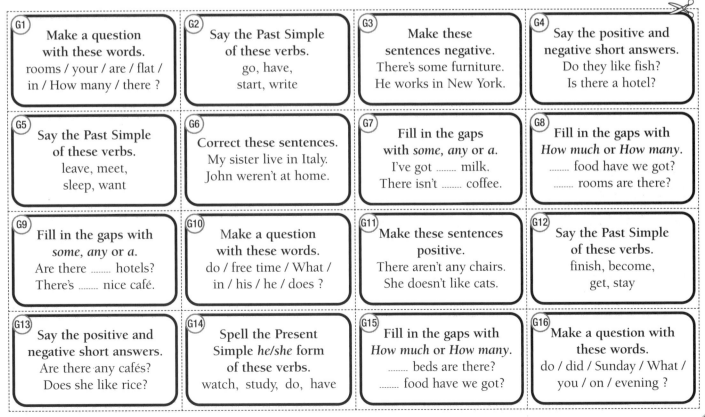

G1 Make a question with these words.
rooms / your / are / flat / in / How many / there ?

G2 Say the Past Simple of these verbs.
go, have, start, write

G3 Make these sentences negative.
There's some furniture.
He works in New York.

G4 Say the positive and negative short answers.
Do they like fish?
Is there a hotel?

G5 Say the Past Simple of these verbs.
leave, meet, sleep, want

G6 Correct these sentences.
My sister live in Italy.
John weren't at home.

G7 Fill in the gaps with _some, any_ or _a_.
I've got .... milk.
There isn't .... coffee.

G8 Fill in the gaps with _How much_ or _How many_.
.... food have we got?
.... rooms are there?

G9 Fill in the gaps with _some, any_ or _a_.
Are there .... hotels?
There's .... nice café.

G10 Make a question with these words.
do / free time / What / in / his / he / does ?

G11 Make these sentences positive.
There aren't any chairs.
She doesn't like cats.

G12 Say the Past Simple of these verbs.
finish, become, get, stay

G13 Say the positive and negative short answers.
Are there any cafés?
Does she like rice?

G14 Spell the Present Simple _he/she_ form of these verbs.
watch, study, do, have

G15 Fill in the gaps with _How much_ or _How many_.
.... beds are there?
.... food have we got?

G16 Make a question with these words.
do / did / Sunday / What / you / on / evening ?

Instructions p128

face2face Elementary Photocopiable

7A My partner's past Past Simple: *yes/no* questions

Student A

		✓ or ✗ ?
1	He/She *went out/stayed in* last Saturday night.	
2	He/She *watched/didn't watch* some sport on TV last weekend.	
3	He/She had dinner *in a restaurant/at home* last night.	
4	He/She *travelled/didn't travel* to another city or country last month.	
5	He/She got up *early/late* last Sunday.	
6	He/She *bought/didn't buy* some new clothes or shoes last weekend.	
7	He/She *went/didn't go* to the cinema last month.	
8	He/She went to bed *before/after* midnight last night.	
9	He/She *played/didn't play* tennis or football last month.	
10	He/She left home *before/after* 8 a.m. this morning.	

Student B

		✓ or ✗ ?
1	He/She *went out/stayed in* last night.	
2	He/She *watched/didn't watch* a DVD last weekend.	
3	He/She *listened/didn't listen* to the radio this morning.	
4	He/She had dinner *before/after* 9 p.m. last night.	
5	He/She *went/didn't go* to a party or a concert last month.	
6	He/She got up *before/after* 8 a.m. this morning.	
7	He/She *met/didn't meet* some friends last Sunday.	
8	He/She *did/didn't do* some sport last week.	
9	He/She had breakfast *at home/in a café* this morning.	
10	He/She *studied/didn't study* English last weekend.	

Instructions p129

Who Where When Why Whose Which What How many How long How old	Name
1 This person is a musician in a band called the Family. He/She plays the .... Question: ....?	
2 This person is a singer. He/She made his/her first album .... years ago. Question: ....?	
3 This person is an actor/actress. He/She has got .... Oscars. Question: ....?	
4 This person was a film director. He/She worked in Hollywood for .... years. Question: ....?	
5 This person is a babysitter. He/She looks after ....'s children. Question: ....?	
6 This person is a journalist. He/She interviewed .... last month. Question: ....?	
7 This person is a teacher. He/She left his/her job last week because .... Question: ....?	
8 This person is a writer. He/She lives in a castle in Scotland. It's .... years old. Question: ....?	
9 This person is a footballer. Last week he/she bought .... Question: ....?	
10 This person is a travel writer. Last month he/she went to .... Question: ....?	

STUDENT A

You're a musician in a band called the Family. You play rock music and you're very famous in your country. Last year your album was number one. You play the guitar and you're also the singer.

STUDENT B

You're a very famous singer in your country. You made your first album three years ago. It was called *Past and Present* and it sold 3 million copies. You sing pop music and rap and you write all the songs and music.

STUDENT C

You're a famous Spanish actor/actress and you live in Hollywood. You usually make thrillers and action films. You have got lots of famous friends, like Leonardo di Caprio and Julia Roberts. You've got five Oscars.

STUDENT D

You were a famous film director, but you retired last year. You worked in Hollywood for 29 years and made over 60 films. Now you live in the mountains and you never watch films on TV or at the cinema!

STUDENT E

You're a babysitter and you look after David and Victoria Beckham's children when they go out in the evenings. You like the children very much and you're good friends with their parents. Three years ago you looked after Madonna's children!

STUDENT F

You're a journalist for a famous newspaper in your country. You interview famous people and write articles about them. Last month you interviewed Brad Pitt. He was very friendly and you went out for a meal together!

STUDENT G

You're a teacher from Australia and you started teaching ten years ago. You left your job last week because you won £5 million on the lottery! Now you want to buy a house in Hawaii and then have a really big party!

STUDENT H

You're a famous British writer and you live in a big castle in Scotland. The castle is 900 years old and it has 43 rooms, but you live on your own there. You write horror stories and the castle is the perfect place for you to work.

STUDENT I

You're a famous footballer in your country. You make a lot of money every week and you love cars. Last week you bought a new red Ferrari. Now you've got three Ferraris – and a Rolls Royce!

STUDENT J

You're an American travel writer. You visit lots of different countries and write travel books. Last month you went to Brazil and two months ago you went to Japan. You love your job – but you hate staying in hotels!

Tourist

British tourists safe

This morning an army helicopter found the two missing British tourists, **Sam Smith and Pat Davis.** The tourists left Kathmandu, in Nepal, nearly two months ago. They wanted to walk across the Himalayas to China, but they never arrived at the border. Both tourists are safe and well.

You are Sam Smith or Pat Davis. A journalist from the News365 website wants to interview you. Make notes on these things to help you in the interview:

- the reason why you got lost
- the place(s) you stayed at night
- what you did in the day
- what you ate and drank
- the clothes you had with you
- people you met
- animals you saw
- how you tried to get help
- other problems you had
- what you want to do now
- other things you can tell the journalist

Journalist

British tourists safe

This morning an army helicopter found the two missing British tourists, **Sam Smith and Pat Davis.** The tourists left Kathmandu, in Nepal, nearly two months ago. They wanted to walk across the Himalayas to China, but they never arrived at the border. Both tourists are safe and well.

You are a journalist for the News365 website. You want to interview Sam Smith or Pat Davis. Write questions to ask about these things.

- the reason why they got lost
- the place(s) they stayed at night
- what they did in the day
- what they ate and drank
- the clothes they had with them
- people they met
- animals they saw
- how they tried to get help
- other problems they had
- what they want to do now
- your own ideas

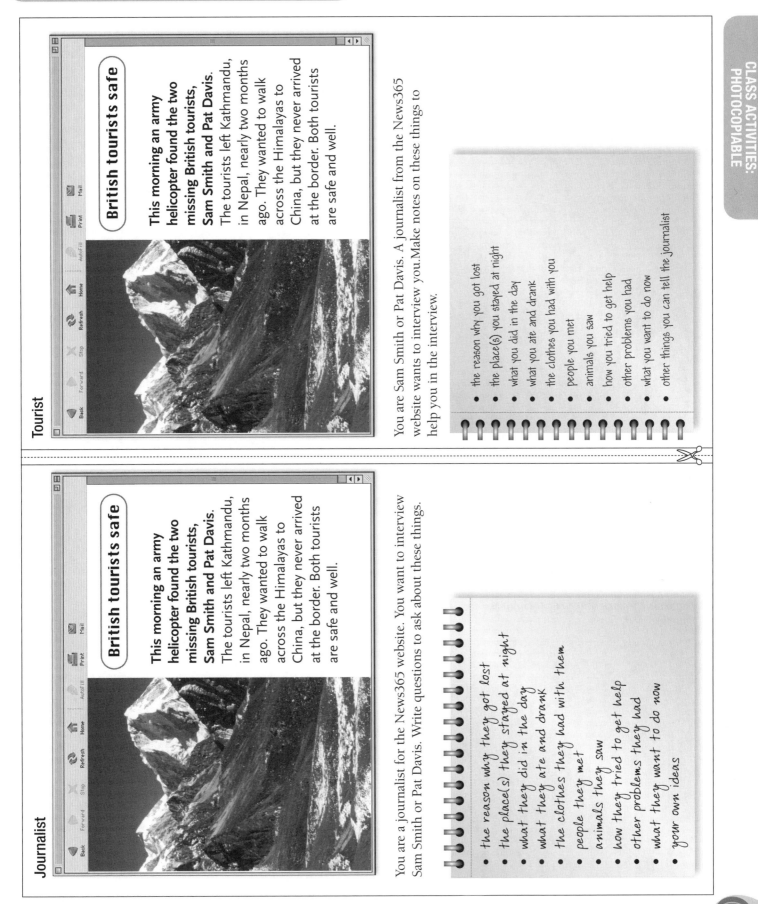

8A Language schools *can/can't* for possibility; holiday activities

Group A

www.whichlanguageschool.co.uk

www.whichlanguageschool.co.uk

**The City Language School
23 Highgrove Road, Liverpool**

The school

- general English courses 20 hours a week
- morning or afternoon courses
- library open from 8.00 a.m. to 9.00 p.m.
- coffee bar and restaurant
- join the theatre club – start acting in English!
- stay in student accommodation (20 mins from school) or with English families

The place

Liverpool is, of course, the home of the Beatles, but there's lots more to this famous old city than John, Paul, George and Ringo!

- visit museums and art galleries (including the Tate Gallery)
- go to a Premiership football match
- see a play at the famous Liverpool Playhouse
- go sightseeing in the city centre
- go dancing in one of the city's famous nightclubs
- go to the Cavern Club, where the Beatles first played!

Group B

www.whichlanguageschool.co.uk

www.whichlanguageschool.co.uk

**English World Language School
Station Rd, York**

The school

- general English courses 15 or 25 hours a week
- morning or afternoon courses
- students' library
- study centre with free Internet
- coffee shop and games room
- stay with English families and practise English at home!

The place

York is a beautiful old city in the north of England, and there are lots of things to see and do there.

- visit the 800-year-old York Minster Cathedral
- go on boat trips along the river
- go cycling or have a picnic in the beautiful Rowntree Park
- hire a bike and explore the beautiful countryside
- go shopping in The Shambles, the city's famous old shopping area
- eat out in traditional English pubs

Instructions p130

Group C

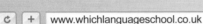

Sea View Language School
Coast Road, Plymouth, Devon

The school

- general English courses 15 or 20 hours a week
- afternoon or evening courses
- school library (open 9 a.m.–7 p.m. every day)
- self-study centre free to all students
- coffee and sandwich bar
- stay with local English families

The place

Plymouth, in the south-west of England, is a great place to come and learn English – and have fun!

- go on boat trips and go fishing in the sea
- go waterskiing and sailing
- go for walks along the coast
- have picnics in the beautiful Dartmoor National Park
- go to the beach and sunbathe
- go for a meal on the seafront

Group D

www.whichlanguageschool.co.uk

Lakeside Language School
Lake Road, Ambleside

The school

- general English courses 10, 20 or 30 hours a week
- morning, afternoon and evening courses
- students' library open from 8.00 a.m. till 9.00 p.m.
- school open on Saturdays
- restaurant and coffee bar
- stay in student accommodation next to the school (flats for four students)

The place

Ambleside is a small town in the Lake District in the north-west of England. It's famous for its beautiful lake and mountains.

- go sailing on Ambleside Lake
- go walking in the mountains
- rent a bike and go cycling to local villages
- eat out in traditional English pubs
- go shopping in local markets
- camp in the beautiful countryside

the USA	Spain	English	Chinese
dogs	cats	your bedroom	your living room
the Beatles	the Rolling Stones	Madonna	Britney Spears
London	Sydney	the River Nile	the River Thames
a Ferrari	a Volkswagen Golf	Brad Pitt	Robert De Niro
your mother	your father	Antarctica	South America
Mount Fuji	Mount Everest	tennis	football
the Pyramids	the Taj Mahal	a CD player	a personal stereo

face2face Elementary Photocopiable © Cambridge University Press 2005

Instructions p131

8D Collocation dominoes collocations review

... **us** when you come to England?	I need to **book** ...	... **a flight** to New York.	You can **get** ...
... **a bus** to the city centre from the airport.	I really like **going for** ...	... **walks** in the mountains.	Do you know where I can **rent** ...
... **a motorbike** for the weekend?	When we were in Paris we **stayed** ...	... **in a nice hotel** by the River Seine.	Mat and Sarah **went** ...
... **skiing** in the Alps last year.	We usually **travel by** ...	... **public transport** when we're on holiday.	When we arrived we **rented** ...
... **a car** and went to visit my aunt.	When I was young I **went** ...	... **fishing** with my father a lot.	They usually **stay with** ...
...**friends** when they're in London.	How much is it to **rent** ...	... **an apartment** in Los Angeles?	My American cousins always **go** ...
... **on holiday** in January.	Last year Tim **went** ...	... **on holiday** with his brother.	Did you remember to **book** ...
... **a hotel room** for Mr Robinson?	When we left the restaurant, we **got** ...	... **a taxi** back to our hotel.	How long did they **stay in** ...
... the north of **Canada**?	Yesterday we **went on** ...	... **a boat trip** to Alcatraz.	Can you tell me how to **get** ...
... **to your place** from the airport?	On Monday Paul **rented** ...	... **a bike** and cycled to the lake.	Susannah wants to **go** ...
... **sightseeing** when she's in Rome.	Excuse me, can I **book**. ...	... **a table** for two for 8 p.m., please?	Today I want to **go to** ...
... **the beach** and sunbathe all day.	Anne and David often **go** ...	... **cycling** at the weekend.	Do you want to **stay with** ...

9A At the park Present Continuous for 'now'

Anna Harry Hassan Remi Jane Polly Rob Lee Mark Laura Bob Jack
Jane and Sarah Tony and Frank John and Alex Elena and Maria

face2face Elementary Photocopiable © Cambridge University Press 2005 Instructions p132

Activity cards

① **Hassan** is sitting outside the café and talking on his mobile.	② **Elena and Maria** are buying ice-creams.	③ **Lee** is sitting outside the café and reading a newspaper.	④ **Bob** is taking a photo.
⑤ **Jane and Sarah** are sitting on the grass and having a picnic.	⑥ **Polly** is having a coffee and a sandwich outside the café.	⑦ **John and Alex** are sitting on the grass and reading a book.	⑧ **Remi** is writing a postcard to his family.
⑨ **Mark** is running away from a dog.	⑩ **Laura** is having a cup of tea and reading a book.	⑪ **Jack** is listening to music on his personal stereo.	⑫ **Rob** is selling ice-cream.
⑬ **Anna** is going into the café.	⑭ **Tony and Frank** are playing football.	⑮ **Jane** is writing an email to her husband.	⑯ **Harry** is playing computer games.

Student B

Hi Fiona

How are you? At the moment Robert and I are sitting in a taxi in the centre of London. We're going a) _____ (Where?) to meet some friends, but there's a transport strike today so it's taking a long time. Robert is reading the newspaper and I'm writing this email on my laptop and eating b) _____ (What?) at the same time!

Life with me is good. I like my new job and the people in the office are nice. But I hate c) _____ ! (What?) I start work at 8.30 and usually finish work at about d) _____ . (What time?) But I'm having a day off today because my friends are coming to visit. Their names are Lucas and Karen, and they live in e) _____ . (Where?) The last time I saw them was six years ago!

Oh dear, this traffic is terrible – we're not moving at all. Now Robert's talking to his sister on his mobile and the taxi driver is f) _____ ! (What?)

There isn't much family news – the children are fine. Tom has tennis lessons every week and he's very good now. Sally doesn't like sport at all, she wants to be g) _____ (What?) when she's older. They both like going to school, but at the moment they're staying h) _____ (Where?) – the schools are closed today because of the strike.

Oh, we're moving again – good. I'll write again soon. Bye!

Love

Olivia

Student A

Hi Fiona

How are you? At the moment Robert and I are sitting 1 _____ (Where?) in the centre of London. We're going to the airport to meet some friends, but there's a transport strike today so it's taking a long time. Robert is reading 2 _____ (What?) and I'm writing this email on my laptop and eating a sandwich at the same time!

Life with me is good. I like 3 _____ (What?) and the people in the office are nice. But I hate getting up in the morning! I start work at 4 _____ (What time?) and usually finish work at about six. But I'm having a day off today because 5 _____ . (Why?) Their names are Lucas and Karen, and they live in Brazil. The last time I saw them was six years ago!

Oh dear, this traffic is terrible – we're not moving at all. Now Robert's talking to 6 _____ (Who?) on his mobile and the taxi driver is reading a book!

There isn't much family news – the children are fine. Tom has 7 _____ (What?) every week and he's very good now. Sally doesn't like sport at all, she wants to be a doctor when she's older. They both like 8 _____ , (What?) but at the moment they're staying at my parents' house – the schools are closed today because of the strike.

Oh, we're moving again – good. I'll write again soon. Bye!

Love

Olivia

Instructions p132

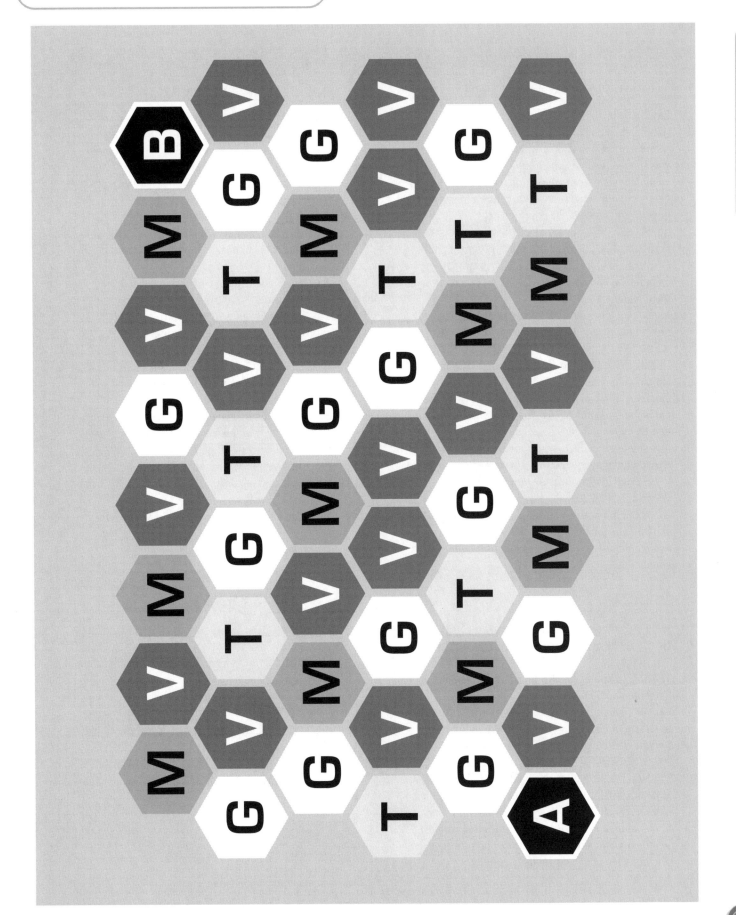

face2face Elementary Photocopiable

169

Team A

Ⓖ Grammar

1 Do we usually use these words/phrases with the Present Simple or the Present Continuous? **at the moment, usually, every week, today** (*Present Simple: usually, every week; Present Continuous: at the moment, now*)
2 Correct this sentence: **Jack plays chess very good.** (*Jack plays chess very well.*)
3 Spell the verb+*ing* form of these verbs: **sit, smoke, play** (*sitting, smoking, playing*)
4 Correct this sentence: **The UK is more expensive Russia.** (*The UK is more expensive than Russia.*)
5 Make the comparative of these adjectives: **crowded, noisy, bad** (*more crowded, noisier, worse*)
6 Fill in the gap with *last, in* or *ago*: **I went to Rome two years ..... with my wife.** (*ago*)
7 Correct this question: **Why Jim went to bed early last night?** (*Why did Jim go to bed early last night?*)
8 Put these time phrases in order from 'now': **three years ago, in 2001, last month, in June last year** (*last month, in June last year, three years ago, in 2001*)
9 Correct this sentence: **They don't watch TV at the moment.** (*They aren't watching TV at the moment.*)

Ⓥ Vocabulary

1 Say the opposite of these adjectives: **crowded, dirty, friendly** (*empty, clean, unfriendly*)
2 Say the Past Simple of these verbs: **choose, tell, say** (*chose, told, said*)
3 What are the adverbs for these adjectives? **easy, bad, fast** (*easily, badly, fast*)
4 Say eight question words in 20 seconds. (*who, where, when, why, whose, which, what, how many, how long, how old, what time, how much, etc.*)
5 Say the Past Simple of these verbs: **lose, break, come** (*lost, broke, came*)
6 Say three things you can **rent**. (*a bike, a motorbike, a car, a flat/apartment, etc.*)
7 In an office, say one thing you can: **sign, answer, take** (*sign a contract/a letter, answer an email/a letter/the phone, take notes/ a message*)
8 Say six types of music in 20 seconds. (*rap, rock music, pop music, classical music, opera, jazz, dance music, reggae, rock'n'roll, etc.*)
9 Say the verbs that mean the same as these phrases: **go by plane, go by car, go by boat** (*fly, drive, sail*)
10 Which is the odd one out and why? **bike, foot, train, bus** (*'foot' because it uses the preposition 'on', not 'by'*)

Ⓜ Mystery

1 Fill in the gaps in these telephone phrases: **Hold ..... a moment. Can I call you ..... ?** (*on, back*)
2 Tell the joke about the dog in the cinema from lesson 7D.
3 Do we use the infinitive (*do*) or the infinitive with *to* (*to do*) with these phrases? **I'd like, I want, I'd rather** (*I'd like and I want + infinitive with to, I'd rather + infinitive*)
4 Say two reasons why the writer Ian Fleming and James Bond's lives are similar. (*They both worked for the British Secret Service, they went to the same school, they were both good at sport.*)
5 Say two ways you can say who you are on the phone. (*This is (John)., It's (John).*)

Ⓣ Talk about

1 Talk about music you like and don't like for 20 seconds.
2 Talk about what you did last weekend for 20 seconds.
3 Talk about things you can or can't do in your town/city for 20 seconds.
4 Talk about what your friends and family are doing now for 20 seconds.
5 Talk about things you usually do on holiday for 20 seconds.

Grammar

1 Correct this question: **When Madonna made her first record?** (*When did Madonna* **make** *her first record?*)
2 What are the questions for these answers? **a) She's a doctor. b) She's sitting on a beach.** (*a*) *What does she do? b) What is she doing (now/at the moment)?*)
3 Spell the verb+*ing* form of these verbs: **write, study, stop** (*writing, studying, stopping*)
4 Correct this question: **How many people there were in the Beatles?** (*How many people* **were there** *in the Beatles?*)
5 Fill in the gap with *last, in* or *ago*: **I played tennis ...... weekend.** (*last*)
6 Put these time phrases in order from 'now': **two days ago, half an hour ago, in January last year, last night** (*half an hour ago, last night, two days ago, in January last year*)
7 Correct this question: **What are your parents do at the moment?** (*What are your parents doing at the moment?*)
8 Make the comparative of these adjectives: **happy, small, interesting, good** (*happier, smaller, more interesting, better*)
9 Correct this sentence: **Spain is more hot than England.** (*Spain is hotter than England.*)

Vocabulary

1 Say the Past Simple of these verbs: **win, put, take** (*won, put, took*)
2 Say three things you can **book**. (*a flight, a room, a table at a restaurant, etc.*)
3 Say six types of film in 20 seconds. (*action film, thriller, horror film, science-fiction (sci-fi) film, cartoon, love story, comedy, historical drama, etc.*)
4 Say eight things you can do on holiday in 20 seconds. (*go fishing, go sightseeing, go shopping, go skiing, go swimming, go cycling, go for walks, go to the beach, go on boat trips, sunbathe, have picnics, rent a car/bike, etc.*)
5 Say three things you can **play**. (*chess, a musical instrument, tennis, football, etc.*)
6 Say three things you can **ride**. (*a horse, a bike, a motorbike*)
7 Say the adverbs for these adjectives: **beautiful, fluent, hard** (*beautifully, fluently, hard*)
8 Say the opposite of these adjectives: **safe, modern, boring** (*dangerous, old, interesting*)
9 Say the Past Simple of these verbs: **fall, buy, find** (*fell, bought, found*)
10 Say eight types of transport in 20 seconds. (*car, plane, train, taxi, bus, tram, bike, scooter, boat, motorbike, etc.*)

Ⓜ Mystery

1 Fill in the gaps in these telephone phrases: **I ...... your message. Call me ...... my mobile.** (*got, on*)
2 Say five of the people or bands whose photographs were in the music quiz in lesson 7B. (*Madonna, U2, Sting, Elton John, the Beatles, Shakira, Elvis Presley*)
3 Where did Luke and Monica go on holiday? Did Monica or Luke want to go there? (*Phuket, in Thailand. Monica wanted to go there.*)
4 Say three of the radio news stories in lesson 7C. (*plane crashed in China, married couple lost on Everest, flood in India, dog won lottery*)
5 Say three things you can do in Regent's Park. (*go to the zoo, listen to music, go to the theatre, go on a bike ride, go on a guided bird walk*)

Ⓣ Talk about

1 Talk about your last holiday for 20 seconds.
2 Talk about films you like and don't like for 20 seconds.
3 Talk about things you can or can't do for 20 seconds.
4 Talk about a place you'd like to go to for the weekend for 20 seconds.
5 Talk about what you did yesterday for 20 seconds.

10A Something in common *How often ... ?* and frequency expressions; prepositions

How often do you ...	Me	Name
1 ... go *in/to/on* the cinema?		
2 ... get *up/ – /for* before 7 a.m.?		
3 ... go *to/in/for* a walk in the park or the country?		
4 ... phone *with/ – /to* your best friend?		
5 ... go *out/up/on* with friends?		
6 ... play *with/ – /on* football, tennis or golf?		
7 ... watch sport *in/ – /on* TV?		
8 ... go *by/to/with* the gym?		
9 ... go *on/for/of* a drink after work/university?		
10 ... listen *for/ – /to* the radio?		
11 ... go *to/ – /on* shopping for clothes?		
12 ... go *in/ – /to* bed after midnight?		

Student A

10C Get well soon! health problems and treatments

Student A

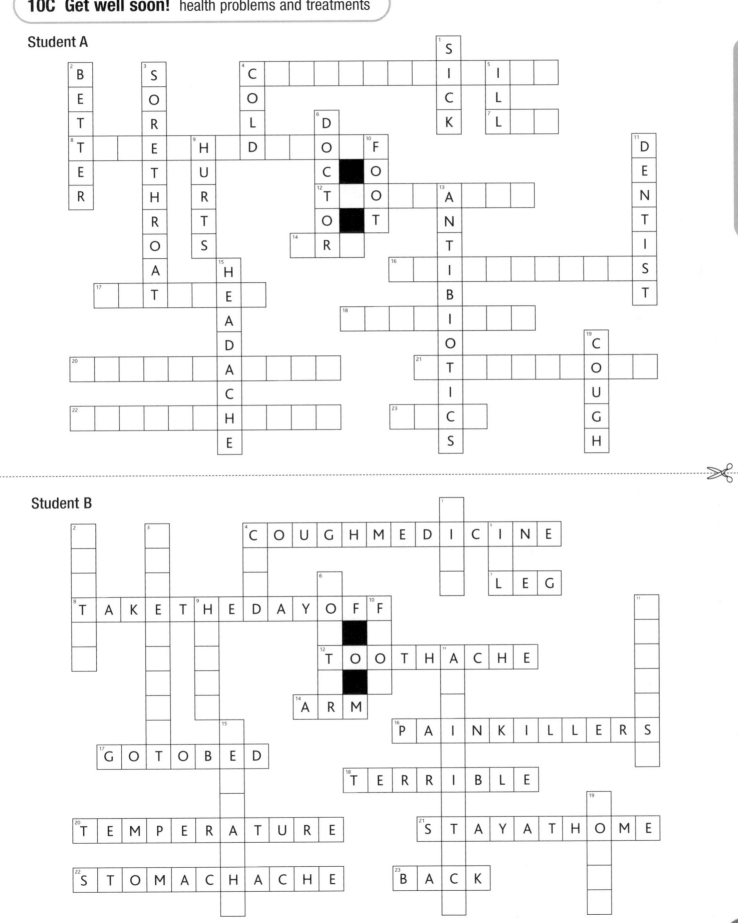

Student B

11A New Year's Day *Wh-* questions with *be going to*

Student A

Tomorrow's New Year's Day, so we've got a lot of things to do. In the morning we're going to buy ¹_____ for the living room and in the afternoon we're going to visit my father. Then in the evening we're going to have dinner at our ²_____ .

Tom and Katrina

It's going to be a busy day. In the morning Gary and I are going to clean the house, then in the afternoon we're going to meet ³_____ for lunch – it's her 30th birthday. Then in the evening my family are going to come for dinner. I'm going to cook chicken, I think.

Rebecca and Gary

On New Year's Day in the afternoon I'm going to see ⁴_____ in London with my cousin. Then I'm going to meet my friend Freddy in town and we're going to buy ⁵_____ . In the evening I'm going to have dinner at my sister's – chicken again, probably!

Daniel

New Year's Day? I'm going to play golf in the morning – it's very good exercise, I think. In the afternoon my ⁶_____ are going to visit me. Then I'm going to have dinner at my granddaughter's in the evening. I hope she doesn't cook chicken again!

Harold

Student B

Tomorrow's New Year's Day, so we've got a a lot of things to do. In the morning we're going to buy a new sofa for the living room and in the afternoon we're going to visit my a)_____ . Then in the evening we're going to have dinner at our daughter's house.

Tom and Katrina

It's going to be a busy day. In the morning Gary and I are going to b)_____ , then in the afternoon we're going to meet my friend Helen for lunch – it's her 30th birthday. Then in the evening my family are going to come for dinner. I'm going to cook c)_____ , I think.

Rebecca and Gary

On New Year's Day in the afternoon I'm going to see a football match in London with my cousin. Then I'm going to meet d)_____ in town and we're going to buy some new CDs. In the evening I'm going to have dinner at my sister's – chicken again, probably!

Daniel

New Year's Day? I'm going to play e)_____ in the morning – it's very good exercise, I think. In the afternoon my son and his wife are going to visit me. Then I'm going to have dinner at f)_____ in the evening. I hope she doesn't cook chicken again!

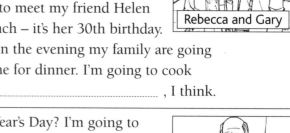

Harold

176

face2face Elementary Photocopiable   © Cambridge University Press 2005   Instructions p134

CLASS ACTIVITIES: PHOTOCOPIABLE

11C The missing lottery ticket asking for and giving directions

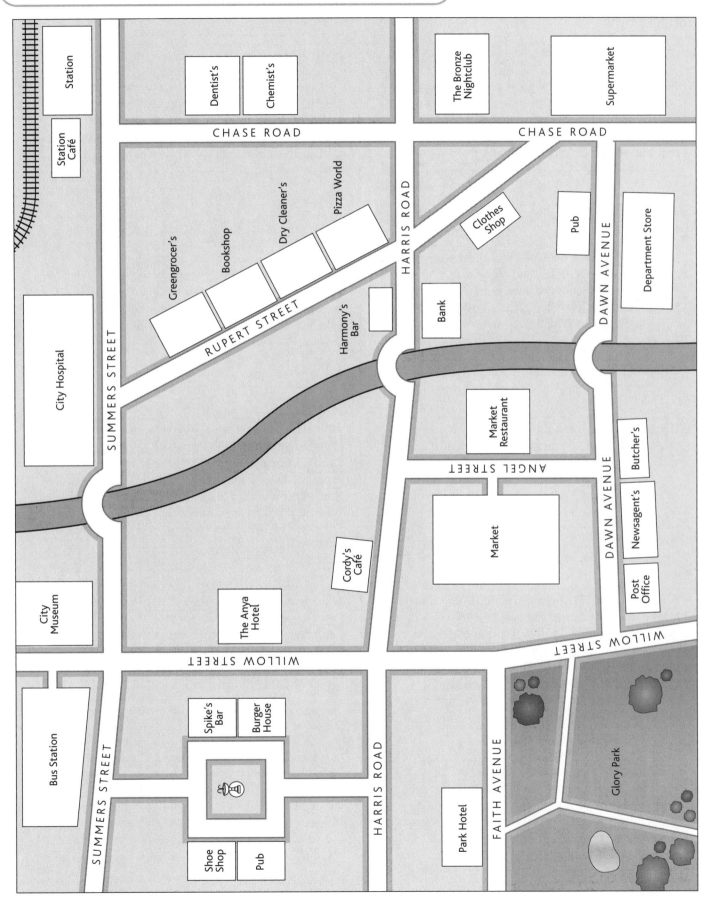

Directions cards

1

OK, you're at the station. good. Go along Summers Street, past the café, and turn left. That's Rupert Street, I think. Go past some shops on your left and then turn right. This place is on your right, opposite the bank. Where are you?

Answer: _____

2

It's not there? Oh, dear. Go out of the bar and turn right. Then go over the bridge and turn left. That's Angel Street, I think. At the end of the street turn right. There's a shop on your left, between the post office and a butcher's. What type of shop is it?

Answer: _____

3

Isn't it there either? OK, go out of the newsagent's and turn left. Walk to the end of the road – Glory Park is opposite you now. Turn right along Willow Street, then turn left. This place is on your right, opposite the park. Where are you?

Answer: _____

4

OK, I know where it is. Go back along Faith Avenue and turn left. Then turn left again – that's Harris Road. Go along this road and turn right. When you get to the square, look for the shop on the left, next to a pub. Which shop is it?

Answer: _____

5

Hmm, I didn't think it was there but I wanted to check. OK, go out of the shoe shop and turn left, and at the end of the road turn right. You're now on Summers Street again. Go along this street and go over the bridge. There's a big building on your left. What is it?

Answer: _____

6

Oh, dear. I'm sure it was there. Go out of the hospital and turn left. Turn right opposite the café and go along Chase Road. Go over Harris Road, past the Bronze nightclub, then turn right opposite the supermarket. This place is on your left opposite the pub. Where are you now?

Answer: _____

7

Sorry about this. I'm sure you're quite tired now! Maybe it's at the next place. Go out of the department store and turn left. Go over the bridge and turn right. Go past the market on your left, then at the end of the road turn left. I had a coffee in the place on the right – what's it called?

Answer: _____

8

Oh, dear, not there either? Well, the next place is quite near to where you are now. Go out of the café and turn right. Then turn right again – that's Willow Street, I think. Go along this road and go over Summers Street – there's a building on the right opposite the bus station. What is it?

Answer: _____

9

Isn't it there? You're joking! Well, go back to Summers Street and turn left. Go over the bridge again, and then turn right opposite the hospital. That's Rupert Street. On your left are some shops. This shop is between a greengrocer's and a dry cleaner's. What kind of shop is it?

Answer: _____

10

Ah, I remember now! Go out of the bookshop and turn left. Turn left again – that's Harris Road. Then after a few metres turn left and go along Chase Road. At the end of the road there's a place in front of you, next to the station. That's where I left it – well done, you found it!

Answer: _____

Instructions p135

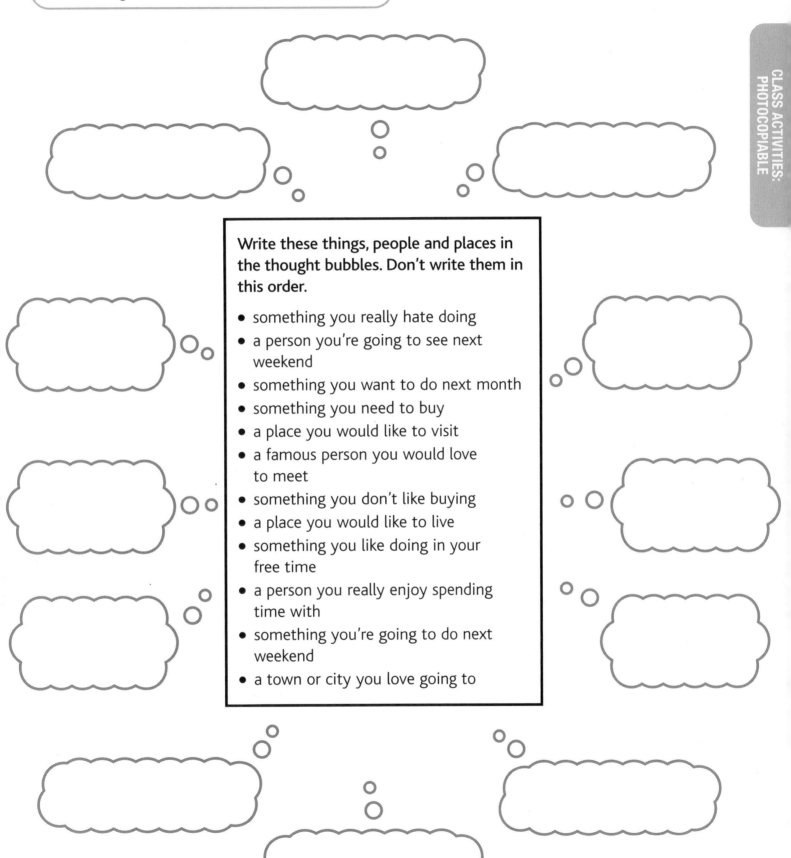

Write these things, people and places in the thought bubbles. Don't write them in this order.

- something you really hate doing
- a person you're going to see next weekend
- something you want to do next month
- something you need to buy
- a place you would like to visit
- a famous person you would love to meet
- something you don't like buying
- a place you would like to live
- something you like doing in your free time
- a person you really enjoy spending time with
- something you're going to do next weekend
- a town or city you love going to

CLASS ACTIVITIES: PHOTOCOPIABLE

Which restaurant ...	Name of restaurant
1 ... is the .... (modern)?	
2 ... is the .... (old)?	
3 ... is the .... (small)?	
4 ... is the .... (big)?	
5 ... has the .... (cheap) food and wine?	Food: Wine:
6 ... has the .... (expensive) food and wine?	Food: Wine:
7 ... is the .... (near) to the tube station?	
8 ... is the .... (far) from the tube station?	
9 ... opens the .... (early)?	
10 ... stays open the .... (late)?	
11 ... has the .... (interesting) menu?	
12 ... is the .... (good) for your evening out?	

The Golden Palace

This traditional restaurant opened in 1979 and is still one of the most popular restaurants in the North London area. Only seven minutes' walk from Finsbury Park tube station, The Golden Palace offers excellent French, Spanish and Mexican food cooked by one of the best chefs in London, with main courses between £13.50 and £18.95 and house wine at £12.50. It's the perfect place to go for that very special night out.

Opening times: 11.30 a.m.–11.30 p.m.   **Tables: 20**

The World Food Café

This exciting restaurant only opened in 2002, but it's quickly becoming one of the favourite places to eat in the area. With food from all over the world – Thai, Brazilian, Indian, Mexican and traditional English – it's a great place for an evening out. Main courses are between £10 and £15 and the excellent house wine is only £9.95. It's 20 minutes' walk from Finsbury Park tube – but you can always get a taxi!

Opening times: 10.30 a.m.–12.00 p.m.   **Tables: 32**

Asia Garden

This small, very friendly restaurant only opened last year, but it's now one of the area's most popular places for a night out. Asia Garden is only 10 minutes from Finsbury Park tube station and offers Chinese, Thai and Malaysian food cooked in traditional style by the restaurant's excellent chef. The main courses are from £7.50–£12.95 and house wine is only £10.50 a bottle. A great choice for that special evening.

Opening times: 12.00 a.m.–11.00 p.m.   **Tables: 12**

La Trattoria

La Trattoria, which opened in 1986, is now one of the most famous restaurants in the area and offers some of the best Italian food in London. And with main courses from £8.95 to £14.50 and house wine at only £7.95 a bottle, it's always very busy. So if you love pizza, pasta and traditional Italian service, then why not try La Trattoria for that special evening out – it's only three minutes from Finsbury Park tube station.

Opening times: 6.30 p.m.–2.00 a.m.   **Tables: 23**

face2face Elementary Photocopiable   © Cambridge University Press 2005   Instructions p135

Have you ever ...	Name	Extra information
1 a) **... / go / skiing?** b) Where / go? c) / have a good time?		
2 a) **... / work / or / study / in another country?** b) Which country / be / it ? c) What / do there?		
3 a) **... / meet / someone famous?** b) Who / meet? c) What / say to him or her?		
4 a) **... / go / to an important football match?** b) Which teams / see? c) / enjoy it?		
5 a) **... / lose / your mobile phone?** b) How / lose it? c) / find it?		
6 a) **... / want / to be in a band?** b) What kind of music / want to play? c) Which instrument / play?		
7 a) **... / go / to the cinema in another country?** b) Which country / be / it? c) Which film / see?		
8 a) **... / work / in a shop?** b) What / do there? c) How old / be / you?		
9 a) **... / write / a diary?** b) How old / be / you when you / start / it? c) / write it every day?		
10 a) **... / walk / more than 20 km in one day?** b) Why / walk so far? c) What / do the next day?		

face2face Elementary Photocopiable

Vocabulary Plus

Instructions

There are twelve Vocabulary Plus worksheets (p187–p198). These worksheets introduce additional vocabulary that is <u>not</u> presented in the Student's Book. The topic of each Vocabulary Plus worksheet is linked to the topic of the corresponding unit in the Student's Book. There is an answer key at the bottom of each worksheet, which can be cut off if necessary. You will need to photocopy one Vocabulary Plus worksheet for each student.

- Use them as extra vocabulary input in class. The instructions give additional communicative stages you can include in each lesson. We suggest you cut off the answer keys and check the answers after each exercise.

- Give them for homework for students to use on their own. You can either leave the answer keys on the worksheets so students can check answers themselves, or cut them off and check answers at the beginning of the next class.

- Give them to fast finishers in class. This is often useful when you have a mixed level class and some students finish longer speaking activities early. Students can then begin the worksheets and finish them for homework if necessary. You can then give the worksheet for homework to the other students at the end of the class.

1 Jobs p187

Language

a businesswoman, a businessman, a nurse, a secretary, a footballer, a pilot, a taxi driver, an artist, a singer, a hairdresser, a journalist, a politician

When to use and time

Use any time after lesson 1B. 10–20 minutes.

Procedure

1 Students do the exercise on their own or in pairs. Check answers with the class (see answer key on worksheet). Drill the words chorally and individually, focusing on word stress. Pay particular attention to the pronunciation of *businesswoman* /ˈbɪznɪsˌwʊmən/, *businessman* /ˈbɪznɪsˌmæn/, *journalist* /ˈdʒɜːnəlɪst/ and *politician* /ˌpɒlɪˈtɪʃən/. Note that there are two different ways to pronounce *secretary*: /ˈsekrɪtəri/ and /ˈsekrɪteri/.

2 Students do the exercise on their own. Check answers with the class. Then put students into pairs. Students cover the words in **1** and take turns to ask their partners about the people. For example, student A points to picture 1 and asks *What's his job?*. Student B replies *He's a footballer*. Demonstrate this with a strong student before students work in their pairs.

3 Students do the puzzle in pairs. You can make this a race and the first pair to find all the words wins. Check answers with the class.

W	B	U	S	I	N	E	S	S	W	O	M	A	N
F	G	T	E	V	U	F	J	O	G	N	O	P	J
E	P	B	C	A	R	T	I	S	T	S	R	O	O
I	I	I	R	Y	S	A	S	V	M	I	W	L	U
P	L	K	E	S	E	B	O	N	T	N	S	I	R
F	O	O	T	B	A	L	L	E	R	G	I	T	N
O	T	U	A	D	J	R	Y	C	O	E	K	I	A
H	A	I	R	D	R	E	S	S	E	R	R	C	L
R	F	J	Y	C	K	O	G	B	D	E	A	I	I
L	T	A	X	I	D	R	I	V	E	R	M	A	S
S	Q	B	U	S	I	N	E	S	S	M	A	N	T

--- **EXTRA IDEA** ---

- Students work in pairs and take turns to mime jobs for their partner to guess. They can mime jobs from this worksheet and from lesson 1B.

2 Personal possessions p188

Language

keys, a briefcase, a handbag, a mirror, an address book, a pen, a hairbrush, make-up, a pencil, a dictionary, a notebook, a purse, a rubber [US: an eraser], tissues, a comb, money

When to use and time

Use any time after lesson 2D. 15–25 minutes.

Procedure

1 Students do the exercise on their own or in pairs. Check answers with the class (see answer key on worksheet). Check students understand that women usually have *purses* and men have *wallets*. Drill the words chorally and individually, focusing on word stress. Highlight the pronunciation of *handbag* /ˈhændbæg/, *mirror* /ˈmɪrə/, *purse* /pɜːs/, *tissues* /ˈtɪʃuːz/, *comb* /kəʊm/, *money* /ˈmʌni/. Also point out that *make-up* and *money* don't have a plural form and are used with a singular verb. (Note that students haven't been introduced to the concept of countable and uncountable nouns yet in the Student's Book, so it isn't advisable to go into this in detail at this stage.)

2 Students do the exercise on their own and check in pairs. Check answers with the class. Then put students into new pairs. Students take turns to ask each other *yes/no* questions with *have got* about the pictures. For example, student A asks *Has Andy got an address book in his briefcase?* and student B replies *No, he hasn't*.

3 Students do the exercise on their own or in pairs. Check answers with the class.

Tell students to look at the pictures for one minute and remember what each person has got. Students then cover the pictures. They then work in pairs or on their own and write down what Madga and Andy have got. The pair or student with the most correct answers wins.

— EXTRA IDEA —

- Students write three true and three false sentences about the pictures with *have/has* got. They then work in pairs and swap papers. Students decide which sentences are true and correct the false sentences, before checking with their partner.

3 Daily routines p189

Language

read the newspaper, go to the shops, watch the news, have a shower, check my email, charge my mobile phone, tidy up the flat, cook a meal, do my homework, do the washing-up [US: wash the dishes]

When to use and time

Use any time after lesson 3D. 20–30 minutes.

Procedure

 Students do the exercise on their own before checking in pairs. Check answers with the class (see answer key on worksheet). Drill the phrases with the class, focusing on natural rhythm and stress. Highlight the stress on *email*, and the pronunciation of *charge* /tʃɑːdʒ/ and *tidy* /ˈtaɪdi/. Point out that we can say *check my email* or *check my emails*. You can also point out that we often use *go to the shops* when we go to buy food and day-to-day provisions, whereas *go shopping* is more often used when we buy clothes, etc. Students can also confuse *do the washing-up* (washing the plates and pans after a meal) and *do the washing* (clothes). Students then work in pairs and test each other on the collocations. For example, student A says *the washing-up* and student B replies *do the washing-up*.

2 a) Check students remember the words for different meals (*breakfast*, *lunch*, *dinner*). Students do the exercise on their own before checking in pairs or groups. Check answers with the class.

b) Students do the exercise on their own. Check answers with the class.

3 Students work on their own and fill in the gaps in the sentences to make them true for them. They then compare sentences in pairs or groups to see how many are the same. Ask students to tell the class some of the things they have in common with other students.

— EXTRA IDEA —

- Review the new collocations by playing Pelmanism (see p22) with the verbs on one set of cards and the noun phrases on another set.

4 Food p190

Language

steak, potatoes, butter, margarine, mushrooms, onions, a lettuce, pasta, beans, lemons, strawberries, pears, salt, pepper, grapes, oil, garlic, tomato ketchup

When to use and time

Use any time after lesson 4D. 20–30 minutes.

Procedure

1 Students do the exercise on their own or in pairs. Check answers with the class (see answer key on worksheet). Drill the words chorally and individually. Pay particular attention to the pronunciation of *steak* /steɪk/, *margarine* /mɑːdʒəˈriːn/, *onions* /ˈʌnjənz/, *lettuce* /ˈletɪs/ and *pears* /peəz/. Highlight the irregular spelling of the plural of *potato*: *potatoes*. You could point out that we also use *beans* for green beans, etc. Students can then work in pairs and test each other on the vocabulary by taking turns to point to a picture and asking: *What's this?* or *What are these?*.

2 Elicit examples of countable and uncountable nouns students already know from lesson 4D in the Student's Book to check they remember the difference. Then ask students to do the exercise in pairs. While they are working, draw the table on the board. When students have finished, elicit the answers and fill in the table. Note that some words in English can be both countable and uncountable: *steak* (the type of meat) and *a steak* (a piece of steak).

3 Students do the exercise on their own. While they are working, write these example conversations on the board:

A I love (garlic).   B Me too./Oh, I hate it.

A I eat (pasta) every day.   B Me too. Oh, I don't.

A I don't often eat (beans).   B Me neither./Oh, I do.

Drill these with the class. Then students move around the room and find one person who agrees with each of the sentences they have completed. When they find someone who agrees with their sentence, they write that student's name on the worksheet. Students then continue moving around the room and talk to a different student. Alternatively, students can do this stage of the activity in groups of four or five.

4 Students work on their own and circle the food words in the puzzle. Check which words aren't in the puzzle (*margarine*, *mushrooms*, *a lettuce*, *grapes*).

— EXTRA IDEA —

- If you have a class of real beginners, bring in pictures of the food items on the worksheet and teach them one at a time at the beginning of the lesson. Then use the matching exercise in **1** to check.

5 Places in a town p191

Language

a tourist information centre, a swimming pool, a travel agent's, a theatre, a hospital, a library, a hairdresser's, a football stadium, an art gallery, a shopping centre [US: a shopping mall]

When to use and time

Use any time after lesson 5A. 15–25 minutes.

Procedure

1 Students do the exercise on their own before checking in pairs. Check answers with the class (see answer key on worksheet). Drill the words chorally and individually, paying particular attention to the pronunciation of *theatre* /'θɪətə/. Note that *library* is a false friend in many languages, and means a place where you borrow books, not a place where you buy them, which is *a bookshop*. You can also point out that the *'s* in *travel agent's* and *hairdresser's* is possessive, and the person who owns each business or works in it is *a travel agent* and a *hairdresser*.

2 Check or pre-teach *holiday, play* (noun), *borrow* and *nurse*. Students then do the exercise on their own before checking in pairs. Check answers with the class. Then put students in pairs to test each other on the vocabulary. For example, student A asks *What's picture f)?* and student B replies *It's an art gallery*.

3 Pre-teach *town/city centre, main street* and *local*. Students do the exercise on their own. Encourage students to use words from the worksheet if possible, but if the words aren't appropriate they can use words from **V5.1** SB p131. Students then compare answers in pairs or groups.

> ┌ EXTRA IDEA ─────────────────────
> * For homework, students can write a description of their town/city, using *there is/there are*, vocabulary from the worksheet and other ideas. You can display the descriptions in the classroom for other students to read.

6 Irregular verbs p192

Language

know/knew, eat/ate, make/made, drink/drank, drive/drove, read/read, send/sent, wear/wore, understand/understood, give/gave, spend/spent, speak/spoke

When to use and time

Use any time after lesson 6D. 20–35 minutes.

Procedure

1 **a)** Students do the exercise on their own before checking in pairs. The aim of this exercise is to check that students know the meaning of these verbs. Check answers with the class (see answer key on worksheet).

b) Students tick the sentences in **1a)** that are true for them, then compare sentences in pairs to find out how many they have both ticked. Elicit sentences from students using *both*, for example, *Both Clara and I usually wear jeans when we're at home*.

2 Students do the exercise on their own in their notebooks, checking irregular Past Simple forms as necessary in the Irregular Verb List, SB p159. If you have a strong class, ask students to do the exercise without checking in the Irregular Verb List. Then ask them to compare answers in groups. Check answers with the whole class. Drill the infinitives and Past Simple forms with the class. Highlight the difference in pronunciation between the infinitive *read* /riːd/ and the Past Simple *read* /red/, and the word stress on *understand* and *understood*. Students then work in pairs and test each other on the Past Simple forms, for example, student A says *give* and student B responds by saying *gave*.

3 **a)** Focus students on the pictures of Jennifer's weekend, then give students time to read the email and put the pictures in order. Check answers with the class.

b) Students do the exercise on their own before checking in pairs. Check answers with the class.

> ┌ EXTRA IDEA ─────────────────────
> * Play Bingo! (see p21) using the Past Simple forms from the worksheet and from unit 6 in the Student's Book.

7 Verb and prepositions p193

Language

look at, listen to, play with, look for, write to, ask for, pay for, talk about, wait for, talk to, go to, spend money on

When to use and time

Use any time after lesson 7B. 15–25 minutes.

Procedure

1 **a)** Students do the exercise on their own or in pairs. Check answers with the class (see answer key on worksheet).

b) Students do the exercise on their own and check in pairs. Then check answers with the whole class. Use the example phrases and pictures to clarify any problems in meaning, particularly with the verbs that can take two prepositions: *look at/for* and *talk about/to*. Drill the phrases chorally and individually. Then put students in pairs to test each other on the collocations. For example, student A says *new clothes* and student B replies *spend money on new clothes*.

2 **a)** Pre-teach *(birthday) present*. Ask students to cover the phrases in **1a)**. Students then do the exercise on their own. Check answers with the whole group.

b) Students answer the questions for themselves, then compare answers in groups. Alternatively, students can work in pairs or groups and take turns to ask and answer the questions. Elicit one or two answers for each question from the class.

┌─ **EXTRA IDEA** ──────────────────
● Play Noughts and Crosses (see p21). Write the verbs in the squares for the students to guess the correct prepositions.
└─────────────────────────────────

┌─ **EXTRA IDEA** ──────────────────
● Making word associations can be a strong aid to memory. Say the British English words one by one to the students, and ask them to write down the first word that comes into their heads, for example, you say *a holiday* and students write *the beach*. Students then look at their list of words and see if they can remember the words you said and the American English equivalents.
└─────────────────────────────────

8 British and American English p194

Language

a holiday [US: a vacation], the bill [US: the check], a mobile phone [US: a cell phone], chips [US: (French) fries], a film [US: a movie], a lift [US: an elevator], a shop [US: a store], a shopping centre [US: a shopping mall], the ground floor [US: the first floor], biscuits [US: cookies], sweets [US: candy], a flat [US: an apartment], trousers [US: pants], a chemist's [US: a pharmacy]

When to use and time

Use any time after lesson 8A. 20–30 minutes.

Procedure

 Check students understand that people in the UK and the USA sometimes use different words for the same things, using *a holiday* and *a vacation* from lesson 8A as an example. Pre-teach *a lift, a shopping centre, the ground floor* and *sweets* (all the other British English words have been taught in the Student's Book). Students then do the exercise in pairs. Check answers with the class (see answer key on worksheet). Drill the words chorally and individually, paying particular attention to the pronunciation of *biscuits* /ˈbɪskɪts/, *trousers* /ˈtraʊzəz/, *chemist's* /ˈkemɪsts/ and *pharmacy* /ˈfɑːməsi/. You may also want to explain that *chips* in American English are very thin fried potatoes, usually sold in packets, which are called *crisps* /krɪsps/ in British English. Also *pants* in British English is underwear for men. Students can then take turns to test each other on the words. For example, student A says *the bill* and student B replies *the check*.

 a) Students read the conversation and do the exercise on their own before checking in pairs. Check answers with the class.

b) Students do the exercise on their own or in pairs. Check answers with the class.

a) Students do the exercise on their own. Check answers with the class.

b) Students tick the sentences that are true for them and make the other sentences true for them. Put students in groups of three and ask them to compare their sentences. Students can then tell the class which sentences are true for all the students in their group, for example, *We all hate going to shopping malls.*

9 Computer vocabulary p195

Language

a document, a printer, a monitor, a website, a screen, a keyboard, a mouse, a scanner, disks, speakers, icons, click on, turn on/off, search, open, close, save, print, download, send

When to use and time

Use any time after lesson 9C. 20–35 mins.

Procedure

 You can begin by asking how many people in the class have got a computer, use one every day, etc. Then students do the exercise on their own or in pairs. Check answers with the class (see answer key on worksheet). Drill the words chorally and individually, paying particular attention to the pronunciation of any words that are similar or the same in the students' own language(s). Students can then test each other on the vocabulary by saying the number of an item in the picture and asking their partner to say the correct word.

 Students do the exercise on their own before checking in pairs. Check answers with the class. Highlight the prepositions in *search for something <u>on</u> (the Internet)* and *download something <u>from</u> (the Internet)*. Check the meaning of these phrases by asking what you can search for, (for example, a company's name, information about famous people, etc.) or download, (for example, pictures, games, etc.). Also check students understand the other words in **bold** in sentences 1–6, such as *open, save* and *print*. Teach students that *the Net* or *the Web* are alternatives to *the Internet*, and these words are sometimes spelt without a capital letter. You can also teach *switch on/off* as an alternative to *turn on/off*.

 Remind students of Emily, the woman who works in the 3DUK office in lesson 9C of the Student's Book. Students then do the exercise on their own before checking in pairs. Check answers with the class. Students can then practise the conversations in pairs.

10 Parts of the body p196

Language

stomach, arm, hand, back, fingers, thumb, knee, leg, shoulder, head, chest, toes, neck, foot (plural: feet), hair, mouth, eye, nose, ear, throat, teeth (singular: tooth)

When to use and time

Use before lesson 10C, if you would like to teach students the parts of the body before doing this lesson on health problems and treatments, or any time after lesson 10C. 15–20 minutes.

Procedure

1 Students do the exercise on their own before checking in pairs. Check answers with the class (see answer key on worksheet). Drill the words chorally and individually. Highlight the pronunciation of *stomach* /ˈstʌmək/, *thumb* /θʌm/, *knee* /niː/, *throat* /θrəʊt/ and the silent letters in *thumb* and *knee*. Students then work in pairs. They take turns to say a letter on the pictures and their partner says the part of the body.

2 Students do this exercise on their own. Put students into groups to check their answers and encourage them to explain why they have chosen a word as the odd one out. Check answers with the class. Ask students to explain their answers. Note that students might have other answers which could be correct.

3 Students do the crossword in pairs. You can make this a race and the first pair to finish wins. Each pair can check their answers with another pair if necessary.

> **EXTRA IDEA**
> - Play Simon Says. Prepare a list of instructions, for example, *touch your head, hold your arm*, etc. Pre-teach any new verbs, for example, *touch, hold*, etc., then explain the game. If you say *Simon says ...* before an instruction, students must do this. If you don't say *Simon says ...* students must do nothing. For example, if you say *Simon says touch your head*, students should touch their heads. If you say *Stand on your toes*, students shouldn't move. Any student who doesn't follow the instructions is 'out'. Continue the game until you have a winner.

11 Prepositions of place and movement p197

Language

out of, through, across, up, down, into, below, above, inside, outside, between, on top of

When to use and time

Use any time after lesson 11C. 15–25 minutes.

Procedure

1 **a)–b)** Write these prepositions from exercise 3 in lesson 11C on the board: *over, past, along, on, opposite, next to*. Ask students which describe movement (*over, past, along*) and which describe place (*on, opposite, next to*). Ask if students can add to these lists, for example, *behind, under*, etc. Students then do **1a)** and **1b)** on their own before checking in pairs. Check answers with the class (see answer key on worksheet), using the pictures to clarify any problems with meaning. Drill the prepositions with the class, highlighting the pronunciation of *through* /θruː/ and *above* /əˈbʌv/. Tell students that people *get into/out of* cars and taxis, but they *get on/off* trains, buses, planes, etc. Also point out that we often use *on top of* for something tall or high, and we often use *inside* and *outside* to mean *inside/outside the house or building*.

2 Students do the exercise on their own before checking in pairs. Check answers with the class.

12 Past participles p198

Language

past participles and Past Simple forms of *drive, break, sleep, eat, fly, read, take, win, ride, sing*

When to use and time

Use any time after lesson 12B. 20–30 minutes.

Procedure

1 Pre-teach *sports car, tent, sushi* and *in public*, and check students remember *helicopter* and *horse*. Students then do the exercise on their own before checking in pairs. Check answers with the class (see answer key on worksheet).

2 Students do the exercise in pairs. While they are working, draw the table on the board. Check answers with the class (see the Irregular Verb List, SB p159). Drill the verb forms in sets of three, for example, *drive, drove, driven*. Highlight the pronunciation of the infinitive *read* /riːd/ compared to the Past Simple and past participle *read* /red/. Students then work in pairs and test each other on the past tenses and past participles. For example, student A says *sleep* and student B replies *slept, slept*.

3 **a)** Students do the exercise on their own before checking in pairs. Check answers with the class.

b) Students answer the questions for themselves and compare answers in pairs. Ask students to share any interesting answers with the class.

1 Jobs

1 Match the jobs to pictures 1–12.

a businesswoman [9]　a businessman [ ]　a nurse [ ]　a secretary [ ]　a footballer [ ]　a pilot [ ]
a taxi driver [ ]　an artist [ ]　a singer [ ]　a hairdresser [ ]　a journalist [ ]　a politician [ ]

2 Look at pictures 1–12 again. Tick (✓) the true sentences. Correct the false sentences.

1　He's a footballer. ✓
2　She's a ~~politician~~. *hairdresser*
3　He's a journalist. _____
4　She's a pilot. _____
5　She's a nurse. _____
6　He's an artist. _____
7　She's a secretary. _____
8　He's a hairdresser. _____
9　She's a businesswoman. _____
10　He's a businessman. _____
11　He's a singer. _____
12　She's a taxi driver. _____

3 Find all the jobs in **1** in the puzzle.

W	B	U	S	I	N	E	S	S	W	O	M	A	N
F	G	T	E	V	U	F	J	O	G	N	O	P	J
E	P	B	C	A	R	T	I	S	T	S	R	O	O
I	I	I	R	Y	S	A	S	V	M	I	W	L	U
P	L	K	E	S	E	B	O	N	T	N	S	I	R
F	O	O	T	B	A	L	L	E	R	G	I	T	N
O	T	U	A	D	J	R	Y	C	O	E	K	I	A
H	A	I	R	D	R	E	S	S	E	R	R	C	L
R	F	J	Y	C	K	O	G	B	D	E	A	I	I
L	T	A	X	I	D	R	I	V	E	R	M	A	S
S	Q	B	U	S	I	N	E	S	S	M	A	N	T

2 Personal possessions

1 Look at the pictures of Magda and Andy's things. Match the words to the things 1–16.

keys 7	a briefcase ☐	a handbag ☐
a mirror ☐	an address book ☐	a pen ☐
a hairbrush ☐	make-up ☐	a pencil ☐
a dictionary ☐	a notebook ☐	a purse ☐
a rubber [US: an eraser] ☐	tissues ☐	
a comb ☐	money ☐	

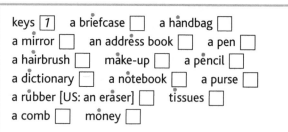

Magda

2 Are these sentences true (T) or false (F)?

1 They've both got keys and a mobile phone. _T_

2 Andy's got a purse and Magda's got a wallet.

....

3 Magda's got some money in her handbag. ....

4 Andy's got a notebook. ....

5 Magda's got an address book. ....

6 They've both got two pens. ....

7 Andy's got some tissues and a hairbrush. ....

8 Magda's mirror is in her make-up bag. ....

3 Write words from **1** in the puzzle. Find the thing (↓).

			↓					
	①	M	O	N	E	Y		
	②	N			B			K
③	H			R			H	
	④	M		R			R	
⑤	P		N		I			
⑥	A			R		S		K
	⑦				R		E	
	⑧				D	B		G
	⑨	C			B			
⑩	D		T			A		Y
⑪	T			S			S	

4 Look at the pictures for one minute. Cover the pictures and write what Magda and Andy have got. How many things can you remember?

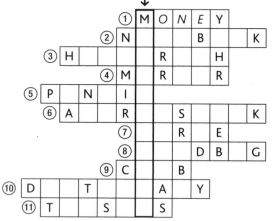

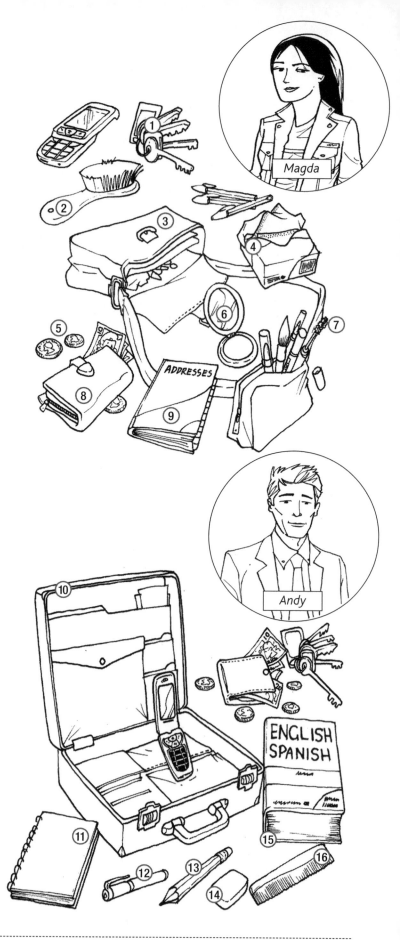

Andy

ADDRESSES

ENGLISH SPANISH

1 a briefcase 10; a handbag 3; a mirror 6; an address book 9; a pen 12; a hairbrush 2; a pencil 13; a dictionary 15; a notebook 11; a purse 8; a rubber [US: an eraser] 14; tissues 4; a comb 16; money 5 **2** 2F 3T 4T 5T 6F 7F 8F **3** 2 notebook 3 hairbrush 4 mirror 5 pencil 6 address book 7 purse 8 handbag 9 comb 10 dictionary 11 tissues ↓ mobile phone

face2face Elementary Photocopiable © Cambridge University Press 2005 | Instructions p182

3 Daily routines

1 Match phrases 1–10 to pictures a)–j).

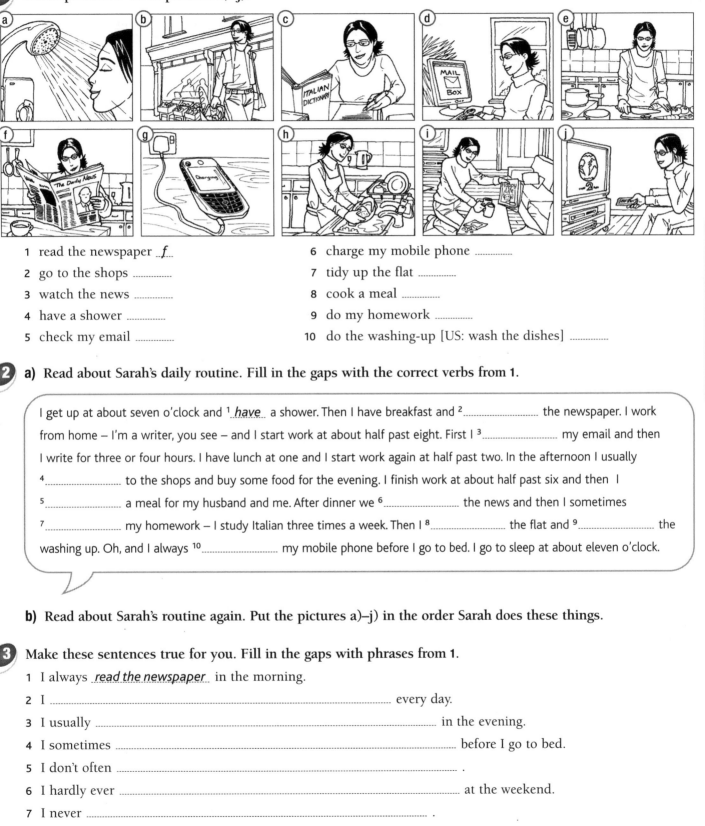

1 read the newspaper _f_
2 go to the shops ....
3 watch the news ....
4 have a shower ....
5 check my email ....

6 charge my mobile phone ....
7 tidy up the flat ....
8 cook a meal ....
9 do my homework ....
10 do the washing-up [US: wash the dishes] ....

2 a) Read about Sarah's daily routine. Fill in the gaps with the correct verbs from 1.

I get up at about seven o'clock and ¹ _have_ a shower. Then I have breakfast and ² .... the newspaper. I work from home – I'm a writer, you see – and I start work at about half past eight. First I ³ .... my email and then I write for three or four hours. I have lunch at one and I start work again at half past two. In the afternoon I usually ⁴ .... to the shops and buy some food for the evening. I finish work at about half past six and then I ⁵ .... a meal for my husband and me. After dinner we ⁶ .... the news and then I sometimes ⁷ .... my homework – I study Italian three times a week. Then I ⁸ .... the flat and ⁹ .... the washing up. Oh, and I always ¹⁰ .... my mobile phone before I go to bed. I go to sleep at about eleven o'clock.

b) Read about Sarah's routine again. Put the pictures a)–j) in the order Sarah does these things.

3 Make these sentences true for you. Fill in the gaps with phrases from 1.

1 I always _read the newspaper_ in the morning.
2 I .... every day.
3 I usually .... in the evening.
4 I sometimes .... before I go to bed.
5 I don't often ....
6 I hardly ever .... at the weekend.
7 I never ....

4 Food

1 Match the words to the food.

steak `10` potatoes ☐ butter ☐ margarine ☐ mushrooms ☐ onions ☐ a lettuce ☐ pasta ☐ beans ☐
lemons ☐ strawberries ☐ pears ☐ salt ☐ pepper ☐ grapes ☐ oil ☐ garlic ☐ tomato ketchup ☐

① ② ③ ④ ⑤ ⑥ ⑦ ⑧ ⑨ ⑩ ⑪ ⑫ ⑬ ⑭ ⑮ ⑯ ⑰ ⑱

2 Put the words in 1 in the table. Write the singular and plural if possible.

COUNTABLE NOUNS

singular	plural
a potato	*potatoes*

UNCOUNTABLE NOUNS

steak	

3 Make these sentences true for you. Fill in the gaps with words from 1.

1 I love ....

2 I eat .... every day.

3 I don't often eat ....

4 I sometimes put .... on my food.

5 I don't like .... very much.

6 I never eat ....

7 I quite like ....

8 I think .... is/are OK.

9 I really hate ....

4 Find the food words. Which four words from 1 aren't in the puzzle?

potatoesaltomatoketchupepperoilemonsteakonionsgarlicpearsbutterpastabeanstrawberries

---

face2face Elementary Photocopiable © Cambridge University Press 2005 Instructions p183

5 Places in a town

1 Match the words/phrases to places a)–j).

a tourist information centre [h]   a swimming pool ☐   a travel agent's ☐   a theatre ☐   a hospital ☐   a library ☐

a hairdresser's ☐   a football stadium ☐   an art gallery ☐   a shopping centre [US: a shopping mall] ☐

2 Match these sentences to the places in 1.

1 People get their hair cut here. _a hairdresser's_

2 There are a lot of pictures on the walls in this place. _____

3 People buy holidays here. _____

4 There are usually a lot of shops in this place. _____

5 People go swimming here. _____

6 You can see a Shakespeare play in this place. _____

7 This is a good place to get a map of the town. _____

8 People go here to read and borrow books. _____

9 Doctors and nurses work in this place. _____

10 People go and see football matches here. _____

3 Make these sentences true for you. Fill in the gaps with words/phrases from 1, or your own ideas.

1 There's a big _____ in my town/city.

2 There's a _____ in the centre of my town/city.

3 There are some interesting _____ in the main street.

4 There isn't a _____ in my town/city.

5 There's a _____ near my home.

6 There isn't a _____ near my home.

7 I go to my local _____ quite a lot.

8 I went to the _____ last week.

Instructions p184   © Cambridge University Press 2005   face2face Elementary Photocopiable

6 Irregular verbs

1 a) Match words/phrases 1–6 and 7–12 to words/phrases a)–f) and g)–l).

1 I **know** — a) to work/university every day.
2 I never **eat** — b) some irregular verbs in English.
3 I don't **make** c) the newspaper every day.
4 I **drink** d) red meat.
5 I **drive** e) two litres of water every day.
6 I **read** f) many mistakes when I write in English.

7 I sometimes **send** g) films in English very well.
8 I usually **wear** h) birthday presents to my friends.
9 I don't **understand** i) English with my friends.
10 I always **give** j) on clothes every month.
11 I **spend** a lot of money k) jeans when I'm at home.
12 I sometimes **speak** l) emails to people in other countries.

b) Tick the sentences in **1a)** that are true for you.

2 Write the Past Simple forms of the irregular verbs in **bold** in **1a)** in your notebook. You can use the Irregular Verb List (Student's Book p159) to help you.

know → knew

3 a) Read Jennifer's email to her friend, Angelica, about her weekend. Put pictures a)–d) in the order she did them.

> Hi Angelica
>
> How are you? It was Carlos's birthday on Saturday and we had a big party for him at my flat. My sister and I ¹ *spent* all afternoon cleaning and then we ² _____ lots of food for the party. Carlos didn't ³ _____ about it, so it was a big surprise for him! There were about fifty people there and I ⁴ _____ my favourite dress – you know, the long blue one. Everyone ⁵ _____ Carlos cards and presents, and it was a very special evening for him, I think. On Sunday Carlos and I ⁶ _____ to his parents' house for lunch in his new car. The food was fantastic and I ⁷ _____ too much as usual! His parents are Argentinian, as you know, and all his family ⁸ _____ Spanish at the table – I didn't ⁹ _____ very much! Then I just sat in the garden, ¹⁰ _____ a glass of wine and ¹¹ _____ my book.
>
> It was a great weekend.
>
> Write soon!
>
> Love
> Jennifer
>
> PS Did you ¹² _____ me an email last week? I didn't get one!

b) Read the email again. Fill in the gaps with the infinitive or the Past Simple of the verbs in **bold** in **1a)**.

face2face Elementary Photocopiable   © Cambridge University Press 2005   Instructions p184

7 Verbs and prepositions

1 a) Match the verbs and prepositions in A to the words/phrases in B.

A	B
look at	a new job
listen to	some photos
play with	music
look for	children

A	B
write to	the bill
ask for	football
pay for	a friend
talk about	dinner

A	B
wait for	your mother on the phone
talk to	new clothes
go to	a phone call
spend money on	an art gallery

b) Match the complete phrases in 1a) to pictures 1–12.

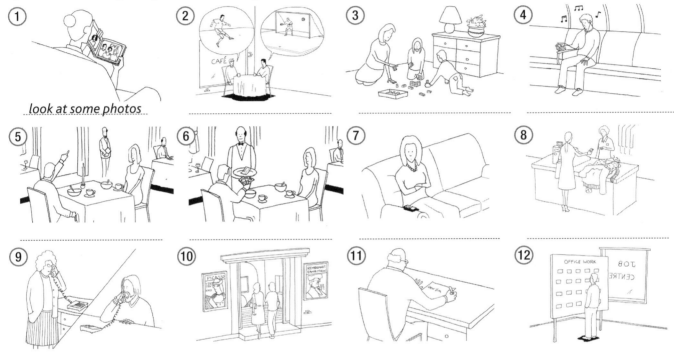

look at some photos

2 a) Cover the phrases in 1a). Fill in the gaps with the correct preposition.

1 What type of music do you listen _to_ ?
2 Who do you like talking _____ on the phone?
3 When did you last pay a lot of money _____ something?
4 Who was the last person you wrote _____ ?
5 What do you hate spending money _____ ?
6 What do you and your friends often talk _____ ?
7 Do you like going _____ the theatre?
8 Did you wait a long time _____ a bus or train this morning?
9 Did you ask _____ any presents for your last birthday?
10 When you were a child, who did you play _____ ?
11 What's the best way to look _____ a cheap car?
12 Do you often look _____ old photos?

b) Answer the questions in 2a) for you.

8 British and American English

1 Match the British English words 1–14 to the American English words a)–n).

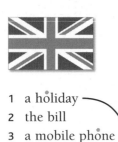

British English	American English
1 a holiday	a) the first floor
2 the bill	b) a cell phone
3 a mobile phone	c) candy
4 chips	d) a vacation
5 a film	e) the check
6 a lift	f) a store
7 a shop	g) cookies
8 a shopping centre	h) an elevator
9 the ground floor	i) pants
10 biscuits	j) a movie
11 sweets	k) (French) fries
12 a flat	l) a shopping mall
13 trousers	m) a pharmacy
14 a chemist's	n) an apartment

DRESS

2 **a)** Read Bob and Pam's conversation. Then choose the correct answers.

1 Pam stayed in *a hotel/her sister's flat*.
2 She *needed/didn't need* to use a lift there.
3 She went to *the cinema/some shopping centres*.
4 She bought *some trousers/a coat*.
5 The waiters always give you *sweets/chips* when you get the bill.
6 When Pam saw her friends they had some *biscuits/sweets*.
7 She talked to her friends on her *mobile phone/sister's phone*.
8 Pam *enjoyed/didn't enjoy* her holiday.
9 She is from *the USA/the UK*.

BOB Hi, Pam! How was New York?
PAM Oh, it was great!
BOB Where did you stay?
PAM In my sister's apartment in Greenwich Village. She hates elevators, so it's on the first floor.
BOB What did you do there?
PAM Oh, I went to the movies a few times, and I went shopping in Manhattan. I didn't go to any shopping malls, but there are some great stores! I bought these pants, do you like them?
BOB Yes, they're nice. And did you eat out much?
PAM Yes, we always go to the same restaurant. The steak and French fries are fantastic there, and the waiters always give you candy when you get the check!
BOB And did you see all your friends?
PAM Well, I saw some of them. One night two friends came to visit me in my sister's apartment and we just talked and ate cookies all evening. And I talked to the others on my cell phone.
BOB It sounds like you had a great time.
PAM Yes, it was a very good vacation.

b) Read the conversation again. Underline all the American English words. Which American English word from 1 isn't in the conversation?

3 **a)** Write these sentences in American English.

1 I hate going to shopping centres.
   I hate going to shopping malls.

2 I eat sweets or biscuits every day.

3 There's a chemist's near my house.

4 The last film I saw was an action film.

5 There are two lifts where I live.

6 I use my mobile phone every day.

7 My last holiday was in March.

b) Tick the sentences in 3a) that are true for you. Make the other sentences true for you.

9 Computer vocabulary

1 Match these words to the things in the picture 1–11.

a document `11`   a printer ☐   a monitor ☐   a website ☐
a screen ☐   a keyboard ☐   a mouse ☐
a scanner ☐   disks ☐   speakers ☐   icons ☐

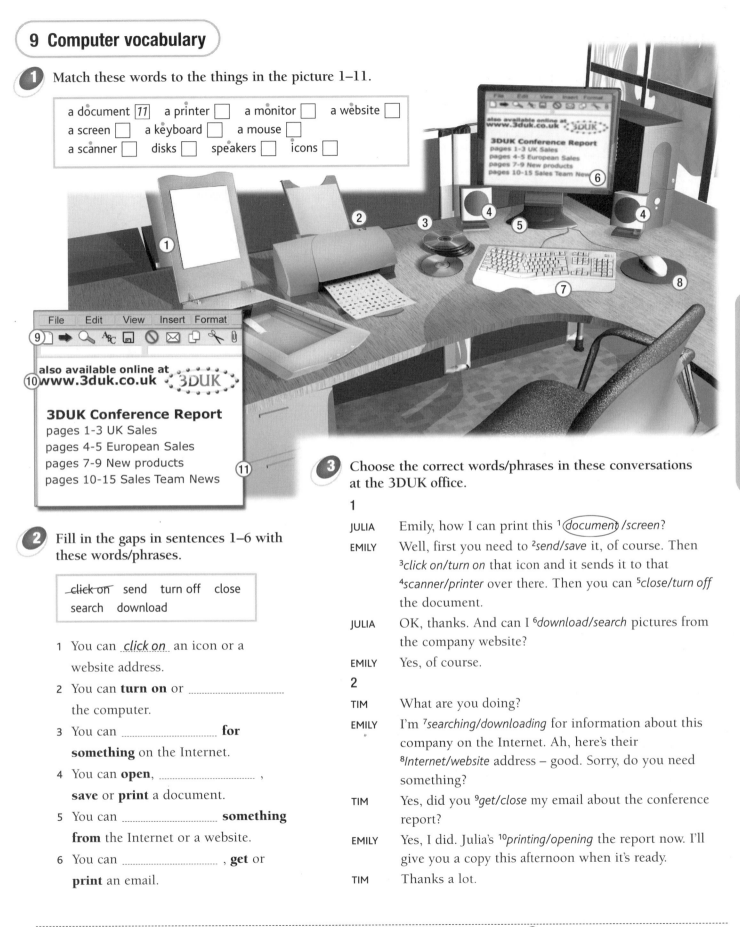

File   Edit   View   Insert   Format

also available online at **www.3duk.co.uk** · 3DUK

3DUK Conference Report
pages 1-3 UK Sales
pages 4-5 European Sales
pages 7-9 New products
pages 10-15 Sales Team News

2 Fill in the gaps in sentences 1–6 with these words/phrases.

~~click on~~   send   turn off   close
search   download

1 You can _click on_ an icon or a website address.

2 You can **turn on** or .... the computer.

3 You can .... **for something** on the Internet.

4 You can **open**, ... , **save** or **print** a document.

5 You can .... **something from** the Internet or a website.

6 You can .... , **get** or **print** an email.

3 Choose the correct words/phrases in these conversations at the 3DUK office.

1

JULIA   Emily, how I can print this ¹*document*/*screen*?

EMILY   Well, first you need to ²*send*/*save* it, of course. Then ³*click on*/*turn on* that icon and it sends it to that ⁴*scanner*/*printer* over there. Then you can ⁵*close*/*turn off* the document.

JULIA   OK, thanks. And can I ⁶*download*/*search* pictures from the company website?

EMILY   Yes, of course.

2

TIM   What are you doing?

EMILY   I'm ⁷*searching*/*downloading* for information about this company on the Internet. Ah, here's their ⁸*Internet*/*website* address – good. Sorry, do you need something?

TIM   Yes, did you ⁹*get*/*close* my email about the conference report?

EMILY   Yes, I did. Julia's ¹⁰*printing*/*opening* the report now. I'll give you a copy this afternoon when it's ready.

TIM   Thanks a lot.

1 a printer 2; a monitor 5; a website 10; a screen 6; a keyboard 7; a mouse 8; a scanner 1; disks 3; speakers 4; icons 9 **2** 2 turn off 3 search 4 close 5 download 6 send **3** 2 save 3 click on 4 printer 5 close 6 download 7 searching 8 website 9 get 10 printing

10 Parts of the body

1 Match these words to the parts of the body a)–u).

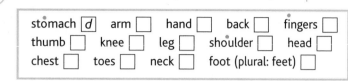

stomach ☐ *d*	arm ☐	hand ☐	back ☐	fingers ☐
thumb ☐	knee ☐	leg ☐	shoulder ☐	head ☐
chest ☐	toes ☐	neck ☐	foot (plural: feet) ☐	

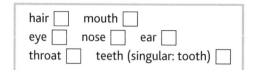

hair ☐	mouth ☐	
eye ☐	nose ☐	ear ☐
throat ☐	teeth (singular: tooth) ☐	

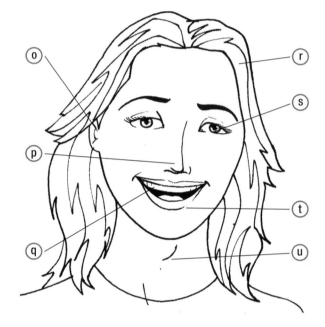

2 Which word is the odd one out? Why?

1 fingers thumb hand (head)

2 shoulder leg mouth hand

3 knee leg hair foot

4 back stomach toes chest

5 nose eye hair knee

6 teeth feet neck fingers

3 Write the words from **1** in the crossword.

11 Prepositions of place and movement

Penny

Rick

Joe

Sue

1 a) Look at the pictures. Fill in the gaps with these prepositions of movement.

out of	through	across	up	down	into

1 Rick is getting __out of__ his car.

2 Penny is getting _____ her car.

3 An old man is walking _____ the street.

4 Joe is walking _____ the stairs.

5 The dog is going _____ the stairs.

6 The cat is climbing _____ the window.

b) Look at the pictures again. Fill in the gaps with these prepositions of place.

below	above	inside	outside	between	on top of

a) The picture is _____ the clock.

b) The clock is _____ the picture.

c) The CD player is _____ the bookcase.

d) The coffee table is _____ the armchair and the sofa.

e) Sue and Joe are _____ .

f) Rick and Penny are _____ .

2 Choose the correct prepositions in these sentences.

1 They walked (across)/*down* the park to the hotel.

2 It was a very cold day so they stayed *outside/inside*.

3 They looked *down/up* and watched the birds fly over the house.

4 Gerry got *into/out of* his car and drove home.

5 You walk *through/below* this door and his office is on your left.

6 Your keys are *on top of/into* the fridge.

7 It took us six hours to walk *up/down* the mountain and only two hours to walk *up/down*.

8 Our restaurant is *between/inside* a bank and a greengrocer's.

9 Samantha got *into/out of* the taxi and walked *through/across* the road to meet her friends.

10 They lived in a small flat *above/across* a shop.

11 Our dog doesn't come in the house, he stays *inside/outside* in the garden.

12 He looked *out of/inside* the window of the plane at the city *above/below* him.

12 Past participles

1 Match phrases 1–10 to pictures a)–j).

1 **drive** a sports car _c_
2 **break** something expensive _____
3 **sleep** in a tent _____
4 **eat** sushi _____
5 **fly** in a helicopter _____
6 **read** a book in English _____
7 **take** something back to a shop _____
8 **win** a lot of money _____
9 **ride** a horse _____
10 **sing** in public _____

2 The verbs in **1** are all irregular. Complete the table. Use the Irregular Verb List (Student's Book p159).

infinitive	Past Simple	past participle
drive	*drove*	*driven*
break		
sleep		
eat		
fly		
read		
take		
win		
ride		
sing		

3 **a)** Fill in the gaps with the infinitive or past participle of the verbs in **2**.

1 Have you ever _slept_ on a boat?
2 Have you ever _____ in a band or in an opera?
3 Did you _____ any money on the lottery last weekend?
4 Have you ever _____ in a small plane?
5 When did you last _____ Italian food?
6 Have you ever _____ your arm or leg?
7 Did you _____ a car last week?
8 Have you ever _____ a motorbike?
9 When did you last _____ a book or a magazine in English?
10 Have you ever _____ any clothes back to a shop?

b) Answer the questions in **3a)** for you.

① 2d) 3h) 4f) 5j) 6i) 7a) 8e) 9b) 10g) ② See the Irregular Verb List (Student's Book p159). ③ a) 2 sung 3 win 4 flown 5 eat 6 broken 7 drive 8 ridden 9 read 10 taken

Instructions p186

Study Skills

Instructions

There are five Study Skills worksheets (p202–p206). The aim of these worksheets is to help students become better and more independent learners. The worksheets are designed to be used in class, offering a change of pace and focus for both teacher and students. You will need to photocopy one Study Skills worksheet for each student.

1 Classroom language p202

Aim

To introduce and practise students' classroom language.

When to use and time

Use any time after the Welcome to the class! lesson. 10–20 minutes.

Procedure

1 Give a copy of the worksheet to each student. Focus students on the pictures and on the example. Students work on their own or in pairs and match the sentences to the pictures.

Check answers with the whole class. At this stage teach these sentences as fixed 'chunks' of language, rather than focus on the grammar of each question.

Model and drill the sentences.

> 2f) 3h) 4c) 5a) 6i) 7d) 8g) 9e)

2 a) Put students into new pairs. Tell them to cover the sentences in **1** with a piece of paper or a book. Students then take turns to point to a picture and their partner says the correct sentence.

While students are working, monitor and help with pronunciation.

b) Students ask you questions using the language from the worksheet.

3 Students write the questions in the front of their notebooks and add a translation in their own language for each question. If you have a monolingual class, you can check the translations with the class. Alternatively, students can do this exercise for homework.

> — EXTRA IDEA —
> • You or the students can make a poster of these classroom language phrases to display in the classroom for easy reference in future lessons. When students want to ask you something but can't remember the correct question, direct them to the poster and encourage them to use it as a reference during lessons.

2 Nouns, verbs and adjectives p203

Aim

To consolidate students' understanding of nouns, verbs and adjectives.

When to use and time

Use any time after lesson 3D. 20–30 minutes.

Procedure

1 a) Students do the exercise on their own. Check answers with the class. You can also ask students to find other nouns and verbs in the sentence in the speech bubble (nouns: *days*, *lot*, *actors*, *home*; verb: *work*).

> 1 hotel 2 live 3 long

b) Students do the exercise on their own or in pairs. The sentences all come from unit 3 in the Student's Book. Check answers with the class.

> 2 verb 3 noun 4 noun 5 verb 6 adjective 7 noun
> 8 adjective 9 verb 10 noun 11 verb 12 adjective
> 13 noun 14 noun

2 a) Students do the exercise on their own or in pairs. While they are working, draw the table on the board and write in the first example in each column (*car*, *have*, *young*). Check answers by eliciting them from the class and writing them in the correct column on the board.

noun	verb	adjective
suitcase	write	difficult
France	see	beautiful
cinema	buy	favourite
laptop	leave	important
aunt	eat	French

b) Students do the exercise on their own, then check answers in pairs. Check answers with the class.

> 2 cinema 3 leave 4 write 5 aunt 6 eat
> 7 France 8 important; difficult

3 a) Check students know these words and teach *cook* if necessary. Point out that many words in English can be both nouns and verbs, and that students need to look at the whole sentence before deciding which part of speech they are.

b) Students do the exercise on their own or in pairs. Check answers with the class.

> 2 noun 3 noun 4 verb 5 verb 6 noun 7 noun
> 8 verb 9 verb 10 noun 11 verb 12 noun

4 **a)** Students write four verbs, four nouns and four adjectives on a piece of paper. Make sure students don't write the words in verb/noun/adjective order or in a table. If necessary, demonstrate by writing twelve words in random order on the board.

b) Students work in pairs and swap papers. Students decide if their partner's words are verbs, nouns or adjectives.

c) Students compare answers in their pairs. Deal with any queries on the board.

> **EXTRA IDEA**
>
> ● Write a list of words from the Vocabulary sections of Language Summaries 1–3 SB p122–p127 on the board. Students work in groups and decide if they are verbs, nouns or adjectives. You can make this into a competition and the group with the most correct answers wins.

3 Using your English dictionary p204

Aim

To introduce students to the information that they can find in a monolingual English dictionary.

When to use and time

Use any time after lesson 6D. 20–35 minutes.

Procedure

1 Students work in groups and discuss the questions. Ask each group to share ideas with the whole class. Find out how many students have a monolingual dictionary, how many have a bilingual dictionary and which type of dictionary they prefer.

2 Students do the exercise in pairs or groups. Check answers with the class. Elicit other examples of dependent prepositions they know, for example, *look at*, *talk about*, *go to*, etc., in order to check they understand question h).

> b)1 c)7 d)4 e)5 f)2 g)6 h)8

3 **a)** Allow students time to read the entries. Ask students whether the definition or the examples were more useful as a guide to meaning. If you have a monolingual class, you can ask the students what the words are in their language. Be prepared with a simple situation or other examples to convey the meaning of these words in case students don't understand the dictionary entries. Note: *apologize* is also spelt *apologise* in British English.

b) Students do the exercise in on their own before checking in pairs or groups. Check answers with the whole class.

> 1 adjective 2 very good 3 bad 4 regular 5 happy
> 6 a pessimist 7 Before a test or exam. 8 No, it's an
> uncountable noun. 9 inviting 10 get, leave

c) Write the words on the board. Focus students on the dictionary entries again and remind students how to find the word stress in a dictionary. Do *optimist* as an example by eliciting the word stress from students and marking it on the word on the board.

Students work on their own and put the stress on the other words.

Check answers with the class and mark the stress on the other words on the board.

> ŏptimist; invīte; mĕssage; apŏlogize; revīsion; pĕrfect

4 Students do the exercise on their own by looking back at the dictionary entries in **3a)**. Check answers with the class.

> 2 I'd like to invite you **to** my party. 3 Can you give him
> a message? 4 He apologized **for** his mistake. 5 I did a
> lot of revision~~s~~ last night. 6 This armchair is perfect
> **for** this room.

4 Recording vocabulary p205

Aim

To show students different ways of recording vocabulary and to encourage them to make their own vocabulary notebooks more useful as a learning and revision aid.

When to use and time

Use any time after lesson 8D. 20–35 minutes.

Procedure

1 Students work in groups and discuss the questions. Ask groups to share their ideas with the whole class. You will probably find that most students write new vocabulary in lists in their notebooks, with the English word or phrase and a translation in their own language. Encourage students who don't yet have a vocabulary notebook to start one.

2 Focus students on the two notebooks. Students work in pairs and discuss what extra information is in notebook B.

Check answers with the class.

> Extra information in notebook B: word stress; part
> of speech; opposite; irregular Past Simple form;
> collocation: break a leg; examples; the indefinite article
> *a* with a countable noun; irregular plural; regular verb;
> common mistake: ~~take the sun~~; uncountable noun;
> American English word; dependent preposition:
> on holiday

3 **a)** Students do the exercise on their own. If they can't remember the meaning of the words, refer them to Language Summaries 7 and 8, SB p136 and SB p138.

b) Students compare their lists for the words in **3a)** in pairs. Write students' ideas for each word on the board (with the translation if you have a monolingual class).

Possible answer:
win (irreg verb, past: won)
My sister won a tennis competition last week.
crowded (adj) (opposite: empty)
The restaurant was very crowded.
a comedy (pl: comedies) = a type of film
have a picnic not ~~make a picnic~~
stay (reg verb) stay in a hotel, stay with friends
an apartment (noun, US) [UK: a flat]
We rent our apartment to some students.

4 a) Focus students on the wordmap. Some visual learners find this approach to recording new vocabulary very useful as a way of organising groups of related vocabulary. Wordmaps can also help as a revision aid. Students do the exercise on their own. Check answers with the class.

> 1 a fridge 2 a sofa 3 a shower 4 a single bed 5 a plant

b) Students work in pairs and organise the vocabulary in **V8.1** SB p138 of their Student's Book into a wordmap. They can organise the words and phrases in any way they like, for example, by verb, by topic (water activities, travelling, accommodation, etc.), town/beach/country activities, etc. You can make this more challenging by telling students that they can only use four or five different categories.

c) Students compare wordmaps with other pairs.

> ┌─ **EXTRA IDEA** ──────────────────────
> • Ask students to write their wordmap on a large piece of paper. You can then display the wordmaps around the classroom for other students to look at. Students can then decide which wordmap they think is the most useful.

5 Word building p206

Aim
To show students that we can often tell which part of speech a word is by its ending (or suffix) and to teach some common suffixes for nouns and adjectives.

When to use and time
Use any time after lesson 10D. 20–35 minutes.

Procedure

1 a) Focus students on the photo. Ask what Julian does (he takes photos). Teach *photographer*.

b) Students read the text and answer the questions on their own. Students check answers in pairs. Check answers with the class.

> 1 He was six years old. 2 He entered/won a photographic competition. 3 Because of the fantastic colours in the pictures. 4 Famous people.

2 a) Students do the exercise on their own or in pairs.
 While students are working, draw the table on the board so that you are ready to check students' answers.

Check answers with the class by eliciting each answer and writing it in the correct place in the table. Highlight the change from *-y* to *-i* in *happiness*. Elicit or teach the stress for each word and mark it on the words in the table. Highlight that the stress is sometimes on different syllables in the 'word family'. Model and drill the words, focusing on word stress.

> 1 friendship
> 2 friendly
> 3 photographer
> 4 photograph
> 5 photographic
> 6 competitor
> 7 competition
> 8 colourful
> 9 happiness

b) Students complete the rules on their own. Check answers with the class. Tell students that these are very general rules and that not every word with these endings is necessarily a person, thing or adjective (many types of word end in *-y*, for example). However, it is useful for students to try and work out parts of speech when they meet a new word, as this allows them to become more independent in their reading and learning outside class.

> • Nouns for people often end in *-er* or *-or*.
> • Nouns for things often end in *-ship*, *-ion* or *-ness*.
> • Adjectives often end in *-y*, *-ic* or *-ful*.

3 Students do the exercise on their own, then check their answers in pairs. Check answers with the class and ask students what part of speech the correct answers are.

> 2 colourful (adjective)
> 3 competitive (adjective)
> 4 photographic (adjective)
> 5 happiness (noun)
> 6 friendship (noun)
> 7 competitions (noun)
> 8 photos (noun)

4 Students do the exercise in pairs. Check answers with the class. With a strong class you can ask students if they know other nouns for people, nouns for things or adjectives with the endings in **2b)**, for example, *lawyer*, *station*, *beautiful*.

> 2A 3A 4T 5T 6A 7P 8T 9A 10T 11P 12T

1 Classroom language

1 Match sentences 1–9 to pictures a)–i).

1 Excuse me, what's that in English? _b_

2 How do you say 'chaise' in English? ....

3 Can you write it on the board, please? ....

4 How do you pronounce this word? ....

5 What does 'map' mean? ....

6 Sorry, I don't understand. ....

7 Which page are we on? ....

8 How do you spell 'Tuesday'? ....

9 Can you say that again, please? ....

2 a) Work in pairs. Cover the sentences in **1**. Then take turns to point to a picture. Your partner says the student's sentence.

b) Ask your teacher a question.

3 Write the questions in **1** in your notebooks. Then write a translation in your own language for each question.

Instructions p199

STUDY SKILLS: PHOTOCOPIABLE

2 Nouns, verbs and adjectives

> We work very **long** days and a lot of the actors **live** in a **hotel**, not at home.

1 a) Look at Sam Dane's sentence from the Student's Book. Fill in gaps 1–3 with the words in **bold**.

1 .... is a noun. 2 .... is a verb. 3 .... is an adjective.

b) Look at these sentences from the Student's Book. Are words 1–14 nouns, verbs or adjectives?

a) The [1]actors [2]have [3]breakfast at the [4]studio.

b) Let's [5]give him the [6]new Simpsons [7]DVD.

c) I'm always [8]happy and I [9]have a lot of [10]energy.

d) This [11]is the [12]glamorous [13]life of a film [14]actor.

1 _noun_	4	7	10	13 ....
2	5	8	11	14 ....
3	6	9	12	

2 a) Look at these words from the Student's Book. Write them in the table.

| ~~young~~ ~~car~~ ~~have~~ |
| difficult write suitcase |
| see France beautiful |
| cinema favourite buy |
| important laptop aunt |
| leave French eat |

noun	verb	adjective
car	have	young

b) Fill in the gaps with words from **2a)**.

1 That's my _favourite_ dress.

2 I always go to the .... at the weekend.

3 What time do you usually .... home?

4 Do you often .... emails to your sister?

5 I've got two uncles and one ....

6 We often .... out on Friday evenings.

7 Pierre's brothers live in ....

8 That's an .... and a .... question.

3 a) Tick the words you know. These words can all be nouns <u>and</u> verbs.

| drink work watch sleep phone cook |

b) Are the words in **bold** nouns or verbs?

1 Do you **watch** TV in the evenings? _verb_

2 I haven't got a **watch**. ....

3 I've got a lot of **work** to do. ....

4 Where do you **work**? ....

5 I don't **drink** beer or wine. ....

6 Would you like to go for a **drink**? ....

7 Have you got a mobile **phone**? ....

8 I **phone** my mother every day. ....

9 I always **sleep** for eight hours a night. ....

10 My baby has a **sleep** every afternoon. ....

11 Do you **cook** every day? ....

12 Our uncle is a very good **cook**. ....

4 a) Work on your own. Write four verbs, four nouns and four adjectives you know on a piece of paper. Don't write them in order.

b) Work in pairs. Swap papers. Are your partner's words verbs, nouns or adjectives?

c) Compare your answers with your partner. Are they correct?

Instructions p199

face2face Elementary Photocopiable

3 Using your English dictionary

1 Work in groups. Discuss these questions.

1 What type of English dictionary have you got?

2 How often do you use a dictionary?

3 What type of information do you look for in a dictionary?

2 Look at these entries for *terrible*, *travel* and *listen* from the *Cambridge Essential English Dictionary*. Match 1–8 to the information a)–h).

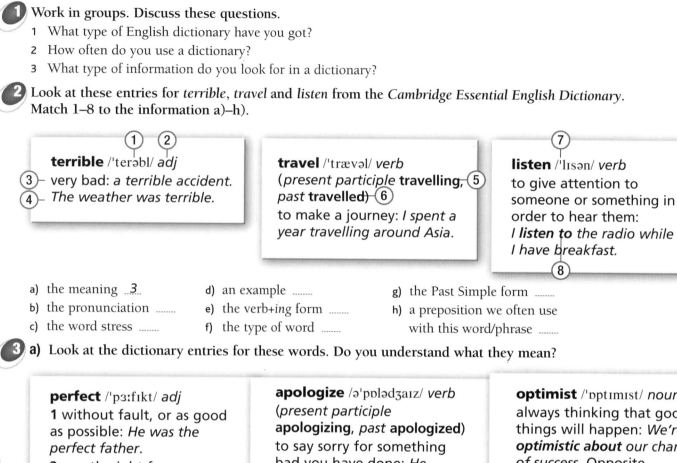

① ②
terrible /ˈterəbl/ *adj*
③ – very bad: *a terrible accident.*
④ – *The weather was terrible.*

travel /ˈtrævəl/ *verb*
(*present participle* **travelling**, ⑤
past **travelled**) ⑥
to make a journey: *I spent a
year travelling around Asia.*

⑦
listen /ˈlɪsən/ *verb*
to give attention to
someone or something in
order to hear them:
*I **listen to** the radio while
I have breakfast.*
⑧

a) the meaning __3__   d) an example ....   g) the Past Simple form ....

b) the pronunciation ....   e) the verb+*ing* form ....   h) a preposition we often use

c) the word stress ....   f) the type of word ....   with this word/phrase ....

3 a) Look at the dictionary entries for these words. Do you understand what they mean?

perfect /ˈpɜːfɪkt/ *adj*
1 without fault, or as good
as possible: *He was the
perfect father.*
2 exactly right for someone
or something: *You'd be
perfect for the job.*

apologize /əˈpɒlədʒaɪz/ *verb*
(*present participle*
apologizing, *past* **apologized**)
to say sorry for something
bad you have done: *He
apologized for being rude.
I **apologized to** her.*

optimist /ˈɒptɪmɪst/ *noun*
always thinking that good
things will happen: *We're
optimistic about our chances
of success.* Opposite
pessimistic

revision /rɪˈvɪʒən/ *noun*
[no plural] *UK* when you
study a subject before
taking a test

invite /ɪnˈvaɪt/ *verb*
(*present participle* **inviting**,
past **invited**)
to ask someone to come to your
house, to a party, etc: *They've
invited us **to** the wedding.*

message /ˈmesɪdʒ/ *noun*
a piece of written or spoken
information which one
person gives to another: *Did
you **get** my **message**? I called
her and **left** a message.*

b) Answer these questions.

1 What type of word is **perfect**?

2 If something is **perfect**, is it very good or very bad?

3 Do you **apologize** after something good or bad happens?

4 Is **apologize** a regular or irregular verb?

5 Are **optimists** usually happy or unhappy?

6 What is the opposite of an **optimist**?

7 When do people do **revision**?

8 Does **revision** have a plural form?

9 How do you spell the verb+*ing* form of **invite**?

10 Which two verbs do we often use with **message**?

c) Put the stress on the words in 3a).

4 Look at the dictionary entries for the words in 3a) again. Correct these sentences.

1 My friend John's ᵃⁿ optimist.

2 I'd like to invite you at my party.

3 Can you give him a mesage?

4 He apologized to his mistake.

5 I did a lot of revisions last night.

6 This armchair is perfect to this room.

STUDY SKILLS: PHOTOCOPIABLE

4 Recording vocabulary

1 Work in groups. Discuss these questions.

1 Have you got a vocabulary notebook? If not, where do you write new vocabulary?

2 How do you write the meaning of new words in your notebook?

3 How do you try to remember new vocabulary?

2 Work in pairs. Look at the vocabulary notebooks of two Spanish students, A and B. What extra information is in notebook B?

A

dangerous = peligroso
break = romper
tooth = un diente
sunbathe = tomar el sol
information = información
holiday = vacaciones

B

dangerous (adj) = peligroso
(opposite: safe)
break (irreg verb, past: broke) = romper
He fell and broke his leg.
a tooth (pl: teeth) = un diente
sunbathe (reg verb) = tomar el sol
not ~~take the sun~~
information (uncountable) = información
I'd like some information.
go on holiday [US: vacation] = ir de vacaciones
I went on holiday last month.

3 **a)** Look at these words from the Student's Book. Write them in your vocabulary notebook. Write extra information about each word.

win   crowded   comedy   picnic   stay   apartment

b) Work in pairs. Compare your vocabulary notebooks. What information did you partner write about each word?

4 **a)** It is often useful to organise new vocabulary into a wordmap. This can help you remember words. Fill in the gaps in this wordmap with the words in the box.

a sofa   a fridge   a shower   a single bed   a plant

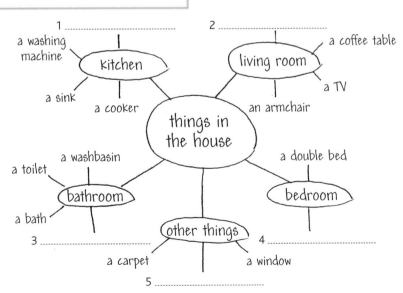

b) Work in pairs. Look at the words/phrases in **V8.1** SB p138. Make a wordmap with these words/phrases.

c) Compare your wordmap with another pair.

Instructions p200

5 Word building

1 a) Look at the photo of Julian. What does he do, do you think?

b) Read about Julian. Answer these questions.
1 How old was Julian when he started taking photos?
2 What did he do when he was eighteen?
3 Why did his pictures win the competition?
4 Who does he take photos of now?

Julian's one of my oldest **friends**. He's a famous **photographer** and he started taking **photos** when he was only six years old. At the age of eighteen he entered an international **photographic competition** and sent in some really **colourful photographs** he took on holiday in India. There were over ten thousand other **competitors**, but Julian won because of the fantastic **colours** in his pictures. He was really **happy** because he won a holiday!

He now takes photos of famous people for magazines and he gets a lot of work because he's always very **friendly** and easy to talk to. We don't see each other very often these days, but our **friendship** still gives me a lot of **happiness**.

2 a) Look at the words in **bold** in the text. Write them in the table. Write the singular form of the nouns.

noun: person	noun: thing	adjective
friend	1	2
3	photo (or 4)	5
6	7	competitive
–	colour	8
–	9	happy

b) Look again at the table. Complete the rules with *adjectives*, *things* or *people*.
- Nouns for .... often end in *-er* or *-or*.
- Nouns for .... often end in *-ship*, *-ion* or *-ness*.
- .... often end in *-y*, *-ic* or *-ful*.

3 Choose the correct words.
1 Joanne is a very *friend*/*friendly* person.
2 She always wears very *colour*/*colourful* clothes.
3 My brother is very *competitive*/*competitor* – he always wants to win!
4 I went to a *photographic*/*photographer* exhibition last weekend.
5 Most people are looking for *happy*/*happiness* in their lives.
6 Mark and I have a very interesting *friendly*/*friendship*.
7 Do you like entering *competitive*/*competitions*?
8 Would you like to see my *photos*/*photographers* of my holiday?

4 Look at these words. Do you think they are people (P), things (T) or adjectives (A)?
1 actor *P*
2 sunny ....
3 helpful ....
4 sadness ....
5 relationship ....
6 useful ....
7 visitor ....
8 invitation ....
9 athletic ....
10 exhibition ....
11 interviewer ....
12 illness ....

Progress Tests

Instructions

The Progress Tests (p211–p224) are designed to be used after students have completed each unit of the Student's Book. Each Progress Test checks students' knowledge of the key language areas taught in the unit. Some exercises and questions may also test students' knowledge of language taught in previous units.

It is helpful for students to have done the Review section at the end of each unit before doing a Progress Test. You can also encourage students to revise for the test by reviewing the relevant Language Summary in the back of the Student's Book, and by doing exercises for that unit on the CD-ROM and in the Workbook. Note that Progress Test 6 also reviews items from units 1–5, and Progress Test 12 reviews items from the whole of the Student's Book.

- Allow students 25 minutes for each Progress Test, apart from Progress Tests 6 and 12, for which you should allow 50 minutes. You may wish to adjust this time depending on your class.

- Photocopy one test for each student. Students should do the tests on their own. You can either check the answers with the whole class at the end of the test, or collect in the tests and correct them yourself. Keep a record of the test scores to help you monitor individual student's progress and for report writing at the end of the course.

- Progress Tests can also be given as homework for general revision.

Listening Tests

There is a listening section in Progress Tests 6 and 12 only. The corresponding recording scripts (R6.13 and R12.14) are in the answer key for the tests.

Both R6.13 and R12.14 have three separate sections. Focus on one section of the recording at a time. Allow students time to read through the questions for that section in the Progress Test before you start. Play that section of the recording without stopping and allow students to answer the questions. Then play the recording again without stopping. With low-level classes you may wish to play the recording a third time. Repeat this procedure for the other two sections.

Answer Key and Recording Scripts

Progress Test 1 p211

1 2 coat 3 watch 4 suitcase 5 umbrella 6 dress 7 wallet 8 shoes

2 2 is 3 aren't/'re not 4 isn't/'s not 5 are 6 Is 7 Are 8 'm 9 're

3 2 Japanese 3 seventeen 4 forty 5 nationality 6 surname 7 engineer 8 musician 9 unemployed

4 2 Turkish 3 Germany 4 this 5 those 6 an 7 They're

5 2 Her 3 she 4 They 5 their 6 Our 7 he 8 we

6 (2 marks each) 2 What's your surname? 3 How do you spell that/it? 4 What do you do?/What's your job? 5 What's your address? 6 What's your mobile number? 7 say that again/repeat that 8 What's your email address?

Progress Test 2 p212

1 2 beautiful 3 short 4 easy 5 slow 6 right/correct 7 good 8 expensive

2 2 Has 3 have 4 Have 5 're 6 hasn't 7 is

3 2 wife 3 uncle 4 grandparents 5 Robert 6 Gloria's 7 father/dad 8 Anna 9 son

4 (2 marks each) 2 I've got a very expensive camera. 3 Has Diana got a new bag? 4 My class is at twenty past ten. 5 What time is the concert? 6 How much is that blue dress? 7 Lisa's books are by the computer. 8 Where's your mother's car? 9 What's he got in his suitcase?

5 2 o'clock 3 quarter ... four 4 half past 5 ten to 6 twenty-five to

6 2 on 3 What time 4 How much 5 How many 6 Who 7 What 8 to 9 Whose

Progress Test 3 p213

1 2 do ... get up 3 start 4 have 5 do ... finish 6 leave 7 do ... get 8 watch 9 go 10 do ... do 11 have 12 go 13 visit 14 have

2 2 in 3 at 4 on 5 every 6 on 7 at 8 in 9 at

3 (2 marks each) 2 I usually visit my family at the weekend. 3 My children never get up early on Saturdays. 4 We often go to the cinema on Sunday afternoons. 5 I hardly ever have coffee with friends in the week. 6 We sometimes stay in on Saturday evenings.

4 2 date 3 shall/can 4 Let's 5 sure 6 What/How 7 idea

5 2 She's 3 him 4 They 5 her 6 us 7 them

6 2 They don't do a lot of sport. 3 I haven't got a digital camera. 4 You aren't/You're not usually late. 5 We don't watch TV in the day. 6 My brother hasn't got a new car. 7 I don't go shopping with my mother. 8 He isn't/He's not an accountant.

Progress Test 4 p214

1 2 take 3 go 4 listen 5 watch 6 read 7 go

2 2 works 3 live 4 love 5 doesn't 6 don't 7 likes 8 goes 9 don't 10 phones

3 2 Her father doesn't work in London. 3 Mia and Luis don't go skiing in January. 4 Sid's sister doesn't like tennis. 5 I don't like shopping for clothes. 6 My uncle doesn't hate cats.

4 (2 marks each) **2** Where does Tim's brother work?
3 What (kind of) music do Mike and Gabi like?
4 What time/When does Julia leave home? **5** Where
do Wendy's parents live? **6** What does Sam do in his
free time?

5 **2** order **3** I'd **4** anything **5** can/could **6** would **7** of
8 bill

6 **2** soup **3** sausages **4** biscuits **5** vegetables **6** orange
juice **7** cereal **8** toast

7 **3** I like ~~a~~ tea but I don't like coffee. **4** Would you
like **a** cheese sandwich? **5** ✓ **6** I never have ~~a~~ milk
in my tea. **7** ✓ **8** I don't often eat ~~a~~ toast.

Progress Test 5 p215

1 **2** there is **3** There's **4** there are **5** There's **6** there aren't
7 Is there **8** there's **9** are there **10** there aren't

2 **2** any **3** any **4** some **5** some **6** any **7** How many
8 How much **9** ones **10** one

3 **2** living room **3** furniture **4** armchairs **5** double bed
6 shower **7** toilet **8** fridge **9** washing machine
10 cooker

4a) **2** skirt **3** boots **4** jumper **5** cap **6** T-shirt **7** dress
8 trousers **9** tie **10** trainers

4b) trousers

5 **2** butcher's **3** chemist's **4** baker's **5** post office
6 department store **7** greengrocer's **8** dry cleaner's

6 **2** have **3** any **4** I'll **5** much **6** can **7** Here

Progress Test 6 p216–p217

R6.13

1

WAITER Would you like to order now?
CUSTOMER Yes, I'd like a pizza, please. A margherita.
W Would you like a salad with that?
C No, thank you.
W And would you like anything to drink?
C Er, yes, can I have a bottle of beer, please?
W Certainly.
C Oh, and I'd like some mineral water.
W Still or sparkling?
C Sparkling, please.
W Right, so that's one pizza margherita, a beer and some
sparkling mineral water.
C Yes, please.
W Was everything OK?
C Yes, very good thanks. Can I have a coffee, please?
W Certainly.
C And can I have the bill, please?
W Of course.

W Here's your coffee and the bill.
C Thank you. How much is it?
W £11.25, please.

C Thanks very much.
W Thank you.

2
MARTIN Hello, Patricia. Were you on holiday last week?
PATRICIA Hi, Martin. No, Peter and I got married!
M Oh, congratulations.
P Yes. I've got a new husband and a new flat in the city centre.
M That's great. Where is it?
P In Green Street.
M Is that near the park?
P Yes, that's right. It's beautiful. It's got two bedrooms and
a big living room.
M So you've got a lot of space then?
P Yes, ninety square metres. And there's a very nice kitchen
and bathroom.
M Is there any furniture?
P There are some armchairs and a sofa, and we've got a new
double bed – but we haven't got a table.
M I've got an old table. Would you like it?
P Yes, please!
M OK. I haven't got a car. Can you come to my house for it?
P Of course. I can come on Saturday morning. What's your
address?
M 24 Water Lane. And my phone number's five double six oh
four three.
P That's great, Martin. Thanks a lot.
M No problem.

3
DAVID Happy birthday, Julia.
JULIA Oh thanks, David. It was your birthday last week, wasn't it?
D Yeah, that's right. April the seventeenth.
J What did you do?
D Oh, I had a really nice time. My family and I went to
Brighton for the day.
J Oh, how many children have you got?
D Two. A boy and a girl.
J Oh yes, of course.
D We went to the beach in the morning and the, er, kids went
swimming in the sea. Then we had lunch at a very nice
Italian restaurant. Er, the food was great and quite cheap.
J Oh yeah? I love Italian food. What's the name of the
restaurant?
D Palms.
J How do you spell that?
D P–A–L–M–S.
J Mmm. And where is it?
D It's on Queens Road near the station.
J Thanks. Maybe my boyfriend can take me there next
weekend.
D Oh, yeah. Good idea!

1a) Margherita pizza; Bottle of beer; Bottle of sparkling
mineral water; Coffee

1b) £11.25

2 **2**T **3**F **4**F **5**F **6**T **7**T **8**F

3 **2** 17th **3** Brighton **4** a son and a daughter **5** to the
beach **6** Italian **7** Palms **8** station **9** boyfriend

4 **2** quiet **3** difficult **4** beautiful **5** crowded **6** intelligent
7 rich **8** friendly **9** interesting

5 (2 marks each) 2 Where did Sally's grandmother live?
3 Where were Trudy and Janet yesterday? 4 Who did
Joe meet last weekend? 5 How old was Greg's father
when he died? 6 How many children did Tom's
grandparents have? 7 What time/When did they get
up this morning? 8 When was your mother born?

6 2 did … live 3 did … go 4 was 5 did … marry 6 got
7 Was 8 left 9 became (was) 10 wrote 11 did … have
12 was 13 had

7 2 start 3 study 4 become 5 write 6 have 7 sleep
8 clean 9 go away

8 2 Oh, great! 3 Wow! 4 Oh, dear. 5 You're joking!
6 What a shame.

9 2 really 3 quite 4 very 5 too 6 quite

10 2 Was 3 at 4 watched 5 on 6 to 7 got 8 don't 9 are
10 My 11 works 12 him 13 for 14 went 15 there

11 2 trousers 3 aunt 4 French 5 wine 6 unemployed
7 newspaper 8 second

12 2 museum 3 newspaper 4 accountant 5 interesting
6 intelligent 7 vegetables 8 banana

Progress Test 7 p218

1 2 thrillers 3 love stories 4 action films
5 horror films 6 comedies

2 2 classical music 3 opera 4 dance music 5 pop music
6 reggae

3 2 They didn't become very rich. 3 He wasn't late for
the lesson. 4 We didn't have a good meal at the hotel.
5 I didn't buy a new dress for the party. 6 Sarah didn't
put her bag under the table.

4 2 Where 3 Why 4 Who 5 Whose 6 How many
7 How long

5 2 were 3 does 4 Were 5 has 6 Do 7 do 8 are

6 2 chose 3 broke 4 took 5 won 6 told 7 found 8 fell

7 2 Which 3 ago 4 in the 5 last 6 in 7 the 8 (one mark
each) a; The

8 2 I wasn't/we weren't 3 they did 4 they don't
5 they haven't 6 it was 7 she didn't 8 there wasn't

Progress Test 8 p219

1 2 skiing 3 fishing 4 sightseeing 5 swimming
6 shopping 7 to the beach 8 cycling

2 2 dirty 3 quiet 4 unfriendly 5 boring 6 safe 7 empty
8 cheap

3 2 booked 3 get 4 rented 5 stayed 6 get 7 rent 8 get

4 2 more expensive 3 hotter 4 older 5 more crowded
6 worse 7 more interesting 8 happier 9 friendlier
10 bigger

5 2 to go 3 have 4 have 5 having 6 go 7 go 8 to do
9 do 10 swim 11 sunbathe

6 2 with 3 by 4 on 5 to 6 in 7 for 8 out 9 in 10 for
11 at

Progress Test 9 p220

1 2 's windsurfing 3 're playing chess 4 's swimming
5 're playing tennis 6 's cooking 7 's sailing 8 's singing

2 2 likes 3 's learning 4 goes 5 isn't/'s not working
6 're skiing 7 go 8 are … doing 9 'm making
10 's … doing 11 doesn't … go 12 's buying

3 2 by 3 take 4 by 5 ride 6 on

4 2 notes 3 sign 4 message 5 customers 6 answer
7 meetings

5 2 It's 3 Can 4 to 5 Hold 6 got 7 Shall 8 I'll 9 call
10 on

6 2 She's a **beautiful** dancer. 3 Why does he always talk
so **quietly**? 4 ✓ 5 They play tennis quite **well**. 6 ✓
7 My children work very **hard** at school. 8 ✓

7 2b) 3c) 4b) 5a) 6c)

Progress Test 10 p221

1 2 get 3 does 4 stopped 5 eat 6 get 7 lose 8 had
9 drink

2 2 a cough 3 a toothache 4 back hurts 5 a cold
6 a stomach ache 7 a temperature 8 leg hurts
9 a headache 10 a sore throat

3 (2 marks each) 2 Do you usually eat fish twice a
week? 3 How much salt do you have every day?
4 I often work more than 60 hours a week. 5 You
should do exercise four times a week. 6 How often
do you go to the gym?

4 2 OK 3 I feel 4 What's 5 Oh, dear. 6 a shame
7 should 8 why don't you 9 hope

5 2 home 3 hair 4 windy 5 sun 6 lazy 7 selfish
8 in 9 Don't 10 He's

6 2 What does he like doing? 3 What does she look like?
4 What's he like? 5 What do you like doing? 6 What
do they look like? 7 What's she like?

Progress Test 11 p222

1 2 'm going to get 3 Is … going to have 4 's going to
move 5 'm going to get 6 'm going to lose 7 'm going
to revise 8 'm going to pass 9 's … going to lose
10 's going to do 11 's going to stop 12 's … going
to start 13 Are … going to do 14 're going to move

2 2 to 3 do 4 passed 5 have 6 harder 7 get 8 eating
9 aren't

3 2 I might 3 going 4 to have 5 to take 6 to stay 7 to be
8 swimming 9 we're going to 10 to move 11 visiting
12 might

4 2 revise 3 college 4 degree 5 opposite 6 university
7 qualification

5 2 near 3 there's 4 along 5 over 6 on 7 next to 8 know
9 along 10 past 11 right 12 opposite 13 miss

Progress Test 12 p223–p224

1

JOHN Are you going to do anything interesting this weekend, Gemma?

GEMMA I might go away. Any suggestions?

J Why don't you go to Norfolk?

G Norfolk! What can you do there? It's empty and boring!

J It's quiet, I know. But it isn't boring. You can go camping, you can rent a boat and go fishing … or sunbathe?

G Sunbathe! It's always cold and cloudy in Norfolk.

J Yes, OK. But it's very interesting. You can go to the Queen's house in Sandringham and see the gardens. Or why don't you go into the country and have tea in a café.

G John, I'm twenty-four not a hundred and twenty-four.

J Right. Why don't you go to London and go to a club?

G That's a much better idea!

2

ANGELA This is Angela Smart's voicemail. Sorry I can't speak to you right now. Please leave your name, number and message after the tone.

BRUCE Angela, hi, it's Bruce. Er I've looked at those application forms for the outdoor centre job and I've chosen two people to interview. We want someone who can do sports but also be in the office, so I think you should interview Susannah and Betina. Susannah can sail and swim and she speaks, um, er, French. She worked here last year. She's very reliable. Betina's a bit older, er, she loves tennis and windsurfing and she can type very fast. Her reference says she's very outgoing. I think they're the best. Good luck. Ring me and tell me who you choose. Bye.

3

NEWSREADER Here is the news at 1 o'clock.
Footballer Peter Conway is in hospital in France after a car accident last night. He hurt his leg, but doctors say that, with painkillers, he can play in England's match against Italy next week. Check-in workers at Heathrow airport went on strike for forty-eight hours from midnight last night. The airport is crowded with people waiting to go on holiday, especially to Spain, Greece and Turkey, as the school holidays started yesterday. This is the second strike by the staff. They are asking for more money.

1 2F 3T 4F 5T 6F 7F

2 2 Two. 3 Yes, she can. 4 French. 5 Yes, she does. 6 Yes, she can. 7 Betina. 8 Angela.

3 2 car accident 3 leg 4 week 5 two days 6 Europe 7 second 8 more money

4 2 trip 3 too 4 will 5 us 6 in 7 on

5 2 Did you have a nice **flight**? 3 Passengers should go to **gate** number forty-one. 4 Can I have a window **seat**, please? 5 Have you got any sharp items in your hand **luggage**? 6 This is your **boarding** card. 7 Show your ticket at the **check-in** desk.

6 2 thinner; thinnest 3 more difficult; most difficult 4 worse; worst 5 nicer; nicest 6 more boring; most boring 7 better; best

7 2 most intelligent 3 most expensive 4 younger 5 most beautiful 6 shorter 7 more crowded 8 oldest 9 earlier 10 most famous

8 2 worked 3 's/has written 4 won 5 's/has … been 6 went 7 Have … met 8 had 9 Did … watch 10 've … seen 11 Have … lived 12 lived 13 was 14 did … stop 15 was

9 2 'm sitting 3 arrived 4 want 5 Have … been 6 don't understand 7 talk 8 met 9 came 10 's doing 11 needs 12 's/has visited 13 knows 14 went 15 saw 16 was 17 's ringing

10 2b) 3c) 4c) 5a) 6b) 7c) 8a) 9b) 10a) 11a)

11 2 take 3 is 4 go 5 take 6 book 7 ride

12 (half a point each) 3 musician 4 breakfast 5 ✓ 6 biscuits 7 ✓ 8 vegetables 9 ✓ 10 ✓ 11 mountains 12 sunbathe 13 ✓ 14 attractive 15 ✓ 16 beautiful

Name _____ Score ☐ 50

1 Write the words for these things.

① diary ② ③ ④
⑤ ⑥ ⑦ ⑧

1 d*iary*   5 u_____
2 c_____   6 d_____
3 w_____   7 w_____
4 s_____   8 s_____   ☐ 7

2 Fill in the gaps in these conversations.

1 A Are you a teacher?
  B Yes, I _am_ .

2 A Is your name Marcus?
  B Yes, it _____ .

3 A Are your children here?
  B No, they _____ .

4 A Is this your suitcase?
  B No, it _____ .

5 A Where _____ we?
  B In Oxford Street.

6 A _____ it Saturday today?
  B No, it's Sunday.

7 A _____ your friends from the UK?
  B No, they're from the USA.

8 A Hello, Maria. How are you?
  B I'_____ fine, thanks.

9 A Are David and Molly here?
  B Yes, they'_____ over there.   ☐ 8

3 Where is the stress on these words?

1 Poland   6 surname
2 Japanese   7 engineer
3 seventeen   8 musician
4 forty   9 unemployed
5 nationality   ☐ 8

4 Choose the correct words.

1 Jaime is from (Spain)/Spanish.
2 I'm Turkey/Turkish. I live in Istanbul.
3 Berlin is in German/Germany.
4 Is this/these your letter?
5 Are these/those your shoes over there?
6 John's a/an engineer.
7 They're/Their from Russia.   ☐ 6

5 Fill in the gaps with a subject pronoun (I, you, etc.) or a possessive adjective (my, your, etc.)

¹ _My_ name's Ute Kuhlmann. I'm a student at the Greenwood School of English. My friend Heiki is also a student here. ² _____ surname's Schmidt and ³ _____ 's from Germany. Pierre and Elisabeth are students here too. ⁴ _____ 're from Paris and ⁵ _____ children are at school in London. We're in an Elementary class. ⁶ _____ teacher's name is Alan and ⁷ _____ 's American. Alan's a good teacher and ⁸ _____ 're good students!   ☐ 7

6 Peter is at the City Car Hire office. Write the woman's questions.

WOMAN Hello, ¹ _what's your first name_ ?
PETER Peter.
W   ² _____ ?
P   Matheson.
W   ³ _____ ?
P   M-A-T-H-E-S-O-N.
W   ⁴ _____ ?
P   I'm a doctor.
W   ⁵ _____ ?
P   16 New Road, Oxford.
W   ⁶ _____ ?
P   My mobile number? It's 07947 336621.
W   Sorry, could you ⁷ _____ , please?
P   07947 336621.
W   ⁸ _____ ?
P   It's pmatheson@webmail.com.
W   Thank you.   ☐ 14

Instructions p207   © Cambridge University Press 2005   face2face Elementary Photocopiable

Progress Test 2 25 minutes

Name .... Score ☐50

1 Write the opposites of these adjectives.

1 old _new_   5 fast ....

2 ugly ....   6 wrong ....

3 long ....   7 bad ....

4 difficult .... 8 cheap ....

☐7

2 Choose the correct words.

1 A Have you got a laptop?

  B Yes, I *am*/(*have*).

2 A *Have/Has* your father got a car?

  B No, but he's got a bike!

3 A What car *have/has* your parents got?

  B It's a Ford, I think.

4 A *Have/Has* you got the time, please?

  B Yes, it's about 3.30.

5 A Those shoes are beautiful!

  B Yes, but they*'ve/'re* £180!

6 A Has Karen got a brother?

  B No, she *haven't/hasn't*.

7 A Whose mobile phone *is/has* that?

  B I think it's Ian's.

☐6

3 Look at the family tree. Complete the sentences.

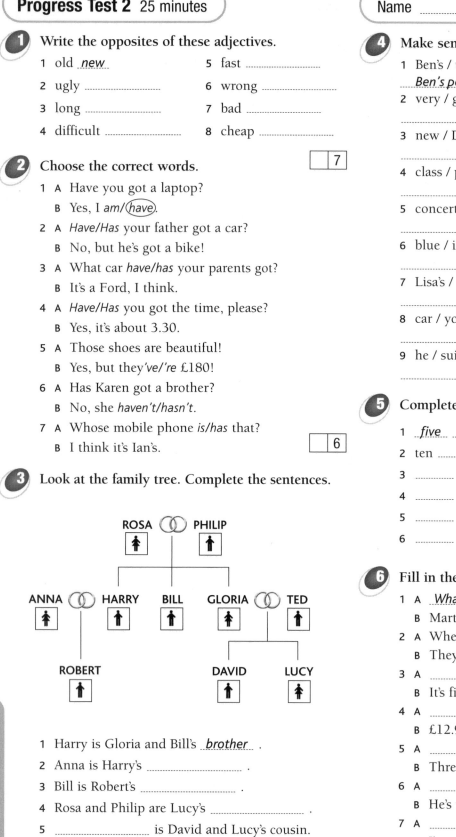

1 Harry is Gloria and Bill's _brother_ .

2 Anna is Harry's ....

3 Bill is Robert's ....

4 Rosa and Philip are Lucy's ....

5 .... is David and Lucy's cousin.

6 Ted is .... husband.

7 Harry is Robert's ....

8 .... is David's aunt.

9 Bill is Rosa and Philip's ....

☐8

4 Make sentences and questions with these words.

1 Ben's / table / on / personal stereo / is / coffee / the .

  .... _Ben's personal stereo is on the coffee table._ ....

2 very / got / expensive / a / 've / I / camera .

  ....

3 new / Diana / a / got / bag / Has ?

  ....

4 class / past / at / ten / My / twenty / is .

  ....

5 concert / is / time / the / What ?

  ....

6 blue / is / dress / much / How / that ?

  ....

7 Lisa's / the / books / by / are / computer .

  ....

8 car / your / Where / mother's / 's ?

  ....

9 he / suitcase / 's / his / What / in / got ?

  ....

☐16

5 Complete the times.

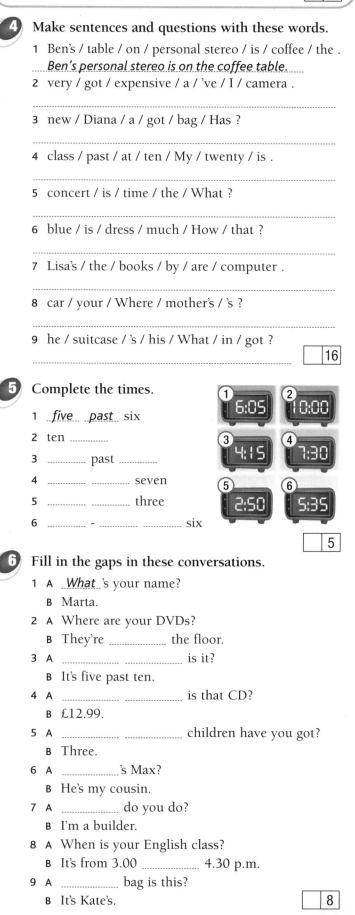

1 _five_ _past_ six

2 ten ....

3 .... past ....

4 .... seven

5 .... three

6 .... - .... six

☐5

6 Fill in the gaps in these conversations.

1 A _What_'s your name?

  B Marta.

2 A Where are your DVDs?

  B They're .... the floor.

3 A .... is it?

  B It's five past ten.

4 A .... is that CD?

  B £12.99.

5 A .... children have you got?

  B Three.

6 A ....'s Max?

  B He's my cousin.

7 A .... do you do?

  B I'm a builder.

8 A When is your English class?

  B It's from 3.00 .... 4.30 p.m.

9 A .... bag is this?

  B It's Kate's.

☐8

Name _____ Score [50]

1 Read about Joe's job in a film studio. Fill in the gaps with the correct form of these verbs.

| do̶ watch get leave |
| have (x 3) go (x 2) start |
| get up finish do visit |

ANN What ¹ _do_ you _do_, Joe?

JOE I'm a waiter in the film studio restaurant.

ANN What time ² _____ you _____ in the morning?

JOE At 5 o'clock. I ³ _____ work at 6 o'clock. The actors arrive at 6.30 and they ⁴ _____ breakfast here.

ANN When ⁵ _____ you _____ work?

JOE We usually ⁶ _____ the studio at 6 p.m. but sometimes it's 9 or 10.

ANN That's very late! What time ⁷ _____ you _____ home?

JOE At about 10.30. I ⁸ _____ TV for an hour, then I ⁹ _____ to bed.

ANN And what ¹⁰ _____ you _____ in your free time?

JOE Well, on Saturdays I usually ¹¹ _____ coffee with friends or ¹² _____ shopping. On Sundays I ¹³ _____ my parents. We always ¹⁴ _____ lunch in a restaurant near their house. And we're always very nice to the waiters! [13]

2 Choose the correct word.
1 I have lunch _in_/(at) 12.30.
2 What time do you have dinner _at/in_ the evening?
3 We get home late _in/at_ night.
4 Do they go out _every/on_ Friday evenings?
5 They go to the cinema _in/every_ week.
6 What time do your classes start _at/on_ Monday?
7 I visit my family _in/at_ the weekends.
8 I don't go out _in/every_ the week.
9 We start work _on/at_ nine o'clock. [8]

3 Make sentences with these words.
1 watch / we / TV / often .
  We often watch TV.
2 my / usually / visit / I / weekend / family / at / the .

  ----

3 children / Saturdays / never / get up / My / early / on .

  ----

4 cinema / to / Sunday / We / go / afternoons / often / on / the .

  ----

5 coffee / the / friends / I / in / have / hardly ever / with / week .

  ----

6 on / evenings / We / stay / Saturday / sometimes / in .

  ----
  [10]

4 Fill in the gaps in the conversation.

KIM This is a photo of Joanne's baby. It's her first birthday ¹ _on_ the 24th.

SUE Oh, what's the ² _____ today?

KIM The 22nd. What ³ _____ we buy her?

SUE ⁴ _____ get her a Disney DVD.

KIM I'm not ⁵ _____ . She's very young.

SUE ⁶ _____ about a dress?

KIM That's a good ⁷ _____ . [6]

5 Choose the correct word.
1 (I)/me have breakfast at 7.30.
2 My sister's a lawyer. _She's/Her's_ in Madrid for a conference this week.
3 He's my favourite uncle but I don't see _he/him_ very often.
4 This is a photo of my children. _They/Them_ both go to Bath University.
5 Sue's parents always phone _she/her_ late at night.
6 Our teachers give _we/us_ a lot of homework.
7 Mike and Sally are great. I go for a drink with _they/them_ every Friday. [6]

6 Make these sentences negative.
1 I'm from France.   _I'm not from France._
2 They do a lot of sport.

  ----

3 I've got a digital camera.

  ----

4 You're usually late.

  ----

5 We watch TV in the day.

  ----

6 My brother's got a new car.

  ----

7 I go shopping with my mother.

  ----

8 He's an accountant. [7]

© Cambridge University Press 2005 **face2face** Elementary Photocopiable

213

Progress Test 4 25 minutes

Name .... Score ☐ 50

1 Fill in the gaps in the phrases with these verbs.

~~play~~ go (x 2) listen read take watch

1 ___*play*___ tennis   5 _____ sport on TV

2 _____ photos   6 _____ magazines

3 _____ dancing   7 _____ running

4 _____ to music   ☐ 6

2 Choose the correct word.

My friend Helen ¹*live*/*lives* in New York. She's married and her husband Brad ²*work*/*works* in a bank. They ³*live*/*lives* in Manhattan and they both ⁴*love*/*loves* living there. Helen ⁵*don't*/*doesn't* work because she's got three young children. Brad and Helen ⁶*don't*/*doesn't* have a lot of free time, but at the weekends Helen ⁷*like*/*likes* playing tennis and Brad often ⁸*go*/*goes* swimming. Helen and I ⁹*don't*/*doesn't* see each other very often, but she always ¹⁰*phone*/*phones* me on my birthday! ☐ 9

3 Make these sentences negative.

1 I go to the cinema every Friday.
   I don't go to the cinema every Friday.

2 Her father works in London.

   ....

3 Mia and Luis go skiing in January.

   ....

4 Sid's sister likes tennis.

   ....

5 I like shopping for clothes.

   ....

6 My uncle hates cats.

   .... ☐ 5

4 Make Wh- questions to ask about the words in bold.

1 They get up **at half past** seven.
   What time do they get up?

2 Tim's brother works **in London**.

   ....

3 Mike and Gabi like **rock** music.

   ....

4 Julia leaves home **at nine o'clock**.

....

5 Wendy's parents live **in Australia**.

....

6 Sam **does a lot of sport** in his free time.

.... ☐ 10

5 Fill in the gaps in the conversation.

WAITER   Would you ¹ *like* to ² _____ now?

SAM   Yes, ³ _____ like a burger, please.

WAITER   Would you like ⁴ _____ else?

SAM   Yes, ⁵ _____ I have a salad, please?

WAITER   Yes, of course. And what ⁶ _____ you like to drink?

SAM   A bottle ⁷ _____ beer, please.
     ... Excuse me.

WAITER   Yes, sir?

SAM   Can I have the ⁸ _____ , please?

WAITER   Certainly.   ☐ 7

6 Write the food and drink.

1 ___*banana*___   5 _____

2 _____   6 _____

3 _____   7 _____

4 _____   8 _____ ☐ 7

7 Tick the correct sentences. Change the incorrect sentences.

1 Do you want a cheeseburger? ✓

2 I always eat ~~a~~ fruit for breakfast.

3 I like a tea but I don't like coffee.

4 Would you like cheese sandwich?

5 He usually has a banana with his coffee.

6 I never have a milk in my tea.

7 I often have meat and rice for lunch.

8 I don't often eat a toast. ☐ 6

Name _____ Score ☐50

1 Fill in the gaps with the correct form of *there is/there are*.

A ¹ *Is there* a lot to see in Cambridge?

B Yes, ² _____ . Cambridge is a beautiful place. ³ _____ a very old university and ⁴ _____ students from a lot of different countries. ⁵ _____ also an interesting market every day and it's very easy to walk around because ⁶ _____ any cars in the market square.

A ⁷ _____ an airport near Cambridge?

B Yes, Stansted is only half an hour away and ⁸ _____ a bus and train station in the city.

A And ⁹ _____ any mountains near Cambridge?

B No, ¹⁰ _____ , but it's nice to walk by the river. ☐9

2 Choose the correct words.

1 Does he wear ⓐ/*any* cap?

2 Have you got *a/any* shorts?

3 I haven't got *any/some* ties.

4 I want to buy *some/a* jeans.

5 I'd like *a/some* bread, please.

6 There aren't *any/some* tissues.

7 *How much/How many* people are there?

8 *How much/How many* milk have we got?

9 A Can I have some envelopes?

   B Do you want these *one/ones*?

10 A Which magazine would you like?

    B This *one/ones*, please. ☐9

3 Read the email and complete the words.

Dear Mum and Dad
Jenny and I are in our new flat, and it's great!
There are five rooms, a ¹k*itchen* , a bathroom,
a very big ²l_____ r_____ and two
bedrooms. There's some ³f_____ as well.
There's a sofa and two ⁴a_____ in the main
room, and in one of the bedrooms there's a
⁵d_____ b_____ and a desk. In the
bathroom there's a bath and a ⁶s_____ , and
a ⁷t_____ , of course! And in the kitchen
there's a ⁸f_____ and a very old ⁹w_____
m_____ , but there isn't a ¹⁰c_____ .
Can we come for dinner on Sunday?!
Love
Ian ☐9

4 a) Write the clothes.

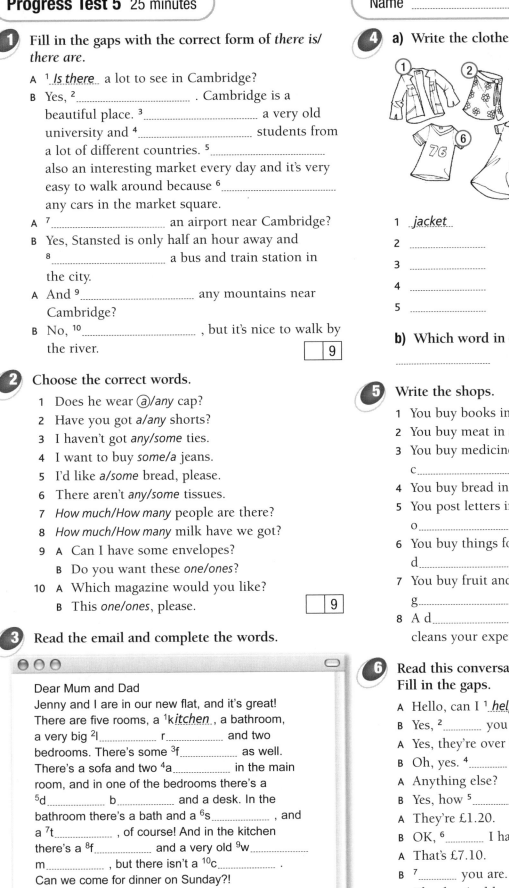

1 *jacket*   6 _____
2 _____   7 _____
3 _____   8 _____
4 _____   9 _____
5 _____   10 _____

b) Which word in **4a)** is always plural?

_____ ☐10

5 Write the shops.

1 You buy books in a b*ookshop* .

2 You buy meat in a b_____ .

3 You buy medicine (aspirins, etc.) in a c_____ .

4 You buy bread in a b_____ .

5 You post letters in a p_____ o_____ .

6 You buy things for the house in a d_____ s_____ .

7 You buy fruit and vegetables in a g_____ .

8 A d_____ c_____ cleans your expensive clothes. ☐7

6 Read this conversation in a newsagent's. Fill in the gaps.

A Hello, can I ¹ *help* you?

B Yes, ² _____ you got ³ _____ maps of London?

A Yes, they're over there, by the magazines.

B Oh, yes. ⁴ _____ have this one, please.

A Anything else?

B Yes, how ⁵ _____ are those big bottles of water?

A They're £1.20.

B OK, ⁶ _____ I have two, please?

A That's £7.10.

B ⁷ _____ you are.

A Thanks. And here's your change. Bye.

B Goodbye. ☐6

© Cambridge University Press 2005 **face2face** Elementary Photocopiable

1 **a)** [R6.13] Listen to the recording of a conversation in a restaurant. Underline the things the customer orders.

Antonio's Restaurant

Food

Neapolitan pizza	£6.50
Margherita pizza	£5.50
Burger and chips	£5.25
Chicken salad	£6.00
Mixed salad	£3.50

Drinks

Glass of wine (red or white)	£2.95
Bottle of beer	£2.50
Bottle of still mineral water	£1.75
Bottle of sparkling mineral water	£1.75
Coffee	£1.50

b) Listen again. How much is the bill?

.... ☐ 5

2 [R6.13] Listen to the recording about Patricia's new flat. Are these sentences true (T) or false (F)?

1 Patricia was on holiday last week. _F_
2 Patricia's new flat is in Green Street. ......
3 There are four rooms in her flat. ......
4 There are some armchairs but there isn't a sofa. ......
5 Patricia hasn't got a double bed. ......
6 Martin has got an old table he doesn't want. ......
7 Martin can't take the table to Patricia's flat. ......
8 Martin's phone number is 556043. ...... ☐ 7

3 [R6.13] Listen to the recording about David's birthday. Circle the correct answers.

1 It was David's birthday *yesterday/last week.*
2 His birthday was on April *7th/17th*.
3 On his birthday he went to *London/Brighton* with his family.
4 He's got *two sons/a son and a daughter*.
5 They went *to the beach/shopping* in the morning.
6 They had lunch in a *Chinese/Italian* restaurant.
7 The restaurant's name was *Parms/Palms*.
8 The restaurant is near the *station/beach*.
9 Julia wants her *boyfriend/husband* to take her to the restaurant. ☐ 8

4 Fill in the gaps in Petra's diary with these words.

> ~~ill~~ beautiful quiet rich crowded interesting difficult friendly intelligent

Saturday 12 August

Sally didn't come to see me today. She was ¹ _ill_ and she stayed in bed for the day. The house was very ² .... because my two noisy little brothers were away. I studied English in the morning but I didn't finish my homework - it was too ³ .... ! In the afternoon I went to the beach. It was a ⁴ .... day, but the beach was very ⁵ .... so I didn't stay. Then I met Miranda, a student from my English class. She's very ⁶ .... - she's always first in our class. She's also from a very ⁷ .... family - her father is a famous musician. But she's really ⁸ .... - she always says hello to me. We went to a Chinese restaurant for dinner and had a very ⁹ .... conversation about her father's job. So it was a really nice day in the end.

☐ 8

5 Write Wh- questions to ask about the words in **bold**.

1 I was born **in Sydney**.

Where were you born?

2 Sally's grandmother lived **in Spain**.

....

3 Trudy and Janet were **at home** yesterday.

....

4 Joe met **an old school friend** last weekend.

....

5 Greg's father was **92** when he died.

....

6 Tom's grandparents had **seven** children.

....

7 They got up **at 6.30** this morning.

....

8 My mother was born **in 1965**.

....

☐ 14

6 Read about William Shakespeare. Fill in the gaps with the correct form of these verbs.

> be born get live leave go be (x 3) become
> marry write have (x 2)

A When ¹ _was_ William Shakespeare _born_ ?

B In April 1564.

A Where ² .... his parents .... ?

B In a town called Stratford-upon-Avon.

A Where ³ .... Shakespeare .... to school?

B In Stratford. He ⁴ .... a very good student.

A Who ⁵ .... he .... ?

B Anne Hathaway. They ⁶ .... married in 1582.

A ⁷ .... he happy in Stratford?

B No, he wasn't. He ⁸ .... Stratford and went to London. He ⁹ .... an actor and a writer, and he ¹⁰ .... 37 plays.

A How much money ¹¹ .... he .... at the end of his life?

B Well, he ¹² .... quite rich. He ¹³ .... a big house in Stratford. | 12 |

7 Fill in the gaps with these verbs.

> get write start clean have
> become study sleep go away

1 _get_ divorced
2 .... university
3 .... law
4 .... a doctor
5 .... a report
6 .... a wonderful time
7 .... until 10.00 a.m.
8 .... the house
9 .... for a couple of days | 8 |

8 Choose the correct response.

1 A I slept for 24 hours.
   B *Oh, right./(Really)?*

2 A I'm really happy – my boyfriend asked me to marry him!
   B *Oh, dear./Oh, great!*

3 A We went to New York for the weekend!
   B *Wow!/Oh, right.*

4 A The restaurant was too crowded so we came home.
   B *Oh, dear./Oh, nice.*

5 A I won £500,000 on the lottery last weekend.
   B *You're joking!/Oh, right.*

6 A I had a bad cold and stayed in bed all weekend.
   B *What a shame./Oh, nice.* | 5 |

9 Choose the correct words.

1 The dress was *quite/(too)* expensive so I didn't buy it.
2 The hotel was great and it was *really/too* cheap.
3 This burger is *too/quite* nice.
4 I loved that film. The actors were *too/very* good.
5 You're 15. You're *very/too* young to get married!
6 The party was *quite/too* good but I didn't like the music very much. | 5 |

10 Fill in the gaps in this email.

Hi Laura

How are you? Did you go ¹ _to_ Steven's party? ² .... it good? I stayed ³ .... home that weekend because I was ill. I ⁴ .... a really boring film on TV ⁵ .... Saturday night and I went ⁶ .... bed early.

Anyway, I've got a new job! I'm a manager in a bookshop and I've ⁷ .... my own office. I usually work six days a week, but I ⁸ .... work on Sundays because the bookshop is closed. I really like the job and the people here ⁹ .... very friendly. ¹⁰ .... boyfriend Richard ¹¹ .... in a bank five minutes from my shop so I often meet ¹² .... for lunch or we go ¹³ .... a drink after work. Last Sunday we visited the British Museum and then we ¹⁴ .... shopping in Oxford Street. It was good fun but ¹⁵ .... were too many people!

Write to me soon!
Lots of love
Fiona | 14 |

11 Which word is the odd one out?

1 January June (Tuesday) March
2 trainers trousers boots shoes
3 brother uncle aunt husband
4 French Italy Turkey Mexico
5 meat cheese bread wine
6 accountant builder unemployed musician
7 newspaper butcher's bookshop chemist's
8 seventeen second sixty fifty-one | 7 |

12 Where is the stress on these words?

1 computer
2 museum
3 newspaper
4 accountant
5 interesting
6 intelligent
7 vegetables
8 banana | 7 |

217

face2face Elementary Photocopiable

PROGRESS TESTS: PHOTOCOPIABLE

Name _____ Score [50]

1 Write the types of film.

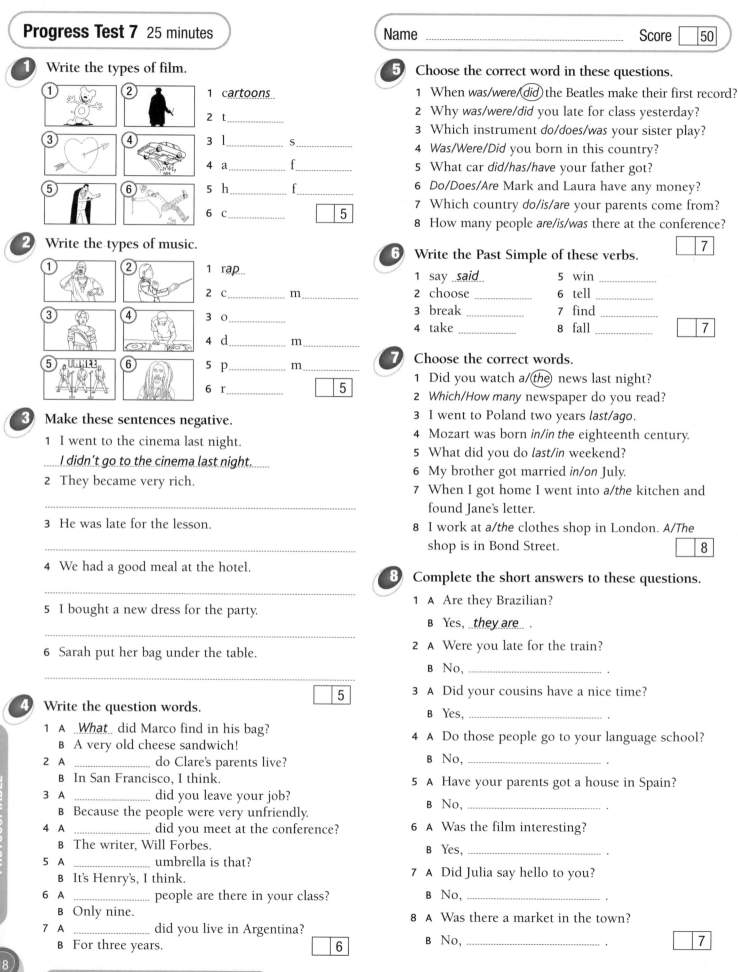

1 c*artoons*
2 t_____
3 l_____ s_____
4 a_____ f_____
5 h_____ f_____
6 c_____   [5]

2 Write the types of music.

1 r*ap*
2 c_____ m_____
3 o_____
4 d_____ m_____
5 p_____ m_____
6 r_____   [5]

3 Make these sentences negative.

1 I went to the cinema last night.
   I didn't go to the cinema last night.
2 They became very rich.
   _____
3 He was late for the lesson.
   _____
4 We had a good meal at the hotel.
   _____
5 I bought a new dress for the party.
   _____
6 Sarah put her bag under the table.
   _____   [5]

4 Write the question words.

1 A *What* did Marco find in his bag?
  B A very old cheese sandwich!
2 A _____ do Clare's parents live?
  B In San Francisco, I think.
3 A _____ did you leave your job?
  B Because the people were very unfriendly.
4 A _____ did you meet at the conference?
  B The writer, Will Forbes.
5 A _____ umbrella is that?
  B It's Henry's, I think.
6 A _____ people are there in your class?
  B Only nine.
7 A _____ did you live in Argentina?
  B For three years.   [6]

5 Choose the correct word in these questions.

1 When *was/were/did* the Beatles make their first record?
2 Why *was/were/did* you late for class yesterday?
3 Which instrument *do/does/was* your sister play?
4 *Was/Were/Did* you born in this country?
5 What car *did/has/have* your father got?
6 *Do/Does/Are* Mark and Laura have any money?
7 Which country *do/is/are* your parents come from?
8 How many people *are/is/was* there at the conference?   [7]

6 Write the Past Simple of these verbs.

1 say *said*   5 win _____
2 choose _____   6 tell _____
3 break _____   7 find _____
4 take _____   8 fall _____   [7]

7 Choose the correct words.

1 Did you watch *a/the* news last night?
2 *Which/How many* newspaper do you read?
3 I went to Poland two years *last/ago*.
4 Mozart was born *in/in the* eighteenth century.
5 What did you do *last/in* weekend?
6 My brother got married *in/on* July.
7 When I got home I went into *a/the* kitchen and found Jane's letter.
8 I work at *a/the* clothes shop in London. *A/The* shop is in Bond Street.   [8]

8 Complete the short answers to these questions.

1 A Are they Brazilian?
  B Yes, *they are* .
2 A Were you late for the train?
  B No, _____ .
3 A Did your cousins have a nice time?
  B Yes, _____ .
4 A Do those people go to your language school?
  B No, _____ .
5 A Have your parents got a house in Spain?
  B No, _____ .
6 A Was the film interesting?
  B Yes, _____ .
7 A Did Julia say hello to you?
  B No, _____ .
8 A Was there a market in the town?
  B No, _____ .   [7]

Name _____ Score [50]

1 Fill in the gaps with the correct words/phrases for these activities.

1 go _on holiday_
2 go _____
3 go _____
4 go _____
5 go _____
6 go _____
7 go _____
8 go _____ [7]

2 Write the opposites of these adjectives.

1 old   _modern_
2 clean   _____
3 noisy   _____
4 friendly _____
5 interesting _____
6 dangerous _____
7 crowded _____
8 expensive _____ [7]

3 Fill in the gaps with the correct form of these verbs. You can use each verb more than once.

    book   rent   stay   get

1 How much is it to _stay_ in that hotel?
2 He phoned the restaurant and _____ a table.
3 Why don't you _____ a taxi home after the party?
4 When she was in Spain she _____ a car.
5 Mike _____ with me for three weeks last January.
6 Can you tell me how to _____ to your place?
7 We want to _____ a flat in north London.
8 How do we _____ to your house? [7]

4 Fill in the gaps in 1–10 with the comparative form of these adjectives.

    ~~small~~ interesting old friendly expensive
    big happy hot crowded bad

1 Oxford is _smaller_ than London.
2 The holiday in Phuket is _____ than the one in Bangkok. Bangkok is only €1240.

3 The weather in the UK is _____ in summer than in winter.
4 My sister is five years _____ than me.
5 The shops are usually _____ on Saturdays than on Mondays.
6 My Progress Test mark is _____ than last month's. This time I only got 25 points.
7 Holidays in cities are _____ than holidays on the beach. There are more things to see and do.
8 Linda's _____ in her new job because the work's interesting and she gets more money.
9 People are often _____ in small villages than in big cities. They have more time to talk to you.
10 Mexico City is _____ than Paris. There are 18 million people in Mexico City and only 10 million in Paris. [9]

5 Read the conversation. Choose the correct answers.

A What do you want [1](to do)/do tomorrow?
B I'd really like [2]to go/go for a walk in the mountains.
A Fine. And we can [3]to have/have lunch in a café.
B I'd rather [4]to have/have a picnic. I love [5]have/having picnics in the mountains.
A OK. And where shall we [6]to go/go on Thursday?
B I know. Let's [7]to go/go on a boat trip to the islands. Would you like [8]to do/do that?
A No, sorry. Can we [9]do/to do something else? I don't like boats because I can't [10]to swim/swim. I'd rather [11]to sunbathe/sunbathe on the beach. [10]

6 Fill in the gaps with a preposition.

1 They travelled _to_ to the island yesterday.
2 He stayed _____ his friends in the country.
3 They always travel _____ public transport.
4 Johann and Susan went _____ holiday last week.
5 They went _____ the beach for the day.
6 We stayed _____ a bed and breakfast near the sea.
7 You can go _____ long walks in the mountains.
8 She loves going _____ with her friends in the evenings.
9 I was born _____ 1983.
10 Chris slept _____ 12 hours last night.
11 I usually work _____ night. [10]

219

1 Complete these sentences about the pictures.

① ② ③ ④
⑤ ⑥ ⑦ ⑧ ♫ ♪

1 She _'s driving_ .
2 He _____ .
3 They _____ .
4 He _____ .
5 They _____ .
6 She _____ .
7 He _____ .
8 He _____ .

☐ 7

2 Read about the Lee family. Put the verbs in brackets in the Present Continuous or the Present Simple.

Mr Lee ¹ _is working_ (work) in the garden. His son, Dan, usually ² _____ (like) helping his father but he ³ _____ (learn) his French verbs at the moment. Dan's brother, Ned, ⁴ _____ (go) to the office on Saturdays, but he ⁵ _____ (not work) today. He's on holiday with some friends. They ⁶ _____ (ski) – they ⁷ _____ (go) there every year. Dan and his sister, Ann, are in the kitchen.

DAN What ⁸ _____ you _____ (do)?
ANN I ⁹ _____ (make) a pizza for lunch.
DAN Great! What ¹⁰ _____ Mum _____ (do)?
ANN She's in town.
DAN Really? But she ¹¹ _____ usually _____ (not go) shopping on Saturday.
ANN No, but she ¹² _____ (buy) a special present for someone today.

☐ 11

3 Fill in the gaps with these words. You can use each word more than once.

ride take on by

1 _ride_ a horse
2 go _____ tube
3 _____ the train
4 go _____ plane
5 _____ a motorbike
6 go _____ foot

☐ 5

4 Complete the words in these sentences.

1 Did you write that r_eport_ for me?

2 It's a good idea to take n_____ in class.
3 Did Mr Tamada s_____ the contract?
4 I'm sorry, Sue isn't here. Can I take a m_____ ?
5 The café had 17 c_____ on the first day.
6 They don't a_____ the phone after 11 p.m.
7 I go to lots of m_____ every day.

☐ 6

5 Choose the correct answers.

IAN Hello, Ian Harris ¹speaks/(speaking).
LISA Hi. ²I'm/It's Lisa. ³Can/Do I speak ⁴to/at Amy?
IAN ⁵Hold/Wait on a moment. I'll get her.
AMY Hi, Lisa. I ⁶got/get your message this morning.
LISA Good. ⁷Shall/Do we go out for a meal this evening?
AMY I'm not sure. ⁸I'll/I want to call you back later.
LISA OK. Or I can ⁹speak/call you ¹⁰at/on your mobile at about 7.

☐ 9

6 Tick the correct sentences. Change the words in bold in the incorrect sentences.

1 I'd like to speak English **fluent**. _fluently_
2 She's a **beautifully** dancer.
3 Why does he always talk so **quiet**?
4 I'm a very **bad** cook.
5 They play tennis quite **good**.
6 Hassan does his homework very **carefully**.
7 My children work very **hardly** at school.
8 He's a very **fast** driver.

☐ 7

7 Choose the correct answer.

1 Can you swim?
   (a) Yes, I can.   b) No, I can.   c) Yes, I can't.
2 Are you working at the moment?
   a) Yes, I work.   b) No, I'm not.   c) Yes, I'm.
3 What do you do?
   a) I'm cooking.   b) Fine, thanks.   c) I'm an actor.
4 Are we leaving now?
   a) Yes, we're.   b) No, we're not.   c) Yes, are we.
5 Do you want to go stay in a hotel?
   a) I'd rather camp.   b) Yes, I want.   c) No, I'm don't.
6 When were you born?
   a) I born in 1986.   b) I borned in 1986.
   c) I was born in 1986.

☐ 5

Name _____   Score 50

1 Fill in the gaps with the correct form of these verbs.

go lose stop drink eat have do get (x 2)

1 I _go_ to the gym every weekend.
2 I'm quite overweight and I want to .... fit.
3 My grandfather .... some exercise every day.
4 I .... smoking about four years ago.
5 I hardly ever .... fried food these days.
6 You shouldn't .... stressed about work.
7 Do you know a good way to .... weight quickly?
8 I .... a heart attack when I was only 41.
9 I didn't .... any alcohol last week.   8

2 Fill in the gaps with the correct health problems.

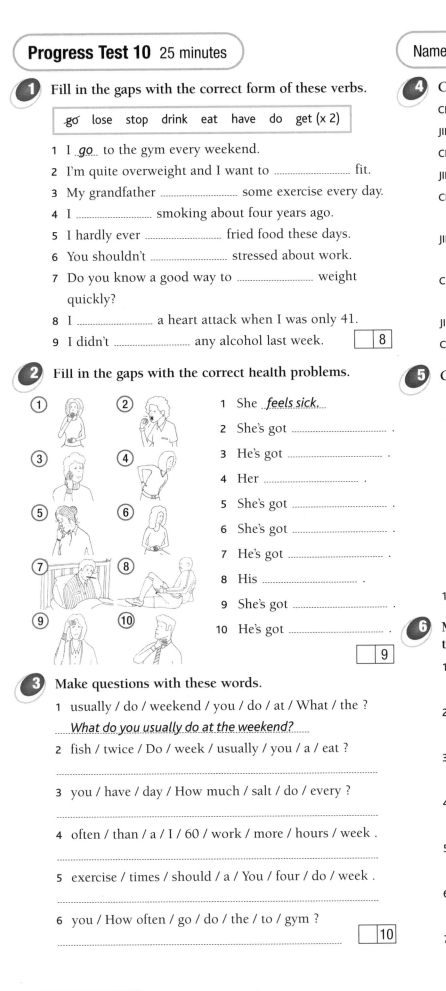

1 She _feels sick._
2 She's got ....
3 He's got ....
4 Her ....
5 She's got ....
6 She's got ....
7 He's got ....
8 His ....
9 She's got ....
10 He's got   9

3 Make questions with these words.

1 usually / do / weekend / you / do / at / What / the ?
   What do you usually do at the weekend?
2 fish / twice / Do / week / usually / you / a / eat ?
   ....
3 you / have / day / How much / salt / do / every ?
   ....
4 often / than / a / I / 60 / work / more / hours / week .
   ....
5 exercise / times / should / a / You / four / do / week .
   ....
6 you / How often / go / do / the / to / gym ?
     10

4 Choose the correct words/phrases.

CHRIS How ¹are you/is it, Jill? Are you ²wrong/OK?
JILL   No, I'm not. ³I'm/I feel terrible.
CHRIS ⁴What's/What the matter?
JILL   I feel sick and I've got a really bad cold.
CHRIS ⁵Oh, great/Oh, dear. That's ⁶better/a shame. You ⁷should/shouldn't take the day off.
JILL   I can't. I've got an important meeting this morning.
CHRIS Well, ⁸you shouldn't/why don't you go home after lunch?
JILL   That's a good idea.
CHRIS I ⁹think/hope you get better soon.   8

5 Choose the correct words.

1 He's got long hair/hair long.
2 I'm going home/to home.
3 My mother's got dark hair/hairs.
4 It's a very wind/windy day today.
5 I don't go out in the sun/sunny very much.
6 My son never helps me. He's very lazy/kind.
7 She's very selfish/reliable. She only thinks about her life, not other people's.
8 I think you should stay in/at bed.
9 Don't/Not go to work tomorrow.
10 He's/He's got bald.   9

6 Make questions with like/like doing/look like for these answers.

1 A _What are they like?_
  B They're very generous.
2 A .... ?
  B He likes going to the gym and playing tennis.
3 A .... ?
  B She's quite tall and slim with blonde hair.
4 A .... ?
  B He's very funny but he's not very generous.
5 A .... ?
  B I love going to the cinema and watching TV.
6 A .... ?
  B They've got long blonde hair and blue eyes.
7 A .... ?
  B She's very friendly and outgoing.   6

PROGRESS TESTS: PHOTOCOPIABLE

Progress Test 11 25 minutes

1 Complete these sentences about these people's plans. Use the correct form of *be going to* and the verbs in the box.

> ~~do~~ move (x 2) have get (x 2) lose (x 2)
> stop do (x 2) start revise pass

a) A What ¹_are_ you _going to do_ this year?

   B I ² .... a new job.

b) A ³ .... Gary .... a holiday this summer?

   B No, he ⁴ .... house.

c) A Have you got any New Year's resolutions?

   B Yes, I ⁵ .... fit and I

   ⁶ .... seven kilos!

d) A When's your exam, Ruby?

   B Tomorrow. I ⁷ ....

   for it tonight, but I don't think I

   ⁸ ....

e) A Tell me, Sue, how ⁹ .... your husband

   .... weight?

   B He ¹⁰ .... more exercise and

   he ¹¹ .... eating chocolate!

f) A When ¹² .... your son Christopher

   .... school?

   B Next year, when he's five.

g) A ¹³ .... they .... an

   English course next year?

   B No, they ¹⁴ .... to England instead!   [13]

2 Choose the correct word.

1 At the end of the road *(turn)/take* left.

2 John moved *to/in* Canada last year.

3 Do you *do/make* some exercise every week?

4 I *passed/failed* my exam. I'm very happy!

5 Did you *have/get* fun last night?

6 Your daughter should work *harder/hardly*.

7 Where did you *find/get* your degree?

8 I think you should stop *eat/eating* sweet things.

9 We *aren't/not* going to work this evening.   [8]

3 Choose the correct answers.

Q What are your plans for the future, Rod?

A I'm going ¹*singing/(to sing)* in Japan in the summer.

Q What about concerts in any other countries?

A ²*I'm going to/I might* go to Australia but I'm not sure.

Q Why not?

A Well, I'm away from home a lot. I love ³*going/go* to different places, but I'd really like ⁴*having/to have* more time with my family. Next year I want ⁵*taking/to take* two months off work.

Q Do you want ⁶*staying/to stay* in London for those two months?

A No. I need ⁷*being/to be* in a very quiet place. I enjoy ⁸*swimming/to swim* a lot, so ⁹*we're going to/we might* rent a house on a small island. We found a house in the Caribbean last month.

Q Would you like ¹⁰*moving/to move* away from London?

A Yes, I really like ¹¹*visiting/visit* New York. I ¹²*want/might* buy a flat there one day.   [11]

4 Where is the stress on these words?

1 exăm   3 college   5 opposite   7 qualification

2 revise   4 degree   6 university   [6]

5 Look at the map. Then fill in gaps 1–13.

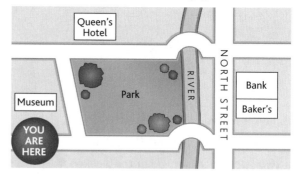

A ¹_Excuse_ me. Is there a bank ² .... here?

B Yes, ³ .... one in North Street. Go ⁴ .... this road and go ⁵ .... the bridge. Then turn left – that's North Street. The bank is ⁶ .... your right, ⁷ .... a baker's.

A Excuse me. Do you ⁸ .... the Queen's Hotel?

B Yes, go ⁹ .... this road and turn left. Go ¹⁰ .... the museum and turn ¹¹ .... The Queen's Hotel is ¹² .... the park. You can't ¹³ .... it.   [12]

1 R12.14 Listen to John and Gemma's conversation about Norfolk, a place in England. Are these sentences true (T) or false (F)?

1 Gemma might go away this weekend. _T_

2 John thinks Norfolk is boring. ......

3 He says you can rent a boat there. ......

4 Gemma thinks the weather in Norfolk is good. ......

5 John says the Queen has a house in Norfolk. ......

6 Gemma is 34 years old. ......

7 She is going to Norfolk this weekend. ...... [6]

2 R12.14 Bruce is the manager of an outdoor centre. Listen to his voicemail message to his secretary, Angela. Answer these questions.

1 Is Angela in the office? _No, she isn't._

2 How many people did Bruce choose to interview?

....

3 Can Susannah sail? ....

4 What language can Susannah speak? ....

5 Does Betina play tennis? ....

6 Can Betina type well? ....

7 Is Susannah or Betina very outgoing? ....

8 Who is going to do the interviews, Bruce or Angela? .... [7]

3 R12.14 Listen to the recording of two news stories. Choose the correct answers.

1 Peter Conway is a (footballer)/tennis player.

2 He was in a *plane crash/car accident* last night.

3 He has a problem with his *arm/leg*.

4 England are going to play Italy next *weekend/week*.

5 The strike at Heathrow airport is for *a day/two days*.

6 Lots of people are waiting to fly to *Europe/the USA*.

7 This is the *first/second* strike at the airport.

8 The check-in workers want *more money/longer holidays*. [7]

4 Choose the correct word.

A ¹(Have)/make a nice holiday and a good ²*fly/trip*!

B You ³*also/too*.

A Thanks, I ⁴*will/have*.

B Send ⁵*we/us* an email.

A Yes, of course. See you ⁶*for/in* two weeks.

B Yes, see you ⁷*in/on* the next course. Bye! [6]

5 Correct these sentences.

    pack

1 Did you ~~put~~ your bags yourself?

2 Did you have a nice fly?

3 Passengers should go to door number forty-one.

4 Can I have a window chair, please?

5 Have you got any sharp items in your hand luggages?

6 This is your board card.

7 Show your ticket at the check-out desk. [6]

6 Write the comparative and superlative forms of these adjectives.

		comparative	superlative
1	long	*longer*	*longest*
2	thin		
3	difficult		
4	bad		
5	nice		
6	boring		
7	good		

[6]

7 Choose the correct answers.

1 I'm quite tall, but my brother's (taller)/tallest.

2 Who's the *more intelligent/most intelligent* person in your class?

3 Wow! That's the *more expensive/most expensive* watch I've ever seen!

4 My sister is two years *younger/youngest* than me.

5 I met the *more beautiful/most beautiful* girl today.

6 Is your husband *shorter/shortest* than you?

7 The bar was *more crowded/most crowded* than usual.

8 We stayed in the island's *older/oldest* hotel.

9 My wife always gets up *earlier/earliest* than me.

10 Which is Shakespeare's *more famous/most famous* play? [9]

8 Put the verbs in brackets in a)–g) in the Present Perfect or the Past Simple.

a) I¹'ve never _stayed_ (stay) in a five-star hotel but I ² .... (work) in one when I was a student.

b) Robert ³ .... (write) some excellent science-fiction stories. He ⁴ .... (win) a prize for one last week.

c) My husband ⁵ .... never .... (go) to Thailand, but I ⁶ .... (go) there on business last month.

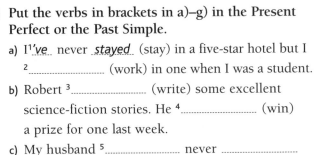

d) A ^{7}_____ you ever _____ (meet) a famous musician?

B Yes, I ^{8}_____ (have) dinner with Sting before he was famous!

e) A ^{9}_____ you _____ (watch) that Japanese film on TV last night?

B No, I ^{10}_____ never _____ (see) a Japanese film in my life.

f) A ^{11}_____ you ever _____ (live) in another country?

B Yes, I ^{12}_____ (live) in Mexico when I ^{13}_____ (be) a child.

g) A When ^{14}_____ your father _____ (stop) work?

B About two years ago, when he ^{15}_____ (be) sixty-five.

| 14 |

9 Read Julia's email. Put the verbs in brackets in the Present Simple, Present Continuous, Past Simple or Present Perfect.

Hi Roberto

How ^{1} _are_ you? I hope you're OK. At the moment I ^{2}_____ (sit) in an Internet café. I ^{3}_____ (arrive) in London two days ago and I ^{4}_____ (want) to do an English course for a month. ^{5}_____ you ever _____ (go) to London? It's an amazing city, but I ^{6}_____ (not understand) the people very well – the problem is they ^{7}_____ (talk) very fast.

I'm here with one of my cousins, Javier. You ^{8}_____ (meet) him last year when you ^{9}_____ (come) to my house for a barbecue. He ^{10}_____ (do) some shopping in Oxford Street at the moment because he ^{11}_____ (need) to buy a new coat. Javier ^{12}_____ (visit) London a couple of times for work, so he ^{13}_____ (know) a lot of good places to go. Last night we ^{14}_____ (go) to a concert in Camden and ^{15}_____ (see) a new band called the Love Doctors – it ^{16}_____ (be) great! Well, my phone ^{17}_____ (ring) – it's probably Javier. I'll write again soon.

Love

Julia

| 16 |

10 Choose the correct answers.

1 It's a very _b_ day today.
   a) rain   b) windy   c) cloud

2 Frederick doesn't like travelling _____ plane.
   a) in   b) by   c) with

3 My _____ , Alex, is my father's brother.
   a) aunt   b) cousin   c) uncle

4 My aunt's very _____ . She often gives me money.
   a) selfish   b) outgoing   c) generous

5 I usually have a _____ for lunch.
   a) sandwich   b) toast   c) soup

6 He left his car _____ the hotel.
   a) on   b) in front of   c) along

7 Mark is a very _____ driver. He drives too fast.
   a) safe   b) noisy   c) dangerous

8 I went to visit a _____ last week.
   a) customer   b) contract   c) meeting

9 I usually buy my meat in the _____ in my road.
   a) baker's   b) butcher's   c) greengrocer's

10 _____ did you stay in the USA?
   a) How long   b) How much   c) How many

11 Would you like to go _____ a drink?
   a) for   b) to   c) on

| 10 |

11 Choose the correct verb in these sentences.

1 How often do you go/*do*/have sport?

2 When did you last take/make/revise an exam?

3 My brother Simon has/is/have twenty years old.

4 How often do you go/make/have shopping?

5 I never take/make/do photos.

6 We should rent/book/call a table at the restaurant.

7 Can you drive/sail/ride a motorbike?

| 6 |

12 Tick the correct spelling. Correct the wrong words.

1 difficult ✓

2 sutcase _suitcase_

3 musican _____

4 brekfast _____

5 swimming _____

6 biscits _____

7 sausages _____

8 vegtables _____

9 chocolate _____

10 fridge _____

11 mountins _____

12 sunbath _____

13 message _____

14 atractive _____

15 toothache _____

16 beatiful _____

| 7 |

Instructions p210